U.S. LABOR
IN THE
TWENTIETH
CENTURY

REVOLUTIONARY STUDIES
Series Editor: Paul Le Blanc

U.S. LABOR
IN THE
TWENTIETH CENTURY

---

*Studies in
Working-Class Struggles and Insurgency*

EDITED BY

JOHN HINSHAW AND PAUL LE BLANC

**Humanity
Books**

an imprint of Prometheus Books
59 John Glenn Drive, Amherst, New York 14228-2197

Published 2000 by Humanity Books, an imprint of Prometheus Books

Inquiries should be addressed to
Humanity Books
59 John Glenn Drive
Amherst, New York 14228–2197
VOICE: 716–691–0133, ext. 207
FAX: 716–564–2711

04 03 02 01 00   5 4 3 2 1

Library of Congress Cataloging-in-Publication Data

U.S. labor in the twentieth century : studies in working-class struggles and insurgency / edited by John Hinshaw and Paul Le Blanc.
        p. cm. — (Revolutionary studies series)
    Includes bibliographical references.
    ISBN 1-57392-865-8 (paper : alk. paper)
    1. Working class—United States—History—20th century. 2. Labor movement—United States—History—20th century. 3. Industrial relations—United States—History—20th century. 4. Industrial mobilization—United States—History—20th century. I. Title : United States labor in the twentieth century. II. Hinshaw, John H., 1963– III. Le Blanc, Paul, 1947– IV. Series.

HD8072.5 .U185 2000
331'.0973'0904—dc21   00–040723
                                                                 CIP

Printed in the United States of America on acid-free paper

This book is dedicated to the memories of four working-class heroes:

Harry Braverman, Genora Dollinger, Ed Mann, and James J. Matles

CONTENTS

PART ONE: THE WORKING CLASS STILL MATTERS

1. Why the Working Class Still Matters
    Paul Le Blanc and John Hinshaw   13

2. The Making of the American Working Class
    Harry Braverman   24

3. Working-Class Studies: Where It's Been Lately
   and Where It's Going
    *Sherry Linkon, Bill Mullen, John Russo,
    Susan Russo, and Linda Strom*   39

PART TWO: DIVERSITY, INSURGENCY, AND FRAGMENTATION

4. Ethnic Organizing: A Double-Edged Sword
    Dan Georgakas   63

5. The *Appeal to Reason* and the Mass Socialist Movement
   Before World War I
    David Riehle   72

7

6. Representations of Women in Narratives
    About the Great Steel Strike of 1919
        David Demarest   82

7. Reflections on the Great Migration to Western Pennsylvania
        Joe W. Trotter   92

8. The Gendered Social World of Steelmaking:
    A Case Study of Bethlehem Steel's Sparrows Point Plant
        Karen Olson   101

PART THREE: THE OPPORTUNITIES OF LABOR RADICALISM

9. Revolutionary Vanguards in the United States During the 1930s
        Paul Le Blanc   129

10. The Role of Women, and of Radicals, in the First Sit-Down Strikes
        An Interview with Genora Johnson Dollinger
        by Kathleen O'Nan   162

11. Opportunities Found and Lost: Labor, Radicals,
    and the Early Civil Rights Movement
        Robert Korstad and Nelson Lichtenstein   178

12. A. Philip Randolph and the Foundations of Black Socialism
        Manning Marable   206

PART FOUR: AFFLUENCE, POSSIBILITIES, AND PROBLEMS

13. Working-Class Lives/Working-Class Studies:
    A Historian's Perspective
        Lizabeth Cohen   235

14. Modest but Adequate: Standard of Living
    for Mon Valley Steelworkers in the Union Era
        Mark McColloch   246

15. We *Are* the Union
        Ed Mann   263

16. Black Workers' Struggles for Jobs and
    Civil Rights in Twentieth-Century Pittsburgh
        John Hinshaw   295

PART FIVE: APPLYING THE LESSONS OF THE PAST

17. Why Unions Matter
    Elaine Bernard   329

18. A Century of Struggle in Homestead:
    Working-Class Responses to Corporate Power
    Irwin M. Marcus   340

19. The Role of Labor Today: Reflections on the
    Past Throw Light on the Road Ahead
    James. J. Matles   359

20. Seeds of a Labor Insurgency
    Peter Rachleff   369

21. The Struggle for Survival
    General Baker   382

    Contributors   393

Part 1

THE WORKING CLASS STILL MATTERS

Since the 1950s, many radical activists have been disappointed in the labor movement as an engine for social change. Its unions were too committed to the Democratic Party; its leadership too bureaucratic, being "partners in progress" with big business; and its rank and file appeared too conservative or racist to truly be a force that could change society for the better. While the last twenty-five years have seen important changes in the character of the labor movement, many scholars and activists have seen other social movements that fought for civil rights, women's rights, gay rights, or against military intervention abroad, and the like, as far more central to progressive projects.

From the 1950s onward, scholars seriously debated whether the working class had in fact disappeared as a result of consumerism, suburbanization, and the decline of manufacturing as a source of employment. The rapid increase in poverty since the 1980s (much of it the result of deindustrialization) has shifted, but not fundamentally changed the direction of academic thought. Since the 1980s, many theorists have emphasized the importance and fluidity of identity in our "postindustrial" or "postmodern" age. Many postmodernists argue against the "outdated" idea that conflicts between labor and capital shape society and social change, insisting that we should look instead to the complexity of identities within society.

In fact, the relative "invisibility" of the labor movement in the media and the universities is an illustration of class conflict. While most newspapers strive for "objectivity," all have lengthy business sections for entrepreneurs, managers, and investors, but none have a section devoted to the interests of those who sell their labor to survive. Of course, despite the media-dominated image that protestors are spoiled rich kids, workers and children of the working class have made up the bulk of social movements, and these demands for "new" kinds of rights actually advance the interest of the working class as a whole. However, because even those from the working class are surrounded by the dominant ideas of our society, the first section of this book examines the question of why the study of the working class is still relevant for our times.

In "Why the Working Class Still Matters," John Hinshaw and Paul Le Blanc argue that conflicts between labor and capital are central to how capitalist societies reorganize themselves in response to changing conditions. Although it is the dominant class, capital must constantly destroy the institutions that it has itself created in the past in order to maximize profits in the new circumstances. In "The Making of the American Working Class," Harry Braverman investigates the ways that capital's reorganization, as well as the struggle of workers themselves, have transformed the working class over the last 150 years.

In "Working-Class Studies: Where It's Been Lately and Where It's Going," Sherry Linkon, Bill Mullen, John Russo, Susan Russo, and Linda Strom investigate working-class studies as a field of inquiry that is emerging out of the work of artists, writers, historians, and educators. These intellectuals are laboring to investigate the experiences and express the aspirations of an extremely heterogeneous working class.

Taken together, these essays argue that the weakness of the labor movement today is not an argument for the end of class conflict, but simply an argument that workers have yet to develop new strategies for our times. Delving into the past can help illuminate the path forward.

1

WHY the WORKING CLASS STILL MATTERS

PAUL LE BLANC AND JOHN HINSHAW

At the beginning of the twenty-first century the outlook of labor looks very bleak indeed. Unions represent only one in six workers. About one-quarter of those in the working class hold low-wage, part-time, dead-end jobs. Since the mid-1970s, the real wages of those fortunate enough to have full-time employment have declined by over 20 percent. Even many unionized workers whose wages and benefits have kept pace with inflation share the common view that the labor movement is dominated by entrenched, self-serving bureaucracies having little positive relevance for the lives of working people. And the condition of labor markets will surely deteriorate as corporations and public employers accelerate the process of eliminating full-time employees in favor of temporary workers or so-called self-employed contractors. Such "structural adjustments" have been occurring not only in smokestack industries but also in high-technology corporations with record profits. The public sector, too, has been getting "lean and mean" at the expense of its employees. Even in the rarified world of higher education, large numbers of academics are receiving an education in the harsh realities of downsizing: 40 percent of university professors are contingent.

On the political front things are equally grim. The labor movement remains shackled within a legal framework written in the 1930s and then subsequently amended, interpreted, and enforced by legions of pro-corporate politicians, judges, and bureaucrats. From the 1930s through the 1970s the

Democratic Party had portrayed itself and had been seen by many as the bulwark of working-class hopes for a society infused by what Franklin D. Roosevelt called The Four Freedoms—freedom of thought, freedom of expression, freedom from fear, freedom from want. Throughout the recent years, despite narrow disagreements over personalities and specific policies (the narcissism of small differences), both the Republican and Democratic parties are relentlessly pursuing the dismantling of the meager welfare state which had been designed—due to considerable pressure from below—to provide a safety net of social programs to protect hard-pressed and disadvantaged layers of the U.S. working class and to ensure a modicum of dignity for all. Politicians cloak their lean and mean policies in populist rhetoric which beguiles significant numbers of working people who feel that "we" shouldn't be taxed to support "them," but such cuts in social programs are bound to erode whatever dignity and security that working people as a whole enjoy.

The mass media, largely owned by a handful of large corporations, treats resistance to downsizing as wrongheaded, as if health-conscious politicians and employers were simply proposing a fitness regime to recalcitrant and overweight workers. At the same time, the media delicately avoids critical scrutiny of lifestyles enjoyed by the top 1 percent of the population that owns 40 percent of the nation's wealth. Downsizing is commonly presented as a commonsense approach to economic necessity—a juggernaut of political inevitability. We have no choice. The ways of the past no longer work. The dream of a society in which there is liberty, justice, opportunity, and a decent standard of living for all—promised by many decades of "great presidents" (the Square Deal of Teddy Roosevelt, the New Freedom of Woodrow Wilson, the New Deal of Franklin Roosevelt, the Fair Deal of Harry Truman, the New Frontier of John Kennedy, the Great Society of Lyndon Johnson) and actually struggled for by the labor movement throughout the history of our country—is simply not possible. If we are to move into the future, we must embrace the market economy which—like "Big Brother" in Orwell's *1984*—loves us all with a very tough love indeed, but from which there is no escape.

WHY STUDY THE HISTORY OF THE WORKING-CLASS MOVEMENT?

Given all of this, and given the fact that the organized labor movement today represents a shrinking minority of the U.S. population, one may wonder why anyone should study U.S. labor history. Perhaps one might have an interest in the labor movement in the way one might study the design of antique cars or stamps, but labor's history would seem to have no clues to solving the problems of a predominantly middle-class country adjusting to a "postindustrial" world.

Part of the answer involves basic definitions of society. Contrary to the dominant view, at least 75 percent of the U.S. population is working class. Most people in our society have no way to make a living except through the sale of the ability to labor (the energy and abilities stored in our minds and bodies, our *labor power*). This includes wage and salary workers—blue and white collar—plus family members who rely on the wages and salaries of "breadwinners," plus those unable to secure such employment (whom Karl Marx termed the "reserve army of labor"). Once this is understood, the history of a movement that has struggled to improve the organization, working conditions, and political power of workers has great relevance to the majority of people in the United States.

More than this, there is an accumulation of "anomalies" which suggest that labor struggles for a better society are not part of an outmoded paradigm. Because railroads supply many of the country's factories with raw materials, the specter of sixty thousand railroad workers withdrawing their labor power in unison is more than enough to bring the U.S. Congress into emergency session to command them back to work. There has been a growing number of militant and radicalizing strikes in recent years—some of which have gone down to defeat after heroic struggles (the Hormel strike, the Staley strike), but some of which could not be vanquished. In the early 1990s, coal miners in Virginia defeated the allied forces of a determined coal company and a state government—but Pittston miners had the advantage of the militant leadership and full support from their national union. Clearly, such unity combined with workers carefully planning their efforts can result in union strike victories, as the Teamsters' confrontation with UPS or the casino workers' six-year strike at the Frontier similarly prove.

In other countries, workers have launched moderately effective general strikes over political and economic issues—in Nigeria, Belgium, France, Russia, and Denmark. In Mexico the challenge of an insurgent movement representing the dispossessed Indians, peasants, and workers has seriously undermined the legitimacy of the government. While Mexico's ruling elite might hope to use troops to eliminate the Zapatista challenge, force appears unlikely to resolve Mexico's underlying economic and political crisis—one that is increasingly shared by its free-trade partners to the north. It is not inconceivable that labor's radical vision (radical in the sense of "going to the root" of our social problems and seeking basic changes that give power to the majority of people) could once again become a force in the political life of our own country.

LABOR'S RADICAL VISION

The cause of labor was aptly summarized in the 1886 founding constitution of the American Federation of Labor (AFL): "A struggle is going on in all nations of the civilized world, between the oppressors and the oppressed of all countries, a struggle between the capitalist and the laborers, which grows in intensity from year to year, and will work disastrous results to the toiling millions, if they are not combined for mutual protection and benefit."

The labor-radical vision of the old AFL constitution—far from being some alien import—has been an organic part of working-class experience, consciousness, and organization at least since the post–Civil War period of the 1860s, and with roots going back to the dual revolution of the late eighteenth and early nineteenth centuries: the democratic ferment associated with the American Revolution, and the social reform currents largely generated by the Industrial Revolution. This egalitarian vision recognized that freedom and opportunity for workers will entail popular control over the political and economic institutions of this country. Such a society can only be accomplished through conflict with the elites and corporations that control the U.S. economic and social order. Of course, more consistent working-class radicals often confronted conservative workers and leaders who favored "pragmatic" bread-and-butter gains, frequently advanced through endorsing racism, sexism, and/or nationalism as the common "bond" with employers or politicians. But the left wing of the workers movement—animated by socialists, communists, anarchists, and other radicals seeking to go to the root of society's problems—has always been a key factor in advances won by organized labor.

Thus a central focus of this volume is the history of the left wing of the workers movement and the relationship of this left wing to the working class as a whole. While the racial, ethnic, and gender diversity of the working class has often frustrated the efforts of left-wing workers to achieve the unity necessary to confront the enormous power of economic elites, common goals and experiences of diverse sectors of the working class have also resulted in stalwart resistance, innovative organizations, and often unexpected militancy. In this book, special attention is given to issues of race and gender, which are essential to understanding the complexities of the U.S. working class. Some of the essays focus on the ways in which capitalism or consumer culture have shaped (and in turn been shaped by) the conscious struggles and daily activities of the working-class majority. And some of the essays focus on working-class organizations, including trade unions but also left-wing groups and parties, that have played an often decisive—though sometimes problematical—role in how the aspirations of working people have been articulated and mobilized. They raise urgent questions about the failure of the radical vision to guide the working class to victory, a failure which has had devastating consequences.

The old cliché of left-wing agitators retains its validity: the working-class majority *is* a slumbering giant "that can bring to birth a new world from the ashes of the old," a more democratic, just, and equitable society. But today's weakened labor movement must come to grips with its legacy of defeats and divisions in order to overcome these limitations in future struggles. This books seeks to advance an ongoing dialogue among workers, activists, and educators as to how to understand and strengthen the cause of labor.

CAPITALISM'S RADICAL VISION

Bertolt Brecht once remarked that the reality of capitalism has generally been more radical than the visions of socialism. By this he meant that capitalists' quest for profits leads them to destroy political and social institutions, industries, and established ways of life that only a few years or decades ago it had itself created; the plans of socialists for workers' control over the economy have seemed a model of social responsibility by comparison (as indeed they are).

Under capitalism, the production of goods and services is organized by the market. This means that almost everything is produced and exchanged not to benefit society as a whole, but instead to make a profit. All businesses from General Motors to the mom-and-pop grocery store strive to produce, buy, or sell things or services in order to make a profit for the owners of the businesses. (While certain parts of the economy may be in the "public" sector or run on a "nonprofit" basis, their organizational form and functions are largely determined by the private sector.) Of course, most people do not own their own business, and to keep a roof over their heads and food on the table, they must work for wages or a salary for those who need to acquire labor power. The labor power of people is just another commodity (like steel, cloth, or computer chips), something that workers sell and employers buy. Even children would recognize that, of course, labor power is comprised of human beings, not objects. This fact is lost on many employers, who treat their employees as if they were so many typewriters, trucks, or copiers.

It has long been fashionable among many economists to deny, with seemingly sophisticated formulations, Adam Smith's truism that labor is the ultimate source of wealth. But historically those more intimately engaged in the realities of economic life have known better. For example, in the early years of the American Republic both slaves and slaveholders in the South knew very well that by controlling the unpaid labor power of African or African American slaves, slaveholders could grow very rich indeed. Northern factory owners found distinct advantages in not owning the source of their labor power: as their laborers got sick or old under the system of "free labor," it was not the employer's responsibility to take care of the workers. But no less than Southern slaveholders, nineteenth-century employers in the industrializing North knew that labor was the source of their wealth. In order to turn land, raw materials, and tools into something that could be sold for a profit, employers needed workers to build the house or the railroad, print the newspaper, mine the coal, forge the iron, sew the clothes, haul the produce, or create whatever they wanted to sell.

Particularly at the early stages of the Industrial Revolution, most employers—lacking intimate knowledge of the production process—had to hire workers who had the necessary skills to make their products. Employers received the *surplus value* of workers' efforts, the value left over once wages were paid. Of course, to get the most out of their investment in labor power, employers must squeeze as much actual labor out of the workers as they could. Once a crew of workers was assembled, employers tried to increase the amount of surplus value they received by lengthening the workday, lowering wages, or getting nine workers to do what ten workers used to do (what unionists called a "speedup"). By the early twentieth century, large industrialists hired time-and-motion "experts" to study and reorganize the production process, to increase efficiency, and to transfer knowledge of and control over this process to the employers.

Industrialists also introduced "labor-saving" machinery (what Marx called "dead labor" because machines are themselves the product of labor power, the repositories of "living labor") to lower their ongoing labor costs. Machinery raised the productivity of labor, which meant that the same or increasing amounts of goods could be produced with less labor, making it possible to sell these goods for less, driving out of business other capitalists unable to maintain such levels of mechanization. Along with this there developed ambitious and increasingly efficient forms of organization: corporations which marshaled sufficient amounts of capital to absorb other companies, achieving vertical and horizontal forms of organization in industry which revolutionized the capitalist firm and made possible hitherto unimagined economies of scale.

Capitalism has been said to develop through "long waves" of expansion and contraction. Periodically, declining profit rates might cause economic slowdowns, and overproduction might glut the market to such an extent that a surge of business failures and massive unemployment might result: a cycle in which "boom" times of economic growth lead to the "bust" of economic depression. Among businesses, only the strong and most efficient enterprises could survive, becoming stronger yet as the economy revived. Through such pitiless mechanisms as these U.S. capitalism was periodically transformed, growing more intensively within the United States while extending its interests and operations—seeking raw materials, markets, and investment opportunities—throughout the world.

By the late nineteenth century, competitive capitalism had been replaced by corporate capitalism (some analysts have called it "monopoly capitalism"). Successful industrialists such as Andrew Carnegie made great fortunes by drawing thousands of workers into large factories. Carnegie and others were able to grab larger shares of the market at the expense of small-scale capitalists, when necessary smashing unions to force down wage rates and often artificially lowering prices in order to destroy competition—only later to raise prices and gouge consumers.

In the early twentieth century, employers such as Henry Ford began to realize that they could make more profit *and* raise wages if productivity rose faster than the cost of labor. Ford paid "responsible" workmen well while ruthlessly driving them to assemble cars more quickly. As a result, the share of Ford cars sold rose as fast as the price of Model T's dropped. The "golden age" of Ford lasted until the late 1920s, and many corporations also sought to increase profits and workers' standard of living (and avoid the formation of unions) via a "welfare capitalism" which provided an array of benefits and inducements to nurture employee loyalty to and dependence on the company. This orientation collapsed with the onset of the Great Depression. Many industrial workers, overcoming the initial shock or fear of unemployment, soon mobilized to protect their interests and better their conditions through militant new industrial unions formed under the banner of the Congress of Industrial Organizations (CIO) in the 1930s. The mass unionization generated in these years and afterward raised wages, but union and company negotiators tied such increases to productivity gains, just as Henry Ford had done. Therefore, some economists call this phase of capitalism *Fordism*.

Although it was the booming military production generated by World War II (1939–1945) which pulled the U.S. economy out of the Depression, the Fordism put in place by the CIO—buttressed by New Deal social programs—helped ensure a consumer buying-power that continued to fuel prosperity in the postwar era. The fact that the United States emerged from the war as the most powerful industrial nation in the global capitalist economy facilitated increasingly far-flung and profitable economic expansion. The threat posed in various countries by a succession of postwar revolutionary upsurges, in some cases intertwined with the spread of Communist influence (and the fear that Western civilization might be overwhelmed by the sinister red menace), generated decades of Cold War. This involved massive military spending which—while distorting U.S. economic and political development and giving rise to what President Dwight D. Eisenhower termed an ominous "military-industrial complex"—constituted a kind of "military Keynesianism" that provided further stimulus to the U.S. economy.

In later decades, the Fordism of the 1950s and 1960s appears like a dream. True, most workers complained that their jobs were boring and alienating. But their pay and benefits were better than they had ever been, and appeared certain to improve over the course of workers' lives. Not only were corporations profitable, and living standards on a seemingly permanent upward swing, but social services—health, education, social security, transportation, unemployment insurance, public assistance, etc.—seemed destined to continue expanding and improving indefinitely. Full employment seemed a reasonable goal, and political leaders confidently spoke of eliminating the last pockets of poverty throughout the country. While small groups of conservatives muttered darkly about "creeping socialism," many workers optimistically believed that labor's vision of social justice was guaranteed by the Fordist-induced prosperity of corporate capitalism.

Times have changed. Faltering corporate profits of the early 1970s collided with the revolution of rising expectations and rising entitlements, leading to a shift in business strategies and government policies. Growing Japanese and Western European economic competition began to erode U.S. supremacy. Global restructuring, "deindustrialization" involving the partial dismantling within the United States of much of the high-wage mass production industries, and a new get-tough policy against unions was matched by a rising crescendo of government cutbacks in social programs—starting in earnest under Democratic President Jimmy Carter, turning into an onslaught during the Reagan-Bush years.

At the close of this period, the world saw the spectacular collapse of the USSR and other Communist countries—in part induced by economic strains generated by the exorbitant costs of the Cold War, and in part brought on by the mismanagement and the popular alienation generated by authoritarian Communist bureaucracies. With the elimination of the foremost global challenger to corporate capitalism, publicity agents and propagandists pulled out all the stops: those who in any way questioned the logic of the market economy were standing against the tide of history itself.

Despite the presidential election of centrist Democrat Bill Clinton, the onslaught of corporate capitalism against previous working-class gains has accelerated in the 1990s. Policies of "structural readjustment" enhance a so-called flexibility in the private sector which benefits wealthy elites at the expense of the bottom 80 percent of the population. Despite pushing and shoving over specifics, President Clinton joined with the triumphalist conservative Republican Congressman Newt Gingrich to proclaim capitalism's new radical vision—the end of big government, the new age of information, the triumph of the market—which translates into slashed social programs, the increasing evaporation of traditionally high-paid industrial jobs, and the unchallenged power of multinational corporations.

LABOR, RACE, AND GENDER

And yet the radical vision of global capital—with its proliferating "high-tech" wonders—cannot undo the system's never-ending need for labor and markets. The working-class majority, denied and degraded but no less there for all that, remains a force to be reckoned with, whatever its dilemmas of the moment.

Although women's labor has always been crucial to households and the paid labor market, since the 1960s, the U.S. labor force has been increasingly "feminized." In part this is because of the expansion of traditionally female sectors such as office work, health care, and services, but also the decline of men's wages. (Also important is that many women do not want to be dependent on the income of another wage earner.) Black sectors of the labor force—always subjected to higher levels of poverty, unemployment, and inferior wages—are now experiencing increasing devastation, but they also seem, in fact, to have paved the way for what increasing numbers of whites are now dealing with. These facts raise, with a new poignancy, unresolved issues of race and gender in the history of the U.S. working class.

As a system capitalism is deeply committed to inequality: the few owners of the economy must be enriched by employing the labor of the many who own nothing but their own labor-power. More than this, while racial and sexual oppression are not new, they have developed over time in step with the development of capitalism. It can be documented that discrimination on the basis of race and gender has been fostered by, and has been immensely profitable for, those who dominate the economy. It has also helped them, in more than one way, to maintain greater social control and political power.

And yet this could not have been so successful if there had not been among white working people often viciously racist perspectives and among male workers deep-held attitudes denying women's full humanity. Such perspectives and attitudes were combated (not always consistently or successfully) by the left wing of the labor movement. As things turned out, racist and sexist policies became notoriously ingrained in many unions. The shattering of left-wing influence during the Cold War period meant that antiracist and antisexist efforts were further weakened. Without a radical wing pushing for a thoroughgoing working-class equality and solidarity, much of the labor movement in some ways became a kind of identity movement of relatively conservative white males.

While important gains were sometimes made for people of color and for women, and while working-class solidarity sometimes successfully overcame divisions based on race and gender, the history of the working class cannot be comprehended without understanding ways in which racism and sexism persisted and often triumphed in labor's ranks. It is not only so-called postmodernist analysts who were consequently inclined to privilege "identity politics" over class politics, rather than seeing the two as inseparable. Struggles to overcome discrimination and oppression around identi-

ties of race, gender, and sexuality many times could only be advanced outside the "official" ranks of organized labor—and sometimes even in open
opposition to the conservative policies of certain unions. One key to
advancing our understanding of U.S. labor history involves the ability to
look beyond the institution of the trade union, recognizing that the trade
union is not necessarily all there is to "organized labor," just as the working
class and the class struggle are not confined simply to the membership of
the organized labor movement. The realities are more complex and more
interesting than that.

The revitalization of the labor movement—historically and recently—
has often involved a radicalism which embraces all members of the working
class, drawing people of color and women into central roles in militant
struggles that transform power relations within the working class as well as
in the workplace and the larger society. This also provides keys to advances
in understanding labor history—and perhaps for comprehending the possibilities of labor's future.

THEMES IN THIS BOOK

Gathered in this volume are contributions by scholars and activists which
illuminate various facets of working-class experience in twentieth-century
America. The case studies focus on two of the most dynamic realms of
experience for workers, union activists, and labor historians. From the auto
industry we have rich narratives of union activists Genora Dollinger from
the 1930s sit-down strikes and General Baker from the 1960s black revolutionary union movement—both of whom relate their hard-won insights to
more recent struggles; suggestion of similar links can be found in the scholarly contribution of Robert Korstad and Nelson Lichtenstein. A higher proportion of contributions deal with experiences relating to the less-
researched steel industry—the remarkable memoir of Ed Mann (again
tracing connections between struggles spanning the 1930s and 1980s), plus
detailed scholarship from Irwin Marcus, David Demarest, Karen Olson,
John Hinshaw, and Mark McColloch.

Working-class experiences from these two realms by no means tell us
all we need to know about workers in other sectors of the economy. The
surveys by Harry Braverman, David Riehle, Dan Georgakas, Paul Le Blanc,
and Lizabeth Cohen place the case studies in broader contexts while at the
same time helping to further clarify some of the themes explored by the
other authors. Intersections of class, race, gender, and ethnicity stand as
one of the major areas of investigation. Another is a concern with experience both in the workplace and in the larger culture and community. Yet
another involves the antinomies and dynamics of working-class conscious-

ness, and the interrelationship of the "conscious" workers animated by insurgent and revolutionary ideologies with broader layers of their class.

The relevance of all this is pressed forward in the challenging essays by Elaine Bernard, James Matles, Irwin Marcus, and Peter Rachleff which conclude this volume. In these essays—as in the previous pieces—there is much ground that is covered. But we are also keenly aware of limitations. Workers' experiences in political parties—whether Democratic or Republican or independent or left-wing—do not receive sustained attention. Nor is there adequate investigation of the state's role in promoting, suppressing, or channeling working-class movements and struggles. Attention should similarly be given to correlations between the "long waves" of capitalist development and developments in working-class culture, consciousness, organization, and struggle. Other important themes, such as the relationship of labor's struggles (or disorganization) with the family, or child labor, or the international economy, are only touched upon. And as we have already emphasized, there is a need to factor in developments in other economic sectors— of coal miners, textile and garment workers, longshore and maritime workers, teamsters, railway workers, food and commercial workers, hospital workers, teachers, government employees, and many others.

There is much more that needs to be explored, articulated, debated. Our goal has been to further the process of dialogue on the history and future of the working-class struggle. We think readers will agree that the contributors to this volume have helped to move that collective effort forward.

2

THE MAKING OF THE AMERICAN WORKING CLASS

HARRY BRAVERMAN

What follows is the transcription of a talk given at a weekend seminar in February 1975 at Empire State College, New York, and aired over Pacific Radio.

What do we mean by working class? Anyone who is inclined to use the term obviously has in mind an immense mass of people—in fact, most of the people of the country. But at first glance the divisions among these tens of millions seem more important than anything that can unify them under a single heading.

First of all, they're divided by sex. Then, when one speaks in terms of genetic origin, they're divided once more among black and white, the Hispanics, the Asians and the Indians, that is, those who were native to the Americas before the coming of Europeans and who contributed heavily to the working class chiefly by way the populations of sub-Rio Grande America.

The population of European origin forms another great mass. Numerically, perhaps the greatest. But this population is again divided according to the nations and regions of Europe from which they or their forebears came, and even more importantly, according to *when* they came to this continent.

Then, this mass of workers is also divided according to the industries and

From the *Monthly Review* 46, no. 6: 19–35. Copyright © 1994 by Monthly Review Inc. Reprinted by permission of the Monthly Review Foundation.

occupations in which they work, and especially by whether they work in factories or offices, transport or warehouses, or retail stores or banks (to name only some of the most important divisions of this kind). And finally, they are divided according to their organizations, their opinions, their moods, their sentiments, and their attitudes toward their own place in society.

But while a description of this diversity is thus of the greatest importance, it seems to me that one must start with its opposite: not with the diversity but with the unity. In other words, we must try to understand what it is that this great mass of people has in common that causes us to call it a class, as we all do in common parlance, and as many of us do in scientific or analytical terms. The discussion of the diversities will then make much more sense.

The single feature that's common to the many people who make up this class is that they do not own the business enterprises in which they work, but are hired to labor there for a stipulated pay. It doesn't usually occur to us to call, for instance, the man and wife who own a small family farm members of the working class, even though they work for long hours and at manual work at that. Why? Because these farmers are the proprietors of small businesses of a special kind. Their labor is thus not hired to others. We see here at once that it is not just the fact that people *work* which makes them part of the working class, but the fact that this work is done within the framework of certain relations.

Consider again, for example, an excavating and earthmoving contractor who owns or leases a few bulldozers and backhoes and employs a few men on and off, alongside of whom he himself works as a machine operator. To the casual observer he seems to spend his days doing much the same thing as the men in his employ. But it wouldn't enter our minds to call him anything but a contractor and the others workers.

Here again, the difference is not in the physical activities in which we may see them engaged, but in their social relationships, in which the contractor represents the hirer of labor and the others the labor hired. Being a worker, therefore, is a condition which originates not primarily in some form of work activity but rather in a social relation. The worker is the hired hand by which capital accomplishes its work, no matter what the particular form of work that may be.

Now we speak tonight of the formation of a class of people of this kind as a process which has been going on throughout U.S. history. The first thing to notice is that it would hardly occur to us to organize a discussion around the formation of many other such social groupings that we know exist in this country. For example, we wouldn't organize a discussion around the formation of the modern class of farmers in the United States, or the formation of a class of retailers, shopkeepers, and artisans—of petty capitalists, in other words. That's not because there are no farmers or no petty capitalists in the countryside and in the cities; it is rather because we all understand—even those of us who know history only from the daily newspapers we have read in our own lifetimes—that these classes are not in process of formation but in process of liquidation, and that what still remains of them is not the special product of capitalism but merely the remnants of formerly numerous classes destroyed by capitalism.

In place of a population consisting, as it did in the past, of people with a fixed and defined place in the economy and with a certain relation to the land, to the artisan guilds, or to commerce, we have today a floating population of separated molecules which are combined and recombined according to the needs of capital. This population exists to serve, as interchangeable parts, a limited number of ever larger corporate enterprises, which in turn exist for the purpose of expanding their capital (and alongside of which exist governmental or semigovernmental organizations having an auxiliary role which are organized in a similar fashion).

The organizing group which owns, controls, and manages these corporations is a small layer of a few percent of the population, and the national structure exists for the benefit of this class of people and to carry out their purposes and designs. The largest part of the remainder of society exists merely to serve these organizations and lives only by striking wage bargains with them—in many cases as individuals, and in many other cases with the aid of organizations which somewhat ameliorate their conditions of life and labor without gaining for them any substantial measure of power or control.

For all of us who have grown up and lived within such a society, it seems to us a natural condition. And in fact, it is probable that most people believe, if they've ever thought about the matter, that things have always been pretty much this way. This entirely false belief is encouraged not only by the tendency of the human mind to accept the appearances presented to the senses (after all, what is science but an attempt to get behind such appearances?), but also by the bias of our educational institutions and the other instruments of information and education.

The educational system, as a rule, is prevented from entertaining and teaching any but the narrowest views on this subject. And the views which both our schools and the other instruments of information accept are those which stress not the very recent appearance and thus possibly transitory character of these social relations, but rather their supposed naturalness, permanence, and of course, superiority to all others.

But the most important single thing to grasp about a society of a tiny owning class and a vast working class is the very recent date of its appearance and the extraordinary swiftness with which it has developed. In the United States, for example, it is only a little more than a century since hired labor became the lot of the majority of the population. At the start of the nineteenth century, at least four-fifths of the nonslave population was self-employed, chiefly in farming.

The slave population again was not hired labor in the modern sense, but rather labor owned outright, in a barbaric throwback to the social relations of antiquity. But the working class was very small, so far as we can judge from all available information, and moreover consisted in large part of household servants rather than workers in capital-expanding enterprise.

Apart from these and from the slaves, most of the population was self-employed in one form or another. And although the United States was exceptional in the matter of the availability of land and other so-called frontier conditions, much the same was true of Europe despite this difference of condition.

If we turn now to the census of the U.S. population taken in 1970, we find that only some 10 percent of the working population of the country was self-employed. That's 10 percent as against 80 percent at the beginning of the last century. Now I must caution that this doesn't mean that all the other 90 percent of the population was working class. It's one of the peculiarities of the modern corporate structure that all persons within it share the same formal relation to it. They're all on the payroll, whether managers or production line workers, engineers or sweepers, department heads or clerks, the chairman of the grievance committee or the chairman of the board. All are carried on the payroll as employees. This has a marked effect on the census figures that I've just mentioned.

Thus, from the 90 percent of the population who are not self-employed, we must remove the officials and the managers perhaps down to the level of foreman, in order to remove from the working class the controllers and organizers of the enterprises and their managerial agents.

Now, one must also take account of the middle layers of employment, those who exercise professional planning, organizing, and other staff functions, because these layers occupy a special position in the social structure which must be analyzed separately. But when one has done this and when one leaves behind only the mass of labor at the truly working-class level (the highest stratum of which, in terms of pay, training, and responsibility, are the skilled craftsmen and craftswomen of the factory and the office, and whose lowest level is made up of the immense mass of people employed in other clerical, production, service, and trade occupations), then there remains, according to one calculation that I attempted in *Labor and Monopoly Capital*, no less than two-thirds and probably closer to three-quarters of the entire employed population. Now, I must emphasize that this estimate includes no teachers, no nurses, and no office workers above the level of secretary or bookkeeper.

In 1970 this embraced, as I have said, close to three-fourths of the population counted by the census as economically active. Only seven censuses earlier, in 1900, an estimate made according to the same principle shows just about half of the population in the working-class category. From this we can see how swiftly the working class grows and how powerful is the tendency of the capitalist mode of production to convert every form of independent work into hired or wage labor.

Thus it's clear that the formation of the working class is by no means a mere matter of population growth. It involves the ruination of other classes and their conversion into raw material for exploitation by capitalist enterprises. In the first instance, at the beginning of the process in the United States, it is the ruin and the urbanization of the farming population that supplies the recruits for the working class. We have already noted that the largest part of the population was, at the beginning of the last century, made up of farmers and farm families. If we now note that all farm employment in this country, including owners, managers, and hired farm labor, is at present below 4 percent of the employed population, we can see how immense this change has been.

I think it is hard for people of the present student generation to understand what an upheaval the United States has gone through in this respect and how recent that upheaval was. When my generation was growing up, this wholesale destruction of a way of life was still going on. Even as recently as thirty or forty years ago, we still thought of the farming population as one of the great classes of modern society. Now, it's a mere remnant of its former self, dominated—in the main—by great corporate farms and embracing a total workforce that is far exceeded even by the number of college students.

The farming population is virtually all gone now. The special farming population of the South, the black population—which after the end of slavery supplied the labor of the whole southern portion of the United States as plantation workers and sharecroppers—converted in large measure into wage labor, in urban industries of all kinds. Almost all the rest of the farm population similarly converted into urban labor of various kinds.

Next we must speak of the ruined and dispersed peasant population of Europe, especially southern and eastern Europe, which have also, in considerable measure, gone into the formation of the U.S. working class. It's interesting to note that the peasantry of these same portions of Europe is today contributing larger masses of workers to the urban labor of northern Europe, particularly Germany, England, to some extent France, the Scandinavian countries, and Switzerland (almost the whole working class of Switzerland is imported labor). These same masses served as the principal reserve army of labor for the United States in the years of the tremendous immigration to this country, especially from roughly 1890 to the First World War. Today, they serve as one of the principal reserve armies of labor for the northern European continent.

Then there are the peasant populations of Puerto Rico, of Mexico, of other countries on our Caribbean and Latin American rim, as well as portions of those trans-Pacific populations in the Philippines, Hawaii, Japan, China, and other areas which have been washed over by the tide of U.S. capital accumulation. All of these have also contributed more or less heavily to the working class of the United States. Especially in the case of Latin America and the Philippines, we see here a typical capitalist world process at work. The penetration of imperialism disrupts age-old ways of life and produces a surplus population which is dispersed from the land and reassembled in the cities of the colonial regions in great poverty and misery.

Next, the overseas capitalist countries draw upon this labor power as raw material for exploitation by importing this labor into the metropolis. Puerto Rico is an almost textbook example of this process. A similar dynamic can be seen in northern Europe, starting with Hitler's Third Reich, which is really the beginning of the period of the imports into Germany of the working population of southern and eastern Europe. Beginning under Hitler and continuing in the post–World War II period, northern Europe has raised this arrangement to a fine art and even has the legal means of regulating the flow of labor not only into their countries but also back home again, in accordance with the varying needs of capital accumulation.

This the United States is trying to emulate today, not by legal but by extralegal means, simply by winking at the arrival of large masses of Latin American labor power when it is needed and starting a campaign to send it back the moment the natural reserves of surplus labor (reserves which are produced by the capital accumulation process at home) grow big enough.

Finally, and in some ways most importantly, still speaking of the populations that went into the formation of the U.S. working class, there is the other sex. Women made up only 18 percent of the so-called labor force at the beginning of this century; they now make up just short of 40 percent. There appears to be no slackening of the trend, and it is clear that it will not be long before women make up half the labor force, or as near to such a situation as makes no difference.

The largest single reason for the vast increase of working women is the same for both waves and the office-trade service wave of more recent decades. In both cases the drawing upon women for mass labor was associated with the opening up of new kinds of jobs and thus accompanied an occupational shift in which new mass occupations were established as so-called women's jobs. The typing of these jobs as jobs for women enabled employers to draw upon a vast pool of low-wage labor—a fact which, more than any other, is responsible for the assignment of these new occupations to women.

For example, clerical work in the United States and in England started out almost entirely as a male occupation. There were hardly any women. It was a much different kind of stratum then. The word *clerk* meant something different; it meant almost a semimanager, certainly an assistant manager of some sort. And clerks were in line for promotions. As clerical labor was transformed into a mass occupation however, although it didn't start out as a female occupation, it was rapidly transformed into one. Today it is overwhelmingly female except for certain types of workers who are listed as clerks, like receiving clerk, postal clerk, and so on, who are mainly men.

The earlier, factory wave of feminization did not in the end stick, except in certain industries. But the present wave obviously is sticking, with the resulting creation of a giant new feminized working class, the future of unionism and social struggles in the United States.

Let me add, also, another reason for the feminization of the working population, and that is the cycle of capital accumulation in the household-related industries. I'll explain what I mean by that. Capital, as we have seen, is extraordinarily jealous of every work activity which is not carried on under its banner and which does not pay tribute to capital. As we've seen in the case of farming—and it's also true in the case of a variety of businesses, like retail trade—capital tends to destroy these as areas of inde-pendent entrepreneurship and recreate them as areas for the profitable investment of capital. In the case of retail trade, the elimination of the small retail store and the growth of the supermarket is the prime instance.

Just so with household work. On the one side, various household aids are developed which shorten the time spent in cleaning, the preparation of food, and so on. On the other hand, these activities are moved outside the household and recreated in profitable form as manufacturing, retailing, and service industries. Thus millions of women now clean, make beds, prepare food, wait on tables, and wash clothes in canneries, restaurants, food shops, hotels, motels, commercial laundries, etc.—doing the same sorts of work that they did in the home in the past, while at the same time much of the cooking, baking, canning, washing, and hospitality formerly done in the home has been moved into such commercial enterprises. Apologists will tell us that this is a more efficient way of doing things, which may or may not be the case. But whether it's the case or not, efficiency is not the reason this shift has taken place.

The reason is that this has enabled capital to divert millions of hours of daily labor to its own purposes; that this labor, formerly done privately and outside the grip of capital, is now done within its grip and, therefore, pays its tribute of profit to capital. This is another important part of the femi-nization of the labor force over the past three-quarters of a century, and one which has not yet run its course.

In the past, therefore, the U.S. standard of living, whatever it was, was typically sustained by one working adult in the family. Today the same standard of living typically requires the wages of two adults. When we con-sider the effect of this on family life and on child-rearing under the condi-tions of the cities today (where no real facilities are provided for such a situation), we may say that in addition to the ruined and dispersed peasant population which formed a source for the U.S. working class, more recently the ruined and dispersed U.S. family also forms a major source for the modern working class.

So much for our discussion of the sources of the working-class population. Let us now consider the nature of its work. The nature of its work must be considered under two headings. First, there's the change in the work processes themselves, brought about by capitalist management. And second, there's the shifting of the working population from some occupations into other different occupations, which of course also represents the change in the nature of the work being done.

Until the capitalist era, that is, for thousands and thousands of years up to only two centuries ago, the history of work was, with certain specialized exceptions, the history of craftsmanship. Throughout human history, and until it was changed by capitalist management, work was accomplished by men and women who spent the entire early part of their lives learning the traditional processes of transforming raw materials into useful objects. The smith fashioned tools, implements, and hardware of iron. The carpenter framed buildings and the cabinetmaker created furniture of wood. The potter made clay vessels; the cordwainer, footware; the weaver, cloth; the tailor, clothing; and so on. Of course, the most widespread craft of all was that of farming.

The typical craft apprenticeship lasted from four to seven years—in precapitalist times, more commonly seven. The farming apprenticeship, which began in earlier childhood, was much longer even than that.

The practitioners of each craft worked independently, that is, they organized their own tools, materials, and processes according to their own judgment. And their own judgment was presumed to be the final authority on the right way to do a job, since they themselves were the repositories of craft knowledge and experience. In this organization of work, both the conception and the execution of the tasks of production are united in the same individual.

In the hands of the capitalist employing a mass of labor under his control, however, all of this has been rapidly changed and, where it has not yet been changed, is rapidly being changed. The capitalist, at first by himself and later with the assistance of a managerial and technical staff, takes over all of the knowledge, the standards, the principles of the labor processes of society, which now become mysteries to the workers. And he parcels out these duties and operations of the process in bits and pieces, a small piece to each individual worker who is now presumed to need no real knowledge or skill other than that required to follow directions and perform one or several special tasks with rapidity and diligence.

The worker now becomes truly that which I defined him or her to be early in this talk, the hand by which capital performs the tasks necessary to make a profit. The ideal organization toward which the capitalist strives is one in which the worker possesses no basic skill upon which the enterprise is dependent and no historical knowledge of the past of the enterprise to serve as a fund from which to draw on in daily work, but rather where everything is codified in rules of performance and laid down in lists that may be consulted (by machines or computers, for instance), so that the worker really becomes an interchangeable part and may be exchanged for another worker with little disruption.

This may be seen most clearly in such a job as automobile assembly, where, as the technology projects of Yale University found in a study, the average operation at one major company takes three minutes, and the learning time for this operation varies from a few hours to a week. Nor is this true only of factory jobs.

Charles Silverman, the *Fortune* editor, cites a recent study (what was called in the jargon of government and sociology, a manpower survey) by the New York State Department of Labor, which concluded that two-thirds of all the jobs in New York State can be learned in a few days, weeks, or at the very most months of on-the-job training.

Now, you will recall that at the onset we saw that the entire working class embraced some two-thirds to three-quarters of all jobs. And thus this survey means that almost all jobs on a working-class level have been reduced to a state of insignificance of content so that those who do them— all the operatives, the laborers, the clerical workers, sales workers, service workers, even many of those who are still called craftsmen—are expected to make a working life of forty or fifty years out of these scraps of duties which, when put together with what everyone else is doing, give the capitalist a result which he and his staff have planned, which they alone understand, and which satisfies only them (by expanding their capital), but satisfies no one else, whether as worker or as consumer.

In the present organization of industry and trade, an increase of knowledge makes the mass of workers not more but less fitted for their jobs, because they enter industry not in order to work (over the years) toward a decent and rewarding mastery over that branch of work into which they've come, but merely in order to serve the production process in limited routines which they've learned quickly, after which their growth as citizens of the world of work comes to an end.

This method of work organization has as its goal the extraction of the largest possible surplus product—that is, product over and above what the worker is paid—from an unwilling working population. That this population is unwilling goes without saying in a capitalist or in any other hierarchically organized society, because the working population has been in advance divested of its stake in the process of production, as it has been stripped of ownership of the means of producing, stripped of ownership of the product, and has no direct interest in the outcome of the process.

That's the starting point of the capitalist organization of production and when, as a result, the workers are next stripped of *knowledge* of the process as a whole and *control* over it and are reduced to the performance of simplified tasks, their alienation from the process is still further increased. The capitalist organization of society makes necessary the capitalist organization of production and the capitalist organization of production then in turn intensifies the need for ever stricter controls over the performance of the worker until the worker ceases to be an autonomous human being in any recognizable sense and becomes a mere instrument.

It is only by such an organization of production, abominable though it may be, that large masses of surplus product may be wrung from an indifferent or hostile mass of people. And it feeds on itself, becoming by its very nature always worse and worse.

This is an abbreviated statement of the tendency of labor processes in our society. I must interpolate here, since I noticed as you went around the room that the incidence of craftsmen and -women in this gathering is probably high (those of you who work as electricians, carpenters, and so on), and maybe you recognize in your own working lives only some of the beginnings of these things. But insofar as craftsmen continue to practice their crafts as autonomous mechanics, true mechanics, they are thus far and to some extent exempt from this tendency, but that's not true of all the rest of the working population and I'm sure it will become increasingly less true of craftsmen, because the story of the tendency of the labor process in capitalist society is the story of the destruction of craftsmanship.

Now, having dealt with this, even if briefly, we're in a position to turn to our second aspect which I've already mentioned, that is, the evolution of work, which is the shift to new occupations. There are many aspects to the rapid occupational shifts which have formed part of the development of capitalism, especially during the past hundred years, and it'll be impossible to cover all of them in this discussion. For this reason, I'd like to take a look at these shifts from a single point of view and only one, because it seems to me the most important single organizing principle.

This is the movement from occupations which are productive to those which are unproductive. By productive, I don't mean anything fancy. There are technical definitions. I simply mean organizations which produce useful objects or use-values, or useful services, not necessarily objects.

I must caution that this definition isn't meant in any narrow sense of separating so-called manual labor from so-called nonmanual labor. As we've seen, it's the tendency of the capitalist mode of production to remove from the shop all the functions of record-keeping, calculation, planning, and so on, in order to reduce labor to its simplest elements, and to perform these tasks in the office. This brings into being small armies of clerks who do things which are necessary for production and which were formerly done on the shop floor as part of production.

So a great variety of clerical work, transportation work, and the like is part of productive labor, even though these workers do not put their hands directly to the product. Nevertheless, and leaving aside these forms of productive work, there has been a tremendous shift of work to unproductive labor in the United States.

Now, the first requirement of such a shift is that the productivity of those who *do* produce useful things or services must rise enormously. As we all know, this has been happening. Since each capitalist combines the resources of science and technology with the resources of management to extract from his workers an ever greater surplus, the effect is the lessening of the working population required to produce useful things and services consumed by the entire society.

Let me give you some indications of the extent to which this has been going on. In manufacturing, mining, and construction industries of the United States (which are, of course, the prime productive industries), employment has risen consistently during the entire period for which records have been kept: from 1820, when the first occupational census was taken, to the present. But the rate of increase has slowed until in recent decades this growing number of workers represents an ever smaller proportion of the working population.

Thus, from 1820 to 1920, the censuses consistently showed about half or perhaps a little less than half of all nonagricultural workers as being engaged in those industries. But after 1920, this percentage began to go down until 1970 no more than one-third of all nonagricultural workers were occupied in the fields of manufacturing and associated industries.

If we compare employment with output in a variety of manufacturing and transportation industries, this tendency of a growing output and a relatively declining number of workers is illustrated even more graphically. I use here a set of figures that deal only with the years 1947 to 1964. Even for this very short period of years, the change is very striking. In these seventeen years of constantly rising production, very small increases of labor or no increases at all typically suffice to produce a much larger output. In those few cases where production actually fell slightly for special reasons, the results for employment were catastrophic.

For example, in bituminous coal mining during that period, production showed a decline of some 20 percent. But in the same period two-thirds of the coal miners were eliminated. In the case of the railroads, there was a very slight decline in ton-miles hauled, a decline of less than 10 percent, but this was accompanied by an employment cut of almost half. In these two industries alone the employment decline was almost one million workers. But even those industries which registered moderate increases in production registered declines in employment. The largest industry of this category, the textile mill, increased its output by more than 40 percent, but employed one-third fewer workers at the end of the period than at the beginning.

Other industries in this category, including iron and steel foundries, malt liquors, lumber and wood products, and footwear, showed production increases of 15 to 40 percent, accompanied by employment drops of 10 to 25 percent. Even some industries which increased their output by as much as two-thirds, up to a doubling of output, had difficulties in maintaining their employment. It was only the industries that had enormous increases in output—for instance, telephone communications, instrument manufacture, electrical equipment and machinery, motor freight, electric power and gas, aluminum, and air transport—that showed any increase in employment; but the increases in employment were typically far smaller than the additional output. For example, the electrical machinery and motor freight industries roughly tripled their production, while adding respectively no more than 50 to 70 percent to their employment. The electric power and gas industry roughly quadrupled its output but added only some 25 percent to its employment.

I don't want to throw too many figures at you, but let me just add what will interest a great many of you because you probably work in construction. In the construction industry, the reduction of the number of workers while output is going up is, of course, harder by virtue of the nature of the processes employed. It's not like a factory process. But even there something of the same sort happened. That is, in these years I've been talking about, the construction industry doubled its output but didn't double its employment; it increased its employment only by half as much, by 50 percent.

Now, all this raises the question, where is all this labor going? What's the outcome of all this increased productivity? It would be easy enough to guess what sort of an outcome such rapidly increased productivity would have, let's say, in a cooperative society of associated producers, who would feel the pressures of work lessening as productivity rose, and who could improve society, improve work itself, the easier it became to turn out the required goods and services. But we are not dealing here with such a society of cooperating associated producers. We're dealing with a capitalist society which has laws of its own according to which it evolved.

In such a society, the pressures of work, of the drive to increase productivity, become more intense the more productivity rises and the huge masses of labor thrown off by the productive industries are absorbed into unproductive labors of a variety of sorts.

What sort of unproductive labors? Let me give you these examples: the banking, the insurance, the investment, the marketing industries; the accounting and control industries, including those operated by the government in the form of regulatory or tax agencies; the relief industries, such as those which deal with unemployment compensation or welfare. The relief industries, by the way, are virtually the only ones which are having a boom in employment right now, while employment in all others or almost all others is going down.

These are some examples of unproductive industries, but furthermore, even manufacturing industries—whose total employment, as we have seen, is shrinking in relative terms—have an increasing number of unproductive jobs on their payrolls. For instance, all manufacturing industries now have swollen marketing sections which employ labor of all sorts and armies of clerks as they compete to enlarge sales of their products. Or as another example, even a good deal of labor that actually goes into working on products can be unproductive, insofar as it is made necessary by marketing considerations rather than by the actual requirements of a solid and useful product. In this class are the model changes in automobiles and other products, as well as various means of shoddy and useless ornamentation, which the demented styling departments proliferate in order to pile up selling points against their competitors.

We must also take into consideration the fact that large amounts of so-called manufacturing labor are really carried on entirely for purposes of marketing. As a prime instance of this, let me cite the printing industry, which produces immense amounts of advertising material in the form of giant newspapers and magazines which alternate one column of editorial matter with ten tons of advertising matter, or the radio and television industry, which is organized according to the same principle even if it cannot be carried to the same extremes.

What we see in all these examples is that the capitalist system has special needs of its own which guide labor into channels that make sense only from the capitalist point of view, not from the point of view of useful labor. These needs are:

(1) The marketing struggle of the corporations to divert consumer dollars to themselves.

(2) The immense accounting needs of a society based not on production but on profits, where the end product is thus not useful objects but money and credit.

(3) The rise of industries which themselves produce nothing (the chief examples are banking and insurance), and which occupy the labors of millions of persons in diverting the surplus to the capitalists who supply capital.

The result of all this is clear, and anyone who has studied the occupational statistics and the way they've been evolving can't come to any other conclusion unless his mind is always working toward making an apology for the way things are, rather than facing the facts. The result is that society increasingly takes the form of an inverted pyramid and rests upon an ever narrower base of productive labor, so that the productive workers are driven ever harder to produce an ever greater product.

This is the end result of a system which regards all labor expended upon production as an intolerable drain on the pocketbook, while labor expended on speculation, marketing, and all such means to divert the surplus products from the hands of one set of capitalists into the hands of another is the real purpose of society.

Now, by all this I don't mean to say that all those in the unproductive enterprises occupy a privileged position in society and live at the expense of productive workers. The workers who have been shifted into enterprises of this kind were not shifted there by their own will but by the evolution of capitalist society, and they're in no better position than the workers in productive enterprises. In fact, since they are still largely unorganized, these workers are, generally speaking, much worse off than workers in productive enterprises. Workers in finance, real estate, and insurance or in retail and wholesale trade are generally paid on a scale below those in manufacturing, mining, and construction.

And if we look at the matter from the occupational standpoint, clerical workers are again more poorly paid than factory operatives, on the average. We've come a long way since a bank, for instance, consisted of a banker with his brother-in-law as the teller. These industries employ great armies of labor organized in a way similar to factory organization—workers who are increasingly used as interchangeable cogs in an increasingly mechanized process and subjected ever more to the same pressures that have long been familiar to the factory worker.

Finally, we must deal with unemployment. Is not another result of the rapid shrinkage of productive labor the growth of unemployment? Well, to the extent that this shrinkage is not compensated by the growth of new industries, either of a productive kind or the unproductive kind we have been describing, an inevitable result is the rise in unemployment. Now, that's not always the case: during rapid upswings of the business cycle, unemployment may be and has been kept down. But I must emphasize that even during a very successful period of growth and capital accumulation, such as we have lived through from the beginning of World War II until just recently, the rate of unemployment which fluctuated in every business cycle still showed a steady and persistent rise throughout the period as a whole. Thus we came out of each recession with a larger pool of unemployment than when we entered, until we arrived at the point where we had higher rates of unemployment in prosperity than we used to have in recession.

A 5 percent unemployment rate, which economists now pronounce themselves absolutely tickled with, and which they would consider a happy prosperity rate today, used to be regarded (in the late 1940s) as an intolerably high recession rate. Moreover, I'm among those who believe that the rise of unemployment even before the present recession has been grossly understated by official figures. But this is another story . . .

[Following a brief passage that could not be transcribed because of a technical difficulty, Braverman summarizes the main factors in the formation of the U.S. working class.]

3

WORKING-CLASS STUDIES

Where It's Been Lately and Where It's Going

SHERRY LINKON, BILL MULLEN, JOHN RUSSO,
SUSAN RUSSO, AND LINDA STROM

The myth of classlessness, that uniquely American culturewide consensual evasion which stresses individual difference over class identification, has been exploded in the midst of economic restructuring, technological unemployment, and regressive legislation. As many individuals find that they are only one job from poverty and surrender their illusions about middle-class existence, classlessness has lost its powers of legitimation. This delegitimation explains the popularity of political appeals by conservative politicians like Pat Buchanan, who can now proudly profess to "Stand up for the working men and women" whose jobs are threatened by unfair trade deals, corporate restructuring, and immigration policy done for the benefits of huge corporations. It also helps explain why the discussion of class in America, and especially the working class, has once again surfaced in political, economic, and academic discourse.

It is generally understood that the absence of discussion of the working class between the end of World War II and the early 1980s was largely the result of the Cold War, progressive legislation, and the lessening of economic inequality in America. Conversely, the massive erosion of economic security in the last fifteen years—job security, health security, retirement security, and purchasing power—brought into question the expanding distribution of wealth and power and issues of class (poverty, equality, opportunity, and deprivation).

Less well understood is how the myths of a classless society were buttressed by the resurgence of individualism in the 1970s and the rise of identity politics and multiculturalism within the liberal and progressive communities. In response to the communitarian ideas of the 1960s, individualism described opportunity, social place, and economic success on the basis of personal traits. The most obvious economic example was the idolatry associated with individual risk taking and financial wizardry in the "go-go" period of the 1980s and the 1990s. In academic circles, attention to individualism surfaced in the form of ideas about subjectivity. While subjectivity questions the existence of the unified individual subject and highlights the influence of membership in various cultural groups on individual consciousness, it nonetheless suggests that each person attempts to negotiate his/her identity individually, not as a member of a class.

Likewise, contemporary discussions of multiculturalism and identity politics defined cultural groups and/or political groups in largely separate terms such as race, gender, ethnicity, sexuality, environmentalism, pro-life, and others. While apparently focusing on collective identities, the emphasis on individuality is retained by emphasizing that each individual negotiates multiple membership in cultural and political groups. In this context, celebrating diversity can mean just the opposite—celebrating individual identity.

During this period, working-class studies was all but ignored except by a handful of "new" labor historians and labor studies professors. On the one hand, many of these same academics were changing the intellectual terrain in the study of class by rejecting traditional notions of class formation and class consciousness in favor of a more dynamic study of the working class which stressed its ability to shape society and their own consciousness. Yet, the role of class as an influence on subjectivity, especially for the working class, was mentioned but rarely fully explored in the discussion of multiculturalism and identity politics.

This neglect of class also spilled into the political arena as many advocates of multiculturalism and identity politics simply ignored the plight of the working class. Many of those who did acknowledge class did so in limited ways, reading working-class experience only through the categories of race, ethnicity, and gender. In fact, as the French political theorist Andre Gorz argues in his book *Farewell to the Working Class*, the working class had been marginalized and coopted by science and technology and replaced by the women's and environmental movements as the central progressive forces in society. Of course, this disregard only made it easier for corporations to deindustrialize and disinvest in the late 1970s and early 1980s with hardly a peep from the liberal community, who largely accepted the restructuring as somehow part of the natural economic order.

The marginalization and sense of betrayal by liberals, the traditional allies of the working class, only intensified feelings of dispossession and anti-intellectualism and fueled existent racism and sexism within many working-class communities. In turn, this lead to a politics of resentment within the working class that supported conservative attacks on liberal economic and social policy. At the same time, the working class was abandoned by both the policy-making right and the academic left. Conservative attacks on "political correctness" helped delegitimize academic discussions of multiculturalism, while the narrow focus of the debate on race and gender allowed academics to ignore class and right-wing policy attacks on the working class. Therefore, ironically, the proponents of multiculturalism, identity politics, liberal sociology, and political economics may have helped to make possible a political consensus that supported conservative economics and politics that was often antithetical to progressive interests.

However, in the last decade, as the cumulative effects of economic restructuring, conservative political climate, and the marginalization of the working class have become apparent, a reconsideration of the relationship between the working class and proponents of multiculturalism and identity politics has begun. Simply put, this involves the exploration of the intersection of multiculturalism, identity politics, and class where class becomes the focus of serious critical attention and a point of linkage between marginalized groups. At the forefront of this reexamination are such scholars as David Roediger, Manning Marable, Bruce Nelson, Paul Lauter, Janet Zandy, George Lipsitz, and bell hooks. The American Association of Colleges and Universities' "American Commitments: Diversity, Democracy, and Liberal Learning" project has led a parallel effort to bring this intersection into college curricula and institutional reform.

The 1995 Working-Class Lives/Working-Class Studies Conference at Youngstown State University (YSU) brought scholars from history, literature, art, sociology, ethnography, and labor studies together with creative artists to enhance our knowledge of working-class studies among various publics and to initiate a Center for Working-Class Studies. One of the most exciting lessons of the 1995 Working-Class Lives/Working-Class Studies conference was the incredible range of creative, scholarly, and pedagogical work being done by artists and academics interested in the working class.

Our own work reflects just a portion of this, and in the remaining pages, we offer a necessarily incomplete survey of contemporary developments in working-class studies and some suggestions for future directions. In work that links working-class studies with multiculturalism, thoughtful analysis of the ways differences of race and ethnicity have played out within the working class offers an important enhancement of labor and working-class history. Representations of working-class life encompass a wide range of genres, including visual arts, performance art, music, theater, film, and writing. Rather than attempt to describe developments in all of these areas, we offer a brief overview of recent work in the visual arts as an example.

Closely related to the arts is critical writing about representations of working-class life and the production and use of such images. A discussion of popular culture criticism highlights several approaches to the study of the relationship between working-class people and popular culture. Finally, we turn our attention to the work of teaching, with a discussion of the needs of working-class students and some of the innovative responses being offered by college teachers inside the academy and beyond. Our goal here is to sketch broadly some of the most interesting and important developments in working-class studies in the 1990s, to suggest some of the directions the field is taking, and to highlight the range of exciting work that remains to be done as well as the challenges of such work.

RACE, ETHNICITY, AND WORKING-CLASS STUDIES

Contemporary scholarship in working-class studies on the interrelation of class, race, and ethnicity has been a welcome and necessary corrective to traditional labor and working-class histories which have naturalized race and racial categories while using a reductive (usually Marxist) class-based analysis which either romanticized or simply made transparent the "whiteness" of U.S. labor history. With some notable exceptions, both old left and new labor history scholarship fell prey to these tendencies.[1] In addition, rigid application of either Marxian or split-market labor theory to worker relations and class formation often diminished or displaced racial and ethnic tensions in the working class, or ignored, as Patricia Hill Collins has noted, those models' failure to take into account undocumented or non-unionized forms of working-class labor such as domestic servitude.[2] Finally, it wasn't until well into the new labor history that concentration on worker agency helped to illuminate both the role of minority workers in the formation of union and working-class consciousness—treating workers of color as "actors, not mere subjects" in Chris Friday's words (6)—and the racism of white ethnic rank-and-filer assumption and protection of white class privilege which earned them what David Roediger has memorably termed the "wages of whiteness."[3]

The primary impetus for recent academic reconsiderations of race and ethnicity in class formation has been the simultaneous shift in the postwar period toward a racially diversified (and increasingly feminized) labor force in the economy, and the not unrelated emergence of liberal multiculturalism in the academy. The belated convergence of these two movements has given rise to the present formation of working-class studies, bringing together emergent work on race, class, and ethnicity in labor history and labor studies with their more theoretical and cultural formulations in the humanities.

Writing on race, ethnicity, and the working class traditionally has been dominated by African American intellectuals and well predates both the new labor history and liberal multiculturalism.[4] The longevity of African American scholarship in the field, the role of slavery in the formation of American working-class identity, black migratory patterns and their contribution to twentieth-century industrial formation and the centrality of black-white tensions in the American labor movement (and the larger society) have subsequently made the African American experience the central site for working-class studies scholarship on race, class, and ethnicity. A controversial contemporary work directing critical attention toward this site is undoubtedly William Julius Wilson's *The Declining Significance of Race: Blacks and Changing American Institutions*. Published in 1978, the book challenged traditional dual-labor market theory and Marxist analysis to argue that black Americans in the postwar period were for the first time more determined by economic than racial factors. Citing exacerbated class stratification among blacks in the economy brought on, ironically, by successful liberal reformism and the civil rights movement, Wilson argued that "in the economic sphere, class has become more important than race in determining black access to privilege and power" (2).

Wilson's argument, though it naturalized race and racial categories and paid little attention to gender differences, helped provoke scholars in both labor history and cultural theory toward reconsideration of race/class connections both historically and in our time. Robin Kelley, in two important books ideologically distinct from Wilson's, helped perform this task. Informed by both classic Marxian analysis, new labor history's attention to worker agency and new historicism's "bottom-up" perspective, Kelley's 1990 *Hammer and Hoe: Alabama Communists and the Great Depression* challenged myopic old left focus on union activity and class consciousness among white workers by making black workers—and their culture—central to discussion of both racial and class consciousness. Kelley's 1994 *Race Rebels: Culture, Politics and the Black Working Class* applied these methodologies to a range of twentieth-century sites, including rap music, arguing convincingly for worker self-activity and agency in places outside the scope of traditional labor and working-class history focus—as in clothing, fashion, and music.[5]

Kelley's work lies squarely in the vanguard tradition of W. E. B. Du Bois and C. L. R. James, and more recently of Manning Marable, whose *How Capitalism Underdeveloped Black America* is perhaps the most thorough and penetrating account of how black workers have been alternately marginalized and impelled toward rebellion. Marable's attention to black women workers has also reflected both the specific influence of the women's movement and its scholarship and a broader inclusivity reflective of emerging 1980s multiculturalism. Those tendencies have converged to produce a number of correctives to male dominance as both subjects and recorders of (white) working-class history. In *Black Feminist Thought: Knowledge, Consciousness and the Politics of Empowerment* Patricia Hill Collins draws from Afrocentric cultural theory to form an analysis of black women's work that transcends both status-attainment and class-conflict models by taking into account African and African American family structures, gender roles, and social differentiation. Collins notes that, "Racially segmented labor markets, gender ideologies in both segmented labor markets and family units, and the overarching capitalist class structure in which Black women's specific race, gender, and social class positions are embedded all structure Black women's work" (46).

Collins's work, what might be called the newest labor history, is somewhat emblematic of tendencies in working-class studies scholarship in Hispanic, Asian American, and even the most recent "white studies" schools. Grounded in multiculturalist appreciation for difference, feminist theory and poststructuralist wisdom on the social constructedness of identity—racial, sexual, or even class—this work points toward a potentially radical polyphony in working-class studies that will be needed to provide a lens on twenty-first-century labor demographics. Key works in Hispanic and Latino working-class studies include the forerunning *The Chicano Worker* by Vernon Briggs, Walter Fogel, and Fred H. Schmidt, a preliminary statistical study of Chicano workers and effects on public policy. Vicki Ruiz's *Cannery Women/Cannery Lives: Mexican Women, Unionization, and the California Food Processing Industry*, like the work of Kelley and Collins, constructs complex labor narratives interrelating worker self-activity and workers' culture. Mexican women workers, according to Ruiz, "did not act in isolation—they were part of a multicultural labor force. . . . Nurtured by gender-based job segregation, extended family ties, and common neighborhoods, intra-ethnic and interethnic groups helped women cope and at times resist the prevailing conditions of work" (xvi).[6] Working-class studies accounts of Asian American workers similarly have attempted to reverse stereotypical emphasis in previous labor histories on worker victimization. Sucheng Chan's *This Bittersweet Soil: The Chinese in California Agriculture, 1860–1910* examines Chinese truck gardeners, farmers, and fruit growers beyond the purview of scholarly focus on Chinese merchants and servants which have sustained accounts of Asian workers as "cheap labor" or victim. Similarly, Evelyn Nakano Glenn's *Issei, Nisei, War Bride: Three Generations of Japanese Women in Domestic Service* rejects "static models of class, race, and sex that would treat Japanese women simply as objects of history" to examine the "active resistance of subordinate groups" like Japanese domestic servants. Glenn's feminist analysis of labor market segmentation, providing examples of how different "cohorts" of Japanese American women fit into the labor market at different times successfully provides a dynamic model of interpretation that moves beyond even new labor historians accounts of traditional worker agency (xii–xiii).[7]

Indeed scholarship on Asian American workers helps point to a full circle completed by scholarship in working-class studies on class, race, and ethnicity. Alexander Saxton's *The Indispensable Enemy: Labor and the Anti-Chinese Movement in California*, published in 1971, was not only one of the first by a white scholar to examine and interrelate minority group work experience oppression, but the first to highlight the role of white workers in that oppression. Echoing W. E. B. Du Bois, Saxton noted that white workers—North Americans of European background—had been shaped by three great racial confrontations resulting from labor recruitment or slavery: with the Indian, the African and the Oriental (1). White workingmen (sic) he noted, have been both exploited and exploiters. On the one hand, thrown into competition with nonwhites as enslaved or "cheap" labor, they suffered economically; on the other hand, being white, they benefitted by that very exploitation which was compelling the nonwhites to work for low wages or for nothing. Ideologically they were drawn in opposite directions. Racial identification cut at right angles to class consciousness (xi).

Saxton's neo-Marxist, poststructuralist, multiculturalist caveat contains in dynamic microcosm the issues that run crosshatch through the present historical moment of scholarship on class, race, and ethnicity in working-class studies. Recent books in labor history like David Roediger's *The Wages of Whiteness: Race and the Making of the American Working Class* and *Towards the Abolition of Whiteness: Essays on Race, Politics and Working Class History* attempt to study the evolution of whiteness as a category emerging out of the experiences of workers, indigenous labor organizations and unions, and labor conflict. While Roediger acknowledges the "tragic past and significant roadblocks to the creation of working class nonwhiteness," he concludes that "consciousness of whiteness also contains elements of a critique of that consciousness and that we should encourage the growth of a politics based on hopeful signs of a popular giving up on whiteness" (Roediger 1994, 3). Returning to the study of the working white majority armed with the insights of both minority labor historians and multiculturalist theorists, working-class studies has come to understand and articulate how power and class privilege often come not from the barrel of a gun but from the ideological constructedness and necessity of race.[8]

REPRESENTATIONS: VISUAL ARTS AND POPULAR CULTURE

The arts and popular culture offer rich materials for understanding the experiences and perspectives of working people. Working-class studies encourages the production and dissemination of artistic work by members of the working class and includes scholarly examination of representations of working-class life and the ways the working class has used these representations. Significant work has been done in publishing and reprinting working-class writing, as witnessed in the University of Illinois's republication of a number of 1930s proletarian novels as well as in contemporary anthologies such as Peter Oresick and Nicholas Coles's *Working Classics*. Paul Lauter, Constance Coiner, Barbara Foley, and others have offered critical reexaminations of working-class literature as well.[9] Comparable work is just beginning in the visual arts, while in popular-culture studies, much recent critical attention has focused on the working class as audience. In both the arts and popular culture, issues of production, distribution, reception, and content take center stage.

The visual-art world has long struggled with issues of class. Bound by a history of tension between "high art" and "low art," i.e., "culture" versus popular culture, art has served as a cauldron of fermenting politics, ideals, and individualistic missions. Positional and hierarchical attitudes are part of the art scene of today as well as that of the past. The art/money knot that cyclically devours the contemporary art scene is only a reminder of how art has always been commodified. The changes that are being effected by technology as visual access to information will serve to exacerbate these tensions, especially as the assimilation of technology impacts the accessibility. Artists with the financial ability to address both the creation of work and the viewing of it through technological means are becoming a class of haves over those who have not the same resources.

Within the hierarchy of visual art, painting and sculpture remain the apex, challenged continually by artists who work either functionally, such as in architecture, design, or crafts, or those who deliberately or intuitively defy commodification by virtue of the media they use. Such an artist is Mike Kelley, whose work is an ode to the ethics of craft. Intentionally utilizing materials such as handmade stuffed animals with the intent of presenting both the visual language of sculpture and the purity of the work ethic that is embodied in craft—especially a craft that makes a literal equation between time and money—he defies the traditional art world. Similarly, many feminist artists have specifically chosen materials for their work that is common, everyday. As Lucy Lippard writes in *The Pink Glass Swan*, women artists have frequently used the materials of their households as well as the techniques of their daily housework to make art. That these processes or materials have been devalued (except when pillaged by the male artists of the pop art school) is no surprise. Many outsider artists fall within this realm, using the materials that surround their daily lives to make art that speaks their unique vision. Theirs is not a political stance, however, as much as an economic need to use the leavings of a consumer culture as the means of making art. The commodification of such naive artists by the sophisticated art scene is symbolic of how workers are used for their profits. Other artists, like sculptor Bryn Zellers, find the abandoned industrial artifacts of their communities a rich treasure trove of materials for art that speaks to and of the history of work.

Artists frequently embody political issues in the content of their work. There is a stratification that exists in the art world concerning form versus content. The mystification of abstract or conceptual artists traditionally places work in those categories at a higher level than art that is content driven. Political protest, environmental concerns, racism, sexism, class—regardless of the issue—art that is inspired by the pain of an underclass is not taken as seriously as the loftier visions of pure form. Painters like Sue Coe, who works prolifically to make her work accessible to workers and who has tackled every imaginable controversial issue that affects the daily lives of ordinary folk, also pays homage to the classism of art by selling those very images that can move the masses, within the context of the New York gallery scene.

Increasingly, narratives about work are becoming visual, viable components of the arts world. The Bread and Roses project sponsored by Local 1199, which commissioned artists to commemorate workers or work issues, is an example of an initiative established *by* workers *for* workers. More commonly, issues of work and the workplace are the subject of individual artists whose commitment to the narrative is intense. Included among these would be artists such as Jerri Allyn, whose *American Dining: A Working Woman's Moment* captured the essence of her work as a waitress in an installation environment. Another artist of this genre is photographer Milton Rogovin, whose compelling images in his series *Portraits in Steel*, a collaboration with oral historian Michael Frish, chronicled the lives and work of steelworkers in Buffalo, New York, over a period of ten years as they lost jobs in the steel industry and created new lives for themselves. But these are not the golden gods of the New York art world. These are individuals whose commitment to or background in a working-class experience has compelled them to communicate visually through their work.

Popular-culture studies examine representations of working-class experience from a more analytical perspective, since few of the creators of popular images come from the working class. Working-class studies of popular culture include a very wide range of scholarship that examines mass media such as television, film, and popular literature as well as sports, hobbies, and other forms of entertainment. The field is best understood not in terms of the various genres it studies (music, popular fiction, television) but as a variety of ways of reading popular "texts," including discussions of the production and dissemination of popular culture, studies of audience responses, and analyses of representations within popular texts. Some popular music critics focus on working-class artists, but most critics focus on identifying the texts that are most popular with working-class audiences and considering their appeal. Still others suggest that working-class consumers operate as active interpreters of the media, creating "popular culture" out of the materials provided by mass culture. A brief survey of contemporary popular-culture criticism will highlight these various approaches, though many studies, like those mentioned below, combine several approaches to offer rich, thorough analyses of the interactions between working-class consumers and popular culture.

Many studies focus on the production and dissemination of popular culture, analyzing the roles working-class artists play in creating new popular forms and the ways popular-culture industries get their products into the hands of working-class consumers. Popular artists of working-class background get most attention in the field of popular music, a reflection of the history of popular music as well as its roots as a folk art. Kenneth J. Bindas, for example, traces the development of swing music in the 1930s to interactions among working-class blacks and immigrants, who found music "a means to make easy money" (76). More important, Bindas argues that class identification and urban life allowed musicians from different cultural groups to interact, thus developing new musical styles as well as audiences for them (78). A similar pattern applies to rock and roll, as George Lipsitz shows in *A Rainbow at Midnight*. Lipsitz outlines the working-class roots of rock and roll and shows how postwar working conditions and the migration of both white and black workers from the south to the north created opportunities for the confluence of white and black working-class musics, rhythm and blues and country swing, to form the new genre. He notes the blue-collar jobs previously held by many early rock-and-roll musicians and describes their movement from truck driving, factory work, and farm labor into music studios and radio playlists. He also traces how the creative work of these musicians was co-opted and refashioned by culture industries, both record and television producers, to downplay the music's oppositional tendencies as well as to mask its working-class history. While this approach highlights the exploitation of working-class artists and dominant resistance to their ideas, Lipsitz argues that popular texts nonetheless provide rich sources for oppositional uses by working-class audiences, comparing rock-and-roll songs with wildcat strikes (330). Moreover, he notes, rock-and-roll music made working-class perspectives available to other groups, including the white, middle-class, suburban teenagers who adopted the music as a sign of their own rebellion.

Lipsitz's work moves from analyzing the production and distribution of popular music to considering the oppositional possibilities of rock and roll for working-class audiences, a critical move that harks back to groundbreaking work by British cultural studies scholars, most notably E. P.

Thompson, Raymond Williams, and Stuart Hall, as well as Antonio Gramsci's concept of hegemony. This emphasis on the working-class audience as resistant, active consumers appears in much contemporary popular-culture criticism. Michael Denning's *Mechanic Accents*, a study of dime novels and their readers, is but one strong example. Dime novels were not created by working-class artists, though he suggests that the books are "marked by the imprint of their working-class audience" (5), presumably because publishers sought to appeal to such readers. Focusing on the working class as audience rather than on the production of dime novels, Denning rejects the notion that such books offered mere escapism. We must, he suggests, ask why working-class readers chose these particular books since, he notes (citing Gramsci), any novel would provide a means of escape from everyday life. He argues that the answer can be found in the resistant readings—what he terms "mechanic accents"—available in mass-produced popular fiction. Such texts can be read in different ways, making them rich sources for active struggle over the meaning of working-class experience. The characters and stories in dime novels function as "a body of representations [of class] that are alternately claimed, rejected, and fought over" (77). He argues that working-class readers neither were manipulated by dime novels nor consistently and successfully resisted the dominant messages contained in such books. Rather, he suggests, we should read popular culture as "a contested terrain, a field of cultural conflict where signs with wide appeal and resonance take on contradictory disguises and are spoken in contrary accents" (3).

As Denning's work suggests, popular culture not only provides opportunities for resistance. It also plays a key role in the construction of working-class identity, not simply by representing working-class life but by offering opportunities for interaction and class solidarity. Eric Lott develops this argument as part of his rich analysis of the relationship between blackface minstrelsy and the antebellum working class in *Love and Theft*. The minstrel show "*staged* class . . . through 'blackness,'" a trope that represented the working class in ways that troubled elite critics and reflected the complex mix of fascination, fear, and revulsion involved in white working-class men's efforts to define themselves as distinct from their black counterparts (64, italics in original). Equally important, the minstrel show was part of the development of a popular theater distinct from the "high-class" entertainments designated for the bourgeoisie. Popular entertainment divided between upper and lower tiers, not within one theater, as in earlier productions, but between different theaters located in different parts of town. As Peter Buckley argues in his analysis of the Astor Place Riots of 1849, which erupted as part of a dispute between elite and working-class theater-goers over appropriate audience behavior and competition between elite and working-class performers, popular entertainment provided "a moment when the mob became a class and when the classes seemed in irreconcilable opposition" (20). For both Buckley and Lott, then, popular culture was not simply the culture consumed by the working class; popular culture made possible the creation of working-class self-awareness in the mid-nineteenth century.

Nan Enstad's study of popular fiction and early film suggests that this class-identity function of popular culture continues in the early twentieth century. In "Compromised Positions: Working-Class Women, Popular Culture, and Labor Politics, 1890–1920," she examines dime novel romances that feature working women as heroines and suggests that turn-of-the-century magazine fiction and early films developed the formulas established in the dime novels. Significantly, Enstad argues, class intersected with gender in these narratives, as female characters enacted versions of heroism of labor usually associated with male roles. Moreover, working-class women appropriated the elements of popular narratives in constructing their own subcultural style, including their own forms of political activism, thus using mass culture for their own ends in ways the producers of such texts may not have imagined.

Critics have also read the relationship between popular culture and class identity from the opposite direction, as in a study by Andrea Press and Elizabeth Cole on working-class women's responses to television programs about abortion. Press and Cole argue that the audience's self-identification correlates closely with their responses both to the issue and the characters. Working-class women who identify themselves as middle-class "accept television's depiction of middle-class life as normal and as normative" (58), while those who self-identify as working-class were more likely to "sympathize with the problems attributed to working-class women and their lives on television" (65). Press and Cole highlight "the multivocality of working-class discourse and identity" which "mark[s] deep divisions within working-class women's experience and in their attitudes toward middle-class life and societal authority" (65), a reminder that studies of working-class audiences must take such differences into account.

Other critics analyze representations of working-class life in popular texts, focusing more on content than on production or reception. For example, in *A Rainbow at Midnight*, Lipsitz includes in his discussion of popular music an analysis of the work-resistant content of early rock and roll, which often included direct commentaries on worker-management relations and the difficulties of blue-collar work. In *Time Passages*, he develops a similar analysis of the representation of working-class life in early television programs, tracing the erasure of working-class identity in sitcoms from the late 1940s to the late 1950s. Considering the mix of ethnic and class identities in shows such as *The Goldbergs*, *Mama*, and *Life of Riley*, Lipsitz argues that these shows served to legitimate the developing consumer culture of the early 1950s, assuring viewers that the key to ful-fillment lay in the path taken by Mama's family—away from blue-collar, ethnic neighborhoods and out to the homogenized suburbs. By the late 1950s, television presented only "a dessicated and eviscerated version of working-class life" (62). As Lipsitz notes, 1970s sitcoms such as *The Jeffersons* reprised many of the trends of early 1950s programs: "legitimation through representations of working-class life and commodification through product-centered plot lines and portrayals of families divided by market interests" (73). As a genre financed and thus driven by consumerism—television peddles its prize commodity, the audience, to advertisers—television is inherently wary of representations that do not legitimate materialism, and working-class culture is thus always at risk in television's version of American life. Stanley Aronowitz suggests that the displacement of working-class experience from television continued in the 1980s. He argues that, in 1988, representations of workers had been "refracted through . . . police shows" (194), a result, in part, of the delegitimization of working-class life presented by shows such as *All in the Family*. The lack of positive, or even authentic, representations of working-class experience "force[s] working-class kids to accept middle-class identities as the only legitimate option" (201), Aronowitz claims. Benjamin DeMott echoes this concern in *The Imperial Middle*, which examines the discounting of class as a viable concept in contemporary media culture. Popular culture fosters a belief that America is a classless society through the use of four ways of seeing class as illusory: class as a fantasy, class as a role that can be taken on or off easily, class as an unreliable source of understanding that is no longer valid, and class as "a veil shrouding the real—i.e., moral/intellectual—differences in our midst" (124). DeMott develops his analysis through discussions of *The Cosby Show*, newspaper reports on inner-city drug dealers, and television news coverage of events such as the surrogate motherhood trial of Mary Beth Whitehead.

As our overview of recent work in the visual arts and popular culture studies suggests, the "working class" in the arts and popular culture may refer to creative artists, the subjects represented, and/or the audience. The emphasis in all areas of arts and media criticism within working-class studies has been on the agency of working-class people, whether as creative artists or as active consumers, but critics also acknowledge the problems of representing the working class in a culture that denies its existence. In analyzing this troubling combination of presence and absence, creative energy and exploitation, working-class studies draw on artistic and academic approaches developed in feminist, labor, and multiculturalist fields. Both artists and critics acknowledge the productive but often contested interactions between race, ethnicity, gender, sexuality, and class and their influence on all aspects of representation.

WORKING-CLASS PEDAGOGY

The stories of the working class evolve out of struggle and strife for recognition and equality in a dominant culture that, traditionally, amplified the voices of the middle and upper classes while muting or silencing the voices of the working class. Through the scholarship and writing of Tillie Olsen, Florence Howe, Paul Lauter, Janet Zandy, and others, the academy is learning to become more attuned to the multifarious voices of workers, and from this awareness working-class studies emerges not as a new area of study but rather as an interdisciplinary field that weaves together threads of labor, gender, African American, ethnic, queer, and American studies. The resulting intersection of different histories, experiences, and stories calls for a pedagogy that, as Zandy explains, "rests on old cultural practices of self-education and group study, union organizing, summer school for workers, and cultural expression" (Zandy 1995, 4). As the Center for Working-class Studies takes shape at YSU, one of the primary goals is the dissemination and development of interdisciplinary teaching strategies and methodologies that bring together theory and praxis, and thus combine old cultural practices with new theories of difference.

To work toward this goal, two of the members of the Working-Class Studies Center in collaboration with the United Steel Workers of America Local 1375, university administrators, and a steel company developed a program for workers that allowed them to take college courses and earn a two-year degree in either business administration or labor studies at the union hall. For the program to succeed, all the participants had to work together to design a structure and a curriculum that put the needs of the steelworkers at the center: courses were offered twice a day to accommodate the rotating shifts of the students and registration, advising, and book sales were done on-site. These initial accommodations made it possible for many of the steelworkers to take college courses for the first time by removing some of the barriers—the commute to campus, bureaucratic red tape, and inconvenient class times—that often prevent working people from entering universities.

The administrative and scheduling changes attracted the students, but for the program to succeed and continue to grow, the curriculum and teaching pedagogy had to reflect and incorporate the collective knowledge and experience the steelworkers—who in some cases had more than twenty-five years' experience working in steel mills—brought to the classroom. With this in mind, we designed the courses using the model of "critical literacy" that Catherine Walsh explains "should relate to the contexts of learners' lives, be interesting, purposeful, engaging, incite dialogue and struggle around meanings, interpretations, and identities and promote among learners a critical understanding of their relationship to a broader society, and of their and its political nature, and transformative possibilities" (17). The writing courses focused on the theme of work and in concert with the labor studies courses gave students the critical tools necessary to locate and analyze their historical place in the larger context of working-class history. Students created projects that ranged in scope from a tracing of the historical role women played in steelmaking to the effect of "downsizing" on industry and the consumer. As the students tailored their writing projects to their own interests, they moved from the position of passive learners to active participants in the creation of knowledge.

In "Living and Learning: Some Reflections on Emergence from and Service to the Working Class," Gregory Mantsios, the director of Worker Education at Queens College, CUNY, comments on the difference between "the great ambitions for accomplished careers, successful business ventures, and recognized professional achievements" of the "younger middle-class" students and the desire of the working adult students for " a decent job and the ability to carry on an intelligent conversation." He observes that "class has a way of reining in the spirit" (233). By placing working-class history and experience at the center of the curriculum and teaching students to use that knowledge to effect change both on an individual and collective level, programs like the one at the union hall and at Queens College provide useful teaching models for loosening the hold that class imposes on many working people and our students from working-class families.

Three recent collections addressing the experiences of working-class academics provide rich material to help college faculty consider how higher education affects students from working-class backgrounds. In *Strangers in Paradise: Academics from the Working Class*, Jake Ryan and Charles Sackrey provide both historical perspective on the increasing number of working-class academics since World War II and a selection of essays, most by white, working-class men, commenting on the experience of entering the academy. Michelle M. Tokarczyk and Elizabeth A. Fay's *Working-Class Women in the Academy* and C. L. Barney Dews and Carolyn Leste Law's *This Fine Place So Far from Home* offer additional personal narratives, including essays reflecting the authors' struggles with the double consciousness and different languages they gained at college and their sense of loss as they found themselves not quite fitting in at school and no longer belonging at home. While these volumes do not address pedagogy directly, they provide useful insights into the educational experiences of working-class students in colleges and universities, reminding us that education can be a mixed blessing and suggesting the value of including discussions of working-class experience in college courses.

As working-class studies becomes an academic discipline, scholars, teachers, and students will need to make it their responsibility, as Mantsios teaches his students, "to make higher education and unions into viable instruments for social change and for a better future" (248). This responsibility can become the underpinnings of our teaching philosophies thus insuring that "working-class culture," quoting Zandy, not "become merely an object of study" but rather "a means of struggle" (Zandy 1995, 8). The coalescing of old cultural practices, the model of critical literacy, and theories of class into new teaching methodologies with roots in feminist and multicultural pedagogues keeps the struggle alive by providing a starting point for conceptualizing the intersection of race, class, gender, and ethnicity.

These teaching practices are evolving at work-site locations and in the university classroom.[10] At YSU we offer courses on campus that examine the representation of working-class culture across the various disciplines of labor, women's, African American, and American studies. This interdisciplinary approach inspires collaboration between teachers, and perhaps more importantly, it encourages teachers to model for students the kind of exchange of knowledge that we want to see enacted in the classroom. It also suggests that the boundaries of working-class studies are fluid and require a kind of poetic vision that is able to create histories that celebrate the past, present, and future of working-class people. Our goal for the center is to contribute to this collective project through our scholarship and our teaching, keeping in mind the debt we owe to those whose visions brought us to where we are today and to those like Zandy who are showing us the way: "What is crucial to retrieving and producing working-class culture is the reciprocal and dialogic dimension of the process. We are generationally interdependent: the past is given voice in our work, but our work would not exist without this class history. It is a conversation of multiple voices across time" (Zandy 1995, 5).

CONCLUSION

We have offered here a sampling of the different types of activities currently emerging out of working-class studies—artistic, scholarly, and pedagogical. Our summary is far from comprehensive. As our experience with the Working-Class Lives/Working-Class Studies Conference showed, working-class studies is a broad and vibrant field, and we have only sketched some of its outlines.

Clearly, part of the project of working-class studies, as it has been with African American studies, women's studies, and queer studies, is to demystify and complicate its own subject of study—class—as a category. But most importantly, what has to be restated is that working-class studies is attempting to develop an ideology that can bring together diverse groups in ways that traditional ideas about class have not. In this light, the recent proliferation of working-class studies texts by white male academics critical of whiteness and class identity gives both life and credence to bell hooks's claim that "Everything changed when white male academics 'discovered' cultural studies" (3). Ideas in working-class history dating to Du Bois suddenly have cachet. The *danger* for working-class studies in this sudden popularization lies in the same challenge facing multiculturalism itself, which hooks articulates as follows:

> What does it mean for us to educate young, privileged, predominantly white students to divest of white supremacy if that work is not coupled with work that seeks to intervene in and change internalized racism that assaults people of color; to share feminist thinking and practice if that work is not coupled with fierce action. . . . To create a culture where those who could occupy the colonizing location have the freedom to self-interrogate, challenge, and change while the vast majority of the colonized lack such freedom is merely to keep in place existing structures of domination. . . . Cultural criticism can be an agent for change, educating for critical consciousness in liberatory ways, only if we start with a mind-set and a progressive politics that is fundamentally anticolonialist, that negate cultural imperialism in all its manifestations. (5–6)

Hooks's warning, applied to working-class studies, is a call to an internationalist perspective that can recover the best of early twentieth-century labor radicalism and syndicalism while devising specific strategies for a *global* labor force and academy of the twenty-first century. Working-class studies must have that *praxis* if it is to avoid the recolonization not only of "new labor history" and "liberal multiculturalism," already threatening to become buzzwords for the millennium, but "working-class studies" itself. Working-class studies must move beyond its own potential institutional propensity toward whiteness and classism by engaging scholars, labor activists, and rank and file from across the spectrum, and by continually imagining the university as one of a number of sites of "work." It must, in short, remain a race (and class) traitor to itself. In the future, the line "an injury to one is an injury to all" should not be just an old saw from the Wobblies, but should represent the need to understand the synchronicity of multiculturalism, identity politics, and class.

NOTES

1. David Roediger provides a sober and insightful review of the treatment (or absence) of race in labor history scholarship in " 'Labor in White Skin': Race and Working Class History" in *Towards the Abolition of Whiteness: Essays on Race, Politics, and Working Class History* (London: Verso, 1994). Roediger generally faults

old left historians, with the controversial exception of Philip S. Foner, for their failure to account for race in the formation of the American labor movement. He credits Du Bois and Alexander Saxton in particular for inspiring his own work and a generation of newer labor historians and cultural theorists for whom race, class, and ethnicity are inextricably linked and central to their work, including: Herbert Gutman, Herbert Hill, Richard Slotkin, Gwen Mink, Manning Marable, Peter Rachleff, and Mike Davis. Among so-called new labor historians he cites Eugene Genovese, Immanuel Wallerstein, and David Montgomery for their calls for increased attention to race and slavery in U.S. labor history. He is sympathetic, but more restrained in appraising the work of Sean Wilentz, whose *Chants Democratic* he presents as an example of a new labor history still underrepresenting race and racism in the creation of American white working-class consciousness.

2. Collins has been a pioneer in conceptualizing race, gender, and class interrelations since her 1984 dissertation *Race, Gender and Labor Market Structure: An Organizational Dynamics and Occupational Stratification in an Urban Political Economy*, a study of Cincinnati. Her 1991 book *Black Feminist Thought: Knowledge, Consciousness and the Politics of Empowerment* (New York: Routledge, 1991) is her most advanced theorization of these issues, and an essential text. See also her *Toward a New Vision: Race, Class, and Gender as Categories of Analysis and Connection*. In addition, see Jacqueline Jones's important *Labor of Love, Labor of Sorrow: Black Women, Work, and the Family from Slavery to the Present* (New York: BasicBooks, 1985).

3. Roediger borrows the phrase and the idea from Du Bois. It refers to the social, economic and psychological benefits white ethnic workers gain from racism within the sphere of labor, stressing "the role of powerlessness at work in opening people to settling for the fiction that they are 'white workers' " (8).

4. W. E. B. Du Bois's 1902 *The Negro Artisan*, a study of discrimination against blacks in forty-three northern unions, is arguably the ur-text of working-class studies works on race and class. See also Du Bois's *Black Reconstruction* and *The World and Africa* as well as numerous essays published in journals like the *Crisis*. Du Bois also helped to inspire major prewar studies of African Americans by black intellectuals, such as C. L. R. James's *Fighting Racism in World War II* and *The History of Negro Revolt*; Horace Cayton and St. Clair Drake's *Black Metropolis* and Richard Wright's *Twelve Million Black Voices* and *Native Son*. While the list of titles on African American working-class experience in the contemporary period is too long to summarize, other significant works include books by Rayford Logan, William H. Harris, Manning Marable, Robert L. Allen, Joe Trotter, Patricia Hill Collins, bell hooks, Charles Denby, and Harry Haywood.

5. Kelley, for example, writes penetratingly of the role of the zoot suit in World War II black urban proletarian culture, citing Malcolm Little's own period as a zoot hipster as a possible sign of hip culture's political significance during the war. See "The Riddle of the Zoot: Malcolm Little and Black Cultural Politics During World War II" in *Race Rebels*.

6. Other noteworthy titles in U.S. Latino and Mexican labor history include Clete Daniel's *Chicano Workers and the Politics of Fairness: The FEPC in the Southwest, 1941–1945* (Austin: University of Texas Press, 1991); *Proletarians of*

the North: A History of Mexican Industrial Workers in Detroit and the Midwest, 1917–1933 (Berkeley: University of California Press, 1993); Camille Guerin-Gonzales's *Mexican Workers and American Dreams: Immigration, Repatriation, and California Farm Labor, 1900–1939* (New Brunswick, N.J.: Rutgers University Press, 1994); Albert Camarillo's *Chicanos in a Changing Society: From Northern Pueblos to American Barrios in Santa Barbara and Southern California, 1848–1930*; Patricia Zavella's *Women's Work and Chicano Families: Cannery Workers of the Santa Clara Valley*. See also *Ethnicity and the Work Force*, ed. Winston A. Van Horne and Thomas V. Tonneson (Madison: University of Wisconsin System, 1985) and *Mexican Women in the United States: Struggles, Past and Present*, ed. Magdalena Mora and Adelaida Del Castillo.

7. See also *Labor Immigration Under Capitalism: Asian Workers in the United States Before World War II*, ed. Lucie Cheng and Edna Bonacich (Berkeley: University of California Press, 1984).

8. See also Eric Lott's *Love and Theft: Blackface Minstrelsy and the American Working Class*; Noel Ignatiev's *How the Irish Became White*; and Bruce Nelson's forthcoming *The Logic, and Limits, of Solidarity: Workers, Unions and Civil Rights, 1935–1974*.

9. For central critical studies of working-class literature, see Constance Coiner's *Better Red: The Writing and Resistance of Tillie Olsen and Meridel Le Sueur* (New York: Oxford University Press, 1995); Barbara Foley's *Radical Representations: Politics and Form in U.S. Proletarian Fiction, 1929–1941* (Durham, N.C.: Duke University Press, 1993); and Paul Lauter's "Working-Class Women's Literature: An Introduction to Study." See also Tillie Olsen, *Yonnondio: From the Thirties* (New York: Dell, 1975) and *Silences* (New York: Dell, 1978); *Radical Teacher* 15 (1979): 16–26; Janet Zandy, ed., *Calling Home: Working-Class Women's Writing—An Anthology* (New Brunswick, N.J.: Rutgers University Press, 1990) and her most recent collection, *Liberating Memory: Our Work and Our Working-Class Consciousness* (New Brunswick, N.J.: Rutgers University Press, 1995). Florence Howe and Paul Lauter were cofounders of the Feminist Press which has reprinted many of the texts by working-class women writers such as Agnes Smedley's *Daughter of the Earth* and Jo Sinclair's *The Seasons: Death and Transfiguration*.

10. For ideas and strategies for teaching working-class studies, see *Radical Teacher* and *Women's Studies Quarterly* 23 (Spring/Summer 1995).

REFERENCES

Aronowitz, Stanley. *The Politics of Identity: Class, Culture, Social Movements*. New York: Routledge, 1992.

Bindas, Kenneth J. "Race, Class, and Ethnicity among Swing Musicians." In *America's Musical Pulse: Popular Music in Twentieth-Century Society*, edited by Kenneth J. Bindas, 73–82. Westport, Conn.: Praeger, 1992.

Briggs, Vernon Jr., Walter Fogel, and Fred H. Schmidt. *The Chicano Worker*. Austin: University of Texas Press, 1977.

Camarillo, Albert. *Chicanos in a Changing Society: From Mexican Pueblos to*

American Barrios in Santa Barbara and Southern California, 1848–1930. Cambridge, Mass.: Harvard University Press, 1979.

Collins, Patricia Hill. *Black Feminist Thought: Knowledge, Consciousness and the Politics of Empowerment.* New York: Routledge, 1991.

DeMott, Benjamin. *The Imperial Middle: Why Americans Can't Think Straight About Class.* New York: Morrow, 1990.

Denning, Michael. *Mechanic Accents: Dime Novels and Working-Class Culture in America.* New York: Verso, 1987.

Dews, C. L. Barney, and Carolyn Leste Law, eds. *This Fine Place So Far from Home.* Philadelphia: Temple University Press, 1995.

Enstad, Nan. "Compromised Positions: Working-Class Women, Popular Culture, and Labor Politics, 1890–1920." Ph.D. diss., University of Minnesota, 1993.

Friday, Chris. *Organizing Asian American Labor: The Pacific Coast Canned-Salmon Industry, 1870–1942.* Philadelphia: Temple University Press, 1994.

Glenn, Evelyn Nakano. *Issei, Nisei, War Bride: Three Generations of Japanese American Women in Domestic Service.* Philadelphia: Temple University Press, 1986.

Gorz, Andre. *Farewell to the Working Class: An Essay on Post-Industrial Socialism.* Boston: South End Press, 1982.

hooks, bell. *Outlaw Culture: Resisting Representations.* New York: Routledge, 1994.

Ignatiev, Noel. *How the Irish Became White.* New York: Routledge, 1995.

Kelley, Robin D. G. *Hammer and Hoe: Alabama Communists During the Depression.* Chapel Hill: University of North Carolina Press, 1990.

———. *Race Rebels: Culture, Politics, and the Black Working Class.* New York: Free Press, 1994.

Lippard, Lucy A., ed. *The Pink Glass Swan: Selected Feminist Essays on Art.* New York: New Press, 1995.

Lipsitz, George. *Time Passages: Collective Memory and American Popular Culture.* Minneapolis: Minnesota University Press, 1990.

———. *A Rainbow at Midnight: Labor and Culture in the 1940s.* Urbana: University of Illinois Press, 1994.

Lott, Eric. *Love and Theft: Blackface Minstrelsy and the American Working Class.* New York: Oxford University Press, 1993.

Mantsios, Gregory. "Living and Learning: Some Reflections on Emergence from and Service to the Working-Class." In *Liberating Memory: Our Work and Our Working-Class Consciousness,* edited by Janet Zandy, 230–48. New Brunswick, N.J.: Rutgers University Press, 1995.

Nelson, Bruce. *Divided We Stand: American Workers and the Struggle for Black Equality.* Princeton, N.J.: Princeton University Press.

Marable, Manning. *How Capitalism Underdeveloped Black America: Problems in Race, Political Economy, and Society.* Boston: South End Press, 1983.

Press, Andrew, and Elizabeth Cole. "Women Like Us: Working-Class Women Respond to Television Representations of Abortion." In *Viewing, Reading, Listening: Audiences and Cultural Reception,* edited by Jon Cruz and Justin Lewis, 55–80. Boulder, Colo.: Westview, 1994.

Roediger, David. *Towards the Abolition of Whiteness: Essays on Race Politics and Working Class History*. London: Verso, 1994.

————. *The Wages of Whiteness: Race and the Making of the American Working Class*. London: Verso, 1991.

Ruiz, Vicki. *Cannery Women/Cannery Lives: Mexican Women, Urbanization, and the California Food Processing Industry, 1930–1950*. Albuquerque: University of New Mexico Press, 1987.

Russo, Alexander. "'No Particular Place to Go: Culture Industries, Youth Culture, and Practices of Teenage Rebellion in the 1950s." Senior thesis, Wesleyan University, 1996.

Ryan, Jake, and Charles Sackrey. *Strangers in Paradise: Academics from the Working Class*. Boston: South End Press, 1984.

Saxton, Alexander. *The Indispensable Enemy: Labor and the Anti-Chinese Movement in California*. Berkeley: University of California Press, 1971.

Sucheng Chan. *This Bittersweet Soil: The Chinese in California Agriculture, 1860–1910*. Berkeley: University of California Press, 1986.

Tokarczyk, Michelle M., and Elizabeth A. Fay. *Working-Class Women in the Academy: Laborers in the Knowledge Factory*. Boston: University of Massachusetts Press, 1993.

Walsh, Catherine, ed. *Literacy as Praxis: Culture, Language, and Pedagogy*. Norwood, N.J.: Ablex, 1991.

Wilson, William Julius. *The Declining Significance of Race: Blacks and Changing American Institutions*. Chicago: University of Chicago Press, 1978.

Zandy, Janet. Introduction. *Women's Studies Quarterly* 23 (Spring/ Summer 1995): 3–6.

Zavella, Patricia. *Women's Work and Chicano Families: Cannery Workers of the Santa Clara Valley*. Ithaca, N.Y.: Cornell University Press, 1987.

Part 2

DIVERSITY, INSURGENCY, AND FRAGMENTATION

The essays in this section investigate how ethnicity, race, and gender have frequently fractured the self-conception and organization of the working class while occasionally providing radicals with a base of social solidarity from which to build a wider movement.

In "The *Appeal to Reason* and the Mass Socialist Movement Before World War I," David Riehle calls attention to the major vehicle of agitation and self-expression for the large-scale socialist movement of that time. While acknowledging the Socialist Party's programmatic limitations and recognizing that many of its members struggled with ethnic, racial, or gender prejudices, Riehle cautions us to take seriously the commitment and contributions of the many working-class revolutionaries of this period.

As the United States experiences another period of mass immigration from Latin America and Asia, Dan Georgakas argues that today's labor activists can learn a great deal about the possibilities and limitations of ethnic organizing from the period from the 1880s to the 1920s. In "Ethnic Organizing: A Doubled-Edged Sword," Georgakas sketches out the ways that immigrant and ethnic culture helped to shape working-class radicalism in the Industrial Workers of the World, the Socialist Party, the Communist Party, and the American Labor Party.

In the early part of the century, most labor organizations were dominated by men. Gender bias also colored perceptions of labor strife, such as in 1919, when steelworkers and their families organized what was the largest strike in U.S. history until the 1930s. David Demarest's "Representations of Women" argues that while some accounts downplay the role of women, female activists and "ordinary" women played a crucial role in the Great Steel Strike. Gender bias was not simply in intellectuals' minds, but was part and parcel of the steelmaking environment. Karen Olson's "The Gendered Social World of Steelmaking" examines how industrialists helped to establish racial and gender hierarchies in turn-of-the-century Sparrows Point, Maryland. Olson argues that steelmaking remained a "gendered world" (as well as a racialized one), greatly influencing the forms of solidarity and division among workers in the mill as well as in their domestic lives.

The migration of Southern rural blacks to industrial cities that began in the 1910s completely transformed the black working class. Southern migrants confronted cities whose jobs, unions, and housing were strictly organized along racial lines. In "Reflections on the Great Migration," Joe Trotter examines how black workers struggled to advance their economic interests and preserve their identities from the ravages of racism in the industrialized North.

Taken together, these articles sketch out some of the ways that workers have confronted the diversity and inequality of their class. Sometimes radicals have been able to use race, ethnicity, or gender to deepen the radical consciousness of large numbers of oppressed people, and ultimately to build movements across these divisions. Capital has often used the diversity of the working class as the basis for fragmenting and limiting their struggles.

4

ETHNIC ORGANIZING

A Double-Edged Sword

DAN GEORGAKAS

Among the various hidden histories of the American Left and American trade unions are how ethnically organized units have functioned within the wider movements to which they adhered. The history of such formations goes back to the early nineteenth century, but reached a period of greatest intensity with the Great Migration of 1880–1924. With some major exceptions, this phenomenon has largely been obscured behind language barriers or in broad-brush labor histories that are relatively oblivious to ethnic groups, often not even bothering to name them. At a time when the United States again finds itself confronting formidable cultural and language diversity, vigorous ethnic studies directly focused on labor and the Left are more relevant than ever. Ethnic organizing will proceed whether or not organizers are aware of the successes and failures of their radical predecessors, but the experiences of the Industrial Workers of the World (IWW), the Socialist Party (SP), the American Labor Party (ALP), and the Communist Party (CP) regarding ethnic-based units are invaluable. They indicate that ethnic units are a double-edged sword to be handled with extreme care.

From *Bulletin in Defense of Marxism*, no. 109 (September 1993). Reprinted by permission.

THE INDUSTRIAL WORKERS OF THE WORLD

The IWW is rightly celebrated as the most indigenous of American radical movements. Nonetheless, during its 1905–1924 heyday, there were many years in which the foreign-born and non-English speakers were in the majority. This was almost always true of the East Coast units. One of the major criticisms the IWW made of the American Federation of Labor was that the AFL considered the new immigrants too undisciplined to be responsible and successful trade unionists. Typical of the early IWW challenge to that view was the 1909 McKee's Rock strike at U.S. Steel. Five thousand workers from sixteen nations took part in this successful action a few miles outside of Pittsburgh. Similar IWW initiatives took place throughout the East Coast and Midwest in the years that followed, culminating in the legendary Lawrence Textile Strike of 1912, in which members of the strike committee represented 25,000 workers from twenty-four national groups speaking twenty-two different languages.

The gains resulting from the strike wave set off by the Lawrence victory were significant. Direct and indirect settlements brought $15 million in wage increases and lighter workloads to some 438,000 workers, the biggest gains going to the 275,000 textile workers in New England. Despite this achievement, the IWW was not able to maintain many of its locals once the strike wave ended. A debate has long raged on the reasons for this failure. Some of the problems directly relate to the peculiarities of the IWW, but an examination of specific locales reveals that fundamental problems arose from the very nature of ethnically organized units.

Although the fervor of a massive strike against indifferent employers was enough to keep diverse groups united for the short haul, language and ethnic differences proved unmanageable for the more mundane routines of trade unionism. The Lawrence Strike Committee, for example, had been composed of 250 to 300 local workers advised by IWW organizers, most of whom spoke more than one language. No means was ever found to transform that unwieldy structure into an acceptable leaner form. Different groups, often concentrated in specific skill areas, broke off to pursue their own ends. Ethnic rivalries reflecting sequence of arrival in the United States or traditional dispute originating in European conditions frequently asserted themselves. Individual members often were more responsive to dynamics without their own ethnic federation than to the needs of the larger trade union movement. Thus, religious disputes might affect union activism as much as workplace conditions.

The IWW proved more successful in handling class/ethnic dynamics in other venues. Positive experiences in Philadelphia, New York City, and the Upper Midwest flowed from three different approaches to similar problems.

The Philadelphia story involved dockworkers. From 1913–1924 the IWW controlled most of the Philadelphia piers, and thereafter, when the IWW imploded, its former Philadelphia unit moved intact into the mainstream labor movement. The peak membership in the unit while under IWW control was about four thousand, half of whom were African Americans. The other members were mainly Lithuanians and Poles. The chief organizer was Ben Fletcher, the most prominent black leader in the IWW, but the local chairmanship was rotated between blacks and nonblacks. This and other relatively simple devices proved sufficient to assuage racial feelings in campaigns that resulted in dramatic gains in wages and working conditions. The unit grew strong enough to support other IWW initiatives in the area, including significant work among Spanish-speaking workers.

Just as the welcome mat put out for blacks provided a basis for success on the Philadelphia docks, the full membership offered Spanish-speakers was key to organizing the Atlantic runs to Latin America. Over half of all the firemen on that run were Spanish speakers, usually Puerto Rican or Cuban. Having been repeatedly denied membership in AFL unions, large numbers of Spanish-speaking seamen joined the IWW in 1913 and 1914. The New York branch alone had nearly five thousand Hispanic members. From this base of strength, the IWW was able to organize in all the major ports of Central and South America. There were even years in which literature for the Chilean and other South American trade unions was printed in Chicago and shipped south via the IWW Spanish-speaking seamen. Spanish-language publications also appeared in American ports with significant Hispanic concentrations. The only downside to this work was that it did not directly relate to other IWW efforts. Its focus remained on specific ports and the Spanish connection.

A more typical ethnic involvement of the IWW was through ethnic federations. These organizations were often the center of life. Their double mission was to preserve the old country culture while acclimating immigrants to the culture of the New World. To those ends federations sponsored plays, lectures, musical programs, health plans, sporting clubs, and other social services. Depending on time and place, the emphasis might be on preserving the old culture or on assimilating to the new. Whatever the circumstances, the IWW sought to find a niche in these ethnic strongholds. Its greatest successes came in the Finnish halls of the Upper Midwest.

Finnish immigrants brought a cooperative tradition with them that melded easily with the IWW's anarcho-syndicalism. Some of the Finnish ethnic halls actually housed the IWW local. Whether or not this was the case, if there was a labor problem, the hall was a place to gather naturally and be safe from the more obvious company spies. In quiet times the Finns were particularly responsive to the class humor in IWW skits and songs. They also placed a high premium on working-class education and were the prime supporters of the IWW-connected Work People's College in Duluth. The most important aspect of these interactions was that the IWW radicals were seen as an integral part of the community, not outsiders. This feeling was buoyed by the IWW disinclination to seek formal control of federations or clubs.

The IWW pattern with the Finns was replicated in many other nationality venues. The IWW songbook and the IWW preamble, its principle mass education tools, were translated into virtually every language spoken by American workers. At its height the IWW published more than a dozen dailies in as many languages, and issued its major pamphlets in more than a score of languages. Although its leadership was English-speaking, the IWW, always prone to intense ideological debates, was relatively free of internal ethnic dispute. This was mostly due to the overwhelming class orientation of the IWW, which honored all cultures but continually underscored class unity and solidarity as its primary principles. Also of relevance was its loose organizational structure which allowed considerable local autonomy and initiative. A less generous explanation may be that the IWW was decimated by government persecution during World War I and ethnic/class tensions never had time to assert themselves in a mature IWW structure

THE SOCIALIST PARTY

Even more than the IWW, much of the success of the SP, particularly in major cities, involved ethnic federations. It is unclear how strongly individual members of federations affiliated with the SP actually felt about socialism per se. What is certain is that the SP had many more foreign-language newspapers and publications than any American radical organization before or since. Years ago James Weinstein observed that many of the SP publications in foreign languages had never been studied, much less translated, meaning that much of SP history remained unknown territory to most labor and radical historians. Many ethnic groups still lack a major monograph, much less a book-length study, of their radical and labor history.

For our present purposes it is instructive to ponder how much of the electoral successes of the SP had an ethnic component as vital as its class or ideological component.[1] An intriguing example is that of Victor Berger, first elected to Congress in 1910 from a German base in Milwaukee. Certainly the Germans there were consciously voting for a socialist, but whether they would have voted for an Irish candidate with the same exact politics is unlikely. Over the long haul, however, the Milwaukee socialists seem to have forged a real fusion of ethnic and class concerns. This is evidenced by the fact that they controlled city hall through to the 1950s, when broader electoral coalitions were needed for success.

A stronger ethnic component marked the congressional races by Morris

Hillquit and Meyer London, when New York City's Lower East Side was a Jewish enclave. Hillquit, a major socialist personality, ran unsuccessfully in 1906 and 1908. Running in the same district, Meyer London almost won in 1910, was elected in 1914, and won twice again thereafter. Although as avowedly socialist as Hillquit, London placed considerably more emphasis on his Jewishness. At the time of his first electoral bid he stated, "I deem it a duty of the Jew everywhere to remain a Jew as long as in any corner of the world the Jew is still discriminated against."

Some historians suggest that London's stronger ethnic emphasis was the decisive factor in his successes, while others believe it took the Jewish community the four years between Hillquit's last defeat and London's victories to get sufficient voters registered to insure electoral dominance. In both instances, voters were clearly voting for both ethnic and ideological reasons, but as the Jewish numerical dominance of the district waned, so did socialist victories. The argument could still be made that ethnic identity and class interests had become thoroughly entwined. This was decidedly not the case with the most successful of all radical politicians, Vito Marcantonio, who represented East Harlem in Congress from 1934 to 1936 and from 1938 to 1950.

THE AMERICAN LABOR PARTY

Vito Marcantonio came to prominence as a campaign manager for Fiorello La Guardia at a time when the Irish and German politicians who ran Tammany Hall would not allow Italians a meaningful place in the Democratic Party. When La Guardia's first bid for Congress on the Socialist line failed, he turned to the Republican Party. Later in his career he would be a fusion candidate of different parties. In like manner, Marcantonio would run under five different political labels, but after 1938, he was most dedicated to building the American Labor Party.

Most historian agree that the Italians of East Harlem, who always gave a majority of their votes to Marcantonio in all the campaigns in which he ran, were more impressed by his personal character, his ethnic sensibilities, and his exemplary performance as a bread-and-butter congressman than by his radical ideas. Unlike the Germans who voted for Berger or the Jews who voted for Hillquit, the Italians seem to have voted for Marcantonio despite his ideology, not because of it. Marcantonio, however, has the unique distinction among these ethnic radicals of having forged a second ethnic base among Puerto Ricans.

As Puerto Ricans began to move into East Harlem, Marcantonio took up their causes as fiercely as he had those of Italians, including the right to seek independence. Although occasionally challenged for these views by

Italians in his district, Marcantonio was steadfast in his advocacy for Puerto Ricans. The Puerto Rican response to him was even stronger than in his solid Italian base. Through the ALP, Marcantonio was instrumental in getting the first Puerto Rican elected to public office in New York. In this instance, his radical ideology had found an ethnic match. Puerto Ricans, in turn, were willing to have a person not of their own ethnic community act as their tribune. Cynics might argue that the Puerto Rican population had not grown large enough to field its own ethnic candidate. What is not disputable, however, is that at the time of Marcantonio's death, his standing in the Puerto Rican community was as high as it had ever been.[2]

Other aspects of ALP history beg for additional study. In a special election in 1948, the ALP elected Leo Isaacson to Congress from the South Bronx. The Jewish ethnic vote was critical to that race although no specific study has yet been made of the contest. More generally, the ALP areas of strength often overlapped with districts where the SP had been able to elect city and state officials, often from a Jewish ethnic base. This suggests that some of the ALP's strength derived from ideological support that transcended narrow ethnic identification.

THE COMMUNIST PARTY

When the Communist Party began to form out of the left wing of the SP, one of the two largest factions was led by the Russian Federation and was mainly supported by other ethnic federations. These groups felt their ethnicity provided insights into what was happening in Russia and made them the logical leaders of an American movement of similar ends and means. By the time the five major factions were united into one party, the leadership agreed it was wise to abandon language groups as too divisive. Nevertheless, many units were composed of a single ethnic group, and those units often published a foreign-language newspaper. Generally speaking, these units were among the most dependable dues-paying sections and loyally carried out the party line, but many of their most energetic initiatives had an autonomous aspect and were concentrated in immigrant bases.

The Greek Communists provide a good example of this general ethnic phenomenon. From 1916 through 1959, a group of Greek radicals published a Greek-language newspaper on either a daily, weekly, or biweekly basis. This group also organized workers' clubs modeled on the Greek coffee house. These clubs primarily served as a means for reaching a broad spectrum of the Greek-speaking working class rather than as centers for recruitment. Later the worker clubs would be used in the larger Communist effort to build the International Workers Order. Through these means some five hundred to a thousand Greek Communists enjoyed significant influence in major industrial areas with Greek concentrations. Among the drawbacks to this approach was that the worker clubs were almost an exclusively male environment and there was great dependency on the Greek language.

For many years the Greek Communists had a Greek-language local in the Communist-led Fur & Leather Workers Union. This local functioned much as the Finnish halls had for the IWW, sponsoring many social events for the broader Greek community and supplying organizers for specific strikes. Approximately a fourth of the local was female, which was a decided advantage in doing work in the community. Further underscoring the complexity of ethnic organizing is the circumstance that the Greek fur workers had been organized by the initiative of Jewish Communists. Led by Communist Ben Gold, most of the fur industry had been organized by the 1920s. Full union control, however, remained elusive because of three hundred Greek-owned shops that had never been approached because of language and cultural barriers. Gold hired Greek Communists who were able to organize the Greek shops in a whirlwind campaign. The partnership between the two ethnic groups remained constant throughout the period of Gold's long leadership.

Several aspects of the Greek experience are typical of other Communists who operated from a strictly ethnic base. A hard-core group was able to sustain itself for decades and reach deeply into the immigrant working class. Greek-language publications and Greek-oriented cultural events were major components of this ethnic connection. Involvement in major trade unions, particularly the CIO, allowed the ethnic group to bring its special ethnic concerns to a wide labor audience. A specific example in the case of Greeks was their ability to rally mass support on behalf of the Greek War Relief campaign.

Balancing these successes are negatives also shared by other groups. Many Greek activities were focused on events in the homeland. At times the cause in Greece seemed to command more fervor than the cause in America. Because of this orientation and the attempt to hold its immigrant base, the newspaper continued to publish almost exclusively in Greek even as second- and third-generation Greek workers came to maturity. These younger workers were not greatly interested in the old country, and they increasingly lacked Greek-language skills. Consequently, the Greek-language Communists did not replenish their ranks. The intense ethnic focus also tended to isolate activists from broader American concerns. There was a marked tendency to be more attracted to activities defending the revolution in Russia than to those that might spread Communism in America. Thus, members barely able to speak English might study technical skills they hoped to eventually take to the USSR, where they could help build "existing socialism."

This Old World focus often linked the fate of the ethnically based Communists to the fate of Communism in their native lands. The Eastern European groups waxed and waned in response to how the USSR was dealing with their homelands. The Ukrainian Communists in America never recovered from the controversies surrounding the Ukrainian famine of the early 1930s, and the Finns, among the most enthusiastic Soviet supporters in the mid-1930s, were devastated by the Soviet invasion of Finland in 1939. The Greeks did well during World War II because of overwhelming community support of the anti-Nazi guerrilla movement in Greece, but were doubly vulnerable in the McCarthy era due to the concurrent civil war in Greece.

TENTATIVE CONCLUSIONS

These briefly considered examples indicate some of the negative aspects of the double-edged sword of ethnically based labor and ideological units. They may be summarized as follows:

1. Much of ethnic organizing is based on the use of a language other than English during the first rush of immigration, when English is a problem for many workers. As time passes, this initial advantage becomes a weakness. Younger generations are not attracted, and older generations, particularly those caught in a language ghetto, can become culturally insular.

2. Ethnic groups inevitably focus on the problems of the old country, and the fate of radical movements in that country are regarded at least as equally important as what is happening in the immediate world of work in America. Although the discourse has an ideological base, the pulse of the organization is nationalistic.

3. Ethnic units consciously or inconclusively perpetuate Old World divisions by the very nature of their organizational form. In addition to traditional enemies, the units may perpetuate regional divisions of the homeland.

4. Ethnic units fit awkwardly into the larger context of an American movement, as class interests are inevitably blurred by an ethnic lens.

None of these problems is insurmountable; but sensitivity to their nature is essential in any effort to find viable short-term and longer-term organizational strategies. Cavalier dismissal of them as inappropriate to the new immigrant wave and to residual ethnic problems is simply foolish. Ethnic-based organizing is a natural impulse that will take place in one form or another. The task for radicals is to create the means for such organizing to be an asset rather than an impediment to the fundamental struggle to reshape the American economic and social order.

NOTES

The general reader can consult some twenty ethnic histories with select bibliographies in Mari Jo Buhle, Paul Buhle, and Dan Georgakas, eds., *The Encyclopedia of the American Left* (New York: Garland, 1990). The first full-length studies of the Polish, Ukrainian, and Greek ethnic Lefts are among thirteen essays in Paul Buhle and Dan Georgakas, eds., *The Immigrant Left* (Albany: State University of New York Press, 1996).

1. The individual careers of all prominent and many lesser-known socialists can be found with selected bibliographies in Bernard K. Johnpoll and Harvey Klehr, eds., *Biographical Dictionary of the American Left* (New York: Greenwood, 1986). Despite the title, this work focuses primarily on the SP.

2. Considerable detail on the Puerto Rican and Italian electoral bases are found in Gerald Meyer, *Vito Marcantonio* (Albany: State University of New York Press, 1989).

5

THE *APPEAL* TO *REASON* AND THE MASS SOCIALIST MOVEMENT BEFORE WORLD WAR I

DAVID RIEHLE

"I received a letter the other day," Jack London wrote in 1905. "It was from a man in Arizona. It began 'Dear Comrade.' It ended, 'Yours for the revolution.' I replied to the letter, and my letter began, 'Dear Comrade.' It ended, 'Yours for the revolution.' In the United States there are 400,000 men, of men and women nearly 1,000,000, who begin their letters 'Dear Comrade,' and end them 'Yours for the revolution.'"[1]

Once in this country, still within the living memory of a very few, there was a time when many thousands of ordinary people, workers and farmers for the most part, were seething with the possibility of a future free of oppression, hunger, and violence, a future based on human solidarity, to be organized through the abolition of private property and collective participation in the work of society for the good of all. They called this future "socialism."

This is not entirely unknown, especially to people who have some knowledge of American history. Even to them this remains for the most part something only dimly perceived, as people in the Middle Ages were faintly aware that there were countries on the other side of the world, but had little or no idea of who lived there or what they were like. But for the most part it is utterly expunged from popular consciousness.

One of the few alive today whose conscious life coincided with this era

From *Bulletin in Defense of Marxism*, no. 115 (April 1994). Reprinted by permission.

is the poet and writer Meridel Le Sueur, born in 1900. Writing in 1984, she recalls the great socialist camp meetings of the Middle West before World War I:

> I got my education at these great picnics, meetings of farmers, lumberjacks, miners, factory workers. They came for miles, some hiking, some in long lines with great banners—"We ask for justice." "We want land." It was a pentecostal of politics. Speakers went up and down the countryside. . . . Everyone was talking, learning, listening. Farmers, mechanics, ranchers, hoboes, wanderers, itinerant workers mounted soapboxes, shouted in wheat fields, passed out leaflets at factory gates. And gaunt, suntanned women who had rarely spoken now rose at meetings and there were singers and everyone could write his own piece and pass it out or pile it on the tables at the meetings. Tongues of flame, witnesses to the agony of the farm evictions. All were touched with prophecy and utterance. The landscape changed, the plow had a new meaning and became alive in the hands of the people who were not going to be silent. . . . Most of all they discovered the fire and wonder of solidarity.[2]

The flame did not just flare for a moment. This great broad movement of the people, of the producers, spanned decades and generations, arising at the close of the Civil War. The socialist mass meetings Le Sueur describes had their roots in the movements of the latter part of the nineteenth century—in the Greenback-Labor Party and the People's Party; the Knights of Labor; the great labor struggles of 1877, 1886, and 1894.

"Everywhere and in all countries the oppressed people are waking up," wrote my great-grandmother, Jennie Jones, editor of the *Workman*, published in the small town of Bloomer, Wisconsin. Their struggles, from Russia to France, to Ireland, to the United States, she said in the cadences of that time, "are synonymous, and all rumbling volcanoes, coming up from the oppressed masses of the people. And they will yet break from the grasp of the oppressor, and will tear his bloody hand from the white throat of labor."[3]

Driven by the stupendous industrialization that swept across the continent, revolutionizing the means of production and creating a modern industrial proletariat, thousands upon thousands of them saw with new insight this gigantic productive machine as something that could be seized by the people and used to build a better world.

"Who are the oppressors?" Mark Twain asked in 1886.

> The few, the king, the capitalist and a handful of other overseers and superintendents. Who are the oppressed? The many: the nations of the earth; the valuable personages; the workers; they that make the bread that the softhanded and idle eat. Why is there not a fairer division of the spoils all around? . . . But when all the bricklayers, and all the machinists and all the

miners and blacksmiths and printers and hod carriers and stevedores and house painters and brakemen and engineers and conductors and factory hands and horse car drivers and all the shopgirls and all the sewing women and all the telegraph operators; in a word all the myriads of toilers in whom is slumbering the reality of that thing which you call power, not its age-worn sham and substanceless spectre—when these rise, call the vast spectacle by any deluding name that will please your ear, but the fact remains a Nation has risen.[4]

At the beginning of the twentieth century these currents of protest and struggle came together in the new Socialist Party. James P. Cannon, who entered political life as a participant in this movement in the first decade of the century under the tutelage of his father, described his father's pioneer socialism as "the predominant mid-Western American socialism of his time—inspired by the great spirit and burning eloquence of [Eugene V.] (Debs). . . . "

"In my opinion," Cannon said, "the modern movement, with its more precise analysis and its necessary concentration on the struggle, would do well to infuse its propaganda with more emphasis on the ultimate meaning of the struggle; speak out, as the old pioneers did, for human rights and human dignity, for freedom and equality and abundance for all. That is what we are really fighting for when we fight for socialism."[5]

Cannon's view on this, which he expressed many times, has had the occasional misfortune of being mistaken for sentimentalism and nostalgia. The movement of that time has likewise had the misfortune of having been described historically too often as a primitive and naive anticipation of various things to come, sometimes the Democratic Party reforms of the New Deal, and sometimes intransigent and hard-hearted Marxism-Leninism, depending on who is doing the describing. In a sense, neither of these is true and both of them are true. There is no doubt that within the Socialist Party of the first two decades of the century can be found the germ of all these things, and others as well. But it was more than that. First of all, it was better than what had come before. Now the goal of a better world, a world of abundance and human solidarity, which was inherent in the great people's struggles that preceded it, could be formulated in a definite, material, and coherent manner, and a social engine for achieving the new society, the working class, could be identified. It could be *explained*. It was not necessary to take it on faith, or accept it as revelation. It was necessary only to be *convinced*.

The people who joined the socialist movement marched, went on strike, contested for elected office, and a myriad of other activities. But central to all their activity they *read* and they *talked*. A 1908 national survey discovered that 54 percent of the rank and file discovered socialism through reading. They studied and discussed *ideas*. "Educate, Agitate and Organize," as it was inscribed on the masthead of my great-grandparents' Greenback-Labor Party newspaper, and a thousand other places. The new mass socialist movement, growing out of the old, could not do otherwise than adopt the old slogan and give it new content.

Who were the people who made up this movement? They had names. They had faces. They had lives. A multitude of us are their descendants, although for the most part we are unaware of it. And, as burns so intensely in Meridel le Sueur's memory, they found their voices in this movement. They were not just simple folk as they have so often been condescendingly portrayed. They were grown-up people responsible for their own lives and for the lives of others. They learned what they could of the world around them and they were educated by a movement that poured out an avalanche of printed material. *And they talked back.*

More than anything, the institution for this reciprocal discussion was the socialist newspaper the *Appeal to Reason*. Published from 1895 to 1922, the *Appeal* was a mass-circulation political medium on a scale and proportion almost unimaginable today, and never exceeded since. At its peak in 1913 the *Appeal*'s regular circulation was over 750,000, reaching as high as three million for special editions. For a long time its circulation was one of the top three or four largest for weeklies in the United States, larger than the *Saturday Evening Post*, for example. In its pages are recorded, more than anywhere else, the voices of the thousands of articulate, inspired, and intellectually awakened human beings who *were* this movement.

We now have the best opportunity presented so far in the historical literature of the American socialist movement to open a window on this era and hear their voices.

Yours for the Revolution: The "Appeal to Reason," 1895–1922, edited by John Graham (University of Nebraska Press, 1990), is both a sensitive and insightful history of the *Appeal* and an anthology of its nearly thirty years of publication.

Graham's superb introduction, accompanying historical and political commentary, and selection of material is done with an evident profound respect for the thousands of men and women who read, circulated, and wrote much of the *Appeal*, as well as for its remarkable editor, J. A. Wayland.

"The editorial policy of 'Tell the *Appeal*' meant that substantial parts of many issues of the paper were written by citizens widely dispersed throughout the United States," he writes.

"Much more than simply a newspaper, the *Appeal* was a participatory counterinstitution that actively represented the socialist movement."

The book contains many examples. *Appeal* readers reported on strikes, free-speech struggles, accounts of workers' life under capitalism, efforts to convince others of the tenets of socialism, and anecdotes from everyday life. A story from Fresno, California, in the February 11, 1911, *Appeal* signed by "Mrs. W. F. Little" reported on a battle for free speech and union organization of the IWW (Industrial Workers of the World) involving herself and other comrades. She reported that over one hundred workers, including her brother-in-law Frank Little, were in jail, arrested for the crime of trying to speak on the streets of Fresno, "in sunny California that you read so much about, where every prospect pleases and only man is vile." In 1917, IWW leader Frank Little was dragged from a jail in Butte, Montana, by a mob of businessmen and lynched from a railroad trestle.

The *Appeal* commissioned and first published serially in the paper Upton Sinclair's *The Jungle*, exposing brutal, oppressive, and unsanitary conditions in the meatpacking industry. The *Appeal* version, in fact, was nearly a third longer than the book published later by Doubleday and Page, and more explicitly political.

Martha Baker wrote in the June 14, 1913, *Appeal*:

> . . . I am uneducated. The greatest desire of my life is denied because poor working people have no chance for education and enlightenment. I am not a member of the Socialist party. I was born and raised in a state where few rights are granted to women, and to talk politics or to have a political opinion is considered unwomanly. But I have been reading the *Appeal* and trying to find out what socialism is. . . . I can see in it a great hope for the millions of working people who are struggling for existence. In the future, under Socialism, I can see equal privileges of life granted to all, the chance to grow and develop physically, mentally, and intellectually. The people will be free from poverty, they will not be robbed of what they produce. I can see the same right to live granted to woman as well as to man and she will not be kept down simply because she is a woman.

Other women discovered that the movement was itself not free of the defects of the world in which it existed. Naomi McDonald Phelps wrote in the April 18, 1903, *Appeal*:

> I would like to answer Comrade Well's suggestion in regard to women, where he says he thinks women ought to be coaxed into the Socialist clubs, as they would talk the old parties to death. . . . The fact is, men have that principle so engrafted in their natures, i.e., speaking of women in regard to public affairs much as they would of imbeciles and children—"ha! ha! Johnny's got on his firstest pair of pants; thinks he will soon be old enough to vote"—that their invitations to women to join their clubs are couched in such a manner, and their treatment of "the talking sex" is so contemptuous that the self-respecting women resent it. We're not babies; we're not fools; if you had been our servants as long as we have been yours . . .—I believe with all my heart that you would have been a sex of blubbering idiots. By what twist of fortune's wheel men became so wise in their own

conceits, fell so in love with their own preponderance of brains, is past finding out of the wisest women.

"But I want to give the male members of all political clubs a recipe for the tolling in of women," Phelps continued.

> . . . Always get the first grip, while you urge her to take hold: see to it that you do the talking, while urging her to talk. Have Jones, Brown, and Brewster all ready for the floor, and see that they keep it from the time your club meeting opens until the motion is made to adjourn. Prove your appreciation for her assistance as a lecturer in the field by running all the consecrated, bifurcated gentry to the front, and filling all the places with the sex that God ordered to till the earth. Finish up by telling her that she's a daisy—when it comes to scrubbing—but it takes you with your wonderful preponderance of brains, to represent her interests.. . . . Well, I hope this will go in the *Appeal*, as men's attitude toward women in regard to the great issues of the day, destroys her usefulness, kills her confidence, enlarges her disgust with self-conceit, and turns the volume of her patriotism back on herself, and though her soul rebel, yet there is no way out of these annoyances that hamper and annoy, until men shall LIVE the gospel they PREACH.

Questions such as this and others were argued out with admirable frankness in the pages of the *Appeal*. The *Appeal* belonged to the movement, and its supporters devoted great energy to making it better, as well as expanding its number of readers and subscribers.

Central to this was the Appeal Army. Readers of the *BIDOM* [*Bulletin in Defense of Marxism*] may be familiar with James P. Cannon's descriptions of the Appeal Army as the medium of his first participation in socialist politics as a teenager, distributing copies of the *Appeal*'s special three-million-copy edition in defense of labor prisoners Bill Haywood and Charles Moyer, leaders of the Western Federation of Miners facing a death sentence in Idaho in 1906. Graham's book gives us a deeper appreciation of the army, and its class content.

Editor Graham describes the Appeal Army as an organization of

> agitators and propagandists who sold subscriptions to the paper and distributed extra copies at public meetings, in barbershops and union halls, on trains and street corners, on porches and doorsteps, wherever the *Appeal* could be read and socialism encountered. Like the *Appeal* itself, the Salesmen Army was a phenomenon like nothing else in American publishing or radical history: at its high point in 1913, *the Army had grown to 80,000 activists, nearly all of whom could be reached in two days time when necessary.* (Emphasis added—D.R.)

The army's activities extended well beyond simply canvassing for subscriptions—in many cases the army preceded and helped organize branches of the SP. The Appeal Army, as noted, could mobilize on short notice and intervene as a political force in its own right into political crises such as the Moyer-Haywood trial with its special editions and thousands of agitators. This was one of the *Appeal*'s many, and mostly unacknowledged, contributions to the movements which came after it. James P. Cannon's conception of a campaign newspaper for socialism which belonged to the rank and file is clearly influenced by his early experiences with the *Appeal*.

J. A. Wayland, the *Appeal*'s editor, did not exempt himself from the task of building the paper's influence and circulation. Wayland reported, for example, in the September 3, 1904, issue: "Last week I rode sixty-five miles, circulating *Appeal* and pamphlets about Girard [Kansas, the small town in which the *Appeal* was located]. One evening after work I made twenty miles and left an *Appeal* and two pamphlets at every farmhouse."

Not everyone in the movement loved the *Appeal*, or the Appeal Army. SP leader Victor Berger accused the members of the army of being "converts . . . who care more for the chance to win some trumpery prize than they do to win the Cooperative Commonwealth." It is true that the *Appeal*, especially at the beginning, offered prizes and premiums to increase circulation. At different times the *Appeal* offered successful subscription-getters prizes such as "a first-class sewing machine," an "art vase, suitably inscribed," and even a ten-acre farm in the heart of the Arkansas fruit belt. It once promised instruments to outfit a complete brass band to the socialists in the city with the highest circulation when the paper's circulation went over seventy-five thousand.

The *Appeal* was a product of its time, as was J. A. Wayland, who had been a successful publisher and real estate speculator before his conversion to socialism. Wayland saw no alternative to using many of the methods of capitalist business to boost the cause. The *Appeal* was not owned by the Socialist Party, which in fact refused on principle to operate an official party newspaper, and accordingly the *Appeal* could only be sustained financially from its own revenue. Wayland agonized publicly many times in the columns of the *Appeal* over the contradiction of the most successful propaganda vehicle for socialism being a private business, and at one time he even offered the paper to the SP, an offer which was declined.

The *Appeal* had its troubles and its inconsistencies, as did the movement it championed and helped in a significant way to create. The limitations of that movement can be examined—they have been before, and will be again—both by those who nostalgically wish it could simply be recreated and by those like Cannon who went beyond it armed with a profound appreciation of those he called the "pioneers."

Another recent book on the *Appeal*—*Talkin' Socialism: J. A. Wayland*

and the Role of the Press in American Radicalism, by Elliott Shore (University of Kansas Press, 1988)—provides an excellent critical history of the great socialist newspaper and its editor. In fact, it is only now, in the last few years, that the first books on the *Appeal* have come out, some seventy years after its cessation. Although the *Appeal,* as noted earlier, was among the largest circulation publications of any kind in the United States in its time, it is entirely absent, as socialist historian Paul Buhle has noted, from any history of journalism in the United States.

John Graham's *Yours for the Revolution* has been criticized as being too celebratory about the *Appeal,* some reviews echoing Berger's contemptuous dismissal of the newspaper, its readers, and supporters. More to the point, in my opinion, is the characterization of the book by Peter Ostenby in the *Illinois Historical Journal* (Spring 1992) as a "marvelous example of the power of a historical anthology." The mighty impulse for human liberation by the workers and farmers of the early twentieth-century United States, which the *Appeal* represented and expressed, *should* be celebrated.

Whatever its flaw and inadequacies, the *Appeal* and its army essentially constituted a movement of equals, whose motivation and reward were the self-sufficient satisfaction of serving the movement. Although many talented and sometimes celebrated writers appeared in the *Appeal,* the paper was not just a forum for the occasional rank and filer, but the place, as a paper that belonged to them, where they spoke to each other. As is inescapable and necessary in a real working-class movement, it was one which collectively educated itself. The hundreds of pamphlets produced in this era by the *Appeal,* by Charles Kerr Publishers, and others, are unmistakably the product of people who have deep mutual respect and seek to educate *each other* as thinking human beings. The histories of the old socialist movement as they have been presented for the most part, do not make this clear enough, with their focus on the socialist municipal administrations, party agitators, union officials, middle-class reformers, professionals, and others who one way or another raised themselves above the ranks. The histories, whatever their merits, tend to be written, consciously or unconsciously, from the perspective of those "higher" types.

John Graham has made a valuable contribution to a deeper understanding of the thinking, conscious human beings who gave this movement whatever value it had, and helps to engender a deeper respect for them—and our class. They, this great tide of human beings who sought to bequeath us a better world, were not only our grandparents and great-grandparents, and uncles and aunts, whether we know it or not, but our brothers and sisters. In my opinion, our understanding is enriched immeasurably by *Yours for the Revolution.* It belongs in the library of every socialist.

As we know, these brothers and sisters of ours did not succeed, and the movement of which they were the foundation faltered and eventually degenerated, and was succeeded by another one, which, too, faltered and degenerated in its turn. But they did not fail.

Meridel Le Sueur said, writing in the name of her parents, Arthur and Marian, about the whole movement:

> If they made a miscalculation, those great rebels of our past, it was the inability to imagine the final brutality of power. . . . But I cannot criticize their heroic warning and their faithful love. It becomes like a turning lighthouse beacon throwing directions to us, maps we never thought of, new social structures of peace and abundance, images of a new reality. How clearly they saw that and showed it on their maps in country schoolhouses and spoke of it from soapboxes on city streets, always threatened by arrest. What they saw and did now appears strong and amazing, moving in new directions, in the enormous battles of the dispossessed to regain and protect our humanity.
>
> Unlike elitists and intellectuals, they never gave up hope, never were addicted to cynicism, disbelief, or philosophical defense of what they called failure. They never failed.[6]

In the present, when the whole perspective of historical optimism, to say nothing of the socialist reconstruction of society, has been shunted to the margins of intellectual and political discourse, it is essential to restudy and penetrate more deeply into the great models of the past. They, and their movement, are not irrelevant historical artifacts. They are not just part of our past, but of our present, if we can blast a passage through to our real history.

That is what Jim Cannon was trying to tell us:

> I think to this day that the spirit, method, and technique of the prewar socialist and IWW movements belong naturally and of necessity to a genuine proletarian movement growing indigenously in the soil of America. The tradition is a rich heritage which the new generation of revolutionary militants must make their own.[7]

In the last analysis, the comrades of the *Appeal* said it as well as anybody. "As the January 5, 1912, issue of the *Appeal to Reason* was being made up, Charles L. Phifer, a columnist and associate editor, paused in the commotion of his work to reflect on the *Appeal*," Graham tells us. Phifer wrote:

> The *Appeal* is not as good as it ought to be. It is crude—I know it. It isn't "literary" or pretty. But it touches souls every week. Sometimes I stand in awe of the fact, sensing the deeper and unexpressed forces and feelings of a nation, of a world, surge upon me, calling for an outlet; and if I thought I did justice to it, I should realize I was inadequate for the position. I like literature; I like art; but sometimes I think the *Appeal*, harsh and ugly as it

is, partial as it is and must be, is after all, the truest literature of the day; tracing the richest art of the soul, and that future bibliographs will go through its files to catch the spirit of an awakening people speaking in broken sentences through it.[8]

NOTES

1. Quoted in John Graham, ed., *Yours for the Revolution: The Appeal to Reason, 1895–1922* (Lincoln: University of Nebraska Press, 1990), ix.

2. Meridel Le Sueur, *Crusaders: The Radical Legacy of Marian and Arthur Le Sueur* (St. Paul: Minnesota Historical Society Press, 1984).

3. Bloomer *Workman*, October 20, 1881.

4. Speech by Mark Twain, "The Knights of Labor, a New Dynasty," March 21, 1886.

5. James P. Cannon, "Farewell to a Socialist Pioneer," June 7, 1947, reprinted in *Notebook of an Agitator* (1958), and in *Bulletin in Defense of Marxism*, no. 115 (April 1994): 21. [Cannon helped to form and lead the Communist movement and later was a founder and leader of American Trotskyism.—Eds.]

6. Le Sueur, *Crusaders*, xxvii–xxviii.

7. James P. Cannon, "In the Spirit of the Pioneers," November 28, 1936, reprinted in *Notebook of an Agitator*.

8. Graham, *Yours for the Revolution*, xi–xii.

6

REPRESENTATIONS OF WOMEN IN NARRATIVES ABOUT THE GREAT STEEL STRIKE OF 1919

DAVID DEMAREST

An unusual number of high-quality "literary" texts have commented on the nationwide 1919 strike in steel. William Z. Foster's *Lessons of the Great Steel Strike* (1920), of course, is a masterpiece of American labor history. William Attaway's novel *Blood on the Forge* (1941), a depressing but powerful and poetic novel, depicts black workers before and during the strike. John Dos Passos in *The Big Money* (1936), the third novel in the *USA* trilogy, describes the ethos of Pittsburgh and the Monongahela Valley in 1919—especially the corporate control of the mainstream press, and the general middle-class scorn of "Hunkies." Thomas Bell's *Out of This Furnace* (1941) has chapters on the strike and its era. The *Interchurch Reports* (1920) are, to my mind, "literary" by virtue of their use of personifying and rhetorical materials: interviews, speeches, letters of appeal.

Despite the masculine image of the steel industry, much of this 1919 literature deals with women, in texts written both by women and by men. Mother Jones's chapter in her *Autobiography* (1925) is memorable: it reads like a series of brilliant from-the-stump speeches. Mary Heaton Vorse's *Men and Steel* (1920) is full of pictorial reportage of women's lives in the steel valleys, especially in Braddock (Braddock and Homestead are the most writer-visited of all

A version of this paper was presented at the Braddock Carnegie Library in Braddock, Pennsylvania, in a September 1994 symposium commemorating the 75th anniversary of the 1919 steel strike.

steel towns). "Mary French," Dos Passos's fictional character, of course, is a *male* writer's version of Vorse and her 1919 strike experience. Other less well known women have created accounts of the martyr Fanny Sellins (a UMW organizer), as well as discussing their own experiences in oral history interviews.

It's these texts about women's lives in the 1919 era that I want to look briefly at here.

I

In the winter of 1919, half a year before the strike started, a simple but powerful episode occurs in Thomas Bell's *Out of This Furnace*. Mary Dobrejcak—a young widow, the mother of four children—lies ill in bed in the family's North Braddock home, just off the Pennsylvania mainline.

> One evening, early, [Mary] was brought out of a tired doze by voices outside, on the railroad. She had left Pauline and Mikie in the kitchen doing the supper dishes; Johnny had gone to a high school basketball game. She sat up in bed and raised the shade. A passenger train's bright-windowed cars were halted before the house. It was an express train for she could see the towels on the seats which identified Pullman cars for her, and one car was a diner. A white-jacketed porter was leaning out of a door and people at tables were peering out into what must have seemed to them a dismal and impenetrable darkness. Men with lanterns and flashlights were moving back and forth along the train's length, and there was a good deal of confused yelling. She hoped there hadn't been an accident and lifted the window as Mikie clumped down the porch steps and crossed the yard.
>
> "Mikie! Don't you go on the tracks. . . ."
>
> Cold air was drenching her and [Mary] lowered the window, coughing. She kept coughing, deep, wracking convulsions that shook her, shook the bed, threw her clawing helplessly against the wall. And then, as though what had been making her cough, the irritant, had finally torn loose, she felt her mouth fill. Even before she took her handkerchief away from her mouth she knew it was blood.
>
> The engineer blew four blasts on his whistle.[1]

This scene is typical of Bell's photographic, documentary style, and it is rich in implications. It is, for instance, a classic depiction of modernity. Two social/economic spheres are brought into sudden, intimate juxtaposition, joined in a moment's (here unwanted) voyeurism. The vignette points to a major theme of the whole book: the contrasts between haves and have-nots—between a comfortable typically Anglo middle and owner class, and the exhausting, dangerous lives of eighty-four-hour-a-week steelworkers, largely Slovak and Eastern European, and their families.

In literature of the Pittsburgh region, Bell's image of Mary at the window begs comparison with Willa Cather's short story "Paul's Case" (written some years earlier), where Paul, after ushering at a concert in Oakland's Carnegie Hall, follows the diva across Forbes Avenue, then stands outside in the rain, watching her at a late-evening party at the Schenley Hotel, its windows brilliantly lit "like the fairy world of a Christmas pantomime." The haves and the have-nots again visually close, tantalizingly so, but worlds apart.[2]

The political question such scenes point to is: Which side are you on? Where is your political allegiance? Obviously Bell's novel puts readers in Braddock and North Braddock, on the side of steelworkers' families. The owners live somewhere else; they travel to, and through, Braddock, simply to exploit its labor and technology.

In *Out of This Furnace*, Bell repeatedly uses framed, photolike images, or windows, to highlight the lives of women—men's view of them and their view of themselves.

Another photo-framing occurs when Mike falls in love with Mary, who is just back from her job as nursemaid for the Dexters, a family that has been summering at the beach:

> She was sitting by the table, her back to the window that looked out on the railroad tracks and the river. She was all in white. . . . She had taken off her hat and put it on the table beside her; it was white too, wide-brimmed and trimmed with flowers. A white parasol leaned against her thigh. She was quite the prettiest and most splendidly dressed young woman that he had ever seen. . . . Here was a girl who looked as though she had stepped out of a magazine advertisement, lovely and cool and strange.[3]

The gaze now is from the male point of view, registering a very conventional, commercial ideal of beauty, but the convention is obviously shared by Mary. This banality, even triteness, is part-and-parcel of Bell's realism: its conventionality pleases the characters and evidently the author too. Bell stays close to popular culture; he never tries to be flashy or avant-garde.

For Mary, of course, her Gibson girl outfit is a glimpse of the American dream. As Mike says, she looked, in her all-white outfit, "like an American girl." This is the upbeat, youthful version of Mary's startling vision into the dining car window twenty years later, now trapped forever on the wrong side of America's tracks. Dying in a sanitarium in 1920 (where "her bed faced the windows"),[4] she thinks back to Mike's hopes when they were courting—how impressed he'd been by the Dexters' home:

> This was the way a man should live. . . . He put his arm around her waist and smiled down at her. "Well, who knows what may happen? I'm still young. We'll work hard, save our money. One of these days . . ."[5]

This classic American dream—hard work, savings—was bound to fail for many like Mary and Mike in the pre-union 1920s (as it has, arguably, for more and more people in the 1990s).

The novel's association of Mary with windows reflects her orientation to domestic, interior, family roles. The most emotionally charged example of this is the announcement of Mike's death during a night turn on the blast furnace. Kracha (the grandfather), sleeping at Mary's home in the front room with the kids, hears a knocking, goes to the window, hears the news, then "sinks down on his knees beside the window." As he turns to the room at the back of the house to tell Mary, he "let out his breath in a shuddering sigh, wondering why God had chosen him to do this dreadful thing to her"—to make *him* tell Mary that her husband is dead.[6] Bell brilliantly stages this scene to emphasize the vulnerability of the home, and of women's lives, to the inhumanity of the industrial workplace. The final twist is that Kracha—a blunt male instrument—has to deliver the news.

Bell presents a gallery of women in *Out of This Furnace*, but Mary is central, an emblem of virtuous family life. Some years ago, Anthony Bell recalled his brother's motive in writing the novel: "About my mother he said once that at the time it didn't make much impression on him, but that when he was in his late twenties he began to recall the years right after my father's death and agonized over the anguish and hardships she experienced in the few years she lasted."[7]

II

Bell's written sources for his 1941 novel included Mary Heaton Vorse's *Men and Steel*, an on-the-scene labor journalist's account of the 1919 strike and its era. This is a good book that is less well known, and less admired, than it deserves to be. It apparently has never been reprinted since its first edition in 1920—overshadowed, I suppose, by the facts-and-figures, no-nonsense (and in fact excellent) analysis of Foster's *Lessons of the Great Strike* and the two volumes by the World Interchurch Movement (to which Vorse contributed research). By comparison Vorse's *Men and Steel* is very simple: emotional and pictorial. I want to suggest that it is a prose version (i.e., without literal photographs) of Dorothea Lange and Paul Taylor's *American Exodus*, or a prose-poem version, perhaps, of Jacob Riis's *How the Other Half Lives*. Again—as with Bell—I'm drawn to the analogy of documentary photography.

Vorse's method, at its best, is very sharp, very disciplined. In *Men and Steel* generalizations are quickly validated by specifics—from the ground up, from the scene, through the camera's eye of the reporter. Set your tripod down, open the shutter. Show, don't just tell.

For nearly half a century Coal and Steel have owned great districts of Pennsylvania, Indiana, Ohio, Illinois. For nearly half a century Steel has been writing its own history in the houses and factories of its towns.

Braddock is one of the oldest steel towns. Here Carnegie Steel was born. Its mills existed before the great mills of Homestead. A ganglion of towns—Braddock, Rankin, Homestead, Bessemer, lined the Monongahela River with steel mills.

All of Braddock is black. The soot of the mills has covered it. There is no spot in Braddock that is fair to see. It has neither park nor playground. It is a town of slack disorder and of scant self-respect. Those who have made money in Braddock mills live where they cannot see Braddock. The steelworkers who can, escape up the hillsides. They go to North Braddock or to Wolftown; but many and many of them live and die in the First Ward.

They live some in two-story brick houses, some in blackened frame dwellings. One set of houses faces the street, the other the court. The courts are bricked and littered with piles of cans, piles of rubbish, bins of garbage, hills of refuse—refuse and litter, litter and refuse. Playing in the refuse and ashes and litter—children. The decencies of life ebb away as one nears the mills. I passed the day along an alley which fronted on an empty lot. Here the filth and refuse of years had been churned into viscous mud. A lean dog was digging. Pale children paddled in the squashy filth and made playthings of ancient rubbish. Beyond was the railroad tracks, beyond that the mills. Two-storied brick houses flanked the brick street. No green thing grew anywhere.

But in the brick courtyard Croatian and Slovak women were weaving rugs. In their villages in Europe they had woven the clothes of their men. In Braddock's squalid courtyards they weave bright colored rugs and sing as they weave. Here and there men bring tables out of doors and play cards. They nod to me in village fashion as I pass. Everywhere were children—Slovak children with flaxen hair and blue eyed; wide-faced Magyar children, Gypsy children. Then I knew that the chief product of Braddock and its sister towns was not steel.

Their principal product is children.[8]

Several things want saying about its skill and effectiveness of a passage like this. One thing to note is the short sentences and four-letter words. At one level, this style may make easier reading. But more important is the feeling of concreteness, of the stripped-down thinginess of reality: of objects seen, encountered, stumbled over. "Piles of cans, piles of rubbish, bins of garbage, hills of refuse"—the words hit the reader in the face like mudballs. The pungency of Vorse's prose reminds one of H. L. Mencken's little essay a few years later, "The Libido for the Ugly," on riding the Pennsy into Greensburg—though unlike Mencken, Vorse stresses that the reign of corporate capitalism has created the squalor of the mill towns.

Another thing to notice is the "I" point of view. Vorse repeatedly presents herself in her writing, in this book and elsewhere, as a visitor—someone who is naively encountering an environment for the first time. The pose is probably true. In this case, at the start Vorse did not know steel-making or steel towns. She also was entering a place like Braddock's First Ward as a middle-class, Anglo-Saxon observer. How to open herself to what she encountered—not override it with class assumptions—is an issue. With her use of "I," Vorse emphasizes her smallness and isolation in this environment. By being up-front about her outsider's ignorance, she is able to underscore her role as fact-gatherer, as a reporter of exactly what she sees. Here she is in contrast, I think, to Jacob Riis. She is more modest than he was, careful *not* to adopt an authoritative, judgmental voice-over.

Another facet of the passage above is Vorse's orientation toward women and their concerns: here the Croatian and Slovak women weaving their rugs, then the rhetorical climax—"Then I knew that the chief product of Braddock and its sister towns was not steel. Their principal product is children." Vorse's book is really mistitled; it should be "Men *and* Women and Steel," because while she does report strike issues and the opinions of steelworkers, she gives at least equal time to women. Women are there repeatedly—in a passage, for example, that Vorse evidently especially liked herself, since she quoted it years later in her memoir *A Footnote to Folly* (1935):

> Women in the steel towns fly a flag of defiance against dirt. It is their white window curtains. You cannot go into any foul courtyard without finding white lace curtains stretched to dry on frames. Wherever you go, in Braddock or in Homestead or in filthy Rankin, you will find courageous women hopefully washing their white curtains.[9]

Vorse's book is full of accounts of her visits to the homes of such women, up and down the alleys and streets of Braddock's First Ward—often with Father Kazincy as her guide, or with a girl who translates. The book ends with such a passage; the book's final image is a kind of Mother Courage figure:

> Weeks after the strike was over I walked again down Braddock's alleys. . . .
> There were no outward changes. The women's curtains were drying on frames. The children played in the litter. Smoke rolled down the valley. . . .
> A woman was sitting beside her door with a child in her arms, another playing at her feet. Her mild eyes gazed on vacancy, as though not seeing the monotony of the squalid street that ended with the red cylinders of the mills . . .
> The woman had the patience of eternity in her broad quiet face.
> "I have waited," she seemed to say. "I am eternal. This strife is about me and mine. If my brothers do not change this, my sons will. I can wait."[10]

I want to turn for a moment—in contrast to these images—to John Dos Passos's character Mary French in *The Big Money*, his version of Mary Heaton Vorse's work during the 1919 strike. Dos Passos's trilogy *U.S.A.* is a great American epic whose dominant theme is the subjugation of American freedoms by the corporate system. Its final mood is captured by the famous prose poem about the execution of Sacco and Vanzetti:

> they have clubbed us off the streets they are stronger they are rich they hire and fire the politicians . . . they hire the men with the guns . . . all right you have won . . . there is nothing left to do[11]

But I would argue that Dos Passos's pessimism leads him to create in Mary French a character very different from Vorse (even though based on her experience)—at least as Vorse presents herself in her writing. Vorse's faith in the cause of labor was indefatigable. Her labor reporting was energized, designed to anger and educate readers. Dos Passos's Mary French is a slightly delicate young woman, definitely middle class and definitely vulnerable. Dos Passos's version of the long passage from Vorse I quoted above shows Mary French walking through a mill town with a Polish steelworker:

> [Gus] made a gesture with his elbow as they turned a corner past a group of ragged kids making mudpies; they were pale flabby filthy little kids with pouches under their eyes. Mary turned her eyes away, but she'd seen them, as she'd seen the photograph of the dead woman with her head caved in [i.e., Fanny Sellins].[12]

Mary Heaton Vorse, as a writer, did *not* turn her eyes away. Dos Passos's Mary French is a naive idealist whom the reader of *U.S.A.* feels admiration for, but also pity. In her personal life, Vorse too was doubtless often tired and sexually vulnerable, but she belonged to a category of tough women agitators and labor campaigners—Mother Jones, Elizabeth Gurley Flynn, Fanny Sellins—whose skills still startle and amaze. Such people ask, above all, to be judged by the merit of their public work. Vorse's skilled writing—like her public career—deserves admiration, not mild condescension, à la Dos Passos.

III

I want to turn briefly to a couple of texts by African Americans, one of them an interview with a longtime Braddock woman resident, the other a novel, William Attaway's *Blood on the Forge*. Again for my purpose here, what interests me in both texts is their representation of the price exacted from women's lives by the industrial workplace in the 1919 era.

Like *Out of This Furnace*, *Blood on the Forge* was published in 1941, but where Bell chose to close his novel with the triumph of the CIO, Attaway focused exclusively on the bitter experience of blacks in the 1919 era: brought north in boxcars by the companies, made the target of rock-throwing kids and shouted insults in the mill towns, and finally used as replacement workers during the strike. Attaway's tale of three "brothers" from the South is a grim memorial to the exploitation of African Americans—in fact, a condemnation of American industrialism in general.

Blood on the Forge invites closest comparison with Richard Wright's 1940 novel, *Native Son*. Both books show how their central characters come to be dominated, and finally destroyed, by violence. In the case of Wright's Bigger Thomas, violence is a product of racism and urban anonymity; it becomes a perverse expression of self-identity. Attaway, in a very Marxist analysis, shows violence resulting directly from the means of production: the feudal overlordism of Southern agriculture, on the one hand; on the other, the Northern factory's mechanization and speedup—all of it sharpened by racism. Big Mat, the eldest brother, is a black Joe Magarac, who works with his muscles, but who turns his anger and frustration into deadly violence.

Anna—a Mexican woman—another cross-continent immigrant to the Mon Valley—is a particular victim of Mat's rage. (There *was*, by the way, a Mexican section in Braddock in 1919—it was described in a 1922 social-work thesis written at Carnegie Tech. Other details in the novel, however, don't fit Braddock; Attaway's fictional mill town seems to be a composite.) Like Mary Dobrejcak in *Out of This Furnace*, Anna has an American Dream, but it is a desperate vision urged on her by her aunt—Sugar Mama—who tells her she should sell her body to an *Americano*. Anna sets the lifestyle of white suburbanites as her goal:

> So she had crept close to one of the white hill houses. Cars had come up the drive. Afraid, she had hidden herself in the bushes at the foot of the hill. All day she was there. Lying on her back, she had watched the house—almost above her where it hung over the hill.[13]

> "Making love in the fields is nothing, [she says.] A man who have a house and will buy high heels and grand things for Anna is big thing. . . ."[14]

> "I look for one big strong fella who will make Anna grand like the Americano . . ."[15]

Of course Mat becomes that "fella." Anna takes Mat's money and goes into the stores and comes out "with rhinestone shoes and dresses like the hostesses wear in the dance halls. . . . [She] wore her new clothes every day and paraded through the Mexican part of town like an overseer's wife."[16]

But Matt cannot keep Anna satisfied for long; she's soon gone through his money. Meanwhile he treats her as a possession, a badge of sexual potency, and is soon frighteningly jealous that she will take on other lovers. Attaway describes the mill towns' culture of prostitution: money as the key to love; love bought by men who must dominate someone in their sexual lives to compensate for abuse they receive at work; love used by women as a way of manipulating men for whatever status they can squeeze out. Attaway spares none of the mill town residents—blacks, Mexicans, Eastern European—from his picture of sexual exploitation.

This "love" is violent. As Anna says at one point: "It's right for the man to beat the woman."[17] After Mat has become a goon for the sheriff, beating up union pickets, he thinks:

> He had handled people, and they feared him. Their fear had made him whole. Now he would go to Anna a whole man. She would fear him too.[18]

Instead [Anna] taunts him:
> "You are a peon . . . I will not live with peon. . . . You are not *Americano. Americano* live in big house back in the hills."[19]

Mat's response is predictable. At the end of the book he beats Anna half to death. Then he goes out in the street, and acting as an agent for the sheriff, kills a union supporter and is killed himself.

As a counterpoint to this bloody sequence, I want to end with a couple of passages from an interview I did with an African American woman in Braddock fifteen years ago. Annie Morgan was eighty then, and she told me how she and her husband came to Braddock in 1917 so he could work at Edgar Thomson (they actually lived in Port Perry, a now extinct village just east of Braddock). Her husband worked during the 1919 strike. She seemed to me a strong, religious, family woman. These are a few of the words she used to sum things up for me:

> [My husband] was working when the union came in to organize—I think [that] was 1919. And he worked [during that strike]. We were in Port Perry, and they would go in the mill and stay in there sometimes two or three days. They could go in from the Port Perry end—the railroad from Port Perry ran right into the mill, you know.
>
> They told the men that they had brought in to work that if they continued to work they would pay them double wages. . . . [Later, during the Depression], of course they joined the union, and [my husband] belonged to the union until he died. . . .
>
> I never did enjoy Braddock at all. I'm from Richmond, Virginia, and I came up here to a different environment altogether. I didn't like Port Perry and I didn't like Braddock.

Of course *you* wouldn't know how Port Perry was. It was just a little space with three or four railroads running through it—smaller than the First Ward. You'll find out that you don't care very much for a place like that. But I made out because I had my husband here and my children. And I've been happy, I guess. There's been some good times, and there's been some really bad times.

My husband liked the mill, he did good in the mill, he had good friends there. I didn't find no fault, I never grumbled. I never told him I didn't like Braddock, because after all he was working and trying to make a living here. And that's enough for a man. I did my job and he did his.

These quotes end my presentation on the right note, I think: on representations of unsung women in the pre-union steel towns—ordinary people—as they come down to us described by good writers, or just in their own voices.

NOTES

1. Thomas Bell, *Out of This Furnace* (University of Pittsburgh Press, 1976), 234–35.

2. Willa Cather, "Paul's Case," in *Collected Short Fiction, 1892–1912*, ed. Virginia Faulkner (Lincoln: University of Nebraska Press, 1970).

3. Bell, *Out of This Furnace,* 128.

4. Ibid., 250.

5. Ibid., 128.

6. Ibid., 207–208.

7. Ibid., 420.

8. Mary Heaton Vorse, *Men and Steel* (New York: Boni and Liveright, 1920), 32–34.

9. Ibid., 36.

10. Ibid., 185.

11. John Dos Passos, *The Big Money* (New York: Harcourt, Brace and Company, 1936), 413.

12. Ibid., 119.

13. William Attaway, *Blood on the Forge* (New York: Monthly Review Press, 1987), 170.

14. Ibid., 149.

15. Ibid.

16. Ibid., 137.

17. Ibid., 168.

18. Ibid., 269.

19. Ibid., 276.

7

REFLECTIONS ON THE GREAT MIGRATION TO WESTERN PENNSYLVANIA

JOE W. TROTTER

A focus on the Great Migration to Western Pennsylvania offers an opportunity for us to reflect on strategies for dealing with crises in the African American community today. We are troubled by the loss of jobs in the industrial sector over the past two decades and the resulting deterioration of our communities, the spread of violence, and the debilitating impact of drugs. For these reasons, we can look at the Great Migration as a response to an even greater crisis in African American life—i.e., the rise of Jim Crow, disenfranchisement, lynchings, and racial segregation in the late nineteenth- and early twentieth-century American South. While a greater appreciation for the past cannot offer immediate solutions, it can highlight the numerous difficulties that African Americans faced and the viable responses they fashioned, and their survival in heart, body, and mind.

The Great Migration to Western Pennsylvania had deep roots in the work, culture, and community experiences of southern blacks. After the Civil War, nearly 4 million slaves gained their freedom in the South. It was perhaps the most optimistic moment in African American history. Yet, in less than twenty-five years, African Americans faced the onset of a new white supremacist regime. During the 1880s and 1890s, the number of recorded lynchings reached an average of about 100 per year. By the early

From *Pittsburgh History* 78, no. 4 (winter 1995/96): 153–57. Reprinted by permission of the Historical Society of Western Pennsylvania.

1900s, African Americans faced systematic exclusion from voting, segregation in the institutional life, and growing economic exploitation.

The sharecropping system dominated the economic sphere. According to Booker T. Washington, sharecropping was a system of debt that resembled slavery. As he put it, sharecropping robbed African Americans of their independence and made them feel "lost and bewildered." African American sharecroppers were by no means passive. Facing the tightening grip of segregation, they adopted migration as a major strategy for changing their lives. They gradually moved into Southern, and then Northern cities.

The migrants came in two waves. During the first, between 1890 and 1910, an estimated 300,000 blacks moved north; some came to Pittsburgh and other industrial towns along the Allegheny, Monongahela, and Ohio rivers. Pittsburgh's black population rose from only 6,000 or so in 1880 to over 26,600 in 1910. The surrounding towns of Homestead, Braddock, Duquesne, and McKeesport also saw increases in their black populations. Most of these early migrants came from the upper South and border states (Virginia, Tennessee, Maryland, and North Carolina) This pre–World War I generation included men such as Jefferson Jackson from King George County, Virginia; James Claggett from Mt. Zion, Maryland; and William Marbley from Beilton, West Virginia. These men found employment respectively at the Duquesne Steel Company, the Carnegie Steel Company, and the Clairton Steel Company, which became part of the U. S. Steel Corporation in 1904.

Early black iron and steel employees worked in a broad range of occupations. As historian Dennis Dickerson notes, not all were confined to jobs such as custodians and common laborers. Some were relatively well educated and gained prestigious and skilled jobs. John Harley, a black graduate of the University of Pittsburgh, became a draftsman at the Crucible Steel Company. Another black graduate of the University of Pittsburgh, William Dennon, joined the engineering department at the Farrell plant of U.S. Steel. William Nelson Page, another early black migrant, served as private secretary to W. G. Glyde, general manager of sales for Carnegie Steel.

At the Black Diamond Steel Works in Pittsburgh, African Americans held such important skilled positions as plumber, engineer, die grinder, and puddler. At the Clark Mills in Pittsburgh, about 30 percent of the firm's 110 black employees worked in skilled jobs—as rollers, roughers, finishers, puddlers, millwrights, and heaters. By 1910, skilled workers made up about 27 percent of Pittsburgh's black iron and steel workforce. Indeed, for a short period, immigrants from Southern and Eastern Europe had fewer of their numbers in skilled jobs than African Americans.

Despite significant progress in the pre–World War I era, however, the number of black employees remained small. By 1910, Pittsburgh's iron and steel mills employed nearly 30,000 workers. African Americans comprised only about 3 percent of the total. American-born whites made up 29 percent of the total, while immigrants comprised 68 percent.

World War I ushered in the second wave of black migration, as blacks moved into Northern cities in growing numbers. An estimated 500,000 blacks left the South between 1916 and 1920, and during the 1920s, another 800,000 to 1 million Southern blacks moved to Northern cities. Unlike the prewar migration, however, most of the new migrants came from the boll weevil-infested cotton regions of the deep South. Between about 1915 and 1930, the number of black farmworkers in Georgia dropped by nearly 30 percent (about 122,500 to less than 87,000). South Carolina, Alabama, and Mississippi experienced similar declines.

Western Pennsylvania, once again, was a major target of the black migration. In 1917, *Iron Age*, a key journal in the steel industry, reported trains "filled with negroes bound from the South to Pittsburgh." According to one contemporary scholar, over 18,000 blacks arrived in Pittsburgh between 1915 and 1917. Pittsburgh's black population increased from 25,600 in 1910 to 37,700 in 1920 (4.8 to 6.4 percent of the total). The black population in the mill towns of Homestead, Rankin, Braddock, and others nearly doubled. By war's end, the black population in the major steel towns of Western Pennsylvania had increased from 29,470 to nearly 50,000, an increase of about 70 percent. By 1930, over 78,000 African Americans lived in Western Pennsylvania (about 7 percent of the total population).

Black migration to the city of Pittsburgh during this period was less intense than elsewhere. Detroit's black population increased by 611 percent; Cleveland's by 307 percent; and Chicago's by 148 percent. Nonetheless, the steel industry in Western Pennsylvania employed African Americans in growing numbers. By 1918, black steelworkers had increased from less than 3 percent of the total to 13 percent. Over 50 percent of these employees worked at Carnegie steel plants in Allegheny County and at Jones and Laughlin's numerous mills in the area.

During the early war years, labor agents from railroads, steel companies, and defense industries facilitated black migration to the region. In the summer of 1916, for example, the Pennsylvania Railroad launched a major campaign to recruit black labor for Northern industries, including its own far-flung operations. Railroad companies provided free transportation passes to black workers, who, upon receiving employment, authorized the railroads to deduct travel expenses from their paychecks.

Northern black newspapers applauded what became known as "The Great Migration" to Western Pennsylvania and elsewhere in urban America. Some Southern black newspapers reinforced the process. A West Virginia editor exclaimed, "Let millions of Negroes leave the South. It will make conditions better for those who remain." The black weekly *Chicago Defender* emerged as the most vigorous promoter of black population movement. The

Defender repeatedly portrayed the South as the land of lynchings, disfranchisement, and economic exploitation. At the same time, the paper appealed to important elements in Southern black religious culture. The *Defender* portrayed the North as the "promised land," and spoke of the migration as a "flight from Egypt," and "Crossing over Jordan." When one trainload of blacks crossed the Ohio River headed North, they knelt to pray and sang the hymn: "I Done Come Out of the Land of Egypt with the Good News."

Although African Americans often expressed their views of the Great Migration in biblical terms and received encouragement from Northern black newspapers, railroad companies, and industrial labor agents, they also drew upon family and friendship networks to help in the move to Western Pennsylvania. They formed migration clubs, pooled their money, bought tickets at reduced rates, and often moved in groups. Before they made the decision to move, they gathered information and debated the pros and cons of the process. As one recent study points out, in barbershops, poolrooms, and grocery stores, in churches, lodge halls, and clubhouses, and in private homes, Southern blacks discussed, debated, and decided what was good and what was bad about moving to the urban North. Historians John Bodnar, Roger Simon, and Michael Weber note in their comparative study of ethnic and racial migration patterns to Pittsburgh that friend and kinship networks played a crucial role in the movement of Southern blacks to Pittsburgh: "As a teenager Jean B. began working at a sawmill near Mobile, Alabama, while living on his parents' farm. It was at the sawmill that he heard mention of Philadelphia, New York, and Chicago. Such conversation prompted him to come north. He decided upon Pittsburgh because two friends were already there. After saving $45, he took a train from Mobile through Cincinnati to Pittsburgh, where his friends obtained a room for him."

Black women played a major role in migration networks. As recent scholarship suggests, they were the primary "kinkeepers." According to historian Peter Gottlieb, black women sometimes chose Pittsburgh over other places and shaped patterns of black migration to the region. In 1919, one black man went to Cincinnati, found a job, and sent for his wife. His wife later recalled her response and the final result: "I wrote him a letter back. My older sister had come to Pittsburgh, and I took her as a mother because I had lost my mother. And I wrote him back and said, 'I don't want to stay in Cincinnati. I want to go to Pittsburgh.' Next letter I got, he had got a job in Pittsburgh and sent for me."

Southern blacks were quite aware of job opportunities in Western Pennsylvania, and that the war in Europe had blocked the flow of European immigrants to Northern cities. Nearly 1,000,000 immigrants annually had entered the country in the years just before America entered the war. During the war years, the annual number dropped to nearly 300,000. Moreover, some immigrants returned to their homelands to fight. Allegheny County lost nearly 20,000 immigrants during the war years. At the same time, the federal government passed the Selective Service Act of 1917 and drafted young men in rising numbers. As the draft (coupled with declining immigration) depleted the labor supply, rural Southern blacks found new opportunities to make higher wages and improve their lives. In a letter to the Pittsburgh Urban League, one man wrote for himself and seven other black men: "We Southern Negroes want to come to the north . . . they ain't giving a man nothing for what he do . . . they [white southerners] is trying to keep us down." Another black man from Savannah, Georgia, wrote, "I want to find a good job where I can make a living as I cannot do it here." From South Carolina, a black woman wrote to the Pittsburgh Urban League for her two sons: "[I have] two grown son[s] . . . we want to settle down somewhere north . . . wages are so cheap down here we can hardly live." A Georgia man wanted to come to Pittsburgh to "make a livelihood, and to educate my children."

African Americans earned between $3.50 and $5 per eight-hour day in the steel industry. In the South, in the cities, they made no more than $2.50 per twelve-hour day. In Southern agriculture, as farm laborers, African Americans made even less, usually no more than $1 per day. According to one recent study, even after accounting for higher rents, life in the Pittsburgh region was better for most blacks than it was in their Southern homes. In their view, migration represented a path leading to upward mobility, citizenship, and a fuller recognition of their humanity. For the first time in American history, blacks entered the industrial mainstream. In doing so, they earned more than they had ever earned before, especially if they came directly from farms in the deep South. In Western Pennsylvania, they also lived in a social environment that contrasted sharply with their Southern homes.

Unfortunately, as blacks entered the region in larger numbers, racism intensified and blocked their mobility. As in the South, employers, white workers, and the state all helped to keep blacks at the bottom of the economic ladder. Compared to prewar counterparts, for example, few black steelworkers gained skilled jobs in the wake of the Great Migration. Employers classified over 90 percent—and sometimes 100 percent—of the new workers as unskilled. This pattern prevailed at Carnegie Steel (all plants), Jones and Laughlin (all plants), National Tube (all plants), Crucible Steel, and others. African Americans took jobs that were the most dangerous, the lowest paying, and the dirtiest. They fed the blast furnaces, poured molten steel, and worked on the coke ovens. They repeatedly complained that their jobs were characterized by disproportionate exposure to debilitating heat and deadly fumes. It is no wonder that the black turnover rate was so high. At A. M. Beyer Company, for example, 1,408 black employees came and went during 1923 to maintain a regular workforce of 223 blacks. Although some employers would later institute social welfare and recreational programs for black workers, they did little to improve the long-term prospects of black steelworkers.

For its part, the labor movement largely excluded blacks, misreading the significance of the Great Migration and losing an excellent opportunity to redefine the African American experience in more explicitly class, rather than racial, terms. As a result, African Americans sometimes served as strikebreakers and undermined the goals of the labor movement. The Great Steel Strike of 1919 is an outstanding example. The strike represented a huge challenge for organized labor. During the war years, the federal government had protected the rights of workers to bargain collectively with employers in exchange for their support of the war effort. As the war emergency passed, however, the federal government exhibited less enthusiasm for protecting the right of workers. Moreover, the triumph of the Communist revolution in Russia unleashed new fears of workers and led to repression of radicals and radical ideas. At the same time, the Great Migration brought racial animosities to the surface; major race riots hit such cities as Chicago and East St. Louis.

Despite these very difficult times and the disappointing record of labor union discrimination, at the outset of the 1919 steel strike African Americans were by no means uniformly hostile to organized labor. They grudgingly accepted segregated unions, using them to fight racial barriers in the labor movement as well as the discriminatory policies of employers. From the outset, the Pittsburgh Urban League urged William Z. Foster and the National Committee for Organizing Iron and Steel Workers to employ black organizers. Although Foster appeared eager to organize black workers, the strike committee as a whole exhibited little interest in the black worker. Comprised of twenty-four international unions, the strike committee itself represented several decidedly hostile and racially exclusionary unions. The machinists and electrical workers barred African Americans altogether, while the blacksmiths relegated blacks to auxiliary lodges under the control of white locals. Understandably, then, in this hostile and at best lukewarm racial climate, few African American steelworkers walked out with their white brothers. In the city of Pittsburgh, fewer than two dozen blacks joined 25,000 white workers in the 1919 Steel Strike. In other plants up and down the Monongahela River, the response was little better. At the huge Homestead, Duquesne, Clairton, and Braddock works, only a handful of blacks walked out with their white counterparts. A similar pattern prevailed in Chicago, Gary, Youngstown, and other northern centers of the steel industry.

The labor movement not only failed to fully organize the existing labor force, it also failed to protect itself against the use of new African American workers as strikebreakers. The importation of new black workers helped to defeat the steel strike. According to the Inter-Church World Movement of North America, managers skillfully utilized black strikebreakers. In a modern-day interview with David Demarest, Annie Morgan recalled how her husband continued to work during the strike: "They would go in the mill and stay in there sometimes two or three days. They could go in from the Port Perry end because . . . the railroad from Port Perry ran right into the mill, you know." Black workers were often shifted from plant to plant, smuggled in at night and mixed with small contingents of white strike-breakers. As Foster put it, thousands of whites, skilled and unskilled, went on strike in their hometowns, but "sneaked away to other steel centers and worked there until the strike was over." After defeating the strike with the aid of black strikebreakers, company officials frequently referred to black workers as "strike insurance" and as a "lifesaver" in times of emergency.

African Americans not only faced restrictions at the workplace, but they also faced constraints on where they could live. Real estate and company officials collaborated in the rise of all-black areas, characterized by overcrowded, dilapidated, and unsanitary conditions. Historian Dennis Dickerson notes that African Americans found housing in carefully desig-nated "Colored areas": Port Perry in Braddock, Castle Garden in Duquesne, Rosedale in Johnstown, and the Hill District in Pittsburgh.

As these areas became overcrowded, other all-black areas also emerged. Making matters worse, African Americans were barred from numerous facilities designed to serve the public. Downtown restaurants routinely excluded black customers. Blacks could only receive food ser-vices in the basement of Rosenbaum Department Store. Theaters con-signed black customers to the balcony. Policemen, judges, and other public officials also treated African Americans with disdain and violated their civil rights. During the early 1920s, local chapters of the Ku Klux Klan emerged in Pittsburgh, Homestead, Johnstown, and other major towns of Western Pennsylvania. At its height in 1924, the Klan claimed a membership of 125,000 in Western Pennsylvania.

In 1923, the most destructive racial conflict occurred in Johnstown, when a black migrant was charged in a shooting incident involving police. The mayor, police, and other town officials blamed the black newcomers for stirring up trouble and ordered them "to pack up" and "go back from where you came." An estimated 500 black steelworkers and their families were forced to leave the area.

But while African Americans faced stiff racial barriers and some were forced to leave the area, most stayed. They not only stayed, but helped to build new institutions and expand their own communities in Western Penn-sylvania. As historian Earl Lewis put it in another context, they helped to transform segregation into "congregation." Black churches, fraternal orders, and newspapers (especially the *Pittsburgh Courier*); organizations such as the NAACP, Urban League, and Garvey Movement; social clubs, restaurants, and baseball teams; hotels, beauty shops, barber shops, and taverns, all proliferated. According to historian Laurence Glasco, "The migrants gave the community a new energy and creativity that quickly attracted attention. Wylie Avenue, Centre Avenue, and side streets in the Hill district 'jumped' as blacks and whites flocked to its bars and night spots."

During the era of the Great Migration blacks not only fueled the engine of industrial expansion with their labor, but also helped to transform the region and the nation. African Americans in Western Pennsylvania helped establish the foundation for the New Deal coalition of the 1930s and 1940s; the new Congress of Industrial Organizations; the Double V Campaign for victory at home and victory abroad during World War II; and new forms of popular culture, especially jazz and blues. In 1941, Richard Attaway opened his powerful novel on black migration to Pittsburgh, *Blood on the Forge*, with a description of the main character, Melody, a guitar player: "He never had a craving in him that he couldn't slick away on his guitar. . . . And maybe that's why his mother changed his name to Melody." The contributions of these Southern blacks would also facilitate the rise of the modern civil rights movement in the 1950s and 1960s.

Our times and conditions are different. The forms of disfranchisement, racial discrimination, and economic inequality have changed significantly since the Jim Crow era of the early twentieth century. Yet, as we move toward the twenty-first century, let us remember that African Americans endured Jim Crow and a massive migration of people with few equals in human history. Their transformation from agricultural people to urban-industrial people created new forms of popular culture and provoked a radical realignment of American political forces. They and their descendants have a great deal to teach.

SOURCES

The author wishes to acknowledge that this essay is based partly upon lectures delivered at the Conference on the 75th Anniversary of the Great Steel Strike (fall 1994) and at the African American Lecture Series of the Historical Society of Western Pennsylvania (spring 1995).

Attaway, William. *Blood on the Forge*. Garden City, N.Y.: Doubleday, Doran & Co., 1941. Reprint, New York: Collier Books, 1970.

Brody, David. *Labor in Crisis: The Steel Strike of 1919*. Philadelphia: Lippincott, 1965. Reprint, Urbana: University of Illinois Press, 1987.

———. *Steelworkers in America: The Nonunion Era*. Cambridge, Mass.: Harvard University Press, 1960. Reprint, New York: Russell & Russell, 1970.

Cayton, Horace R., and George S. Mitchell. *Black Workers and the New Unions*. Chapel Hill: University of North Carolina Press, 1939.

Dickerson, Dennis C. *Out of the Crucible: Black Steelworkers in Western Pennsylvania, 1875–1980*. Albany, N.Y.: State University of New York Press, 1986.

Foner, Philip S. *Organized Labor and the Black Worker, 1619–1973*. New York: Praeger, 1974.

Foster, William Z. *The Great Steel Strike and Its Lessons*. New York: B. W. Huebsch, 1920.

Glasco, Laurence. "Double Burden: The Black Experience in Pittsburgh." In *City at the Point: Essays on the Social History of Pittsburgh*, edited by Samuel P. Hays. Pittsburgh: University of Pittsburgh Press, 1989.

Gottlieb, Peter. *Making Their Own Way: Southern Blacks' Migration to Pittsburgh, 1916–30*. Urbana: University of Illinois Press, 1987.

Spero, Sterling D., and Abram L. Harris. *The Black Worker: The Negro and the Labor Movement*. New York: Columbia University Press, 1931. Reprint, New York: Atheneum, 1968.

Trotter, Joe W., Jr., ed. *The Great Migration in Historical Perspective: New Dimensions of Race, Class, and Gender*. Bloomington: Indiana University Press, 1991.

8

THE GENDERED SOCIAL WORLD OF STEELMAKING

A Case Study of Bethlehem Steel's Sparrows Point Plant

KAREN OLSON

There are few sectors of American life that have been more closely linked with men, manliness, and a masculine work culture than the steel industry. Most of the studies of the steel industry take this for granted. The seminal works in labor history—from David Brody's *Steelworkers in America: The Nonunion Era* to the current array of books analyzing American steel's expansion and precipitous decline—have, without exception, examined steel as an arena in which men worked, organized unions, resisted the authority of management, and accommodated the harshest of working conditions, all without the intrusion of women. Consequently, because women were not present in large numbers in steelmaking, scholars assumed that an analysis of gender was irrelevant. The reality of steelmaking has been far more complicated.

As we shall see, women played an important role in the social production of steel and steelworkers at Bethlehem Steel's Sparrows Point, Maryland, mill from the end of the nineteenth century until the present. Women's unpaid labor at home (and occasionally their paid labor as cooks and housekeepers in boardinghouses) was crucial to making men's labor in the mill possible. Because of the long hours spent at work, even the toughest men relied on women to cook their meals and clean their clothes so that the hours not spent in the mill could be devoted to sleep—a particularly important consideration since almost all steelworkers worked in rotating shifts or "turns."

Furthermore, men's own gender (how their masculinity was expressed) shaped not only the work culture of steel mills but also deeply affected the configuration of family life in steelmaking communities. Prior to World War II, during the first four decades of Sparrows Point's existence, all women—both black and white—outside the managerial class were heavily burdened with the unpaid yet essential work of providing domestic services to steelworkers. After World War II—when union wages, labor-saving devices, and the end of the boardinghouse system eased the domestic burdens of steelmakers' wives—virtually all white steelworkers earned enough to provide for a wife who "did not work"—that is for wages outside the home. Because of systematic discrimination, this was an unrealistic expectation for most black men, but even in the African American community some men were proud of the claim that their wives were not in the paid workforce.

In the 1970s, women began to enter the mill. Their experiences help to highlight the ways that masculine identities influenced the meanings with which male workers imbued their labor. As we shall see, workers' gender influenced their relationships with each other and with management as well. The modernization of Sparrows Point in the 1980s and the concomitant reduction in employment in steel transformed the work and family roles and identities of many steelworkers and their families. Traditional relationships and expectations changed—sometimes painfully. Steelworkers' gendered world helps to highlight not only the importance of gender, but the ways in which it was shaped by the demands of industrial production. The actual gender and race relationships in and around Sparrows Point were not simply the result of choices workers made for themselves, but also a response to a company looking to maximize its profits and its control over its workforce.

Sparrows Point, Maryland, was designed in 1887 as a company town by Frederick and Rufus Wood, founders of the Maryland Steel Company, an integrated steel-producing mill that became part of the Bethlehem Steel Company in 1916 and by the 1950s was the single largest steel complex in the world.[1] The collaboration of the Wood brothers on the Sparrows Point project is well documented by correspondence between the two brothers in which Rufus Wood, who resided in Sparrows Point, sought to apprise his brother, Frederick, who remained in New England, of progress made and problems encountered at the new Maryland steelworks. Their letters show a conscious decision by capitalists to set in place a gendered social world in which men's work would be sharply segregated from women's work (and in which whites and blacks would also be segregated from each other). The Wood brothers' vision would shape the community of Sparrows Point for the first century of its existence.

Foremost in the planning calculus of Sparrows Point were the principles of efficiency and order, a concept designed to maximize profits, and one to which Rufus Wood assigned four major corollaries. First, the meticulous design of the company town accommodated a workforce that was segmented by skill, ethnicity, regional origins, race, and gender. Second, using what they believed to be a highly enlightened system of community management, the Wood brothers instituted a system of education that instructed students discriminately in those skills that would best serve the needs of their steel mill. Third, women, though not permitted in the works, were assigned an essential role at Sparrows Point as the providers of domestic services to men whose hours outside the mill were limited to eating and sleeping. Finally, the engineers of this planned community imposed legal restrictions on the consumption of alcohol within the environs of Sparrows Point that were intended, along with the company-sponsored churches, to ensure sobriety among their overworked steelworkers.

Race and class divisions were explicitly delineated in this planned industrial community by a hierarchical arrangement of east-west streets lettered from A to K with four major divisions separating the socially significant groups. Mill superintendents occupied the choicest lots and finest homes on B and C Streets where private gardens and personal servants marked the social elite of the town. On D Street churches and stores were built, and that street served as the first divide between social classes.

North of D Street were located the modest homes of skilled white workers, an area that accommodated 2,189 men, women, and children who were provided with dwellings that the company proudly described as "substantially built, having baths supplied with hot and cold water, inside closets and sanitary plumbing, as well as ranges and kitchen equipment."[2] Houses in this section of Sparrows Point were 13 feet by 28 feet with six rooms and a backyard, and the average household size was 7.4 people including one or two boarders.[3]

The white community of Sparrows Point ended at Humphrey's Creek, a natural barrier that would be used by the town's architects for the purposes of racial segregation. An 838-foot walkway extended across Humphrey's Creek unto the isolated stretch of land that contained Sparrows Point's black housing, where 1,066 men, women, and children crowded into sixty-four houses. In keeping with the social hierarchy of the community, houses in this section were smaller and lacked the amenities of running water and indoor plumbing. Most of Sparrows Point's African American families took in several relatives or boarders or both, and in this densely crowded black community an average of 11.3 people lived in each house.[4] Blacks were relegated to the hottest, most debilitating, and lowest-paid positions in the mill. In a measure that helped to compensate for the low wages of their husbands, most black women provided domestic services for an exceptionally large group of boarders whose rent money supplemented the family's income.

The sexual division of labor at Sparrows Point followed a pattern of segregation that paralleled the segregation of housing in the town. Women were segregated by an industrial work system that required a devoted crew of laborers in domestic service. The segregation of women was, of course, not a residential system, but it nonetheless was firmly embedded in the original plans for the Sparrows Point community.

When Rufus Wood designed the village where steelworkers were to be housed, educated, and serviced by company-owned or -sponsored stores, churches, fire, and police forces, he also had in mind a fully elaborated plan for molding desirable workmen who would be "sober," "industrious," "reliable," "steady," and "willing to work."[5] A report on the company school, written in 1894, announced proudly that through its vocational education the "older boys are so thoroughly fitted in the use of the wood-worker's tools that when graduated, they are placed on the roll of employees to take places when men drop out. . . ."[6]

Even more revealing of the conventions of gender in this steelmaking community is the report's much more detailed outline of female education:

> The idea at Sparrows Point is not only to mould the girls into women but home planners and home makers. Even girls ten years old go into the training kitchen, don their aprons, roll up their sleeves, and do such things as knead dough for bread and biscuit, make coffee that is clear and fragrant.
>
> On her little one-burner alcohol stove, a girl cooks a breakfast of oatmeal, omelette or bacon and eggs, perhaps biscuits or toast. . . . A wife who is a good cook is a "joy forever" to her husband, though she may not be a "thing of beauty." . . . The girls are shown how to use the broom and duster in a way that will not strain their backs. A model laundry with stationery [sic] tubs gives them practice in washing so they can tell how clothing should be washed without tearing.[7]

The founders of the Sparrows Point mill hoped to cultivate standards of masculinity and femininity that would accommodate the organization of work in a mill that required that workmen with specific skills work long hours on continually changing shifts at low wages. This would be possible with an educational system that provided men with the industrial skills required in the steel mill, and provided women with the domestic skills necessary to maintain frugal households.

Wood's plan for workers' education assumed that married couples would locate in Sparrows Point although, in reality, the labor requirements of the new mill recruited mainly single men from the rural areas of Virginia, Pennsylvania, and Maryland. Men outnumbered women three to one, but the domestic skills of women who lived in the community contributed to the maintenance of 1,114 boarders in addition to the 434 husbands who were employed as steelworkers. Sixty-five percent of Sparrows Point's male population lived in shanties or boardinghouses or boarded with families; 41 percent of the male boarders were housed in crowded, dormitory-style accommodations where laundry was washed and meals provided by young women who either lived with relatives or boarded with Sparrows Point families. Only 28 percent of the men who lived in Sparrows Point in 1900 headed their own households.

The census indicates that the 189 single women who lived in Sparrows Point in 1900 were either servants, seamstresses, or laundresses. The census fails to indicate an occupation for any of the 434 women who were listed as Sparrows Point wives, although undoubtedly these women were responsible for caring for children, as well as preparing meals and doing laundry for the husbands, adult sons, and boarders, virtually all of whom had jobs in the steel mill. Either as wives or servants, the 623 adult women who lived in Sparrows Point in 1900 provided domestic services for a predominantly male population that worked in the mill on shifts of between eleven and fourteen hours a day.[8]

In a community overwhelmingly composed of young single males, an ethos of manliness emerged in the Sparrows Point community that centered on the qualities of physical strength, courage, and rowdiness.[9] The masculine identity constructed for the jobs provided in Bethlehem Steel's Sparrows Point plant was based in part on the conditions of work in steelmaking, which were physically difficult, dangerous, and involved particularly long hours.[10] On the other hand, most women were married and lived in households with large numbers of children, boarders, parents, and in-laws. Their responsibilities for maintaining their households led to a female role complementary to that of single males whose long hours in the mill and constantly changing shifts made it necessary for them to rely on the services of women to provide food, clean laundry, and a properly managed household. The result was a community sharply segregated by sex. Men's lives were centered in the mill while women's lives were centered in households where they contributed to the family economy with unpaid domestic labor. The lives of both white and black women in Sparrows Point were, consquently, considerably more household-centered than were the lives of those women from the immigrant working class in nearby Baltimore city who worked outside their homes in the garment and canning industries.[11]

The masculine identity constructed for the jobs provided in Bethlehem Steel's Sparrows Point plant was based in part on the conditions of work in steelmaking, which were physically difficult, dangerous, and involved particularly long hours. In their dedication to efficiency and profits, Frederick and Rufus Wood organized the labor force into two shifts in order to maintain operation of the mill around the clock, seven days a week. The day shift worked eleven hours a day, seven days a week. The night shift worked thirteen or fourteen hours a day, and on Sunday when the shifts changed the night shift worked twenty-four hours straight.[12]

Under these conditions a code of behavior developed at the Point that emphasized the manly qualities required to work in the steel industry. Camaraderie with fellow workers was accentuated in a situation where trust and teamwork were necessary in the face of danger, and recreational rowdiness came to characterize the little bit of leisure time that was permitted after the long shifts at the Point. Much as Rufus Wood had planned for a sober, industrious workforce, he complained incessantly about outbursts of rowdiness that plagued his idyllic workers' community:

> I drove by Dorsey's yesterday and they were having a regular circus & carusal [sic]. Men lying in the gutter & on the fences, others yelling & hooting & Birmingham complains of the noise and disorder, while the neighbors are afraid to go by especially after dark. . . . [I]t appears that a good many cases of bad women especially across the creek have just turned up.[13]

Dorsey's was one of several taverns where steelworkers from the Point consumed alcohol in defiance of management's regulations. Drinking and carousing with "bad women" were two of the ways in which steelworkers participated in masculine rituals that proved one's virility.

Women were considered taboo within the plant—a dangerous, polluting intrusion that would disrupt the masculine order—and rough language sprinkled with insults, accusations, and gratuitous put-downs composed a discourse among steelworkers that suggested "this is men's work, can you handle it?"

This sharp segregation of female and male worlds would continue for eighty years after the founding of the Bethlehem Steel plant at Sparrows Point. Through two world wars, the Depression and New Deal, and the unionization of the plant in the 1940s, steelmaking continued to be "men's business." Starting in World War I two hundred young, white, mainly immigrant women were employed in production jobs at Sparrows Point as tin floppers, a job that involved inspecting the finished sheets of tin, and one that was considered suitable for women because it required a sensitive touch and quick movements of the hand. Tin flopping was a segregated female niche within a male industry, and until the 1950s women who did this job were required to wear demure uniforms and were protected from flirtatious male steelworkers by an imperious forelady who also assumed responsibility for teaching her "girls" the appropriate feminine conventions of hair style, makeup, and ladylike behavior.[14]

Not even Rosie the Riveter was able to gain entrée in significant numbers at the Sparrows Point mill. Only 700 women took production jobs at the Point during World War II, compared to 35,000 who entered Baltimore's shipbuilding, aircraft, and machinery industries.[15] Mary Anderson, the director of the Women's Bureau of the U.S. Department of Labor, forwarded the following report to Secretary of Labor Frances Perkins explaining why so few women had gone into the steel industry:

> Steelmaking traditionally has been men's business. Steelmaking is a heavy and dirty business and women workers have been taboo. . . . [I]ntense heat and equipment are necessary in processing. These marked characteristics of the industry and inherent hazards have tended naturally to shut out women, with their lesser strength and endurance. . . . [W]omen have constituted only a fraction of 1 percent of the employees in the steel industry. Steelmen—both managers and workers—generally did not welcome the advent of women into their mills and feared that women would not be able to do a full job and would be a disrupting element and liability. . . . Also, there was a deeply rooted prejudice and tradition against women workers in the steel mills similar to that which prevails in the mining industry.[16]

The post–World War II campaign by the Steel Workers Organizing Committee (SWOC) likewise failed to challenge gender segregation in the steel industry. Women made up only about 2 percent of the membership of SWOC, and later in the United Steel Workers of America (USWA), both of which pursued the politics of white male bread-and-butter unionism. Through the 1970s the union's newspaper, *Steel Labor*, acknowledged its female readers with a monthly dress pattern and set of recipes, and acknowledged the gender consciousness of its male readers with a monthly bikini-clad pinup who met the two necessary qualifications of being full-breasted and a member of one of the unions that served traditionally female occupations like airline stewardesses or waitresses. Only a handful of articles referred obliquely to the feminist issues of the decade, and none of them discussed the desirability of hiring more women on production jobs in steel.[17]

A daily drama of dominance and hierarchy is clearly evident in the voices of the men who have worked at the Point during the post–World War II period. The women who gained production jobs during the 1970s and 1980s echo the portrayal of the mill as an aggressive and combative work environment. Risks of injury, conflicts with management, harassment of women, and endemic racial tensions are embedded in the stories that steelworkers—black and white, female and male—tell of their day-to-day work lives. Collectively their stories document a harsh work environment, but also a work environment that is palpably masculine, that is immediately perceived by everyone who enters its gates as "a man's world."

The dangers of working at the Point are extreme. Early accounts of the mill include a series of gruesome accounts of steelworkers who died on the job, and today, when safety standards are much higher than in the 1890s, deaths still occur on a regular basis. A steelworker who is involved in a new safety program at the Point described an accident that prompted company action:

> This guy was standing on lumber that covered a tank filled with sulfuric acid. The tank cover was being changed plank by plank. When he stepped on one of the old planks it gave way and he fell into the acid and was killed. Everybody was shocked by it. We all were thinking, "My God, that could have happened to any one of us."[18]

The constant threat of injury is one of the most stressful conditions of work in steel. A steelworker with fifteen years of experience at the Point angrily listed the conditions that he finds intolerable:

> There are places in the mill where the gas levels are 1,000 times the federal standards. You see guys everywhere who are missing fingers or even limbs. At times we are working with makeshift tools that are unsafe, and there are heat alerts when the temperature gets up into unsafe regions, but often the company doesn't tell us, and then you get heatstroke deaths. Of course, there is always the danger of explosion; I've seen guys burned to death down there.[19]

Because of the dangers and hardships of working at the Point, there is a camaraderie among the men who are employed there that is expressed in pranks, practical jokes, and name-calling. Men who are new to the Point are put through an initiation that tests their suitability to the toughness in the mill:

> When a new employee comes on to one of the mill crews, we look them over and give them a hard time. Somebody will say something like, "Look what the cat dragged in today," letting them know that they'll have to prove themselves to fit in.[20]

In a system that "baptizes" workers at the Point as members of a family of steelmen, nicknames are assigned that make each worker stand out as a character in the ongoing drama of making steel:

> Everyone gets a nickname in the steel mill, because over the years a lot of characters have gone through there. The superintendent had a nickname, but no one called him by his nickname to his face. His nickname was "Pinky" because he had a red mustache. Then there was "Glow Worm," "Road Apple Andy," "Bones," "Locker-room Lou," "Powder Room Pete," "Rubber Jaws," "Squirrel," "Twitchy," "Hot Rod," "Tater Head," "The Preacher," "Green Bean," and "Rag Top." My nickname was "The Hatchet Man."[21]

Steelworkers have always been subject to the frequent and unpredictable layoffs that their families must accept and accommodate. Many steelworkers even relish the periodic layoffs as a vacation (albeit unpaid) from the grueling work in the mill. But whether a layoff is welcomed or resented, it is a constant reminder to steelworkers that they have little control over their jobs but are at the mercy of a large, impersonal company and an even more impersonal economy.

Shift work is another constant reminder to steelworkers that they are not the masters of their own lives. A man who has worked at the Point for twenty years described the schedules in the mill:

> Some workers do work a regular daylight shift from 7 A.M. to 3 P.M. They are mostly maintenance workers and lower-paid laborers. A relatively small number of workers are on permanent 3 P.M. to 11 P.M. or 11 P.M. to 7 A.M. shifts or "turns." The majority of the plant population works rotating shifts to cover continuous production lines. Some only learn their schedule on Thursday for the following week. They could be scheduled any day, any hour. Others have a regularly rotating schedule. I'll give you mine as an example:

SUN	M	T	W	TH	F	SAT
OFF	OFF	3-11	3-11	3-11	3-11	3-11
3-11	3-11	OFF	OFF	7-3	7-3	7-3
7-3	7-3	7-3	7-3	OFF	11-7	11-7
11-7	11-7	11-7	11-7	11-7	OFF	OFF[22]

The absence of a routine schedule makes the life of a steelworker unpredictable and causes both sleep disorders and disorders of digestion. One steelworker expressed with resignation how it feels working the 11 P.M. to 7 A.M. shift: "Even if you stay in bed for twelve hours the next day, you wake up feeling like you didn't have any sleep. Anyway you cut it, with shift work you don't get enough sleep."[23] When asked how other members of the family would describe the effects of the swing shift on family life, a steelworker confessed:

> It just wrecks your life, but it wrecks your family more, if you're an essential member. Most steelworkers have given up on being central members of their families. Their sense of responsibility to their families is earning money to buy the things their families need. The rest is up to their wives.[24]

Long hours and changing shifts leave steelworkers exhausted and excluded from a central role in family life, and these arduous conditions also foster drinking after work as a convenient and habitual way to unwind.

Drinking at the end of the shift, even drinking on the job, have long been a part of the work culture at the Point. Every man who works at the

Point is familiar with the bar culture that exists immediately outside the mill gates. Just as Dorsey's tavern was a thorn in the side of Rufus Wood as he tried to organize a sober, disciplined workforce, bars like Mickey's, Gail's, Hogameyers, Pops Tavern, and The White House continue to lure steelworkers from the Point to drink and relax at the end of their shifts. There is an obligation to prove one's masculinity on a day-to-day basis through heavy drinking:

> Drinking is a part of the mystique of being a steelworker. Every guy feels overworked, and this is a good way to relax as well as a chance to indulge in a lot of bravado—joking and challenging and bragging about sexual prowess. I can remember standing on the lot at Mickey's challenging some guy to drink a pint faster than me.[25]

A former steelworker who had worked at the Point for eighteen years before being laid off in 1984 described his own devotion to "drinking with the guys":

> What my kids remember of me when I worked at the Point was a drunken father who would stumble into the house at all hours. When they left in the morning I was in bed. It was hard on family life because most of the guys drink a lot, and I joined the crowd because it was the macho thing.[26]

Participation in family life could not compete with the work culture that included constantly changing shifts and obligatory drinking, and in another sense, being a participant in family responsibilities was in competition with the obligation to prove one's masculinity on a day-to-day basis through heavy drinking.

A more benign, but no less pervasive expression of masculinity at the Point is the costume that steelworkers wear proudly. While hardhats are a safety requirement and casual clothes make sense in a workplace filled with dirt and grime, one man emphasized the image created by the clothes that steelworkers wear: "At the Point you could dress the part: dungarees, steel-toed boots, plastic helmet, cut-off shirts. It gave the appearance of a real macho."[27]

A thirty-five-year-old steelworker concluded that for many men working in the steel industry was a proof of manliness:

> A lot of guys who work at the Point are still in the stage of improving their manhood. They can say, "Hey, I work in a steel mill." What better image of manhood is there? It's dangerous and it's hard physical work. You're not going to have soft hands. Why, just the word "steel" implies toughness. Look at Superman, he's the "Man of Steel."[28]

Many steelworkers experience a debilitating level of hostility that pervades day-to-day interactions in the mill and makes egalitarian or cooperative relationships impossible. One man who spent twenty years at the Point consoled himself about being laid off: "Sometimes, though, I think losing my job at the Point was a blessing in disguise. Now I have a chance to get a job in a place where people are nice to each other."[29] There are several reasons why the Point is a work environment where people are rarely described as "nice to each other." The heat, the noise, and the danger encourage a defensive response of gruffness and bravado, but some of the antagonism is most closely related to the competition for steel's highest-paying jobs. Much of this competition is expressed in racial tension and antagonism.

The organization of labor at Sparrows Point has a long history of excluding African American workers from higher-paying, skilled jobs. In his initial design of the mill Rufus Wood identified black men as the workforce of choice for the hottest, most strenuous laboring jobs at Sparrows Point, and for much of the history of the mill white steelworkers have held tenaciously to their monopoly of the best jobs at the Point. It was only in the 1960s that black steelworkers were able to successfully organize a campaign, aimed at both the company and the union, to challenge job discrimination based on race at Bethlehem Steel. The divisiveness generated by seven decades of racial separation still holds a stubborn grip on the men who work at the Point, and black and white steelworkers talk of deep racial antagonisms.

There is a teamwork poster prominently displayed at Bethlehem Steel that shows a black hand shaking a white hand, but black steelworkers—and an occasional white sympathizer—insist that it is, in their words, "window dressing that the company displays to make you think things are good."[30] In reality racial antagonism is widespread and is generally described as either part of the competition over desirable jobs, or part of the effort to maintain a pecking order that has an acceptable place for white men.

Black steelworkers are well aware of the history of job discrimination based on race at Bethlehem Steel, and for some it continues to be a painful reality. For most of the mill's history only a handful of blacks worked in any job category other than laborer, and the coke ovens—the hottest and dirtiest area of the mill—were all-black departments that came to represent a pariah status for African American steelworkers.[31] In the words of one black steelworker:

> They put us in the coke ovens, which is like working in hell! There is constant smoke, constant gas, constant pollution, and the smells are sickening. You are always covered with grime, and from the day you start there until the day you quit, it never gets out of your skin.[32]

They cite numerous examples of having been bypassed for a promotion that went to a white man, and their universal lament is, "Why did the white guy come in eighteen and clean-faced and get all of the good jobs?"[33]

White steelworkers, on the other hand, steadfastly deny that any discrimination against blacks exists in the mill, insisting that blacks are treated equitably, "as long as they are willing to work," implying that any inequities that exist are the result of the inferior competence or work discipline of black coworkers. White steelworkers stand the accusation of discrimination on its head, complaining that lost opportunities for promotions are the result of favoritism to blacks.

A few white steelworkers are willing to admit that the presence of black men working in steel is perceived as a dangerous threat to job security. One white man admitted that the desire to keep blacks in a subservient position is pervasive and he cited as an example the story of a black steelworker who made the mistake of showing up at a party given at the home of a white coworker:

> All night long the white guys were hollering, "Hey, Mike, we're going to get you a lantern and make you stand in front of the house." It was good-natured kidding, but with a meaning behind it. There's nothing they would like more than to have Mike standing out front with a lantern—to have blacks be in a certain place beneath the white man.[34]

Most African American steelworkers avoid this kind of harassment by "voluntarily" segregating themselves both on the job and in the socializing that goes on after work.

The message that black steelworkers report most resentfully is that many of their white coworkers consider them to be interlopers in an occupational niche that most rightfully belongs to white men. Because black steelworkers are a numerical minority—they continue to represent about one-third of the workforce at Sparrows Point—they are subject to the opinions of the dominant, white male group. Those opinions can most accurately be viewed as a brand of white croneyism, the pervasive and tenacious folk belief that the steel mill is most appropriately an employment resource for white men who live in the surrounding community. One black steelworker expressed it well:

> . . . white guys who went to the local high school act like Sparrows Point is their place. They're opinionated and narrow-minded and they let you know that they don't think you should be where they are. To their way of thinking, blacks aren't supposed to be successful.[35]

The language of many white steelworkers reiterates this idea that black men "don't fit in," "don't want to work," "don't do well at the Point."

Black steelworkers have similar complaints about the quality of race relations in the USWA, and are convinced that their grievances are not pursued vigorously by the white union leadership. Even black men who are active in and enthusiastic about union affairs report that there are bigots in influential places in the organization. One black man who is a shop steward lamented the hypocrisy of some union officials:

> There is this one grievance committeeman who is very friendly to my face, always slapping my back, and talking about "Doc, my boy." But the minute I walk out the door he starts telling nigger jokes. This kind of guy is, in my book, an opportunist. You have to take it in stride, although some black guys stay away from the union because of this.[36]

While there are many white union members who sincerely believe in the importance of racial equity, there has never been a strong enough majority of union membership willing to support initiatives that would end discrimination against and harassment of African American steelworkers.

There is an interesting parallel here with the harassment of women who work at the Point. While both the union and the company take an official stand against sexual harassment, there are many forms of harassment that go unchallenged. A woman who has worked at the Point for more than twenty years and who is ordinarily not afraid to stand up for herself admitted resignation on the issue of pinups:

> I went to one of the women in management and asked her to do something about the posters with naked women that are all over the plant, but she said, "Forget it, there's no way we're going to get those pictures down." I got the same response from the union, so I figured it was a lost cause.[37]

Black steelworkers face a similar form of chronic, personalized harassment. Explicit racist epithets, being called "nigger" or "boy" are considered unavoidable hardships of working at Bethlehem Steel, and black men acknowledge with resignation that "you have to accept the fact that some of the guys you work with hate blacks."[38]

Black steelworkers are sophisticated about the different levels of white supremacist consciousness that they must maneuver around in their workplace. They make a distinction between Klansmen—whites who stay away from blacks and talk about "the nigger that's getting on their nerves"—and bigots who "call me black when I'm in the room, but when I leave I'm a nigger."[39]

No one even considers reporting these indignities to the union or the company, and most men acknowledge that there is a level at which interracial combativeness is merely another ritualized way in which steelworkers assert masculinity and toughness. A white steelworker was emphatic that racial epithets were a "group thing":

> If I'm talking to one other white guy, most likely we'll call the black guys on our crew "black," but if a third white guy walks up it's a group thing, and we start talkin' about "niggers." If we used the word "black" somebody would say, "What's this black shit? When did you turn into a nigger-lover?"[40]

This kind of peer pressure to conform to racist bantering stands in the way of real cooperation between black and white steelworkers and contributes to a work environment that is tense and hostile.

After seven decades of excluding women from production work at Sparrows Point and restricting the ability of women to even walk inside the mill, there are now women working in this masculine domain. Women who do production work at the Point provide a unique perspective on the kind of environment that exists inside the mill. Women who have spent time working in steel differ in their assessment of the experience, of course, and while some find it challenging and rewarding, others describe harassment and assaults that ultimately drove them from their steel jobs.[41] Whether or not women working at Bethlehem Steel describe their experience as rewarding or difficult, the environment that women describe is a uniformly masculine one: "I'm a woman working in a man's world. It's nothing to be walking along and see some man urinating against the wall. Men have been left alone in that mill for a long time, and some of them are barbarians."[42] That phrase, "It's a man's world," is repeated by almost every woman who has worked at the Point. It is undoubtedly the most powerful impression that any woman gets when she first walks into the mill: "I was walking into a man's world. There were calendars with nude women hanging up, and when I went there weren't even any facilities for women because no women had ever worked there before."[43] Some women are intimidated by the heavy machinery and intense heat of the steel mill, but many women relish the idea of working in such a dangerous workplace: "There is a lot of satisfaction in doing the hard physical work in a place as dangerous as a steel mill, seeing the molten steel pour into the slabs, risking your life, controlling all of that, those tons of melted metal."[44]

The sense of power implicit in that description is new for almost all of the women who entered Bethlehem Steel in the 1970s. These women describe a transformation from the feminine world they live in outside the steel mill, into a uniform that protects them both physically and psychically: "I wear no makeup, put my hair up under my hat. You lose all vanity in there. You're sweating constantly, and there is no glamour in that."[45] For this woman, the need to be glamorous has been replaced by a sense of pride in a more "masculine" appearance that is required by the difficult work she performs.

The language used at Sparrows Point also marks a work culture that is inimical to women, and controlling that language or tempering it becomes one of the issues that women have to deal with:

The men test you with language. They talk filthy if you let them. It's f——
this and f—— that. Or a guy will go on about what he did to his girlfriend or
wife last night. I look them dead in the eye and say, "How you talk is not my
business, I'm not your Mommy, but don't direct it at me."[46]

Along with sexually aggressive language, pinups are a symbol that male
steelworkers use to mark the steel mill as "a man's world" where women
can be freely denigrated as sexual objects:

I walk into offices and I'm shocked by the posters of nude women they
have hanging up. If I don't go in they'll have accomplished what they want
to accomplish, which is to keep me out. There is a culture down there that
says "I'm a real man." It's a badge. A lot of guys can't read *Playboy* at home,
but he's got his locker stuffed with them.[47]

Women steelworkers view the rough talk and the pinups as part of a "cult
of masculinity" inside the mill, a kind of group behavior the purpose of
which is to impress other men:

The men are out to impress each other. They talk different when women
aren't around. They need to prove their masculinity. You'll find yourself
talking about gardening with a man, but if another man walks up they
catch themselves and start talking about "Let's go for a beer."[48]

Female steelworkers are aware that even after working at the Point for
many years some men consider them outsiders: "There is a lot of rejection
toward women. There is such a masculine factor in this job. Some guys will
say right out that they don't want to work with me."[49]

Male steelworkers regard themselves as breadwinners who make enormous sacrifices in order to earn a high wage that provides for family needs.
The breadwinner concept goes hand-in-hand with the macho reputation, and
working side-by-side with women reminds every male steelworker that his
wife might one day get a job and displace his breadwinner status. The accusations launched at women at the Point are direct and fierce: "I don't think you
belong here. How old is your baby? Don't you have no sense? Why don't you
get home where you belong? You don't belong down here."[50]

Some men refuse to speak to the women in their work units, regardless
of how well those women perform or how hard they work. They are
adamant that steelmaking is a man's job, in much the same way that they
are adamant that it a white man's job: "I just don't think you should be
here. I don't think women can do the work, and they make it harder on
everybody else."[51]

This struggle to maintain the Sparrows Point steel mill as a masculine
domain is based in part on the desire to maintain the relative privileges of

a "traditional" gendered world. In a workplace that for eighty years was devoid of female workers, the harshness of social relationships between male steelworkers and the hostility directed toward women contribute to a gendered workplace environment that is masculine, combative, and hostile to interlopers.

In its heyday in the 1950s and 1960s, employment and production at Sparrows Point were at a peak, wages were improved by the success of unionization in the 1940s, and the jobs of white steelworkers were able to comfortably support a breadwinner/homemaker family structure. This period is the "Golden Age" that many old-timers in Dundalk look back upon wistfully as an era of prosperity and good fortune.

It is important to note that during this time African American families in the communities surrounding Sparrows Point experienced a "Golden Age" that was both quantitatively and qualitatively different from that of their white coworkers. By this time the residential community of Sparrows Point had expanded to include Dundalk and Turners Station, two newly developed residential areas as deliberately segregated by race as Sparrows Point had been by the Humphrey's Creek barrier.

The workforce at Sparrows Point continued to be about one-third African American, as it had been at the turn of the century. Despite the increased wages that the USWA won for steelworkers, black men continued to be excluded from the highest-paying skilled jobs but nonetheless had access to a more prosperous lifestyle that sometimes included a wife who did not work outside the home. The wives of black steelworkers were, however, much more likely to be in the paid workforce, and the conventional wisdom for African American families in the 1950s and 1960s was that, "If you worked at Sparrows Point and your wife worked for Social Security, you had it made."

It was extremely unusual for a white woman living in Dundalk at this time to be in the paid workforce unless she was widowed. Despite enjoying the luxury of being supported by a relatively well-paid husband, Dundalk women do not extol the life in the 1950s and 1960s as a good time for steelworkers' wives. Whether they are describing themselves or their mothers, Dundalk women emphasize the extent to which being married to a steelworker meant being a prisoner to the swing shift.

By the 1950s steelworker wives in Sparrows Point and Dundalk had smaller families, more labor-saving devices, and no boarders. During that period of relative prosperity in Dundalk, the wives of steelworkers enjoyed leisure, financial security, and a standard of living far beyond what earlier generations of Dundalk women had ever dreamed of. For a family that could remember when electricity and indoor plumbing were new conveniences, it was possible to buy a new car, a recreational boat, an automatic washer and dryer.

The availability of high-paying steelmaking jobs at the Point in the decades after World War II are remembered as a great boon to this blue-collar community, but easy access to jobs in steel also perpetuated a gendered social world that sent Dundalk men into the mill immediately after high school, and sent Dundalk women to the altar with few job skills and little access to paid employment. From both steelmen and their wives, the Point claimed big sacrifices.

The testimony of men who have worked at the Point is filled with clues that their jobs took a toll, and that behind the masculine pride of having tackled a dangerous and difficult task is also distress at the long hours and debilitating working conditions. For wives of steelworkers the price that was paid was less obvious, but can also be heard in the reflections of the adult sons and daughters who watched their mothers maneuver a role that economists would have us envy: the homemaker wife of a highly paid blue-collar worker.

In the 1950s and 1960s, the wife of a steelworker had money to spend—on groceries, on clothing and home furnishings, and on a family vacation. This, measured on a materialistic scale, should have made her content. But her sense of personal power, within her household, within her family, and within her community, was often severely restricted by the gender consciousness and gender relations reinforced by the organization of work at the very steel mill that she was indebted to for affording her family a relatively high standard of living.

Although she might go her entire life without entering the gates of the mill, the wife of a steelworker was not insulated from the harsh working conditions that accompany the production of steel. She had to accommodate the continually changing schedule that results from the swing shift, and accept the fact that her husband would be away from home for long, irregular hours that make a routine home life impossible.

The compensation earned for overtime in the mill conflicted with family cohesiveness, since the more a steelworker was absent from home, the more prosperous the family would be. The combination of her husband's erratic schedule and his ability to earn high wages colluded to keep the wife of a steelworker homebound, out of the workforce, and economically dependent:

> Since many of the straight shift jobs, like seven-to-three, were also the lowest paying, spouses often were forced to trade family normalcy for money, upward mobility. Since overtime paid so much more than most women were capable of making, many women married to steelworkers stayed home within the limited horizons of the block, the school, and the market.[52]

The accommodation of husbands and fathers who worked in the steel mill was a particularly burdensome imposition because of the erratic schedule that the swing shift imposed on family life. The children of steelworkers recall growing up eating in the middle of the afternoon and tiptoeing around the house so that they wouldn't wake up their fathers. One woman in her mid-fifties remembered that:

> My father came home at the end of his shift covered with red dust and dead tired. My mother made him peel off his clothes at the door so that he wouldn't get the whole house dirty. Then he would take a bath and fall into bed like a dead man. That's what I remember of my father.[53]

At the turn of the century the twelve- to fourteen-hour shifts in the steel mill dictated that steelworkers were either working or sleeping, but even the shorter shifts that were mandated for the steel industry in the 1920s did little to make steelworker husbands available as partners in home-centered activities and tasks. Highly paid overtime replaced the twelve-hour shift in a system that seduced steelworkers into working very long hours. Abundant overtime resulted in fat paychecks that enhanced the reputation of Bethlehem Steel as a desirable employer, but it also kept steelworkers away from their families and removed from household activities:

> When I was growing up my father's work at the Point kept him away a lot. There was just so much pressure on him when a boat was ready to go out. He'd come home and he really didn't want to talk to anybody, and not because he was angry, it was just because the pressure was so much. He'd go in at four o'clock in the morning and get home at eight o'clock at night. He would just pretty much come home, take a bath, sit down for about an hour to try to unwind, go to bed, and he'd be up and out before I even got up.[54]

The extreme inconvenience of shiftwork was perhaps the clearest example of the ways in which the organization of steelmaking placed constraints on gender roles and made it difficult for blue-collar families to negotiate more flexible gender relations. Juggling shiftwork and family life was fraught with problems:

> For couples who wanted to build relationships which were healthy, shiftwork was always a challenge. He comes home at 11:00 P.M. with energy to burn. She has had a bruising day at home, wants to sleep. They try to share some responsibilities, but when he's working three-to-eleven, most of the work of ferrying kids around, etc., falls on her.[55]

Women insist that work outside the home was almost impossible for a woman whose husband was working swing shift. The tasks involved in fixing meals, getting children ready for school, caring for them when they weren't in school, and maintaining a family life fell upon the wives of steelworkers as a full-time occupation. Theresa Porsinsky paints a vivid picture of what it has been like for her being the wife of a steelworker: "It's a very difficult life. Shift work means that I can never count on Tom being here at a certain time. We are both sort of prisoners of his schedule. But over the years I've gotten used to it. No, you never get used to it, you just put up with it."[56]

The accommodation of shift work puts other substantial strains on steelworker families. Men who work swing shifts have work schedules that change every week, and having a hot meal ready at the end of a constantly changing shift has traditionally been an important component of the home-making responsibilities of Dundalk wives. One woman recalled her husband's work schedule:

Oh, God! It was the pits! He would swing every week between three shifts, seven-to-three, three-to-eleven, and eleven-to-seven. When he worked nights I'd have to try to keep the kids real quiet while he slept in the back bedroom. And no matter when the shift ended I'd have a hot meal waiting for him, even if it was eleven o'clock at night.[57]

A woman in her late forties considered the extent to which her husband's shift work had kept her out of the workforce: "Jimmy doesn't want me to work with his shift work. He likes me to have dinner when he gets home, and I figure he's entitled to that after working ten or twelve hours. Maybe I'll go to work when Jimmy retires."[58]

Dundalk wives who did work in the 1950s and 1960s generally did so as a stop-gap measure when their husbands were laid off or out on strike for long periods of time. Part-time jobs as waitresses, sales clerks, and telephone operators were generally the kinds of jobs women took to "fill in" financial gaps that were considered temporary. One woman described the way her mother's employment was linked to the schedule at the Point:

My father and his three brothers all worked at Bethlehem Steel, and everything in the family revolved around the mill schedule. My mother would work only during a strike. In 1959 there was a big strike that lasted for an extended period, maybe four or five months, and my mother worked for the telephone company as an evening operator.[59]

Working during a strike was common for steelworkers' wives, but entering the full-time workforce was unnecessary when steelmen were bringing home good wages.

The prosperity that this steelmaking community enjoyed during the 1940s and 1950s is remembered by Dundalk women as a double-edged sword. The economic security that was seen as a great advantage of working at the Point was also a vehicle for keeping wives of steelworkers out of the workforce. One woman recalled her mother's situation:

> We felt protected because my father worked at Bethlehem Steel and those were very good jobs. We never had any financial problems, but I think my mother suffered, because during a big strike in 1957 my mother was forced to go to work in the personnel department at City Hospital. When my father went back to work she had to quit her job and I know she felt defeated. I remember her saying that the job at City Hospital had given her her own identity.[60]

The "very good jobs" at the Point were a source of protection for steelworkers' families, but they also kept Dundalk women locked into homemaker roles and locked out of opportunities to participate in the full-time workforce.

Even part-time, temporary jobs could be curtailed if they failed to accommodate family and shift-work schedules, as in the case of a Dundalk woman whose seasonal job at a downtown department store was put to an end by her steelworker husband because she arrived home late one day:

> One Christmas my mother wanted to get a part-time job because she wanted to buy some extra things for Christmas, so she got a job and she worked three days in the jewelry department. On the third day she missed the bus and got home late and I was sitting at the back door waiting for her. When my father got home he just said, "That's it. That's it." The next day she quit her job.[61]

For the wife who is told she must quit her job because it is interfering with family responsibilities there is perhaps nothing more than a loss of independence and personal identity. But a Dundalk woman faced a more serious disadvantage if she became widowed. Since there was general agreement that marriage to a highly paid steelworker meant that a woman didn't need to develop any job skills of her own, Dundalk women were especially vulnerable to economic disaster if a husband died:

> When my mother was widowed she had to support herself because my dad's benefits weren't enough. She had never planned on working and had no skills so she went to work in the cafeteria at Dundalk Junior High where she ended up working for thirty years.[62]

Like others of her generation, this woman had never anticipated that there would come a time when she would not be supported by a breadwinner husband.

In discussing the family dynamics they grew up with, many Dundalk women recall their fathers as breadwinners and money managers who expected a whole array of entitlements because of their role in the work-force:

> . . . the thing I remember most vividly was my father taking naps on the couch after his night shift and everyone was supposed to be quiet. He insisted that my mother have a meal ready for him whenever he came home, but sometimes after she fixed it he would say he didn't want it.[63]

In breadwinner/homemaker marriages there was always the potential for men to use their economic power to exercise control over their wives. In many families the result was a kind of tyranny that kept women dependent and homebound:

> My mother-in-law never worked. She never did anything or went any-where. Her husband saw himself as the moneymaker, therefore he got what he wanted. He would take naps on the couch and everyone was supposed to be quiet. He made my mother-in-law beg for money, and when she started getting a small social security check he was angry. He begrudged her that check.[64]

This example of a breadwinner's claim on economic control reveals the power of the paycheck in steelworker households. Audrey Hartman remem-bered that her mother's economic dependence was so apparent in their family that it became the focus of mother-daughter tensions:

> My mother had no money of her own. It was all the money that my father made at Bethlehem Steel. I can remember getting angry one time and saying to her, "You don't make any money, you don't put any money in the bank, that's all Daddy's money in there."[65]

A steelworker wife who had "no money of her own" lost respect within her family as well as power in the public world. As long as homemaker wives could be supported by the relatively high wages of breadwinner husbands, there were definite constraints on the possibilities that Dundalk women could negotiate for more egalitarian marriages.

Steelworker families faced other work-related circumstances that made it difficult for women to achieve a semblance of autonomy within their mar-riages. Steelmen endured long hours and physically debilitating work and expressed a pride in their willingness to make sacrifices of health and com-fort in order to provide adequately for their families. Making those sacri-fices, in turn, entitled steelworkers to certain loyalties, including round-the-clock service from their wives. Hard-working breadwinners felt justified in making a claim on their wives' leisure-time activities and choice of companions. One Dundalk woman remembered with bitterness that her father begrudged his wife the smallest of personal pleasures: "The only thing that woman did was go bowling on Wednesday morning. And that night we would have hot dogs and my father would complain, "If she didn't bowl, we'd have a real meal.' "[66] Bowling was perceived by the family breadwinner as interfering with one of his wife's primary responsibilities—the preparation of a suitable evening meal that he could enjoy after a hard day at work. Another Dundalk woman explained that her husband felt that he had a legitimate claim on her social interactions: "My husband doesn't want me to run with the girls. Everything we do he wants to do together. If we go to a party he doesn't like it if I get to talking to other people and ignore him."[67] In exchange for sacrifices made at work this breadwinner assumed the right to his wife's attention during his leisure time.

Ironically, the circumstances that propelled wives of steelworkers into the job force in the 1950s and 1960s were also the circumstances that made it least likely that their husbands would be receptive to a more egalitarian marital relationship. Being laid off periodically was a condition of working in the steel industry that workers and their wives had to endure, despite the fact that it radically disrupted their lives and caused considerable mental anguish. Cyclical unemployment had an impact on steelworker households that was complicated and that had a different affect on wives and husband. Thelma Porsinsky was quick to realize that having her husband, Tom, laid off was a double-edged sword: "I went back to work when Tom was laid off, and he took care of the house and kids. It was great in a way, but he was so depressed about not having a job and not bringing home a paycheck that I couldn't really enjoy my job very much."[68]

Women generally understood the dilemma they were in. If their husbands were working at the Point and making a good wage, wives would have considerable financial security and be able to stay at home with their children, but the conditions of shift work would make it extremely difficult for them to participate in any regular educational, occupational, or social activities outside their homes. Having husbands laid off might propel the wives of steelworkers into an expanded social context of work outside their homes. Often, however, this resulted in psychic battles with men who had been stripped, if only temporarily, of their breadwinner role. A Dundalk woman explained this phenomenon as she had experienced it: "Men need to control, and when they lose their job it is not just the job that's gone, their whole world is out of control and it's usually the woman who pays for it. When a man loses his job he's much more likely to hassle the woman he lives with."[69]

A man whose father was a welder at the Point remembered witnessing bouts of domestic violence when his father was laid off:

My father looked down on my mother because he was making the money and she wasn't. But when he was laid off he did a lot to her, he really beat her down. I can remember getting up in the morning and finding the coffee table smashed to pieces. They would say it was an accident, but I knew my dad had been tearing into my mom.[70]

The dilemma that faced the wives of steelworkers was a sobering one. Employed husbands are unavailable as partners in family life, and unemployed husbands were too vulnerable to make the partnership work.

This study has argued that it is a mistake to assume that simply because an industry (in this case steel) has been largely male that gender was an unimportant part of workers' lives. For most of the history of Sparrows Point, women did not work inside the gates of the mill, but their lives and labor were intimately tied to steel—and vice versa. Many steelworkers benefited from the fact that women's labor had little monetary value. For historians to also ignore the important role that women's labor played in the steel industry robs them once again of the value of their labor. Gender also shaped men's lives in profound ways. Their masculine ethos was in some ways a survival mechanism adapted to the harsh realities of work in a steel mill. There was a rough camaraderie in steelworkers' masculine work culture—but also a strong individualistic streak that arguably helped to retard higher levels of solidarity.

The examination of the origins of the gendered social world of Sparrows Point reminds us that this community, its way of life, and its family structures were set in place not to accommodate women, not to accommodate families, not even to accommodate men, but to accommodate the profitable production of steel. The patriarchal family structure that was characteristic of Sparrows Point fit the demands of the steel industry and had a profound effect on the organization of family life and the relationships between women and men in this community. That so many workers internalized the values of a system designed to maximize the exploitation of their labor by dividing men from women and whites from blacks remains a tragedy.

NOTES

1. The discussion of Maryland Steel and the town of Sparrows Point between 1887 and 1907 is based on the Maryland Steel Company Papers of Frederick W. Wood (henceforth FWW Papers), Accession 884, Hagley Museum and Library, Greenville, Delaware; the 1900 Manuscript Census for the United States, and sixty Sparrows Point steelworkers and their spouses. See also Mark Reutter, *Sparrows Point: Making Steel; The Rise and Ruin of American Industrial Might* (New York: Summit Books, 1988).

2. Typescript statement of Maryland Steel Company, 1907, FWW Papers.

3. United States. Census Office. Twelfth Census, 1900.

4. Ibid.

5. Rufus Wood to Frederick Wood, 18 September 1890, Maryland Steel Company Papers of FWW Papers.

6. Typescript statement of Maryland Steel Company, 1907, FWW Papers.

7. Ibid.

8. Population statistics are calculated from United States, Twelfth Census. Among this relatively young population the median age of Sparrows Point wives was thirty-three; the median number of children for Sparrows Point mothers was three; and of the 73 percent of households that had boarders the median number was five.

9. Population statistics are calculated from United States, Twelfth Census.

10. There is only a sparse, though growing, body of work on masculinity, most of it focused on white, middle-class men. For a historical reckoning of manliness in working-class communities see Sean Wilentz, *Chants Democratic: New York City and the Rise of the American Working Class, 1788–1950* (New York: Oxford University Press, 1984). For a superb ethnographic and theoretical discussion of manliness and working-class culture, see Paul Willis, "Shop Floor Culture, Masculinity and the Wage Form," in *Working-class Culture: Studies in History and Theory*, ed. John Clarke, Charles Critcher, and Richard Honson (London: Hutchinson, 1979), 185–98.

11. See Roderick N. Ryon, " 'Human Creatures' Lives': Baltimore Women and Work in Factories, 1880–1917," *Maryland Historical Magazine* 83 (Winter 1988): 346–64.

12. Long hours were characteristic of the entire American steel industry, though not of European steel companies where the hours of labor were generally nine or ten, and steelworkers rested on Sundays. Complaints about the long hours imposed on American steelworkers were widespread but ineffective until the 1930s when New Deal standards reduced the hours to eight. Sparrows Point steelworkers still complain that they are asked to work excessively long hours of overtime, a system that enables Bethlehem Steel to hire fewer full-time employees. For a description of working conditions at Sparrows Point at the turn of the century, see U.S. Bureau of Labor, *Report on Conditions of Employment in the Iron and Steel Industry* (Washington, D.C.: Government Printing Office, 1913).

13. Rufus Wood to Frederick Wood, 21 April 1890, FWW Papers.

14. Reutter, *Sparrows Point*, 360–78.

15. For a discussion of women working in Baltimore's war industries during the World War II period, see *Women's Work in the War*, Bulletin of the Women's Bureau, no. 193 (Washington, D.C.: Government Printing Office, 1942); U.S. Department of Labor Women's Bureau, *Baltimore Women War Workers in the Postwar Period* (Washington, D.C.: Government Printing Office, 1948); and Karen Anderson, *Wartime Women: Sex Roles, Family Relations, and the Status of Women During World War II* (Westport, Conn.: Greenwood Press, 1981).

16. The best published description of women in the steel industry during World War II is in Ethel Erickson, *Women's Employment in the Making of Steel, 1943*, Bulletin of the Women's Bureau, no. 192-5 (Washington, D.C.: Government Printing Office, 1944).

17. *Steel Labor: Voice of the United Steelworkers of America* 1, no. 1 (August, 1936) through vol. 44, no. 11 (November 1979).
18. Interview with Hannah Taussig, 19 January 1993.
19. Interview with Robert Wosnowski, 28 July 1989.
20. Interview with Howard Cook, 17 December 1992.
21. Ibid.
22. Interview with Larry Sayles, 5 March 1993.
23. Interview with Helen Taussig, 19 January 1993.
24. Ibid.
25. Interview with Peter Wallace, 10 May 1990.
26. Interview with Douglass Ivey, 17 July 1989.
27. Interview with Richard Lane, 5 January 1993.
28. Interview with Douglass Ivey, 17 July 1989.
29. Ibid.
30. Interview with William Bennett, 6 March 1990.
31. The concentration of African Americans in laboring jobs in the blast furnaces and coke ovens has been common throughout the steel industry. In 1910, 73.6 percent of all black steelworkers in the United States were laborers compared to 8.2 percent who were skilled workers and 10.7 percent in the semiskilled category. In 1935 in the Eastern district, which included Sparrows Point, 26.4 percent of blast-furnace workers were black as compared to only 12.0 percent of the workers in the rolling mills. The statistical information on African American men in the steel industry is from the *Thirteenth Census of the United States*, 1910, quoted in Horace R. Cayton and George S. Mitchell, *Black Workers and the New Unions* (Chapel Hill: University of North Carolina Press, 1939), 24; and Herbert R. Northrup, *Negro Employment in Basic Industry: A Study of Racial Policies in Six Industries* (Philadelphia: Wharton School/Industrial Research Unit, 1970), 258–59.
32. Interview with Peter Wallace, 1 May 1990.
33. Interview with William Bennett, 6 March 1990. For a discussion by both historians and sociologists of the efforts to exclude black workers from skilled jobs, see William Harris, *The Harder We Run: Black Workers Since the Civil War* (New York: Oxford University Press, 1982); Howard Rabinowitz, *Race Relations in the Urban South, 1865–1890* (New York: Oxford University Press, 1978); Peter Rachleff, *Black Labor in the South: Richmond, Virginia, 1865–1890* (Philadelphia: Temple University Press, 1984); and Charles Wesley, *Negro Labor in the United States, 1850–1925* (New York: Russell & Russell, 1927). In 1943, 7,000 of Bethlehem Steel's white workers walked out in protest over the company's plan to train fifteen black welders; see Sherry Olson, *Baltimore: The Building of an American City* (Baltimore: Johns Hopkins University Press, 1980), 364.
34. Interview with Sam Taylor, 7 August 1989.
35. Interview with Peter Wallace, 1 May 1990.
36. Interview with Douglass Ivey, 10 July 1989. The most successful interracial working relationships at the Point are reported among members of the labor gangs and within the union. Between 1937 and 1941 the Steel Workers' Organizing Committee actively recruited the black members it needed to win union recognition at Sparrows Point, and blacks are often influential in determining the outcome of

union elections and frequently hold office. Nonetheless, blacks tend to view the union, like the company, as a white institution. For a discussion of black leadership in the effort to unionize steel, see Nell Painter, *The Narrative of Hosea Hudson: His Life as a Negro Communist in the South* (Cambridge, Mass.: Harvard University Press, 1979).

37. Interview with Hannah Taussig, 19 January 1993.
38. Interview with Robert Albright, 1 August 1989. For a discussion of the mechanisms used by African Americans to maintain cohesion and protect their values and self-esteem in the face of white racism see bell hooks, *Talking Back: Thinking Feminist, Thinking Black* (Boston: South End Press, 1989); and Lawrence Levine, *Black Culture and Black Consciousness: Afro-American Folk Thought from Slavery to Freedom* (New York: Oxford University Press, 1977).
39. Interview with Douglass Ivey, 17 July 1989.
40. Interview with Sam Taylor, 7 August 1989.
41. For a discussion of women hired into traditionally male, blue-collar jobs, see Julie A. Matthaei, *An Economic History of Women in America: Women's Work, the Sexual Division of Labor, and the Development of Capitalism* (New York: Schocken Books, 1982), 293–300.
42. Interview with Karen Grant, 10 August 1989.
43. Interview with Ramona Smith, 25 July 1989.
44. Interview with Karen Grant, 10 August 1989.
45. Ibid.
46. Ibid.
47. Interview with Hannah Taussig, 19 January 1993.
48. Interview with Karen Grant, 10 August 1989.
49. Ibid.
50. Ibid.
51. Ibid.
52. Interview with Larry Sayles, 5 March 1993.
53. Interview with Mildred Frantz, 8 September 1985.
54. Interview with Audrey Hartman, 13 April 1993.
55. Interview with Larry Sayles, 5 March 1993.
56. Interview with Thelma Porsinsky, 25 May 1989.
57. Ibid.
58. Interview with Pauline Van Dial, 25 April 1985.
59. Interview with Carol Pearson, 10 September 1991.
60. Interview with Jean Edwards, 15 May 1991.
61. Interview with Amy Hanson, 13 April 1993.
62. Interview with Edna Samson, 21 September 1991.
63. Interview with Jean Edwards, 15 May 1991.
64. Ibid.
65. Interview with Audrey Hartman, 20 April 1993.
66. Interview with Pauline Van Dial, 25 April 1985.
67. Interview with Martha Randal, 6 September 1988.
68. Interview with Thelma Porsinsky, 25 May 1989.
69. Interview with Mildred Frantz, 8 September 1985.
70. Interview with Stewart Crane, 26 May 1989.

Part 3

THE OPPORTUNITIES OF LABOR RADICALISM

T he decades following World War II have been unkind to the cause of labor radicalism. After the consolidation of unions into the New Deal order, unions were largely dominated by leaders pursuing the conservative policies of "business unionism." Politically, labor became the very junior partner within the Democratic Party rather than an independent force. Nevertheless, labor radicals played a decisive role in shaping the direction of workers' struggles at the birth of the New Deal in the 1930s as well as during other points in this century.

In "Revolutionary Vanguards in the United States in the 1930s," Paul Le Blanc argues that Leninist organizational theory sheds light both on the left-wing contributions to the rise of the CIO and on why radical organizations were eclipsed by conservative ones in that critical decade. While the militancy and radicalism of thousands of workers was a crucial ingredient in the creation of mass unionism, equally important was the role of organizations which coordinated and directed workers' actions. A serious examination of the role and nature of such organizations as the Socialist Party, Communist Party, and Socialist Workers' Party can illuminate more than speculative theorizing about the "inherent conservatism" of American workers.

One labor radical who helped to shape the course of the 1930s was Genora Johnson Dollinger. Her keen sense of justice as well as her organizational skills and connections with socialists allowed "ordinary" women to play an important role in the militant Flint sit-down strikes. Kathleen O'Nan interviews her about her activities in Flint and why in the 1990s she worked to build a Labor Party.

In "Opportunities Found and Lost: Labor, Radicals, and the Early Civil Rights Movement," Robert Korstad and Nelson Lichtenstein investigate how labor radicals were able to use unions in the 1940s as a base to fight for civil rights. The rise of the Cold War ended that experiment. The Cold War, as well as the policies of the major socialist organizations, made for a difficult birth for black socialist politics. In "A. Philip Randolph and the Foundations of Black Socialism," Manning Marable examines the important role that this labor radical had on the house of labor and on the evolution of the movement for civil rights.

9

REVOLUTIONARY VANGUARDS IN THE UNITED STATES DURING THE 1930s

PAUL LE BLANC

I want to explore here the relationship of Leninist organizational theory—particularly the concept of the revolutionary vanguard—to one of the most spectacular working class upsurges in the history of the United States. I believe Leninist theory can help us solve a puzzle about this labor upsurge. On the other hand, an examination of the upsurge may provide us with some insight into the meaning of Leninist theory. In a sense, this essay is also designed to meet a challenge posed by the title we have chosen: were there actually any revolutionary vanguards in the United States during the 1930s, and were such vanguards in fact possible at that time?

LABOR'S GIANT STEP DURING THE TURBULENT YEARS

In James R. Green's valuable history *The World of the Worker: Labor in Twentieth Century America*, published in 1980, we are provided with an image of a powerful working-class insurgency during the Great Depression:

> . . . the gains [U.S.] workers made in the 1930s were enormous. During the decade, when powerful workers' organizations fell before the Fascist threat in Germany and Spain and foundered in democratic countries like Britain, workers in the United States made historic advances despite the effects of

129

the Depression and the cumulative effects of corporate oppression. In organizational terms alone, the growth of the CIO [Congress of Industrial Organizations] and the revival of the AFL [American Federation of Labor] were impressive. The number of unionized employees tripled from 2,805,000 in 1933 to 8,410,000 in 1941. During the strife-ridden decade, the proportion of workers enjoying union rights jumped from 9 to 34 percent in manufacturing, 21 to 72 percent in mining, 23 to 48 percent in transportation, and 54 to 65 percent in construction. A new kind of workers power had been mobilized in countless factories and communities. For the first time, millions of industrial workers asserted rights that had to be respected, and created organizations that finally gave them some control over their world.[1]

In the title of his classic second volume on the history of workers during the Great Depression, Irving Bernstein calls the 1930s the *Turbulent Years*. Noting the expansion of union membership, he observes that this resulted in material payoffs for the working class as a whole. Bernstein points to "a direct relationship between the percent in unionization and the percent in increase in earnings," but goes on to write that "unions also raised the wages of unorganized workers by setting standards of equity for them and their employers and by prodding the latter into granting higher wages in order to keep the union out." He also emphasizes the importance of at least a certain amount of job security and on-the-job dignity provided by the seniority system, union-imposed work rules, and grievance procedures.[2]

More than this, as political scientist Michael Goldfield has recently demonstrated, "labor influence was central to the structure of the political situation in 1934 and 1935, both because of its insurgent and disruptive activities and because of the growing strength of highly organized radicalism." Pushing President Franklin D. Roosevelt's New Deal policies in a leftward direction, the battles of these "turbulent years" brought about what Bernstein terms a transformation of "the distribution of power in American society" through "unemployment relief, a variety of attacks on joblessness, unemployment insurance, old-age pensions, welfare programs, wage, hour, and child labor standards, and protection of the right of workers to organize [unions] and bargain collectively." The very structure of American politics was transformed with Roosevelt's second electoral victory, Bernstein tells us. "In all probability," he comments, "no national election in American history was so class-based as that of 1936. The Republicans gained solid backing from the bankers, the industrialists, and the newspaper publishers; the Democrats received the votes of the urban working class."[3] This liberal-labor alignment—especially in Northern industrial centers—continued to be a major feature of U.S. politics for many years to come.

At the same time, another respected labor historian named Melvyn Dubofsky, combing through statistics on union-organizing drives and strikes in the 1930s, observed that the overwhelming majority of working people during this period were simply *not involved* in these union struggles. He focuses attention on two years of the most intense struggles—1934 and 1937.

The year 1934 saw general strikes in three cities: Toledo, Ohio; San Francisco, California; and Minneapolis, Minnesota. In Toledo workers at the Auto-Lite Company, and their allies in the militant Unemployed League, battled the company and the National Guard, with the support of the city's central labor council and under the leadership of A. J. Muste's left-wing American Workers Party, including Louis Budenz, Sam Pollack, and Ted Selander. In San Francisco longshoremen and other workers, following Harry Bridges and a left-wing leadership—especially militants of the Communist Party—were also backed by the city's central labor council, fought company goons and local police, and here too confronted the National Guard. In Minneapolis and neighboring St. Paul, the radicals providing leadership to the workers' battles were members of the Communist League of America, followers of Leon Trotsky, such as Carl Skoglund, Vincent Raymond Dunne, his brothers Miles and Grant, and Farrell Dobbs. Here the city's teamsters, supported by the central labor council and masses of unorganized and unemployed workers, and nearby small family farmers, faced down the city's powerful employers, fought police, and—here too—their struggles brought in the National Guard. The stunning union victories in these three cities generated the mass organizing drives of industrial workers and launched the CIO.[4]

The year 1937 is described quite well by Dubofsky:

> The year began with the famous Flint sit-down strike in which the United Auto Workers conquered General Motors; saw United States Steel surrender to the Steel Workers Organizing Committee (SWOC)-CIO without a struggle less than three weeks after the General Motors strike ended; and culminated in the late spring with perhaps the most violent and bloodiest national strike of the decade: the Little Steel conflict that led to the Memorial Day "massacre" [by police against masses of peacefully protesting workers] outside Republic Steel's South Chicago plant. In between Flint and Little Steel, more than four hundred thousand workers participated in 477 sit-down strikes [involving the occupation and takeover of factories by strikers]. Twenty-five sit-downs erupted in January, forty-seven in February, and 170 in March. "Sitting down has replaced baseball as a national pastime," quipped *Time* magazine.[5]

THE RIDDLE OF "NONTURBULENCE" AMONG THE MAJORITY OF WORKERS

While there were only 840 strikes in 1932, in 1933 there were 1,700, in 1934 there were 1,856, in 1936 there were 2,200, and in the peak year of

1937 there were 4,740, and these strikes affected every major mass-production industry—steel, auto, rubber, coal, electrical goods, and more. Often these dramatic figures, clearly showing a class-struggle upsurge, have given the impression that all workers, or most workers, or at least a bare majority of workers were engaged in strikes and union-organizing drives. Nothing could be further from the truth.

In July 1934, for example—the month of the San Francisco and Minneapolis general strikes—only seven-tenths of 1 percent (only one in a thousand) of all U.S. workers were involved in strikes. In 1937, only 7.2 percent of employed workers were involved in strikes, and their absence from work represented only 0.043 percent of all time worked—which means that less than five workdays in a thousand were lost due to strikes in that year. Asking "what the other 93 percent of the labor force" was doing during the great strike waves, Dubofsky notes that

> the continental size of the United States . . . could, and did, easily dilute
> the impact of industrial conflict nationally. . . . When teamsters tied up
> Minneapolis and longshoremen closed down San Francisco in July 1934,
> truckers continued to deliver goods in Chicago and Los Angeles, and
> waterfront workers remained on the job in New York, Baltimore, and San
> Pedro. For trade unionists and radicals it was exceedingly difficult . . . to
> transform well-structured local and regional organizations into equally
> effective national bodies.[6]

There are also explanations that go beyond simple geography. Writing in the late 1930s, the perceptive radical journalist Louis Adamic wrote: "I know, or have known, hundreds of unskilled workers, particularly in the smaller industries, whose apathy and resignation are something appalling. Where no union has appeared to rouse them, most of them are basically indifferent to the conditions they have to endure. Because certain conditions exist, they see no possibility of having them altered. There is a dead fatalism." Contemptuous of left-wing cant, Adamic denied that capitalist oppression would naturally breed militant class consciousness. "The exploitation is outrageous, but the workers merely grumble," he wrote. "When unionization is suggested, they oppose it: it might lose them their jobs! Yet they hate their jobs. That hate expresses itself in subversive talk, sabotage, defeatism." Adamic added: "Most American workers have little or no conception of jobs outside their fields. They are unaware of the interdependence of the workers' functions, and so ignorant of their importance, the indispensability of their work. Many tend to deprecate their functions, if not orally, then to themselves and perform listlessly, as workers, as human beings . . . and the general public, as uninformed as they are concerning what makes the wheels go round, tends to agree with them."[7]

This corresponds to the findings of other contemporary observers. In their studies of Muncie, Indiana, in the 1920s and 1930s, which they called "Middletown," Robert and Helen Lynd found labor organization weaker, and the business class apparently more united than ever and determined to keep Muncie a predominantly nonunion town. They noted the stirrings of discontent among workers, but they added that "fear, resentment, insecurity, and disillusionment has been to Middletown's workers largely an *individual* experience for each worker, and not such a thing generalized by him into a '*class*' experience." They added that "such militancy as it generates tends to be sporadic, personal, flaccid; an expression primarily of personal resentment rather than an act of self-identification with the continuities of a movement or of rebellion against an economic status regarded as permanently fixed." They concluded that "the militancy of Middletown labor tends, therefore, to be easily manipulated, and to be diverted into all manner of incidental issues."[8]

To gain greater insights into the so-called average worker who may (or may not) have been involved in union struggles, social historian John Bodnar has directed our attention to "the masses of rank-and-file toilers who were reared in strong, family-based enclaves" of largely immigrant working-class communities. Particularly as mass-production techniques were being developed by employers in the early decades of the twentieth century—largely to eliminate the power of potentially radicalizing skilled workers—recently arrived unskilled immigrant laborers were absorbed as mass-production workers, and often they found jobs in their workplaces for needy friends and relatives as well. Family and ethnic ties became intertwined with occupational patterns, creating what Bodnar calls "kinship-occupational clusters" in which "familial concerns were strongly reinforced." This cut across the competing ideologies of capitalist-oriented upward mobility through "rugged individualism" on the one hand and a revolutionary proletarian class-consciousness on the other. "Clearly," Bodnar writes, "family obligations dominated working-class predilections and may have exerted a moderating influence on individual expectations and the formulation of social and economic goals."[9]

In fact, he concludes (largely on the basis of in-depth interviews with working-class participants in 1930s union activity in Pennsylvania) that "immigrants, blacks, and native-born toilers entered the mines and mills of Pennsylvania prior to 1940 not on their own behalf but because of the needs of their kin. . . . Personal satisfaction, the control of production, equality and mobility were usually secondary concerns." A "family-oriented culture continued to serve necessary functions and define the framework of individual lives" of most workers, according to Bodnar, leading to a preoccupation with survival strategies that focused on family welfare: "Families generally searched for ways to make ends meet, achieved little savings, sent their children to work early in life and valued steady employment," and this orienta-tion "muted individual inclinations and idealism in favor of group survival." At times this would be compatible with support for the new industrial unionism, of course—but even when it was, there was a conservative brake which was introduced. "If workers agitated for job security more than social equality and demonstrated a realism which disappointed those who would have preferred a greater groundswell of social idealism," Bodnar writes, "it was because equality and even mobility were largely personal goals while job security was the key to family sustenance."[10]

It is interesting to note that the interviews gathered by Bodnar are qual-itatively different from those that were gathered by Staughton and Alice Lynd of working-class organizers, mostly from the 1930s, in their excellent book *Rank and File*. The Lynds write: "The rank and filers in this book felt . . . that there had to be basic social changes. They were both militant, in demanding changes within their unions and workplaces, and radical, in the sense that they tried to democratize the larger society. They imagined both a union and a society which were more just, more humane, more of a community."[11] In fact, most of the veteran working-class activists they interviewed had been members of Socialist, Communist, or Trotskyist organizations.

Bodnar's comments on all of this are interesting. "Our interviews with Pennsylvania workers do not specifically refute the assertion by Lynd and others that a tradition of working-class democracy aimed at humanizing society at large was operative or that strains of mobility and self-improve-ment pervaded the industrial working class," he writes. "It should be emphasized, however, that such conclusions followed from analyses that concentrated largely on articulate, working-class leaders and intellectuals and stopped short of penetrating the temper of rank-and-file objectives." Bodnar writes that "brief flirtations with larger social visions emerged, but they were seldom sustained among the rank and file." He argues that "the limits to the ground swell of union activity in the 1930 . . . may have been determined by family priorities, which continued to direct the objectives of most workers."[12]

THE MULTIFACETED VANGUARD: REVOLUTIONARY AND NOT

To the extent that the picture of the American working class presented by Louis Adamic, Robert and Helen Lynd, and John Bodnar is accurate, how did it come to pass that hundreds of thousands of workers *did* throw them-selves into the struggles of the 1930s which transformed U.S. society and politics? Dubofsky brings our attention to the dialectic between conscious working-class militants (the focus of Staughton and Alice Lynd's interviews) and the larger rank and file. He writes: "[M]ore often than not, action by militant minorities (what some scholars have characterized as 'sparkplug Unionism') precipitated a subsequent collective response." His portrait of a multilayered working class is worth presenting in full:

> Even the most strike-torn cities and regions had a significantly internally differentiated working class. At the top were the local cadres, the sparkplug unionists, the men and women fully conscious of their roles in a market-place society that extolled individualism and rewarded collective strength. These individuals, ranging the political spectrum from Social Democrats to Communists, provided the leadership, militancy, and ideology that fostered industrial conflict and the emergence of mass-production unionism. Beneath them lay a substantial proportion of workers who could be transformed, by example, into militant strikers and unionists, and, in turn, themselves act as militant minorities. Below them were many first- and second-generation immigrant workers, as well as recent migrants from the American countryside, who remained embedded in a culture defined by traditional ties to family, kinship, church, and neighborhood club or tavern. Accustomed to following the rituals of the past, heeding the advice of community leaders, and slow to act, such men and women rarely joined unions prior to a successful strike, once moved to act behaved with singular solidarity, yet rarely served as union or political activists and radicals. And below this mass were the teenage workers caught halfway between liberation from their parental families and formation of their own new households, more attracted to the life and rituals of street gangs and candy-store cronies than to the customs and culture of persistent trade unionists and political activists.[13]

The reality of the working class was even more complex than this, though Dubofsky's rough categorizations are useful as an initial approximation. The piece of the analysis that I want to focus on, at this point, is the militant minority that he seems to subdivide, at one point, into political radicals and militant trade union activists, who together played an indispensable "vanguard" role.

There has been considerable discussion, over the years, especially of the role of the Communist Party in the organization of the CIO. According to Martin Dies, first chairman of the notorious House Un-American Activities Committee, "hundreds of Communist organizers were employed by the CIO to organize the workers into industrial unions, according to much testimony before the Committee. . . . The Communist organizers proved their ability to recruit workers into these organizations. But having accomplished this purpose, they set about to use the unions for their own revolutionary purposes." The ex-radical Eugene Lyons, in his 1941 polemic *The Red Decade*, was sharply critical of the decision made by CIO president

John L. Lewis, who was relatively conservative politically, to utilize organizers with Communist Party backgrounds; Lyons commented that "the communist cancer in the CIO grew in malignancy with every passing month." There is, of course, Lewis's comeback that implied his own mastery of the situation: "Who gets the bird, the hunter or the dog?"[14]

The conclusion of such seasoned commentators as Saul Alinsky and Bert Cochran—who themselves had considerable trade union and political experience—was that, given their decision to lead the newly formed CIO in building the new unions, Lewis and those nonradical union leaders grouped around him "had no choice but to accept the support of the Communists," as Alinsky put it, since "every place where new industrial unions were being formed, young and middle-aged Communists were working tirelessly." He added: "It was the left-wingers who kept fighting against the disillusionment and cynicism that swept the workers [in the face of bureaucratic ineptness by the American Federation of Labor]. It was they who kept organizing and organizing and organizing." Cochran agrees that Lewis "could not do without the support of the radicals—and in the 1930s, radicals meant primarily the Communists. It was not that man-for-man Communists were necessarily superior organizers or agitators than non-Communist radicals. The contrary was demonstrated in the Minneapolis and Toledo strikes. But whatever their qualities, non-Communist radicals were few in number." This is illustrated by a look at left-wing membership figures in the mid-1930s. The Trotskyists—even after they merged with Muste's American Workers Party—had about 700 members. The rightward-leaning Communist dissidents following Jay Lovestone had perhaps 1,000. Even the Socialist Party, fluctuating around 10,000, had only 1,300 trade-union members—including in the garment and auto industries, where many were in the process of defecting from the organization. The Communist Party, on the other hand, had about 30,000 members, of whom 15,000 were union members.[15]

For the moment, however, we can set aside the question of specifically which left-wing organization played what role in the class struggles and union-organizing drives of the Depression decade. The dynamic between the two components of the "militant minority" or "working-class vanguard"—the political radical and the nonradical trade-union activist—is worth giving attention to, because it may reveal something about the more general process of working-class organization.

To explore this question further, I want to draw from another contemporary source, a 1938 study by journalist Ben Stolberg, who had extensive left-wing and trade union contacts. His book *The Story of the CIO* stands as a problematical source which is—in some ways—at odds with itself, blending brilliant insight with bitter cynicism. But there are aspects of his analysis which can be helpful.

Stolberg begins with a generalization based on the experience of the

U.S. labor movement up to the 1930s. The old American Federation of Labor under Samuel Gompers, before the First World War, had a very strong left wing, led by members of the Socialist Party of America, at that time a mass working-class organization led by Eugene V. Debs. The wartime and postwar repression (combined with internal splits) shattered this left wing—thereby doing serious damage to the AFL as a whole, in Stolberg's opinion. "For even the most conservative trade union oligarchy flourishes far more on its sound compromises with its own Left than on its necessary compromises with the boss," he wrote. "Forward movements grow on their inner tensions. Hence a trade union movement which crushes all Left criticism finally dies from sheer inanition. When soon after the war our socialist movement splintered into various impotent factions, the A.F. of L. lost all vitality, and finally deteriorated into a sort of independent company unionism."[16]

The AFL was handicapped because it was, for the most part, based on unions of skilled workers organized along craft lines—yet American industry had become restructured on the model of mass production, utilizing unskilled and semiskilled labor in a manner that interconnected into a single enterprise a variety of different "crafts." In addition, the narrowly conservative "pure and simple" trade unionism of the Gompers variety—assuming that businessmen would take care of business and trade unionists would simply bargain for "more"—was overwhelmed by problems generated by the crisis of the traditional free-market economy. This crisis has been attributed by some to overproduction (competing manufacturers eventually glutting the market with their products) and by others to underconsumption (workers not getting paid enough to provide a market capable of absorbing consumer goods), but the bottom line was a devastating economic depression.

Stolberg explained that "the CIO is an effort on the part of American labor to revitalize itself and to modernize its outdated structure. This it cannot do without the stimulus of political and social radicalism. Mere trade unionism as such, without left agitation, cannot recast its point of view or remodel itself functionally." He elaborated on this with an ingenious argument:

> Trade unionism as such is only the economic organization by and for itself—in crafts, or by industries, or in a mixture of both—within the logic of the economy in which it works and deals. Hence, trade unionism everywhere is a purely practical affair. And being a practical day-to-day, collective bargaining movement, it has always attracted and developed practical leaders. The average trade union leader the world over, not only in the A. F. of L., is essentially a business unionist. He is the representative and the broker of labor power in the labor market, who is guided primarily by the daily pressures of that market.[17]

Stolberg notes that in periods of economic catastrophe ("not at the depth of the depression, but when the business cycle begins to crawl up from the bottom"), "[T]he workers begin to realize that their conservative trade unions were unable to protect them from the ravages of the catastrophe. They begin to gauge the lag between the stationary character of business unionism and the ever-advancing industrial process. That lag has meant to them unemployment and hunger." The old ideology of the AFL exposes itself as utterly inadequate. Stolberg makes a generalization about the masses of workers: "Their restlessness becomes social awareness. And this class consciousness, no matter how vague and simple, turns to social radicalism for leadership." This leads to shifts among some of the nonradical trade unionists, according to Stolberg: "Then the progressive and alert union leader breaks away from the conservative union hierarchy, and puts himself at the head of the forward movement. And he necessarily opens the doors to the radicals, whom he needs as agitators and organizers."[18]

There is a question as to whether these "alert union leaders" are steering or being pulled along by dynamics not under their control. This question is raised by Stolberg, perhaps unconsciously, when he writes: "If a new and more left orientation had not been the propelling motive of the CIO, it never would have split from the A.F. of L. in the first place. And once the CIO was on its way, its leaders found it necessary to battle every reactionary force in American life. If the CIO had used only the old-fashioned trade union organizers, it could not possibly have organized over 3,000,000 workers in two years."[19]

CONTRADICTIONS OF VANGUARDISM

There are problems with the concept of "vanguardism" that we can't afford to ignore. There is the crude description of the concept offered, for example, by sociologist Daniel Bell: "Only the organized group counted, and only a mass base could exert social leverage in society. But a mass requires leadership. . . . Lenin . . . argued that the masses, by nature, were backward. Only the vanguard party, aware of the precarious balance of social forces, could assess the play and correctly tip the scales in the revolutionary direction. . . . A line was laid down by the [party] leadership which was binding on all."[20] This constitutes a serious distortion of Lenin's views, but it also provides a useful summary of a very common interpretation of those views both by anti-Leninists and some would-be Leninists. More than this, it suggests a critique, a warning about the undemocratic qualities inherent in so-called vanguardism, that is worth considering. On the other hand, it obscures the more general application of the term utilized in this paper: a vanguard (or leadership) may or may not be revolutionary.

There is another problem. The nonrevolutionary vanguard that we have been referring to—the nonradical trade union activists—as well as the self-consciously "revolutionary" (anticapitalist, socialist) labor activists have a somewhat problematical track record, to say the least. One of the classic critiques of both types of vanguard is offered in Jeremy Brecher's book *Strike!* and it will be helpful to look at his argument.

Brecher notes the importance of informal work groups which spontaneously form in industrial (and presumably other) workplaces, which helps to humanize the labor process. More than this, however, "the work groups created their own ways of getting work done, contradicting those of management." They "are communities within which workers come into opposition to the boss, begin acting on their own, and discover their need to support each other and the collective power they develop in doing so." Naturally challenging the authority and leadership of management, they become transformed into embryonic trade unions, and are in fact the building blocks for any vital union activity.[21]

"Trade unions often started when the industrial work groups we described above simply formed into permanent organizations," Brecher writes. "As they grew, their character changed, however, and they became quite separate from the workplace, controlled from above by professional officials kept in office by their own political machines. Bound by the contractual agreements arrived at with company officials through the collective bargaining process, the trade union officials then play a policing and disciplinary role, seeking to guarantee that the individual workers and informal work groups abide by the company/union contract. There is also a grievance procedure established, of course, for workers to challenge company violations—although this is often clogged to the point of ineffectuality by red-tape and bureaucracy." In any event, the nonradical union "vanguard" becomes a conservative force, separated from the rank-and-file workers, playing anything but a vanguard role.[22]

Brecher goes on to argue that the self-styled "revolutionary vanguards" have not

> played a qualitatively better role in the history of the American labor movement: They have generally been preoccupied with building their own organization, whether party or union, and have seen the significance of mass movements in their possible addition to the membership or support for such organizations. They have done little to clarify the possible revolutionary significance of mass actions or to develop their more radical potentialities. . . . When radical leaders have succeeded in gaining organizational control over unions, the unions have operated within the framework of orderly collective bargaining.[23]

From a somewhat more conservative perspective, one of the most respected U.S. labor historians, David Brody, has similarly commented that "radicalism served trade union needs, not the reverse." The left-wing ideology of some of the trade union militants gave them "an education, a cultural experience, and a sense of community," which helped fuel and facilitate their organizing efforts. "[John L.] Lewis's famous distinction between hunters and hunting dogs—who gets the bird—in part bespoke the man's towering arrogance," Brody argued, "but it also reflected a fact of life about the labor movement. Communists might hold offices of great power, but only so long as they functioned as trade unionists."[24]

Melvyn Dubofsky has stressed another aspect of the deradicalization of working-class vanguards in the 1930s, pointing to the electoral arena:

> Paradoxically, the one experience during the 1930s that united workers across ethnic, racial, and organizational lines—New Deal politics—served to vitiate radicalism. By the end of the 1930s, Roosevelt's Democratic Party had become, in effect, the political expression of America's working class old-line Socialists, farmer-labor party types, and even Communists enlisted in a Roosevelt-led "Popular Front." Blacks and whites, Irish and Italian Catholics, Slavic and Jewish-Americans, uprooted rural Protestants and stable skilled workers joined the Democratic coalition, solidifying the working-class vote as never before in American history. Roosevelt encouraged workers to identify themselves as a common class politically as well as economically. . . . By frightening the ruling class into conceding reforms and appealing to workers to vote as a solid bloc, Roosevelt simultaneously intensified class consciousness and stripped it of its radical potential.[25]

Defending the record of the Communist Party in regard to both trade union policy and electoral policy, Roger Keeran, in his history of *The Communist Party and the Auto Workers Unions*, writes: "While prominent among the union's leaders and organizers, Communists and other left-wingers represented only a tiny minority; many workers, recent migrants from the South or members of ethnic enclaves, remained under such conservative influences as the Ku Klux Klan or the Catholic church." If Communists had followed more independent and radical trade union policies or "pressed more aggressively . . . for independent political action, they would have isolated themselves or provoked a split in the union," Keeran insists.[26]

This presents us with a vision that is the opposite of what Bell warns about: that of a "vanguard" which can do relatively little to lead people forward (or to lead them astray, in the opinion of Bell). It is also different from the view of Brecher that the alleged "vanguard" actually retards the development of the masses—rather, it is the masses that retard (and reverse) the development of the vanguard!

THE POSSIBILITY OF A REVOLUTIONARY VANGUARD

We are now in a better position to confront the challenge embedded in the title: "Revolutionary Vanguards in the United States During the 1930s."

The meaning of the term *vanguard*, which we have been employing in a manner that approximates the Leninist usage, can be summarized as: a minority with a higher level of *political* commitments, knowledge, and organizational skills than the majority, a political elite of a special kind. Such a vanguard is not a little political group, but actually constitutes a significant layer of the working class. Lenin believed that as much of this vanguard as possible should be organized into a revolutionary party. "The party was to lead and inspire the mass of workers; its own membership was to remain small and select," E. H. Carr has written, adding: "It would, however, be an error to suppose that Lenin regarded the revolution as the work of a minority. The task of leading the masses was not, properly understood, a task of indoctrination, of creating a consciousness that was not there, but of evoking a latent consciousness, and this latent consciousness of the masses was an essential condition of revolution." Antonio Gramsci has stressed that this vanguard had the goal of creating the conditions that would eliminate its elite status (by educating, mobilizing, and empowering the majority), and C. L. R. James once pointed to the essential *interactive* aspect involved here: "Lenin fought for the Bolshevik principles and *won*. He was constantly winning, which means that he expressed ideas which stood the test of practice. The proletariat as a whole, at all critical moments, followed the Bolsheviks. More important, however, is the fact that the Russian proletariat taught and disciplined Lenin and the Bolsheviks not only indirectly but directly."[27]

There are three important distinctions to be noted. First, there is a distinction between vanguard elements which are consciously revolutionary and those which are consciously nonrevolutionary, each of which will draw out different elements that are latent in the consciousness of workers. Second, there is a distinction between different revolutionary vanguard organizational formations (Socialists, Stalinist-Communists, Trotskyists, Lovestoneites, etc.) competing with each other to provide revolutionary leadership. Third, there is a question of whether a self-proclaimed revolutionary vanguard organization does (or can) in fact provide revolutionary leadership, whether it will be capable of "being taught and disciplined" by the working class in a manner that allows it, in turn, to provide leadership—that is, to relate to certain latent consciousness and possibilities in the working class in a manner that leads the struggle in a revolutionary direction.

It is worth giving attention to the perceptions of another revolutionary who believed in the need to build, as she put it, "a proletarian vanguard conscious of its class interests and capable of self-direction in political activity." Surveying the great democratic upheavals of the nineteenth and early twentieth centuries, Rosa Luxemburg commented that "for the first time in the history of civilization, the people are expressing their will consciously and in opposition to all ruling classes. But this can only be satisfied beyond the limits of the existing system." She went on to point out that "the mass [of workers] can only acquire and strengthen this will in the course of the day-to-day struggle against the existing social order—that is, within the limits of capitalist society." This created a framework fraught with difficulties for the proletarian vanguard:

> On the one hand, we have the mass; on the other, its historic goal, located outside of existing society. On the one hand, we have the day-to-day struggle; on the other, the social revolution. Such are the terms of the dialectical contradiction through which the socialist movement makes its way.
>
> It follows that this movement can best advance by tacking betwixt and between the two dangers by which it is constantly being threatened. One is the loss of its mass character: the other, the abandonment of its goal. One is the danger of sinking back to the condition of a sect; the other, the danger of becoming a movement of bourgeois social reform.[28]

Luxemburg and other Marxists termed the one danger sectarianism and the other danger opportunism. And she added another important thought— that working-class activists can overcome such dangers not solely by absorbing Marxist theory (the realm of intellectual abstractions); that it was only possible to overcome them "after the dangers in question have taken tangible form in practice." She concluded: "Looked at from this angle, opportunism appears to be a product and an inevitable phase of the historic development of the labor movement."[29]

What this suggests is that it was not within the realm of possibility that the U.S. working class could have made a revolution in the 1930s. Such a possibility requires the development of a consciously revolutionary vanguard layer of the working class, a certain percentage of workers who believe that their class can and should take political power for the purpose of democratically transforming the economy. As matters actually stood in the 1930s, it was necessary for the active layers of the working class to educate themselves through taking the nonrevolutionary path of social reform until increasing numbers of workers finally ran up against the hard fact that their goal could only be reached "beyond the limits of the existing system." On the other hand, it was not a foregone conclusion that everything had to happen just as it happened. David Brody has written of "the problem of inevitability" which "always raises difficulties for the historian." As Brody puts it: "He knows the end of the story, and so is under a strong compulsion to see events as a steady and direct march to that end. The history of labor during the New Deal seems to be a subject especially prone to this kind of treatment. We have tended to write as if only one set of results were possible. And this, of course, has deadly effect on the interpretive potential of the subject."[30] In fact, such determinism makes it impossible to comprehend the actual dynamics and possibilities not only of historical reality, but of reality in general. In fact, what individuals, groups, and revolutionary-minded organizations do or fail to do often makes a difference on the way things turn out—for those individuals, groups, and organizations, as well as for more general historical events and developments.

The leader of one of the U.S. vanguard formations of the 1930s, the Trotskyist James P. Cannon, spoke to this question when he asserted that "the fate of every political group—whether it is to live and grow or degenerate and die—is decided in its first experiences by the way in which it answers two decisive questions. The first is the adoption of a correct political program. But that alone does not guarantee victory. The second is that the group decides correctly what shall be the nature of its activities, and what tasks it shall set itself, given the size and capacity of the group, the period of the development of the class struggle, the relation of forces in the political movement, and so on." He explained that "if the group misunderstands the tasks set for it by the conditions of the day, if it does not know how to answer the most important of all questions in politics—that is, the question of what to do next—then the group, no matter what its merits may otherwise be, can wear itself out in misdirected efforts and futile activities and come to grief."[31]

This brings us to the trickiest part of historiography—the realm of "what might have been." First, we should quickly review the record of the actual groups that sought to play the role of revolutionary vanguard.

Many would-be revolutionary sects of the 1930s, expecting imminent working-class revolution and functioning accordingly, came to grief and faded away. Members of other organizations—particularly those in the Socialist Party, Social-Democratic Federation, and the Lovestoneite Communist Party Opposition (which evolved into the more moderate Independent Labor League)—in their quest for relevance, increasingly adapted to the less radical elements latent within the working class and even more to the nonradical trade union officialdom, ending up as forces for "bourgeois social reform," to use Luxemburg's term; in the period of the Cold War, many of them became "State Department socialists" in the crusade against Communism, while helping to secure the hold of the procapitalist Democratic Party on the labor movement.[32]

There were a number of labor-radicals who didn't fade away, but the only two left-wing vanguard organizations of any substance that persisted were the Stalinist-oriented radicals in and around the Communist Party and the Trotskyists who were, for the most part, in and around the Socialist Workers Party. Although the Trotskyists had been able to develop some influence in the auto and maritime industries, and to a lesser extent in other unions such as those of the steel and electrical workers, it was only in the Teamsters union of the Midwest—especially in Minneapolis—that they were able to provide anything approximating clear-cut revolutionary leadership in the class struggle. While they wrote inspiring and instructive lessons in the annals of labor and radical history, however, as a group that never grew beyond 2,000 people, they were not able to become a serious pole of attraction for masses of workers on a national scale. Finally, the combined assaults of the employers, the conservative union bureaucrats, and the U.S. government destroyed even their power base (though never quite obliterating their influence) in Minneapolis.[33]

The Communist Party, on the other hand, *did* appear to have the potential for building a mass revolutionary base in the labor movement. According to Earl Browder, the undisputed Communist Party leader throughout the Depression decade, "with the rise of the CIO the Communists rose with it as a trade union power." Referring to CP influence in "steel, auto, electrical, marine, transport, and other fields," he recounted: "By the close of the decade the Communists and their closest allies had predominant influence in unions representing approximately one-third of the membership, and various degrees of minority influence in another third. Added to this was their 'understanding' with the centrist leadership [of the CIO] to complete the isolation of the open anti-Communists."[34] The influential publicity director of the CIO, Len De Caux, who maintained close ties with the Communist Party, has described the expansive radicalism associated with the early CIO, which was not simply a new labor federation but "a mass movement with a message, revivalistic in fervor, militant in mood, joined together by class solidarity." On Labor Day 1937, "conservative" CIO chieftain John L. Lewis, in order to express the CIO message, intoned: "This movement of labor will go on until there is a more equitable and just distribution of our national wealth. This movement will go on until the social order is reconstructed on a basis that will be fair, decent, and honest. This movement will go on until the guarantees of the Declaration of Independence and of the Constitution are enjoyed by all the people, and not by a privileged few." Writing in 1938, labor journalist Mary Heaton Vorse commented: "Labor has shown in its struggles an inventiveness, intelligence, and power greater than anything before in its long history. Whole communities of workers have been transformed." Looking back on this period, De Caux elaborated:

> As it gained momentum, this movement brought with it new political attitudes—toward the corporations, toward police and troops, toward local,

state, national government. Now we're a movement, many workers asked, why can't we move on to more and more? Today we've forced almighty General Motors to terms by sitting down and defying all the powers at its command, why can't we go on tomorrow, with our numbers, our solidarity, our determination, to transform city and state, the Washington government itself? Why can't we go on to create a new society with the workers on top, to end age-old injustices, to banish poverty and war?[35]

The mass base of socialist workers that could have been created—assuming the accuracy of these observations—did not come into being, however. The failure to make a revolution may not be a serious criticism, but the failure to build such a base in this somewhat turbulent decade cannot be shrugged off. There are indications, in fact, that this failure flows from mistakes made by the Communist Party.

COMMUNIST PARTY FAILURES

In the opinion of a leading Communist trade union veteran, William Z. Foster, there was a tendency for CP trade unionists "to overestimate the progressive character of the top leaders of the CIO," and CP trade unionists also "shied away from actively recruiting Party members in the basic industries, for fear that this would antagonize the top CIO leaders." This was, at least in part, a retrospective judgment. In 1939, Foster himself supported a policy in which "Party members do not now participate in groupings or other organized activities within the unions. The party also discountenances the formation of progressive groups, blocs, and caucuses in unions; it has liquidated its Communist fractions, discontinued its shop papers and is now modifying its system of industrial branches." The rationale for this was that "Communists are policy making and administrating on an unknown scale . . . building the highest type of trade union leadership based on efficient service and democratic responsibility to the rank and file." According to Stanley Aronowitz, the CP "abandoned its own political identity in the labor movement," and "Communist trade unionists became indistinguishable from their liberal colleagues" in the labor movement (except for their muted expressions of support for the eventual goal of socialism and for the "socialist homeland" in the USSR). Aronowitz argues that "important trade union cadre became union bureaucrats for whom an independent rank and file was anathema."[36]

What's more, the line of the Communist Party and of the trade unionists who were close to it in regard to political action involved a fundamental subordination to Franklin D. Roosevelt and the Democratic Party. "Today we are emphasizing that Roosevelt's programmatic utterances of 1937, when combined with the legislative program of the CIO (his main labor support), provides a People's Front program of an advanced type, that the organization of the majority of the people for the struggle to realize this program is the main road today to the creation of the People's Front," in the words of Earl Browder. Years later, Browder explained that "the New Deal, with its inadequacies and mistakes . . . had put America on the road to the welfare state and thereby had cut the ground from under both the Socialist and Communist parties—yet it certainly had the enthusiastic support of the latter. . . . The Communist party . . . rapidly moved out of its extreme leftist sectarianism of 1930 toward the broadest united front tactics of reformism for strictly immediate aims. It relegated its revolutionary socialist goals to the ritual of chapel and Sundays on the pattern followed by the Christian Church. On weekdays it became the most single-minded practical reformist party that America ever produced." One of the foremost historians of American Communism, Theodore Draper, agrees: "The Popular Front did not serve as an example of 'socialist tactics'; it used non-Socialist tactics in deference to a strongly capitalist society." (Far from reflecting a break from Stalinism, however, this represented loyal adherence to the line that the Soviet leader himself was helping to impose on the Communist International; E. H. Carr has demonstrated that the Popular Front policy was, in fact, inseparable from the practical foreign policy objectives of the USSR and from the consolidation of Stalin's personal power.)[37]

A serious problem with the subordination of labor's radical vanguard to Roosevelt's Democratic Party was that it involved subordination to limitations imposed by the Southern racist element that was a powerful component within the New Deal coalition. Harry Haywood later complained that Communist Party organizing efforts in the South were moderated by a desire not to "frighten off our new democratic allies: the Roosevelt New Dealers, the Southern moderates, and the CIO leadership." There was, in fact, a strong black nationalist current among African Americans in the rural areas of the deep South as well as in northern cities—manifesting itself in the desire of blacks to concentrate in organizations under their own control, and to concentrate on uncompromising struggles for black rights and for a growing measure of black control over black communities. The black Trotskyist theorist C. L. R. James emphasized that this African American militant activism "has a vitality and validity of its own," that it "is not led necessarily either by the organized labor movement or the Marxist party," and that "it has got a great contribution to make to the development of the proletariat, and . . . is in itself a constituent part of the struggle for socialism." But such a view was inconsistent with Communist Party perspectives. In Alabama the militant African American mass-based Share Cropper's Union was seen as an obstacle to the Popular Front priority of developing a racially integrated CIO plus political alliances with white liberal elements, and as Robin Kelley notes, this contributed to "the destruction of the Communist-led rural movement." Further declines in membership were generated by the Alabama CP leadership's "initial willingness to subordinate its militancy, particularly on racial issues," to the requirements of the Popular Front. Birmingham Communist Hosea Hudson recalled that "in this New Deal period the Party was different from before," with close-knit CP units being replaced by larger and more heterogeneous clubs, "a regular goulash" which undermined the earlier sense of comradeship: "But these clubs begin to deteriorate, the Party begin to deteriorate by not having this close contact, like in the units." In Harlem—former CP organizer Abner Berry recalled—"the blacks wanted to be together. They didn't mind on occasion being integrated, but in general, they wanted to be involved in something they could call their own, something they organized and led." Highly respected as a skilled coalition builder and as a "layman's theoretican" in Communist circles, Berry later drew upon black nationalist insights in explaining that "this was not a 'hate whitey' thing," but rather that "society had evolved in such a way that you had a separate people, and they had some things they wanted to discuss by themselves, for themselves. The Party was dead set against this." The subordination of African American struggles to "larger" aspects of U.S. and international politics produced a negative reaction among many African American workers—in the words of one Detroit autoworker: "When I talk to Negro Stalinists, I know and feel that it is the party first, second, and always. With this the question of Russia is always tied in. But it is never the Negroes first, no matter what they say."[38]

About 15 percent of the CP's 50,000 membership at the end of World War II was African American, Haywood explained, "largely due to the outstanding reputation the Party had built for itself during the campaigns of the thirties . . . and its yeoman work in building the CIO and organizing the unorganized." But the persistence "of the 'coalition concept' . . . affected not only the work among Blacks, but all areas of mass work, the trade unions in particular," as efforts were made to continue "tailing the liberal and reformist leaders." The persistence of this orientation, in the opinion of Haywood and others, contributed to the later success of the conservative 1950s and 1960s trade union bureaucracy in maintaining divisions between white workers and more militant African Americans—ensuring that struggles for black liberation would be advanced independently of, and sometimes even against, the mainstream of the organized labor movement. As C. L. R. James had argued, African Americans "are potentially the most revolutionary elements of the population" and capable of being "the very vanguard of the proletarian revolution," which meant that "the Negroes are able by their activity to draw the revolutionary elements and more powerful elements in the proletariat to their side." To the extent that this was true, tendencies to subordinate the African American struggle to the perceived needs of a liberal-labor political coalition would necessarily undermine any effort to maintain a strong left wing in the labor movement.[39]

The subordination of labor activists in and around the Communist Party to Roosevelt's New Deal is clearly indicated in a popular history of the labor movement which reflects the general approach of pro-CP trade unionists. "The purpose of F.D.R. and his New Deal was the saving of the menaced capitalist system and yet in a very real sense it was a people's movement too," wrote Richard Boyer and Herbert Morais in *Labor's Untold Story.* "A high point in American democracy, the New Deal was the necessary answer to the people's insistent demands. FDR became a world figure because he moved to meet the people's needs. There was an élan to all his acts, a shining challenge that rallied labor, farmers, and the Negro people to a fighting unity in which there was neither witch hunt nor red scare."[40]

During World War II, when Roosevelt switched from being "Dr. New Deal" to "Dr. Win the War," the Communist Party—once the USSR was part of the global wartime coalition—became an even more enthusiastic supporter of this capitalist savior. Hosea Hudson described it this way:

> Our line of discussion in those days was that people talk about shortage of houses, shortage of coal, rations of food, couldn't get no heat, we said, "After the war, we're going to have everything." Browder had us through this thing. We said, "We'll have plenty of houses, going to build houses, going to have plenty of jobs." That's how far we had gone. He had left the line of Marxism and Leninism. That was our talk.
>
> I had more battles in Birmingham with workers [who were dissatisfied with this conciliationist line] . . .
>
> I believed it, sure I believed it! I thought the bosses going to lay down with the workers, the wolves with the lambs going to lay together. I was teaching that, I was preaching that everywhere I went, in the union and everywhere. Not only me, but the union leaders was preaching that stuff. We'd work together, you had what you call in the unions "labor relations committees," where the company and the men and the union would get together, discuss the problems, would iron out their differences without strikes and strifes.[41]

But at last the witch-hunt and red scare *did* come. At the conclusion of World War II, the victorious U.S. business community and government (encompassing leadership of both the Democratic and Republican Parties) moved to establish their hegemony in the world and to rebuild war-torn Europe and Asia on a firm capitalist basis. The Soviet Union and insurgent Communist movements in various parts of the world became transformed from wartime allies against Hitler's Axis into the deadly enemies in a global Cold War confrontation. The American Communist Party—loyal to the world movement of which it was part, and continuing to follow the leadership of the Communist Party of the Soviet Union—suddenly found itself isolated. The left-wing trade union leaders of the CIO now paid a high price for their failure to distinguish themselves from their liberal colleagues in the labor movement, especially for their disinclination to build a substantial socialist-minded base among the organized industrial workers. Communist Party influence in the CIO was quickly smashed.[42]

If we define "revolutionary vanguard" as something that could have brought about a socialist revolution in the United States during the 1930s, such a vanguard was not able to come into existence. On the other hand, it might well have been objectively possible for revolutionary socialists to build a substantial organization capable of playing a key role in building the CIO, *without failing to build a conscious socialist base among a significant number of workers*. Such a vanguard might well have facilitated the growth and proliferation of independent caucuses, militant shop papers and other such activities among rank-and-file union members, as well as organized left-wing groupings to embrace and help develop the expansive if embryonic radicalism described by Len De Caux as existing among many workers during the heady "social movement" period of the early CIO. It also would have sought to advance working-class political independence by consistently educating and agitating around the need for a labor party—something which, according to such different observers as Art Preis and Len De Caux, might have been a possibility at the end of the decade.[43]

Such an orientation, which is not out of harmony with the actual historical experience that we have examined, could have contributed to the growing numbers and influence of a revolutionary vanguard but in a manner that might not have made it as vulnerable and weakened as the Communist Party became in the late 1940s and 1950s. It is possible that the left wing of the labor movement might have ultimately been larger and more durable, and it is conceivable that a labor party might have been formed. All of this could have provided a basis for further development of a working-class socialist movement that eventually—through the accumulation of experience by the working class as a whole—could reach its goal beyond the limits of the existing system.

CONCLUSIONS

It may be helpful to sum up the conclusions of this exploration in thesis form.

1. The experience of the United States in the 1930s demonstrates that while millions of working people may be profoundly affected by the same kinds of social and economic problems, they do not all think and act in the same way, and consequently they do not spontaneously organize themselves, in their majority, as a cohesive, combative economic and political force. In the most tumultuous years of the Great Depression, only a

minority of workers were actively involved in the class-struggle activities which transformed U.S. life and politics. This "vanguard" percentage of the working class may not have constituted more than 10 percent of the labor force at any one moment.

2. An essential element in the cohesion and mobilization of this working-class vanguard was the existence of activist organizations. The individual members of these vanguard organizations were able to develop the vision of an alternate reality to that of the status quo, a vision infused with idealism but also based on knowledge and experience not readily available to every member of the working class. This small minority was able to transcend, to some degree, the toils of everyday life, family commitments, and conformity to one's immediate community in order to make an essential commitment of time and energy for the substantial organizational work required to appeal effectively to and mobilize the larger working-class vanguard.

3. The activist vanguard organizations were diverse. Some were consciously nonrevolutionary, consisting largely of "mainstream" trade union formations committed to developing working-class power in order to protect workers' interests within capitalist society. Others were committed to developing working-class power to the extent that capitalist society would finally be overthrown and replaced by socialism. This socialist vanguard was, in turn, divided among various competing groups. Cooperation between the nonrevolutionary and revolutionary components of the activist vanguard was essential for the dramatic growth of the "mainstream" trade unions during the crisis of the 1930s.

4. It was not possible to make a working-class socialist revolution in the United States during the 1930s, if for no other reason than the absence of an experienced revolutionary leadership with authority among masses of workers. For all of the dramatic transformations that it experienced and underwent, the working class did not have sufficient time to go through the experience that would make it a self-consciously revolutionary force, and the various socialist vanguard organizations did not have sufficient time to develop the necessary experience and authority to provide leadership in such a revolution; more than this, a fragment of the capitalist class was able to forge a popular coalition for social reform which cut across working-class political independence and hegemony. This created a dilemma for the competing socialist vanguard organizations.

5. Among the socialist vanguard organizations, those which were more sectarian and unrealistic in their expectations simply disintegrated, while others (particularly the Socialist Party, the Social-Democratic Federation, and the Lovestoneites) eventually adapted to policies of nonrevolutionary trade unionists and forces of bourgeois social reform to such an extent that they were absorbed. The Trotskyist fragment of the Communist movement demonstrated some effectiveness in blending political realism with revolu-

tionary perspectives, but its forces were so small that it was incapable of competing for working-class leadership on a national scale, and finally it was forcibly suppressed in the one area (Minneapolis) where it was able to provide such leadership.

6. The Stalinist wing of the Communist movement, on the other hand, was substantial enough to become the major left-wing force in the labor movement, but it was fatally undermined by certain internal deficiencies which resulted in what was to become a self-destructive policy. While not totally absorbed into its nonsocialist milieu in the manner of most other left currents, it adapted to nonrevolutionary trade unionists and to the forces of pro-capitalist social reform to such an extent that it failed to build a conscious popular base significantly to the left of the capitalist political mainstream. This made it vulnerable to eventual isolation and destruction by an alliance of nonrevolutionary trade unionists, the powerful business community, both liberal and conservative pro-capitalist politicians, and the state apparatus.

7. The existence and efforts of the left-wing vanguard organizations were essential for the revitalization and giant step forward of the labor movement in the 1930s, and when combined with the vitality, the native intelligence, the creative energy, and anger inherent in the working-class majority, this giant step may have been inevitable, given the objective conditions brought on by the Great Depression. The eventual elimination of the left-wing vanguard, however, was not an inevitable result of objective circumstances—least of all was it a result of some alleged "backwardness" or deficiency or other characteristic innate to the U.S. working class. It is conceivable that an organization of the size and with the resources of the American Communist Party at the beginning of the 1930s could have followed a somewhat different political program than was in fact pursued. If this different program was applied intelligently—with a sensitivity to, a learning from, a respectful interaction with various layers of the U.S. working class—then it is possible that a stronger, more durable working-class left-wing movement would have emerged from the Depression decade.

8. It is conceivable that a successful program for a left-wing organization in the 1930s could have included not only a flexible and energetic united-front policy in building the new industrial unions, which the Communist Party displayed, but also: (a) a greater internal democracy and less sectarianism toward other left-wing groups; (b) a critical independence from the Stalin regime in the USSR; (c) an independence from the Democratic Party and consistent support for the development of an independent labor party—while recognizing and living with the fact that many friends and allies in the labor movement would be drawn into the New Deal (at least for a time); (d) an understanding of the revolutionary but relatively independent character of the African American struggle, which—far from

being subordinated to the needs of a liberal-labor coalition—should be supported as essential for the radicalization of the working class as a whole; and (e) persistent education and recruitment of newly unionized workers and others to an understanding of the class struggle and the need for workers' power and socialism.

NOTES

I am grateful to the late Frank Lovell and John Hinshaw for the careful critical reading they gave to this essay; their encouragement and criticial suggestions contributed to this final version. I should also mention the influence of anthropologist Carol McAllister, with whom I discussed many of these ideas over a period of years. The thesis advanced here was presented at a panel of the 1993 Socialist Scholars Conference, and I would like to thank copanelists Elaine Bernard and Dan Georgakas, and moderator Michael Frank—plus the audience participants—for valuable feedback. The panel presentations appeared in *Bulletin in Defense of Marxism*, and a shortened version of the present article has also been published in *Against the Current*: my thanks to the editors of both publications. Thanks are also due to my teacher David Montgomery, who inspired me to pursue such studies, and especially to my late parents, Gaston (Gus) Le Blanc and Shirley Le Blanc, who were part of the story that is recounted here, and who first taught me about the labor movement.

1. James R. Green, *The World of the Worker: Labor in Twentieth-Century America* (New York: Hill and Wang, 1980), 172–73.

2. Irving Bernstein, *Turbulent Years; A History of the American Worker, 1933–1941* (Boston: Houghton Mifflin Company, 1971), 775.

3. Michael Goldfield, "Worker Insurgency, Radical Organization, and New Deal Labor Legislation," *American Political Science Review* 83, no. 4 (December 1989): 1278; Irving Bernstein, *A Caring Society: The New Deal, the Worker, and the Great Depression* (Boston: Houghton Mifflin Company, 1985), 275, 285, 286, 298.

4. These strikes are described succinctly and passionately in a chapter titled "Three Strikes that Paved the Way" in Art Preis's classic, *Labor's Giant Step; Twenty Years of the CIO* (New York: Pathfinder Press, 1972), 19–33. In the *Turbulent Years*, Irving Bernstein's much longer chapter on these events (217–317) is entitled, simply, "Eruption."

5. Melvyn Dubofsky, "Not So 'Turbulent Years': A New Look at the 1930s," in *Life and Labor: Dimensions of American Working-Class History*, ed. Charles Stephenson and Robert Asher (Albany: State University of New York Press, 1986), 209.

6. Ibid., 213–15.

7. Louis Adamic, *My America, 1928–1938* (New York: Harper and Brothers, 1938), 446–47.

8. Dubofsky, "Not So 'Turbulent Years,'" 215–16; Robert S. and Helen Merrell Lynd, *Middletown in Transition; A Study in Cultural Conflicts* (New York: Harcourt, Brace and World, 1965), 41.

9. John Bodnar, *Workers' World: Kinship, Community, and Protest in Indus-*

trial Society, 1900–1940 (Baltimore: Johns Hopkins University Press, 1982), 166, 180, 182; John Bodnar, "Immigration, Kinship, and the Rise of Working-Class Realism in Industrial America," *Journal of Social History* 14, no. 1 (fall 1980): 47, 48, 50, 53, 55.

10. Bodnar, "Immigration, Kinship, and Working-Class Realism in Industrial America," 56, 57, 58–59.

11. Alice and Staughton Lynd, eds., *Rank and File: Personal Histories by Working-Class Organizers* (Boston: Beacon Press, 1973), 4–5. See also Staughton Lynd, ed., *American Labor Radicalism; Testimonies and Interpretations* (New York: John Wiley & Sons, 1973).

12. Bodnar, *Workers' World*, 183.

13. Dubofsky, "Not So 'Turbulent Years,'" 218, 219.

14. Martin Dies, *The Trojan Horse in America* (New York: Dodd, Mead & Co., 1940), 146–47; Eugene Lyons, *The Red Decade; The Stalinist Penetration of America* (Indianapolis: Bobbs-Merrill Co., 1941), 223; Bert Cochran, *Labor and Communism: The Conflict that Shaped American Unions* (Princeton: Princeton University Press, 1977), 97.

15. Saul Alinsky, *John L. Lewis, An Unauthorized Biography* (New York: Vintage Books, 1970), 152–55; Cochran, *Labor and Communism*, 98–99. On membership figures, see George Breitman, Paul Le Blanc, and Alan Wald, *Trotskyism in the United States: Historical Essays and Reconsiderations* (Amherst, N.Y.: Humanity Books, 1996), 72; Robert J. Alexander, *The Right Opposition: The Lovestoneites and the International Communist Opposition of the 1930s* (Westport, Conn.: Greenwood Press, 1981), 29–30; David A. Shannon, *The Socialist Party of America* (Chicago: Quadrangle Books, 1967), 249; Harvey Klehr, *The Heyday of American Communism: The Depression Decade* (New York: BasicBooks, 1984), 153, 225.

16. Benjamin Stolberg, *The Story of the CIO* (New York: Viking Press, 1938), 124.

17. Ibid., 124–25.

18. Ibid., 127.

19. Ibid., 127–28. For sharply different (yet in some ways compatible) portraits and evaluations of Stolberg by contemporaries, see the friendly comments in Adamic, *My America*, 72–86, 329, 425, 654, and the unfriendly ones in Len De Caux, *Labor Radical; From the Wobblies to CIO, A Personal History* (Boston: Beacon Press, 1970), 204, 207–208, 314, 406.

20. Daniel Bell, *The End of Ideology; On the Exhaustion of Political Ideas in the Fifties*, rev. ed. (New York: Free Press, 1965), 293–94.

21. Jeremy Brecher, *Strike! The True History of Mass Insurgencies in America from 1877 to the Present—As Authentic Revolutionary Movements against the Establishments of State, Capital, and Trade Unionism* (San Francisco: Straight Arrow Books, 1972), 234.

22. Ibid., 252–53.

23. Ibid., 257. A similar argument is advanced by George Lipsitz in his generally excellent study *Rainbow at Midnight: Labor and Culture in the 1940s* (Urbana: University of Illinois Press, 1994), 9, 10, 197—but Lipsitz confuses Leninism with Stalinism and, like Brecher, fails to prove his antivanguard assertions.

24. David Brody, *Workers in Industrial America: Essays on the Twentieth Century Struggle* (New York: Oxford University Press, 1980), 133, 165.

25. Dubofsky, "Not So 'Turbulent Years,'" 221. The importance of "old-line Socialists" in the deradicalization of the labor Left is demonstrated—in different ways—by: David Dubinsky and A. H. Raskin, *David Dubinsky: A Life With Labor* (New York: Atheneum, 1978); Steven Fraser, *Labor Will Rule: Sidney Hillman and the Rise of American Labor* (New York: Free Press, 1991). This process can also be traced in various contributions to Melvyn Dubofsky and Warren Van Tine, eds., *Labor Leaders in America* (Urbana: University of Illinois Press, 1987). In *The Politics of U.S. Labor: From the Great Depression to the New Deal* (New York: Monthly Review Press, 1982), 121–38, David Milton shows that—although the Communist Party "controlled unions [that] contained 25 percent of the CIO's total membership and Communists wielded considerable influence in unions with another 25 percent," through skillful maneuvering (and with assistance from such figures as Hillman, and the Communists themselves)—left-wing influence was undermined and Democratic Party influence expanded to such an extent that by the early 1940s one could assert: "Roosevelt Captures the CIO." The complex dialectical interplay between radicalism, nonradicalism, radicalization, and deradicalization among rank and file and leadership is explored in various works already cited, as well as: Nelson Lichtenstein, *Labor's War at Home: The CIO in World War II* (Cambridge: Cambridge University Press, 1982); Gary Gerstle, *Working-Class Americanism: The Politics of Labor in a Textile City, 1914–1960* (Cambridge: Cambridge University Press, 1989); Lizabeth Cohen, *Making a New Deal: Industrial Workers in Chicago, 1919–1939* (Cambridge: Cambridge University Press, 1990); Steve Rosswurm, ed., *The CIO's Left-Led Unions* (New Brunswick: Rutgers University Press, 1992).

26. Roger Keeran, *The Communist Party and the Auto Workers Unions* (Bloomington: Indiana University Press, 1980), 202–203. The truth in Keeran's argument corresponds to a point made in David Saposs's classic *Left-Wing Unionism* (New York: International Publishers, 1926), 190: if radicals "regard these unions merely as a vehicle for propagating their doctrines rather than as agencies that must attend to the daily economic problems of the workers then they will lose the masses and dwindle down to propaganda nuclei. Their allegiance can be retained only by effective disciplinary machinery and tangible current economic benefits and services. The union must not only serve as an emotional outlet." But in *Left-Wing Unionism* we find the thought that it would be possible for "the communists [to] demonstrate the knack of co-ordinating the idealistic with the practical," a notion that seems to get lost in Keeran's argument.

27. E. H. Carr, "A Historical Turning Point: Marx, Lenin, Stalin," in Richard Pipes, ed., *Revolutionary Russia: A Symposium* (New York: Anchor Books, 1969), 371–72, 374; C. L. R. James [writing as A. A. B.], "Philosophy of History and Necessity: A Few Words with Professor Hook," *New International* (October 1943): 276. Related points on the Leninist variant of "elitism" as being profoundly different from that of other political theorists can be found in George L. Mosse, *The Culture of Western Europe* (Boulder, Colo.: Westview Press, 1988), 297–312; and Antonio Gramsci, "The Modern Prince," in *Selections from the Prison Notebooks* (New York: International Publishers, 1973), especially 133–36, 144–47, 152–53, 204–205. See also Ernest Mandel, "The

Leninist Theory of Organization," in *Revolutionary Marxism and Social Reality in the Twentieth Century: Collected Essays by Ernest Mandel*, ed. Steve Bloom (Amherst, N.Y.: Humanity Books, 1994), 77–197; and Paul Le Blanc, *Lenin and the Revolutionary Party* (Amherst, N.Y.: Humanity Books, 1990).

28. Rosa Luxemburg, "Organizational Question of Social Democracy," in *Rosa Luxemburg Speaks*, ed. Mary-Alice Waters (New York: Pathfinder Press, 1970), 119, 128–29.

29. Ibid., 129. For surveys on theories of the labor movement, see: Simeon Larson and Bruce Nissen, eds., *Theories of the Labor Movement* (Detroit: Wayne State University Press, 1987); and Tom Clarke and Laurie Clements, eds., *Trade Unions Under Capitalism* (Atlantic Highlands, N.J.: Humanities Press, 1978). The theories must, of course, be tested against empirical reality, some of which is documented in James Green, ed., *Workers' Struggles, Past and Present: A "Radical America" Reader* (Philadelphia: Temple University Press, 1983); and James Green, *The World of the Worker: Labor in Twentieth-Century America* (New York: Hill & Wang, 1980).

30. Brody, *Workers in Industrial America*, 136.

31. James P. Cannon, *History of American Trotskyism* (New York: Pathfinder Press, 1972), 80, 81.

32. Aspects of the moderate Socialist trajectory are approvingly traced in Ben Stolberg's glowing portrait of the International Ladies Garment Workers Union under David Dubinsky, *Tailor's Progress; The Story of a Famous Union and the Men Who Made It* (Garden City, N.Y.: Doubleday and Doran, 1944); and in Irving Howe and B. J. Widick, *The UAW and Walter Reuther* (New York: Random House, 1949). Additional insight and information is offered in Nelson Lichtenstein, *Walter Reuther: The Most Dangerous Man in Detroit* (Urbana: University of Illinois Press, 1997); in Frank Marquart's fine memoir, *An Auto Worker's Journal: The UAW From Crusade to One-Party Union* (University Park: Pennsylvania State University Press, 1975); and in the important contribution by Sol Dollinger and Genora Johnson Dollinger, *Not Automatic: Women and the Left in the Forging of the Auto Workers Union* (New York: Monthly Review Press, 2000). Harry Fleischman's *Norman Thomas; A Biography: 1884–1968* (New York: W. W. Norton, 1969) describes the Socialist Party leader's accomodation (by the late 1940s) to the predominant domestic and foreign policies of U.S. capitalism—concluding, first of all, that Roosevelt's New Deal, "while advancing the country toward a welfare state, destroyed the possibility of building a strong electoral Socialist Party," and, secondly, that "the outstanding conflict today is between democracy, with all its human and capitalist imperfections, and totalitarian despotism" represented by Communism (248, 254). A fragment of the Trotskyists, which broke away in 1940 under the leadership of Max Shachtman, also ended up in the moderate Socialist trajectory described here—a story told in Peter Drucker, *Max Shachtman and His Left: A Socialist's Odyssey Through the "American Century"* (Amherst, N.Y.: Humanity Books, 1994), 185–320. The general political orientation is documented and critically dissected in two essays to be found in Burton H. Hall, ed., *Autocracy and Insurgency in Organized Labor* (New Brunswick, N.J.: Transaction Books, 1972) by knowledgeable left-wing veterans: Sidney Lens, "Labor Lieutenants and the Cold War," and Julius

Jacobson, "Coalitionism: From Protest to Politicking," 310–45. The even more rightward trajectory of the Lovestoneites is traced in Alexander, *The Right Opposition*, and in Ted Morgan, *A Covert Life: Jay Lovestone, Communist, Anti-Communist and Spymaster* (New York: Random House, 1999). Paul Buhle's *Taking Care of Business: Samuel Gompers, George Meany, Lane Kirkland and the Tragedy of American Labor* (New York: Monthly Review Press, 1999) provides an analysis of the broader context in which such deradicalization took place.

33. The memoir of an experienced union organizer who, as a young radical, went to Minneapolis in 1936, gives a vivid sense of the Trotskyists there: "The toughness of the leaders was combined with a hard, spare, ascetic quality that became a model for all of us. . . . The very intensity and grimness of the radical movement in Minneapolis left little room for errors or weakness. After only a few weeks in Minneapolis, I understood very well how it was possible for this group of men to successfully run the teamsters' union and why the Minneapolis general strike had been run like a military operation: Ray Dunne and the people around him were very serious revolutionists" (Paul Jacobs, *Is Curly Jewish? A Political Self-Portrait Illuminating Three Turbulent Decades of Social Revolt—1935–1965* [New York: Atheneum, 1965], 52–53). In the pamphlet *Trade Union Problems* (New York: Pioneer Publishers, n.d. [1940?], 35–37), a veteran of the Minneapolis experience named Farrell Dobbs outlined the Trotskyist approach:

> To win the confidence and respect of the workers it is necessary to show them capabilities of leadership through practical demonstrations of ability. A leader must strive to be the most useful member of the union. He must be efficient even in the smallest details of union work and must not be afraid to do the Jimmy Higgins duties. The workers respect most those who volunteer their service on any and all union business and who are at the same time courageous fighters on the picket line.
>
> The flippant use of trite names, hackneyed language, and patent formulas should be avoided. Terms such as "bureaucrat," "faker," "sell-out," "betrayal," are dangerous if lightly used. Laziness of thought is caused by this tendency to substitute a catch-phrase for a serious analysis. The workers are not very much impressed by bombastic language. They respond much better to a penetrating analysis and the resultant convincing arguments. Any other presentation is apt to discredit the critic instead of the criticized.
>
> There are no patent policies for the handling of trade union questions. That which applies in one case may work with opposite effect in another. One must study the industry in which he is organizing. . . . Policy in the trade unions must flow from a careful analysis of specific conditions and the resultant general conclusions. . . . It must be remembered that not all who practice class collaboration in one form or another are conscious class collaborationists. The question is one of level and direction of development. . . . A worker who through ignorance scabs today may be a militant striker another day. A leader who at one time supports reactionary policies may at a later time become a progressive. The ideology of human beings is

not a static thing, especially in the labor movement. . . . Ways and means must be found to attempt to cause each individual in the movement to voluntarily, or if necessary involuntarily, play a certain progressive role.

It must be remembered that each trade union is a tiny mirror which reflects a small though distorted image of the whole class. On the right stands the class collaborationists, the conscious reactionaries. On the left are the elements who stand for the class struggle. Between these two forces lies the great mass of the trade union membership, deceived by false education, poisoned by vicious propaganda, chained to the wheel of capitalist exploitation, ground down by the struggle for their daily bread, dreaming of freedom but failing to understand the only road to its realization. The progressive seeks to guide these masses along the road of the class struggle. The class collaborationists seek not only to block this road, but also to drive the progressives out of the leadership, and if necessary, out of the unions. In spite of this brake upon them the workers surge forward in struggle, only to recede again into a period of passivity. The progressive must learn to understand the moods of the masses and he must adjust his tactics to them.

The rise and fall of this revolutionary socialist current in the International Brotherhood of Teamsters is recounted in four richly detailed volumes by Farrell Dobbs: *Teamster Rebellion* (New York: Monad Press, 1972), *Teamster Power* (New York: Monad Press, 1973), *Teamster Politics* (New York: Monad Press, 1975), *Teamster Bureaucracy* (New York: Monad Press, 1977). A Trotskyist "insider's" account of struggles in the maritime industry can be found in Frederick J. Lang [Frank Lovell], *Maritime! A Historical Sketch and a Workers' Program* (New York: Pioneer Publishers, 1943), and a similar perspective is applied to a broader scope of experience in Tom Kerry, *Workers, Bosses, and Bureaucrats: A Socialist View of Labor Struggles Since the 1930s* (New York: Pathfinder Press, 1980). A snapshot of the Trotskyists in 1938 is offered by an informative interview with George Breitman on pages 17–36 of *The Founding of the Socialist Workers Party: Minutes and Resolutions, 1938–1939*, ed. George Breitman (New York: Monad Press, 1982). Valuable material can be found in Paul Le Blanc, ed., *Revolutionary Labor Socialist: The Life, Ideas and Comrades of Frank Lovell* (New York: Smyrna Press, 2000). See also Preis, *Labor's Giant Step*, as well as Breitman, Le Blanc, and Wald, *Trotskyism in the United States*.

34. Earl Browder, "The American Communist Party in the Thirties," in *How We Saw the Thirties*, ed. Rita James Simon (Urbana: University of Illinois Press, 1967), 230, 231. There are controversies over Communist Party gains in the union-organizing drives of the 1930s and the precise nature of its working-class base. In *The Communist Party of the United States: From Depression to World War II* (New Brunswick, N.J.: Rutgers University Press, 1991), 154, Fraser Ottarelli cites CP reports that party membership rose from 37,000 to 60,000 in 1937, and 50 percent belonged either to the AFL or the CIO, but he adds that there were complaints from CP leaders in mid-1938 that the total membership of approximately 75,000 included only 27,000 union members. In *The Heyday of American Communism*,

Harvey Klehr writes that the percentage of CP members in unions rose from 20 percent in 1934, to 36 percent in 1935, to 40 percent in 1936—fluctuating at that level for the rest of the decade, concluding: "In 1938 it was necessary to add the unemployed members of the Workers Alliance to get '50 percent of the active in trade unions and unemployed organizations'" (378).

Nathan Glazer argues in *The Social Basis of American Communism* (New York: Harcourt, Brace and World, 1961), 114, that although "the upsurge in union organization . . . did create for the first time a large number of unions under Communist control," even in industries where the party had a powerful base, "it did not have what might be called a mass membership" except in the marine and longshore unions. However, Glazer's assertion that "in many respects the party was less of the working class in the late thirties than in the early thirties," that it was transformed instead into a "middle-class" organization, strikes me as somewhat dubious—being largely based on the assertion that "the professional and white-collar membership of the party rose even faster than the working-class membership." The "middle-class" occupations cited by Glazer—accounting for 44 percent of CP membership in 1941—include teachers, office workers, sales clerks, all of whom sold their labor-power to employers in order to make a living, the classic definition of a proletarian. On this theoretical issue, see Martin Oppenheimer, *White Collar Politics* (New York: Monthly Review Press, 1985). See also Harry Braverman, "The Making of the U.S. Working Class," *Monthly Review* (November 1994), reprinted in this volume.

The occupational diversity within the working class—and the consequent variations in class consciousness—is a complex issue, complicated further by the fact, noted by Burton J. Bledstein, that in 1940 "79.2 percent of the population considered itself to be middle class, a group that included industrial workers, white-collar service employees, civil servants, technologists, professionals, small and big businessmen" (*The Culture of Professionalism: The Middle Class and the Development of Higher Education in America* [New York: W. W. Norton and Co., 1976], 3). The fact remains that the great majority of those in the "vanguard" organizations we have discussed were—in Marxist terms—"objectively" part of the working class, and that they had significant influence in the struggles and within the new unions of militant layers of the working class in the 1930s.

35. Mary Heaton Vorse, *Labor's New Millions* (New York: Modern Age Books, 1938), 294–95, 285; De Caux, *Labor Radical*, 242–43.

36. William Z. Foster, *History of the Communist Party of the United States* (New York: International Publishers, 1952), 348; Stanley Aronowitz, "Trade Unionism and Workers' Control," in *Workers' Control: A Reader on Labor and Social Change*, ed. Gerry Hunnius, G. David Garson, and John Case (New York: Vintage Books, 1973), 91–92. One Communist Party leader who was expelled in the late 1940s, Max Bedacht, later "argued strongly . . . that the abolition of the fractions led to the withering of the Communist rank-and-file in the trade unions, and the strengthening of the power of the Communist trade-union officials," writes Nathan Glazer in *The Social Basis of American Communism* (219). At the 1950 convention of the Communist Party, Henry Winston offered a devastating portrait of the once-militant Communist trade union leader who—as time went on—"did not see the need for a mass Party in the industry [represented by his union] because, said

he, the union leadership is more capable, more effective in bringing the policies of the Party to the workers" through "smart moves" and shrewd maneuvers, coupled with effective union policies which "got gains for the workers without much difficulty and little struggle" (Henry Winston, *What It Means to Be a Communist* [New York: New Century Publisher, 1951], 6–7). A powerful business counterattack after World War II suddenly brought the labor movement under intense pressure, and Cold War anti-Communism threatened left-wing union leaders who had been accepted by the bulk of their (yet-to-be radicalized) unions' members in spite of the leaders' radical politics. In many cases the "progressive" union officials eventually shifted away from their left-wing commitments. In others, the withering of a left-wing base left them vulnerable to attack and removal—or where they survived made it impossible for them to mobilize the union ranks around more radical issues.

37. Earl Browder, *The People's Front* (New York: International Publishers, 1938), 13; Browder, "The American Communist Party in the Thirties," 236, 237; Theodore Draper, "American Communism Revisited," in *A Present of Things Past: Selected Essays* (New York: Hill and Wang, 1990), 141; E. H. Carr, *Twilight of the Comintern, 1930–1935* (New York: Pantheon Books, 1982), 152–55, 403–27.

Left-liberal journalist Louis Fischer was close to top government and Comintern sources in Moscow, and a strong supporter of the new policy. He reports that Stalin's government, "pursuing its own interests" in developing "allies among foreign governments and foreign popular movements" in order to overcome its isolation in the face of a growing threat from Nazi Germany, changed the orientation of Communists throughout the world; they now "forsook active advocacy of revolution and extended their hand to all parties and persons who wanted to stop Fascist aggression. . . . The Popular Front . . . was an acceptance of the social status quo in capitalist states. It meant not revolution but, instead, collaboration with nonrevolutionary and reformist parties which wanted social change by democratic means." See Louis Fischer, *Men and Politics, An Autobiography* (New York: Duell, Sloan and Pearce, 1941), 305, 308, 311.

According to Sam Darcy, a U.S. Communist in Moscow in 1935–36, Stalin was among the first in the Comintern to conclude that his American comrades should support Franklin Roosevelt as part of the Popular Front effort (Klehr, *The Heyday of American Communism*, 189).

38. Harry Haywood, in *Black Bolshevik: Autobiography of an Afro-American Communist* (Chicago: Liberator Press, 1978), 533; C. L. R. James, "The Revolutionary Answer to the Negro Problem in the United States," in *C. L. R. James and Revolutionary Marxism, Selected Writings of C. L. R. James 1939–1949*, ed. Scott McLemee and Paul Le Blanc (Amherst, N.Y.: Humanity Books, 1994); Robin D. G. Kelley, *Hammer and Hoe: Alabama Communists During the Great Depression* (Chapel Hill: University of North Carolina Press, 1990), 157–75; Robin D. G. Kelley, "Birmingham, Alabama," *Encyclopedia of the American Left*, ed. Mari Jo Buhle, Paul Buhle, and Dan Georgakas (Urbana: University of Illinois Press, 1992), 89; Hosea Hudson, with Nell Irvin Painter, *The Narrative of Hosea Hudson, His Life as a Negro Communist in the South* (Cambridge, Mass.: Harvard University Press, 1979), 245; James Wrenn, "Abner Winston Berry (Babu Sufu) (1902–87)," *Encyclopedia of the American Left*, 85–86; Mark Naison, *Communists in Harlem During*

the Depression (Urbana: University of Illinois Press, 1983), 280; Charles Denby, *Indignant Heart, A Black Worker's Journal* (Boston: South End Press, 1978), 163.

39. Haywood, *Black Bolshevik*, 548, 557, 630; C. L. R. James, "The SWP and Negro Work," in Breitman, *The Founding of the Socialist Workers Party*, 357; James, "The Revolutionary Answer to the Negro Problem in the United States," in McLemee and Le Blanc, *C. L. R. James and Revolutionary Marxism*, 185–86. See Daniel Guerin, *Negroes on the March: A Frenchman's Report on the American Negro Struggle*, trans. and ed. Duncan Ferguson (New York: George L. Weissman, 1956), which offers a well-informed critical analysis of CP policies within the broader and thoughtful discussion of African American realities. A more positive account is offered in Gerald Horne, *Black and Red: W. E. B. Du Bois and the Afro-American Response to the Cold War, 1944–1963* (Albany: State University of New York Press, 1986), esp. 289–311.

40. Richard O. Boyer and Herbert M. Morais, *Labor's Untold Story* (New York: Cameron Associates, 1955), 274–75. Whatever its limitations, this book contributed greatly to the education of many thousands of working-class activists and others; the particular copy I utilize was inscribed in 1960 by an old left-wing garment worker, Harry Brodsky, to his great-grandson Paul.

41. Hudson, *The Narrative of Hosea Hudson*, 307. Such perspectives generated harsh judgments among some militant blacks, such as Detroit radical Dr. Edgar Keemer: "Obviously, the 'Communist' Party had been diverted in its aims for Marxist replacement of an exploitive world capitalist system into a mere tool of the leaders of the Soviet Union. The current political line now came first, ahead of the needs of the multiracial world's working class" (*Confessions of a Pro-Life Abortionist* [Detroit: Vinco Press, 1980], 110). For a time Keemer became a member of the Socialist Workers Party—see C. L. R. James, George Breitman, Edgar Keemer, and others, *Fighting Racism in World War II*, ed. Fred Stanton (New York: Monad Press, 1980).

42. David Caute, *The Great Fear: The Anti-Communist Purge Under Truman and Eisenhower* (New York: Simon and Schuster, 1978), 349–400. Also see Ann Fagan Ginger and David Christiano, eds., *The Cold War Against Labor*, 2 vols. (Berkeley: Meiklejohn Civil Liberties Institute, 1987); for a more critical perspective, consult Cochran, *Labor and Communism*, 248–331.

Harry Haywood, in *Black Bolshevik*, noted that the policy of adhering to "the Roosevelt-labor-democratic coalition" was a political line around which "the Party remained spellbound" from the late 1930s until well after 1945, poorly preparing the Communists for what was about to happen: "So-called progressive-center labor leaders like Walter Reuther and Phillip Murray bolted with lightning speed to the side of the imperialists. The NAACP leaders involved themselves in a vicious red-baiting campaign, as the government began gearing up for full enforcement of the Smith Act" (558–59). Former CP seaman Bill Bailey later concurred that the Party had helped to set itself up for a fall, recalling that he had been uncomfortable but acquiescent in the early 1940s "when the Party was gloating about some Trotskyists being rounded up and jailed during the war and charged with conspiracy under the Smith Act. Oh, how the Party cheered the government on! But only a few years later the government would be doing the same thing to the leadership of our Party as we screamed our heads off that it was harassment" (Bill Bailey, *The Kid From Hoboken: An Autobiography* [San Francisco: Circus Lithographic Repress; distributed by Smyrna Press, 1993], 418).

A quite valuable survey of this period is offered in George Lipsitz, *A Rainbow at Midnight*. Well worth reading is a novel presenting a case study of the U.S. working class and labor movement from the mid-1940s to mid-1950s: K. B. Gilden (Katya and Bert Gilden), *Between the Hills and the Sea* (Ithaca, N.Y.: ILR Press, 1989).

43. Preis, *Labor's Giant Step*, 80–81; De Caux, *Labor Radical*, 356–67. The political radicalization within the working class transformed political life throughout the country. Much of this flowed into support for Franklin D. Roosevelt since "many individual workers and CIO officials hoped to accomplish working-class objectives through the Democratic Party," as Lizabeth Cohen points out, although the Democrats would actually prove to be committed to "less progressive goals" (Cohen, *Making a New Deal*, 366). But potential clearly existed for this expression of independent working-class politics.

Eric Davin offers detailed examination of how class-struggle dynamics in Western Pennsylvania workplaces and communities resulted in a "political revolution"—with militant workers taking over the Democratic Party and, interpreting Roosevelt's New Deal policies with a radical "blue-collar democracy" twist—profoundly altered power relations in a region previously dominated by conservative Republicans. (See Eric Leif Davin, "Blue-Collar Democracy: Class War and Political Revolution in Western Pennsylvania, 1932–1937," *Pennsylvania History* 67, no. 2 [spring 2000]: 240–97.) He has also demonstrated that this radicalizing ferment took form in other contexts of widespread sentiment for the formation of an independent labor party among a fairly broad range of CIO activists throughout the country. He documents that powerful forces, especially in the upper echelons of the CIO, ultimately channeled this into the Democratic Party. (See Eric Leif Davin, "The Very Last Hurrah: The Defeat of the Labor Party Idea, 1934–36," in *"We Are All Leaders": The Alternative Unionism of the Early 1930s*, ed. Staughton Lynd [New York: Monthly Review Press, 1996], 117–71.)

The force that could have consistently and effectively kept the labor party idea alive, in the face of such pressures, was the Communist Party. Some latter-day commentators have been inclined to argue that it would not have been possible for the Communist Party to maintain its alliance with less radical CIO leaders, let alone to enjoy any authority among the masses of CIO rank and file, by holding back from the Democratic Party. But this is not clear from the historical evidence. It is instructive to note that in 1936—while giving roundabout support to Roosevelt—the Communist Party had yet to abandon its support for a labor party based on the trade unions, and in many cases it aggressively ran its own local candidates on the Communist ticket, sometimes winning substantial numbers of votes. As Harvey Klehr—by no means a radical enthusiast—has pointed out, in the earlier period when the Communists opposed orienting to the Democrats, they had demonstrated their skill in the electoral arena in being able to "differ . . . without getting estranged from" CIO allies who had thrown themselves fully into the Democratic Party (Klehr, *The Heyday of American Communism*, 188, 195–96).

10

THE ROLE OF WOMEN, AND OF RADICALS, IN THE FIRST SIT-DOWN STRIKES

An Interview with Genora Johnson Dollinger

KATHLEEN O'NAN

The interview was done on February 4, 1995, transcribed by Lee DeNoyer, and edited by Kathleen O'Nan for publication in the Bulletin in Defense of Marxism. *O'Nan has been the chapter organizer of the Los Angeles Metro Chapter of Labor Party Advocates (LPA). At the time of the interview, Genora Dollinger was in her eighties and an active member of the LPA chapter, along with her husband, Sol Dollinger, who worked at the Chevrolet Assembly Plant in Flint, Michigan. Genora Dollinger was born on April 20, 1913, and died on October 11, 1995.*

Genora Dollinger played a pivotal role in the formation of the United Auto Workers (UAW) and the crucial strikes of 1936–37 in Flint, Michigan. It is often said that without her work during the auto sit-down strikes, the UAW might not exist today. Dollinger was recently inducted into the Michigan Women's Hall of Fame. At the ceremony, Sophie and Victor Reuther said:

"Genora is of the great tradition of Mother Jones, who in an earlier generation was to the Mine Workers what Genora became to the Auto Workers. A living legend in her own time."

Dollinger was only twenty-three years old when the strike against Gen-

From *Bulletin in Defense of Marxism*, no. 123 (March 1995). Reprinted by permission.

eral Motors began. She immediately saw the necessity of developing a support system for the beleaguered strikers and started a Women's Auxiliary, in which women played a role beyond the traditional one of setting up soup kitchens, the main role of women's support groups of the time. She saw that it was necessary to explain that the spouses of the strikers had as much to lose or gain as the strikers themselves and therefore had as much business on the picket lines as the striking men.

The police and the company escalated their tactics to try to break the strike, in what became known as the Battle of Bulls Run, which left thirteen unionists shot and many others injured. Dollinger likewise escalated the tactics of the women, founding the militant Women's Emergency Brigade. These women became the backbone of support for the strikers, with duties ranging from walking the picket lines, even when attacked with billy clubs and tear gas, to outreach in Flint and other GM cities to gather broader support.

Just after leaving the Dollinger household, having completed this interview, I turned on the radio and caught part of a speech by a UAW retiree, who was talking about how changes have come about in America. He said he had been reminded recently of how the UAW had been formed. His story is dramatically different from Genora's: he said that Henry Ford had vowed that he would shut down all of his factories all over the world before he would ever "permit" a union to exist in one of them. His wife, "that sweet, quiet woman," looked at him and "with gentleness, but firmness" said: "Henry, if you do that, I shall have to leave you." The speaker applauded the courage of Mrs. Ford and credited her with being the critical factor in the strikers' victories. I think that the account which follows is a much more accurate reflection of history and of truth.

—Kathleen O'Nan

Q: *You were a founding member of the United Auto Workers Union (UAW) in 1936, and you were a leading figure in the 1936–37 Flint, Michigan, sit-down strike. Can you give us a little background on how both of those events occurred, the formation of the union, and the reasons behind the strike?*

A: I think everybody knows that during the Great Depression of that period workers were in a state of fermentation. They were talking about needing better conditions not only at home and in the streets but in the shops, where they were treated with less care and less respect than the machines in the automobile factories. Having read again just recently a reminder of what the conditions were in those shops, I remember that the men would complain—and I say men in this case because there were only men employed in the shop in the Flint area where the sit-down strike first began and where it was won—so I'm talking about this one part of the UAW which decided the great victory of the organization.

The men in the shop were recalling in the fifty-eighth anniversary issue of their union paper that the conditions in the shop then were so vile that they were not only coming down with diseases, like tuberculosis, and injuries, like losing fingers and hands, but the air was so thick with black fumes and smoke, and so bad from the fumes of the chemicals in the shop, that even when they took a bath and washed off and put on clean clothes, when they perspired they had brown sweat because of the chemicals that had gone into their system.

WORSENING CONDITIONS

The worsening of conditions in the shops made these men feel that they could no longer live this way. And of course their families suffered just as much, because they were not getting adequate wages for their long, long hours and unpaid overtime. They had no control over the hours they worked in the shop. If production was low, they were called in for two hours, then they were sent home, no call-in pay, no nothing. Or they could be asked to work twenty hours. Just keep them right on the job.

So they had no feeling of any human dignity at all—whether inside the shop or in the streets outside the shop. If a man became ill—and this happened of course in my case too—and called in and said he was ill (and he had to be very ill to miss a day in the shop), they would send a man out to investigate, and I mean with a gun. They would send a man out from General Motors, and he would come up on your porch and demand to come in your house and see the employee who was ill.

It was a threatening situation, where you had no power. The city was controlled lock, stock, and barrel. The city council and all of the courts and all of the city administration were controlled by General Motors. You had no feeling of security on the job at any time. If you made some remark or some stool pigeon attributed some remark to you, the boss could come in and just fire you. No question about it. You had no rights, and you had no seniority. Whether you had been there a long time or a short time, they put you on any job they decided they wanted you on.

TOTAL COMPANY CONTROL

If you had to go to the bathroom, these men had to wait for a relief man sometimes so long that their kidneys and their bladder systems were really wrecked. You were clocked from the moment you left the line when you went to the bathroom—a pretty dignified name for this hole in the wall. There was only one bathroom on each floor of this huge plant employing thousands of workers. Immediately after you came out someone would pop in to see if there were any cigarette butts in the toilet bowl, to see if you used a couple of extra minutes to smoke a cigarette.

So tremendous speedup was occurring. General Motors wanted more and more production. There was less and less consideration for the workforce. And the speedup became so bad that men were actually cracking up on the job. They would take a wrench and go after the foreman. Then they would have to appear before a committee in the city, and they would be sent to what in those days was called an insane asylum, in another city close by. We had a lot of autoworkers committed just because they were strung out so bad that at the least little thing they would react violently. They had some shutdowns in departments over such incidents, and this was a harbinger of the future, but it didn't make any difference to GM. There was no discussion with the workers about anything, any of the conditions under which they had to work.

It became so unendurable that one plant sat down for a few hours and got away with it the first time. This encouraged everybody else, because they realized that as one person there was nothing they could do, but as a department or a group organization they had more strength.

Q: *Let me go back for a minute. Did you say there was one sit-down that lasted several hours? What did it accomplish?*

A: There were several incidents like that, for immediate solution of a problem on the job. One was over a couple of brothers, the Perkins brothers, who were fired by Fisher Body Company without any reason whatsoever. The workers just decided that was it. And they sat down and refused to work. They sat down at their workbenches and on the line and refused to work until those boys were brought back in and reinstated. They were two young men, and General Motors actually had to send people out all over the city to locate those guys and bring them back into the department and show that they were on the job again in order for that section of the plant to start operating again.

It was always a local issue: it was the speedup, it was somebody getting injured unnecessarily because the machine wasn't functioning properly. And these were the things that began to encourage workers to thinking that if you got a group to demonstrate, you got results a hell of a lot quicker than just by pleading and begging on your own.

THE ROLE OF RADICAL ORGANIZATIONS

During this whole period of ferment, there is one thing that many historians don't stress. I'm sure they have been told about it many times, but they think that this is something separate and aside from the general development. That was that in Flint we had a number of organizations of minority political parties. I was a member of the Socialist Party. I was one of the founding members of a branch that was reconstructed after a lapse of several years. We had had a socialist mayor (John Menton) elected in that city in 1911. And we had a Communist Party, and during the period of their "red trade union" days they actually organized a walkout at one Fisher Body plant and they were chased by the police over the county line.

The Proletarian Party had classes constantly, around the clock, in Marxism, in genuine Marxist study, of *Das Kapital*, volume one, volume two, etc. That didn't include the majority of the workers, of course, but you had a group in the Proletarian Party that was very active in Fisher Body in talking to workers, telling them why these things were coming about and what had to be done.

The Socialist Party organized classes in labor history. It happened that the headquarters for the Socialist Party, the Proletarian Party, and the Socialist Labor Party were all in the same big historic building where the union offices were on one floor. It was an old, rickety building, but it was something we could afford. And workers were coming up to find out what could be done and we would get to know them. We gave classes in labor history to let them know that there were gains that had been made and that there were labor leaders who had given their lives for the organization of labor.

Then we had a number of old-time Wobblies, the Industrial Workers of the World (IWW), who were coming to Flint to work in the factories, and they were not so much political as what you'd call just damn good "rabble rousers." That was a very affectionate term for anyone who had the courage and the guts to get up there and blow off against the corporation and dared them to do something about it.

THE WORKERS GET SOME TRAINING

In the beginning the people who came down to the union hall were very new and were intimidated by the corporation and the whole city apparatus and felt threatened. Many of them were followed when they would come to talk with the unionists, and when they came out they were beaten badly and would end up with black eyes and broken bones. In our first strike we noticed that the secondary leaders in the plant and groups of people, especially in Chevrolet, who had gone to classes in labor history, parliamentary procedure, and public speaking and had all this training before, that they played a big role. We knew that was part of the reason why we had such a tremendous victory in our first strike against the corporation.

I'm emphasizing the political preparation that was made for such an event, a strike such as this. For instance, the Reuther brothers, who have become famous now because of their role in the UAW from the beginning to even the present day (in the case of Victor Reuther), all attended the Brookwood Labor College, which was a socialist college, and many of the speakers who were there were also active in an organization called the League for Industrial Democracy.

From 1934 to 1936 we socialists organized these big meetings. We held them in the basement of the largest Methodist church in this area, and the biggest meetings would be close to five hundred people. We used to get good turnouts for them. Great discussions were held on the sidewalks after the meetings. We had such speakers as Norman Thomas, Harry W. Laidler—he was a fine educator. And these speakers were good. They gave the workers a vision of a possible society beyond their suffering day in and day out and made you feel that there was something there if you were organized. So this was a preparation that was very important.

BACKWARD ATTITUDES TOWARD WOMEN

We had a few women that would come down to these meetings, but they were most generally not welcome because they were not members of the union, and so they were not involved from the beginning in the union organization. If women came and wanted to help set up the strike, they were sent to the kitchen. You know, that's where they "belonged," carrying on the same duties that they did at home.

That's what happened to me. The people in charge of assigning volunteers, men and women, didn't know me. I was known to the workers in the shop and I was known by all of the political elements, but these people told me to go to the kitchen. They didn't know that I was trained as a public speaker and I was an organizer. I just shook my head and said, "I see you've got a lot of skinny men who say they can't stay too long on the picket lines and you can send them out to the kitchen. They can peel potatoes just as well as a woman."

And so I started talking to the women. Many of them had just come from the deep South and they had very little formal education or political activity outside of what they got from us at the union hall. Also the women of the Socialist Party became active. I got them involved on the union activities instead of just coming to political meetings for a lecture, and they began to talk to other women. The first time that the shops went down was

December 30, 1936, and there were some angry women who came down and said to their husbands, "You come on out of there. You're going to lose your job. You're not going to have your house, your family, or anything else." And they threatened divorce.

Q: *So is this when you formed the Women's Auxiliary?*

A: Yes. I was down there that night and I saw these men come down with their tails between their legs like a beaten dog and their buddies up there sitting down, shutting the plant down, hooting at them. And I realized that such women had a lot of power in the home, and unless somebody got to them, it would weaken the strike. Of course, General Motors had the newspapers and the radios and all other means of information—the union had very little money. So we made the announcement at the big mass meetings that we were organizing the Women's Auxiliary. The core group decided that whereas all of the other AFL auxiliaries were called Ladies Auxiliaries and they had their box socials and little parties and things like that, but really didn't know anything about labor or conditions in the country, we decided we were *women* and we didn't want any of this *lady* stuff, so we called ourselves for the first time in the American labor movement the Women's Auxiliary of the UAW.

The UAW wasn't really yet formed and hadn't had elections. It had workers from Chevrolet, from Fisher Body, from AC Spark Plug, from Buick, and so on, but they hadn't even separated into their locals yet. We were able to organize and elect our officers and bylaws and things like that and start up classes and start a child-care center and a first-aid station with a registered nurse who had joined our ranks. She used to come down there in her white uniform, and after we formed the militant part of the Auxiliary she'd come down in her red beret and red armband on her white uniform and she was treating people who were injured on the picket lines.

Q: *At the height of the activity, how many strikers were there and how many women were in the Women's Auxiliary?*

A: I can tell you that at the height of our organization there was close to one thousand. This is a difficult figure for me to give or for historians because, for instance, we would get letters, maybe unsigned, or maybe signed by one person who represented a whole department of young women. And they wanted us to know about them, and they would give us one number in case of emergency, and they would come immediately. They wanted to be part of our organization.

Q: *So these were women workers?*

A: Yes. In the shops.

Q: *Plus there were women who were spouses?*

A: Or grandmothers, or daughters. In the Auxiliary we had young women from the age of about sixteen or seventeen, daughters or sisters of workers in the shop, up to women in their late sixties. They were considered old women in those days.

Q: *How many people were on strike in Flint?*

A: We had seventeen GM plants that eventually went down after we shut down Plant No. 4. There were fourteen thousand workers alone in the ten Chevrolet plants. The Fisher Body Plant No. 1, which made bodies for Chevrolet, I think would be about two thousand or three thousand. They were smaller because Chevrolet had plants in other parts of the country. Buick probably had around twelve thousand. AC Spark Plug had probably about seven thousand. This was an auto company town. Either you were an autoworker or you were just eating peanuts.

Two Fisher Body plants went down on December 30. The smaller Fisher Body plant went on strike because of some big grievance, some aggravation they couldn't take any more and just shut the plant down, sat down. General Motors thought, Don't pay too much attention to them. We've got other body plants. We can handle it. But then the big Buick Fisher Body plant had a lot of accumulated grievance, too, and the same thing happened when they found out that the smaller Fisher Body plant went down.

Q: *When the sit-down strikes were going on what role did the women actually play, and why did you form the Women's Emergency Brigade?*

A: We wanted to get the women involved, because we knew that was a big factor, and many husbands knew that they were—in the home it became impossible because the women were so frightened. They had to put the food on the table for the children. They had to have the milk. They couldn't just say, "Your dad isn't working." They became very frightened, and they were very much against the union for shutting off their income. And for some men it was a big problem that needed to be solved.

But other men remained as macho as ever and as chauvinistic as ever. They said, "This is our fight and these damn women don't know what's what." They didn't discuss these things with their wives, and they kept them at home even though women could come up to the union hall and could even sit in on the meetings and listen, but they wouldn't let them.

We had to work on the men. And I did that primarily by going in when they were having their mass meetings, when the "rabble rousers" would get them going, rah rah rah and singing "Solidarity Forever" and so on. I would go in there with the same enthusiasm and tell them, "We're going to win this and we're going to win it together and we're going to give you hell till you bring your wives down here and we'll convince them that we're going to have a victory." Many of the men began to encourage their wives to come down. After so many years of men telling them it's none of your damn business what we do at union meetings they came down thinking, "What can I do about it? I don't belong here, I don't work in the plant."

Then we told them, "Well, you can get a lot of other women to come along with us and we can walk the picket lines and we can encourage and show the city of Flint that they're not going to smash our strike."

UNION DAY-CARE CENTERS

As we brought them in, if they had children, for instance, they could bring them to our day-care center. The woman in charge of the day-care center was pregnant with her ninth child, and she would be there with these mothers and their babies and she would be all enthused—she was a socialist, too—and she would tell them, "We're the ones concerned with what we have to live with in the home and we haven't enough to get a washing machine in our home." And the others would start talking and saying we don't have this and we don't have that. There were only about 30 percent of the homes in Flint that had actual plumbing and bathrooms in them. We still had outhouses and things like that in this city, this great company town!

They didn't have a number of things that would make women's lives easier. There was no possibility of their older children thinking about going to college. They couldn't afford such a thing. The minute one would turn eighteen he or she would stand in the long lines and try to get a job. There were times when you could drive past these great big factories and see hundreds of men sitting out on the lawn in front of the factories just waiting for somebody to come to the company door and call them in, maybe for three or five hours of work. So if the children, when they grew up, could get a job, they considered it a great success. It was another income, and young people were very proud to become an autoworker. What else was there in that city?

THE WOMEN BECOME ACTIVE

The women became very active. The only thing that they had been active in before was perhaps their churches and that sort of thing but never where they had a chance to get up and speak or to convince somebody else to join. That wasn't their job in their churches. The Pentecostal churches from the South and the big churches, all of them with the exception of one, were preaching against the unions—they would tell them this was Communism coming right over from godless Moscow, that all the union leaders were influenced by Communism—and they were preaching this every Sunday. Of course, you've heard of Father Coughlin and the Church of the Little Flower, the Catholic Church. He had a radio program that had thousands and thousands of listeners, and they were militant antiunionists. Then they began an organization called the Flint Alliance, which were all the scabs, and they were signing them up and giving them special privileges and promises and so on.

So we needed the women, and the women knew that. Participation in the union began to make it much easier for the women within the family. And the husbands wouldn't mind the children getting taken care of in the neighborhood and getting a second car.

There's another factor here. At the time of the strike the president of the bus drivers' local called a strike, so it was very difficult for some workers to get into work. Because even in this auto town there were an awful lot of workers who couldn't get a second car. Women on the outskirts of town would have to organize cooperatives where some of them would stay and take care of the children, and the men would have to organize as to how many of them could get a ride or how many women could get downtown. It was not an easy thing for them, and when they came down they wanted to make the most of their time and we wanted that too. So we put them in classes, and we had the most wonderful group of women who were changing almost day by day. You could see them standing a little taller and talking to the men a little more sure of themselves.

Many of the men, not all of them, had this chauvinism that went right straight through this strike and the whole period. Some of them thought women shouldn't be there at all, and we were called dykes, and some of them said the young women were just down there seeking out a man. And all kinds of things were said by some of the men. But others who were really men and were much more open to having the forces to build a union and to win a strike were very grateful and told us many times how happy they were in their homes since their wives got active. And some of the wives, believe me, got very active!

BATTLE OF "BULLS RUN"

There was a police attack on the Fisher Body Plant No. 2 strikers. The police came down there and started throwing tear gas canisters into the plant, and picket lines were formed to hold the police back, and barricades were set up, and we had an ensuing battle for a number of hours, into the early morning. It was affectionately called the Battle of Bulls Run, because at the end of it the bulls (the cops) ran.

I happened to be the only woman on the picket line at the time when they started firing buckshot and bullets and throwing fire bombs and tear gas canisters. All that the workers in the shop and on the picket lines had were big heavy car hinges (the kind they used to have on the old cars). They would throw those at the police. And they had water hoses that they got from the plant and they would shoot water at the police. Now this was in about sixteen degree weather—very cold—and water along the curb would freeze. As the battle raged on, the men were urging the people on the sidelines to join them, telling them what they were really fighting for, because the radios were saying that revolution had practically broken out in the city of Flint.

People came and gathered in big groups on the sides of the barricades, but they were afraid of the firing. My parents came down because they thought sure as hell revolution had broken out and I was a socialist and we were having a revolution! (My father was very antiunion.) Then Victor Reuther came over to a group of us at one point. Victor came over, and he said—to try and prepare us—that we may lose this battle but we're going to win the war, so don't worry about it. And why we were going to lose this battle was because the batteries in the sound car were running down and we might not be able to keep this source of inspiration for the strikers going.

When he told me that I thought, My God, this is terrible. Because I had just seen the president of the transportation workers jump over the curb that had water on it and about the time he looked down blood was running down his leg into the water, and I thought, After all of this sacrifice. There was something like sixteen union people injured that night, either shot or beaten, and a number of cops injured by the hinges and things.

APPEAL TO WOMEN TO JOIN THE STRIKERS

I decided that the only way we could get out of this was to get more women down, and if we ever got up and made an announcement that mothers of children were fired on I knew that the men would break in from the sidelines. I said I wanted to give a speech while the sound was still working. I started out talking to the women of Flint—first I called the cops cowards for shooting into the bellies of unarmed men and into the mothers of children—and then I asked the women to break through. I said, "Stand with your brothers and your husbands and your sweethearts. Come down here and stand with us." And one woman started to cross the barricade. A cop grabbed her from the back, but she slipped out of her coat and got away from him and started walking down toward us—in that weather, and without a coat—and when other men and women saw this they entered the battle and the police decided not to shoot the women in the back. As a result of that the fight was won.

THE WOMEN'S EMERGENCY BRIGADE

I put out announcements to all the women, "Meet at the union hall tomorrow. We've got to have an emergency meeting." And I thought, What in hell am I going to tell them? How are we going to organize these women? And I thought about organizing a military group of women that would march in between the police guns and the men, and I didn't know what to call it. I just took charge and said, "We're organizing the Women's Emergency Brigade!" Then I made the speech so bloody that it would scare most people off. I told them that they could not join unless they got up and swore in front of all the other women that they were willing to take the chance and if they were holding the hands of one of their sisters and she was shot and went down in blood, that they wouldn't get hysterical or pass out. I said, "We can't have that. This is going to be a military organization!"

It sounded very dramatic and the women were, of course, by this time very inspired, and all the ones that were working in the Auxiliary were thrilled about it, too. At first there were about fifty women—you should have heard the speech—it's a wonder I got ten! But there were about fifty who came up and signed their names publicly in front of everybody else, and the next day there were women coming down who had heard about this military brigade and wanted to be a part of it.

I had five lieutenants. You didn't want a whole lot of hierarchy who you had to refer things to if an action came up, if something was needed at AC, for example, or no matter where. When we got the invitation one lieutenant would take a group in one car or two cars and go out there right away with these red berets and armbands. Oh, the women got busy sewing these white "EB" letters on their red armbands, and we were passing them out to the members of the brigade only. Then we found out that some of the Auxiliary members who didn't have the courage to join the Brigade were going down to the stores and buying red berets themselves and wearing them on the picket lines so it looked like we had a lot more than we really had. Because it was an easy thing to get a beret at that time, one dollar or something like that.

I think that on the sign-up paper we actually had between three hundred and five hundred, but that's a big gap; we didn't really have any good record. It was very difficult because this was something that was going on all day and all night—all the activity around that hall—and was very tense.

Reports were coming in all the time. It was such a big area to cover, with plants spread out all over the city.

Some of us slept there at night. The young girls were always wanting to take care of me. They were always finding a cot for me to sleep on. [Genora needed treatment for tuberculosis, but put it off because of the strike, and later lost the use of a lung.—*K.O.*] The big kitchen was at the south end of town, where the big Fisher plant was, so at the union hall we would have a bologna sandwich and coffee, just to sustain us. Someone in the union hall couldn't get all the way out to the kitchen. Anyone walking the picket lines was given a card and given big meals and good meals, but we had the bologna sandwiches and cheese sandwiches and coffee at the union hall. That's what I was existing on. Sleeping at night, if you could sleep, and sitting around planning and plotting and talking.

Q: *You were pretty young yourself.*

A: I was twenty-three.

Q: *What inspired you to choose a military-type formation?*

A: Well, the conditions that were going on around the whole city. Men were getting beaten up. You'd see them coming up to the union hall with their faces all puffed out. General Motors had recruited a vigilante squad of about five hundred men who would beat up unionists. I felt we had to organize to counter that. Some of the men were very afraid of getting too militant on the streets, fighting and so on, because they were being charged with being Communists all the time and that was a big threat. If you got blacklisted at one of the plants, they sent it all over to Chrysler and Ford and so on, so that in Michigan you wouldn't be able to get a job. They were very afraid of getting their names right out in front in the newspapers. They did have those flying squads, a group of wonderful men that would go out and do their duty, but the women were quite dramatic.

The papers made it sound especially dramatic because they had never had this before in the history of labor that women came out and fought. Some of the papers said that we came out with our mops and our brooms and our rolling pins to defend our men. That wasn't true. We had clubs. We had big clubs. We had them trimmed down so that they were easy for us to handle, to fit a woman's hand. We also carried bars of hard-milled soap in a sock, usually a man's sock, and when you gave it a good hard whip and hit somebody on the side of the head it could really be very painful. So the women went around with bars of soap in one pocket and socks in the other. I think the police got reports and knew what we were doing, but it wasn't a weapon, so they couldn't arrest us on that.

Q: *What was the effect of the strike that was won, or the series of strikes, in Flint? What was the effect on the city of Flint and the people of the city?*

A: Well, to begin with, the people had been paralyzed with fear, because this was the hand that fed them, you know. They came up to Flint to get good wages from General Motors. Good wages would amount to anywhere from fifty-nine cents to maybe a dollar an hour for men, because this was the industrial workers, not the skilled workers, not the tool and die workers. At first they were paralyzed with fear, men and women. But later, when they saw great numbers coming in and increasing our strength and heard our sound cars going down the street, which was our only avenue of expression really, then they all began coming up to the union hall and wanting to join. And we accepted them. They didn't have to be auto-workers. They could be janitors or they could be anything. We were very happy to have the people of Flint working with us, walking our picket lines, and showing General Motors that we had numbers and strength publicly.

In the Brigade, after we got so that we were functioning well, if someone called for our support, we would go. For instance, a number of girls who worked in a department store, J.C. Penney, sat down; they wanted a union. The Brigade that was going around to groups went down there and talked with them, and by this time the women had a lot of confidence in themselves. Very often they would go right up and talk to the bosses of the stores or other enterprises and all of them in the store would sign up and these stores were organized that way. Not by the employees themselves, but by these other women coming in and mobilizing their forces and demanding that the company sign a union contract, and women did that.

Q: *This kind of broadening of the union movement beyond the auto-workers was a very important effort of the kind we don't see much today. How would you compare in general the union today to the unions of the 1930s and 1940s?*

A: Oh, there's very little good comparison that you can make because that happens in every part of history. When you elect people to higher positions, with both salaries and better acceptance in society and so on, there people begin to feel that their interests are more aligned with people with money than they are with the workers they are supposed to represent. This happened in our union. Take the case of Walter Reuther, who finally became the president of the international union. He and his brother Victor went to Russia in the early 1930s and helped organize the Russian workers in the Soviet Union in the auto factories—helped make their production more up-to-date, more like American production—then they came back and worked on forming a union here. They were socialists, and they came from a staunch socialist and union family.

Walter Reuther finally became the leader of a very powerful organization that had a lot to say about national, state, and local politics, and by the time he was granted the great honor of coming to the back door of the White House and consulting with the president of the United States this changed this man completely. Completely. Then he wanted to control. No wildcat strikes, no this, no that. And he got very good control. In fact he was the one who took away the union dues being paid to stewards in the shop and instead he negotiated the dues checkoff system. It came right out of their checks, so that we lost contact between the stewards and the workers on the plant floor. They never had that same contact, talking as they turned over their dues about what's happening and so on. The checkoff system gave the union officers a guaranteed wage. Nice salaries and traveling and all kinds of prestigious things that they never had before.

This happens with many, many movements. The bureaucrats develop as a result of the pressure of capitalist society. This we have to guard against no matter when and how we organize a political movement of the workers.

Q: *Before we get to that, what do you think can be done by workers today to change their unions back to the militant fighting instruments that they had then?*

A: Education, education, education! And I think we've got to have the understanding, plain and clear, with workers that you've got to have your own voice up there in the United States government. You've got to have your own political party. You've got two parties for the bosses, and you know what *we* get out of it each time. Nothing. We've got to form our own political party with our own leaders and our own demands, our own program, and if we do, then the strikes themselves will have much more significance. Because when we organized the industrial union movement what we were lacking was a labor party.

By the way, the Congress of Industrial Organizations (CIO) didn't become a "Congress" until this great strike was victorious. Before that it was the Committee for Industrial Organization—John L. Lewis and his Committee. As soon as we showed them that we had the power to bring the world's largest industrial corporation down to the bargaining table and to be recognized as a union, then it spread from the autoworkers to the rubber workers to the steelworkers and to all the other industrial unions and it changed the face of America. And John L. Lewis's Congress of Industrial Organizations then became a very powerful force.

But what have we got today? We won a great number of economic gains, but politically we never did anything to secure them and so they're easily legislated away. Many have been legislated away or are in the process now of being taken away in this period very rapidly, and there's no other solution but a labor party. You can say, "We'll improve the unions, throw out the old ones, and bring in new ones," and so on, but that's only a fight for economic betterment. It's not a fight for political control of your life, and that's what we've got to do, and there's only one way that's on the field right now and that's Labor Party Advocates.

Q: *Let me ask you a question about that. Along with your massive history of being first this and that, you are also a founding member of Labor Party Advocates. Tell us a little bit about it and why you decided to promote LPA.*

A: Well, anybody who believes it is possible to someday have a socialist system of equality without wars and starvation and all of the things man had suffered since the beginning of time knows that we must do it in stages of education. And so I have always been in favor of a labor party for working people. In the Chevrolet local following the strike, we set up a labor party committee, ran candidates in the city, and had a very favorable response, but that was only local. During World War II, Emil Mazey, who was on the executive board of the UAW at the time, and I and several other secondary leaders of the UAW organized the Michigan Commonwealth Federation patterned after the Canadian Commonwealth Federation, which was a labor party. In Canada, it turned into the New Democratic Party, and it's having great problems with the bureaucracy and the same thing that infests all organizations. Even in church organizations and small organizations there's always this business of bureaucracy that sets in and gains control over the members. And they're having a great many problems right now with their New Democratic Party, but even so I think a labor party is the answer.

You can't stand on a soapbox in this powerful United States of America, which rules the world, and say, "We want a revolution," and expect it to come about that way. The process of education is going to be in the workers going into their own labor party, electing their own representatives, putting up their own program of action, and that's the only way you're going to change the unions. I don't think there's much opportunity within the union itself. The Teamsters was an exception, but they are not yet successful.

11

OPPORTUNITIES FOUND AND LOST

Labor, Radicals, and the Early Civil Rights Movement

ROBERT KORSTAD AND NELSON LICHTENSTEIN

Most historians would agree that the modern civil rights movement did not begin with the Supreme Court's decision in *Brown* v. *Board of Education*. Yet all too often the movement's history has been written as if events before the mid-1950s constituted a kind of prehistory, important only insofar as they laid the legal and political foundation for the spectacular advances that came later. Those were the "forgotten years of the Negro Revolution," wrote one historian; they were the "seed time of racial and legal metamorphosis" according to another. But such a periodization profoundly underestimates the tempo and misjudges the social dynamic of the freedom struggle.[1]

The civil rights era began, dramatically and decisively, in the early 1940s when the social structure of black America took on an increasingly urban, proletarian character. A predominantly southern rural and small-town population was soon transformed into one of the most urban of all major ethnic groups. More than two million blacks migrated to northern and western industrial areas during the 1940s, while another million moved from farm to city within the South. Northern black voters doubled their numbers between 1940 and 1948, and in the eleven states of the Old South black registration more than quadrupled, reaching over one million by

From *Journal of American History* 75, no. 3 (December 1988): 786–811. Reprinted by permission.

1952. Likewise, membership in the National Association for the Advancement of Colored People (NAACP) soared, growing from 50,000 in 355 branches in 1940 to almost 450,000 in 1,073 branches six years later.[2]

The half million black workers who joined unions affiliated with the Congress of Industrial Organizations (CIO) were in the vanguard of efforts to transform race relations. The NAACP and the Urban League had become more friendly toward labor in the depression era, but their legal and social work orientation had not prepared them to act effectively in the workplaces and working-class neighborhoods where black Americans fought their most decisive struggles of the late 1930s and 1940s. By the early forties it was commonplace for sympathetic observers to assert the centrality of mass unionization in the civil rights struggle. A Rosenwald Fund study concluded, not without misgivings, that "the characteristic movements among Negroes are now for the first time becoming proletarian"; while a *Crisis* reporter found the CIO a "lamp of democracy" throughout the old Confederate states. "The South has not known such a force since the historic Union Leagues in the great days of the Reconstruction era."[3]

This movement gained much of its dynamic character from the relationship that arose between unionized blacks and the federal government and proved somewhat similar to the creative tension that linked the church-based civil rights movement and the state almost two decades later. In the 1950s the *Brown* decision legitimated much of the subsequent social struggle, but it remained essentially a dead letter until given political force by a growing protest movement. In like manner, the rise of industrial unions and the evolution of late New Deal labor legislation offered working-class blacks an economic and political standard by which they could legitimate their demands and stimulate a popular struggle. The "one man, one vote" policy implemented in thousands of National Labor Relations Board (NLRB) elections, the industrial "citizenship" that union contracts offered once-marginal elements of the working class, and the patriotic egalitarianism of the government's wartime propaganda—all generated a rights consciousness that gave working-class black militancy a moral justification in some ways as powerful as that evoked by the Baptist spirituality of Martin Luther King Jr. a generation later.[4] During the war the Fair Employment Practices Committee (FEPC) held little direct authority, but like the Civil Rights Commission of the late 1950s, it served to expose racist conditions and spur on black activism wherever it undertook its well-publicized investigations. And just as a disruptive and independent civil rights movement in the 1960s could pressure the federal government to enforce its own laws and move against local elites, so too did the mobilization of the black working class in the 1940s make civil rights an issue that could not be ignored by union officers, white executives, or government officials.[5]

This essay explores two examples of the workplace-oriented civil rights militancy that arose in the 1940s—one in the South and one in the North. It analyzes the unionization of predominantly black tobacco workers in Winston-Salem, North Carolina, and the ferment in the United Auto Workers in Detroit, Michigan, that made that city a center of black working-class activism in the North. Similar movements took root among newly organized workers in the cotton compress mills of Memphis, the tobacco factories of Richmond and Charleston, the steel mills of Pittsburgh and Birmingham, the stockyards and farm equipment factories of Chicago and Louisville, and the shipyards of Baltimore and Oakland.[6]

WINSTON-SALEM IN THE WAR

Winston-Salem had been a center of tobacco processing since the 1880s, and the R. J. Reynolds Tobacco Company dominated the life of the city's eighty thousand citizens. By the 1940s whites held most of the higher-paying machine-tending jobs, but blacks formed the majority of the workforce, concentrated in the preparation departments where they cleaned, stemmed, and conditioned the tobacco.[7] The jobs were physically demanding, the air was hot and dusty, and in departments with machinery, the noise was deafening. Most black workers made only a few cents above minimum wage, and benefits were few. Black women workers experienced frequent verbal and occasional sexual abuse. Reynolds maintained a determined opposition to trade unionism, and two unsuccessful American Federation of Labor (AFL) efforts to organize segregated locals had soured most black workers on trade unionism.

But in 1943 a CIO organizing effort succeeded. Led by the United Cannery, Agricultural, Packing and Allied Workers of America (UCAPAWA), a new union drive championed black dignity and self-organization, employing several young black organizers who had gotten their start in the interracial Southern Tenant Farmers Union. Their discreet two-year organizing campaign made a dramatic breakthrough when black women in one of the stemmeries stopped work on June 17. A severe labor shortage, chronic wage grievances, and a recent speedup gave the women both the resources and the incentive to transform a departmental sit-down into a festive, plant-wide strike. The UCAPAWA quickly signed up about eight thousand black workers, organized a committee to negotiate with the company, and asked the NLRB to hold an election.[8]

The effort to win union recognition at Reynolds sparked a spirited debate about who constituted the legitimate leadership of the black community in Winston-Salem. Midway through the campaign, six local black business and professional men—a college professor, an undertaker, a dentist, a store owner, and two ministers—dubbed "colored leaders" by the

Winston-Salem Journal, wrote a long letter to the editor urging workers to reject the "followers of John L. Lewis and William Green" and to remain loyal to Reynolds. In the absence of any formal leadership, elected or otherwise, representatives of Winston-Salem's small black middle class had served as spokesmen, brokering with the white elite for small concessions in a tightly segregated society. The fight for collective bargaining, they argued, had to remain secondary to the more important goal of racial betterment, which could only be achieved by "good will, friendly understanding, and mutual respect and cooperation between the races." Partly because of their own vulnerability to economic pressure, such traditional black leaders judged unions, like other institutions, by their ability to deliver jobs and maintain a precarious racial equilibrium.[9]

The union campaign at Reynolds transformed the expectations tobacco workers held of the old community leadership. Reynolds workers responded to calls for moderation from "college-trained people" with indignation. "Our leaders," complained Mabel Jessup, "always look clean and refreshed at the end of the hottest day, because they work in very pleasant environments. . . . All I ask of our leaders is that they obtain a job in one of the factories as a laborer and work two weeks. Then write what they think." W. L. Griffin felt betrayed. "I have attended church regularly for the past thirty years," he wrote, "and unity and cooperation have been taught and preached from the pulpits of the various Negro churches. Now that the laboring class of people are about to unite and cooperate on a wholesale scale for the purpose of collective bargaining, these same leaders seem to disagree with that which they have taught their people." Others rejected the influence of people who "have always told us what the white people want, but somehow or other are particularly silent on what we want." "We feel we are the leaders instead of you," asserted a group of union members.[10]

Reynolds, the only major tobacco manufacturer in the country not under a union contract, followed tried-and-true methods to break the union. Management used lower-level supervisors to intimidate unionists and supported a "no union" movement among white workers, whose organizers were given freedom to roam the company's workshops and warehouses. That group, the R. J. Reynolds Employees Association, sought a place on the NLRB ballot in order to delay the increasingly certain CIO victory. Meanwhile, the white business community organized an Emergency Citizens Committee to help defeat the CIO. In a well-publicized resolution, the committee blamed the recent strikes on "self-seeking representatives of the CIO" and warned that continued subversion of existing race relations would "likely lead to riots and bloodshed."[11]

In earlier times, this combination of antiunion forces would probably have derailed the organizing effort. But during World War II, black workers had allies who helped shift the balance of power. The NLRB closely supervised each stage of the election process and denied the company's request to divide the workforce into two bargaining units, which would have weakened the position of black workers. When local judges sought to delay the election, government attorneys removed the case to federal court. In December 1943 an NLRB election gave the CIO a resounding victory. But continued federal assistance, from the United States Conciliation Service and the National War Labor Board, was still needed to secure Reynolds workers a union contract in 1944.[12]

That first agreement resembled hundreds of other wartime labor-management contracts, but in the context of Winston-Salem's traditional system of race relations it had radical implications, because it generated a new set of shop floor rights embodied in the seniority, grievance, and wage adjustment procedures. The contract did not attack factory segregation—for the most part white workers continued to control the better-paying jobs—but it did call forth a new corps of black leaders to defend the rights Reynolds workers had recently won. The one hundred or so elected shop stewards were the "most important people in the plant" remembered union activist Velma Hopkins. They were the "natural leaders" people who had "taken up money for flowers if someone died or would talk to the foreman [even] before the union." Now the union structure reinforced the capabilities of such workers: "We had training classes for the shop stewards: What to do, how to do it. We went over the contract thoroughly." The shop stewards transformed the traditional paternalism of Reynolds management into an explicit system of benefits and responsibilities. They made the collective bargaining agreement a bill of rights.[13]

The growing self-confidence of black women, who constituted roughly half of the total workforce, proved particularly subversive of existing social relations. To the white men who ran the Reynolds plants, nothing could have been more disturbing than the demand that they negotiate on a basis of equality with people whom they regarded as deeply inferior—by virtue of their sex as well as their class and race. When union leaders like Theodosia Simpson, Velma Hopkins, and Moranda Smith sat down at the bargaining table with company executives, social stereotypes naturally came under assault, but the challenge proved equally dramatic on the shop floor. For example, Ruby Jones, the daughter of a railway fireman, became one of the most outspoken shop stewards. Perplexed by her newfound aggressiveness, a foreman demanded, "Ruby, what do you want?" "I want your respect," she replied, "that's all I ask."[14]

By the summer of 1944, Local 22 of the reorganized and renamed Food, Tobacco, Agricultural and Allied Workers (FTA) had become the center of an alternative social world that linked black workers together regardless of job, neighborhood, or church affiliation. The union hall, only a few blocks from the Reynolds Building, housed a constant round of meetings, plays, and musical entertainments, as well as classes in labor history, black history, and current events. Local 22 sponsored softball teams, checker tournaments, sewing circles, and swimming clubs. Its vigorous educational program and well-stocked library introduced many black workers (and a few whites) to a larger radical culture few had glimpsed before. "You know, at that little library they [the city of Winston-Salem] had for us, you couldn't find any books on Negro history," remembered Viola Brown. "They didn't have books by Aptheker, Du Bois, or Frederick Douglass. But we had them at *our* library."[15]

The Communist Party was the key political grouping in FTA and in Local 22. FTA president Donald Henderson had long been associated with the Party, and many organizers who passed through Winston-Salem shared his political sympathies. By 1947 Party organizers had recruited about 150 Winston-Salem blacks, almost all tobacco workers. Most of these workers saw the party as both a militant civil rights organization, which in the 1930s had defended such black victims of white southern racism as the Scottsboro boys and Angelo Hearndon, and as a cosmopolitan group, introducing members to the larger world of politics and ideas. The white North Carolina Communist leader Junius Scales recalled that the "top leaders [of Local 22] . . . just soaked up all the educational efforts that were directed at them. The Party's program had an explanation of events locally, nationally, and worldwide which substantiated everything they had felt instinctively. . . . It really meant business on racism." The Party was an integrated institution in which the social conventions of the segregated South were self-consciously violated, but it also accommodated itself to the culture of the black community. In Winston-Salem, therefore, the Party met regularly in a black church and started the meetings with a hymn and a prayer.[16]

The Communist Party's relative success in Winston-Salem was replicated in other black industrial districts. In the South a clear majority of the party's new recruits were black, and in northern states like Illinois and Michigan the proportion ranged from 25 to 40 percent. The party's relative success among American blacks was not based on its programmatic consistency: during the late 1940s the NAACP and other critics pointed out that the wartime party had denounced civil rights struggles when they challenged the Roosevelt administration or its conduct of the war effort, but that the party grew more militant once Soviet-American relations cooled.[17] However, the party never abandoned its assault on Jim Crow and unlike the NAACP, which directed much of its energy toward the courts and Congress, the Communists or their front groups more often organized around social or political issues subject to locally initiated protests, petitions, and pickets. Moreover, the Party adopted what today would be called an affirmative action policy that recognized the special disabilities under which black workers functioned, in the Party as well as in the larger community.

Although there were elements of tokenism and manipulation in the implementation of that policy, the Party's unique effort to develop black leaders gave the Communists a special standing among politically active blacks.[18]

Tobacco industry trade unionism revitalized black political activism in Winston-Salem. Until the coming of the CIO, NAACP attacks on racial discrimination seemed radical, and few blacks risked associating with the organization. A 1942 membership drive did increase branch size from 11 to 100, but most new members came from the traditional black middle class: mainly teachers and municipal bus drivers. The Winston-Salem NAACP became a mass organization only after Local 22 conducted its own campaign for the city branch. As tobacco workers poured in, the local NAACP reached a membership of 1,991 by 1946, making it the largest unit in North Carolina.[19]

Unionists also attacked the policies that had disenfranchised Winston-Salem blacks for more than two generations. As part of the CIO Political Action Committee's voter registration and mobilization drive, Local 22 inaugurated citizenship classes, political rallies, and citywide mass meetings. Union activists challenged the power of registrars to judge the qualifications of black applicants and insisted that black veterans vote without further tests. The activists encouraged the city's blacks to participate in electoral politics. "Politics IS food, clothes, and housing" declared the committee that registered some seven hundred new black voters in the months before the 1944 elections.[20] After a visit to Winston-Salem in 1944, a *Pittsburgh Courier* correspondent wrote, "I was aware of a growing solidarity and intelligent mass action that will mean the dawn of a New Day in the South. One cannot visit Winston-Salem and mingle with the thousands of workers without sensing a revolution in thought and action. If there is a 'New' Negro, he is to be found in the ranks of the labor movement."[21]

Organization and political power gave the black community greater leverage at city hall and at the county courthouse. NAACP and union officials regularly took part in municipal government debate on social services for the black community, minority representation on the police and fire departments, and low-cost public housing. In 1944 and 1946 newly enfranchised blacks helped reelect Congressman John Folger, a New Deal supporter, against strong conservative opposition. In 1947, after black registration had increased some tenfold in the previous three years, a minister, Kenneth Williams, won a seat on the Board of Aldermen, becoming the first black city official in the twentieth-century South to be elected against a white opponent.[22]

CIVIL RIGHTS MILITANCY IN DETROIT

The social dynamic that had begun to revolutionize Winston-Salem played itself out on a far larger scale in Detroit, making that city a center of civil rights militancy in the war years. Newly organized black autoworkers pushed forward the frontier of racial equality on the shop floor, in the political arena, and within the powerful, million-member United Auto Workers. Despite increasing racism among white workers, union goals and civil rights aims largely paralleled each other in the 1940s.

In 1940 about 4 percent of all autoworkers were black; the proportion more than doubled during the war and rose to about one-fifth of the auto workforce in 1960. Although proportionally less numerous than in Winston-Salem, blacks were nevertheless central to the labor process in many of Detroit's key manufacturing facilities. Excluded from assembly operations and skilled work, blacks dominated the difficult and unhealthy, but absolutely essential, work in foundry, paint shop, and wet-sanding operations.[23]

Ford Motor Company's great River Rouge complex contained the largest concentration of black workers in the country. More than half of its nine thousand black workers labored in the foundry, but Henry Ford's peculiar brand of interwar paternalism had enabled blacks to secure some jobs in virtually every Ford department. The company therefore proved a mecca for black workers. Those who worked there proudly announced, "I work for Henry Ford," and wore their plant badges on the lapels of their Sunday coats. Ford reinforced his hold on the loyalty of Detroit's black working class by establishing what amounted to a separate personnel department that recruited new workers on the recommendation of an influential black minister. That policy, which continued until the early 1940s, strengthened the pro-company, antiunion attitude of most churchmen and reinforced the hostility shown the early CIO by leaders of the Detroit Urban League and the local NAACP branch.[24]

UAW leaders recognized that unless black workers were recruited to the union they might undermine efforts to consolidate UAW power in key manufacturing facilities. The danger became clear during the racially divisive 1939 Chrysler Corporation strike when management tried to start a back-to-work movement spearheaded by black workers, and it proved even more apparent during the 1940–1941 Ford organizing drive, when black workers hesitated to join the union. During the April 1941 Ford strike, several hundred scabbed inside the plant. In response, UAW leaders made a concerted effort to win over elements of the local black bourgeoisie who were not directly dependent on Ford's patronage network. The ensuing conflict within the Detroit NAACP chapter was only resolved in favor of the UAW after Ford's unionization. Thereafter black workers, whose participation in union activities had lagged well behind those of most whites, became among the most steadfast UAW members. The UAW itself provided an alternative focus of power, both cooperating with and challenging the black church and the NAACP as the most effective and legitimate spokesman for the black community.[25]

Many talented, politically sophisticated black officers and staffers emerged in the UAW during the mid-1940s, although never in numbers approaching their proportion of union membership. Blacks were a majority in almost every foundry and in most paint shops, so locals that represented manufacturing facilities usually adopted the United Mine Workers formula of including a black on the election slate as one of the top four officers. Locals with a large black membership also elected blacks to the annual UAW convention, where the one hundred and fifty to two hundred black delegates in attendance represented about 7 or 8 percent of the total voting roll. And almost a score of blacks also secured appointment as highly visible UAW international representatives during the early 1940s.[26]

Ford's River Rouge complex overshadowed all other Detroit area production facilities as a center of black political power. Although most blacks had probably voted against the UAW in the NLRB elections of May 1941, the unionization process, particularly radical in its reorganization of shop floor social relations at the Rouge, helped transform the consciousness of these industrial workers. With several hundred shop committeemen in the vanguard, workers intimidated many foremen, challenged top management, and broke the company spy system. "We noticed a very definite change in attitude of the working man," recalled one supervisor "It was terrible for a while . . . the bosses were just people to look down on after the union came in." For the next decade, Rouge Local 600 proved a center of civil rights militancy and a training ground for black leaders. The Rouge foundry sent more than a score of black delegates to every UAW convention, provided at least half of all black staffers hired by the UAW, and customarily supplied Local 600 with one of its top officers. Foundryman Shelton Tappes, a 1936 migrant from Alabama, helped negotiate a then-unique antidiscrimination clause into the first UAW-Ford contract and went on to serve as recording secretary of the sixty-thousand-member local in the mid-1940s.[27]

The Rouge was also a center of Communist Party strength in Detroit. The radical tradition there had remained unbroken since World War I when the Industrial Workers of the World and other radical union groups had briefly flourished. Skilled workers from Northern Europe had provided most members during the difficult interwar years, but after 1941 the party recruited heavily among blacks, and at its peak in the late 1940s it enrolled 450 workers, almost half from the foundry. The Rouge was one of the few workplaces in the country where Communists, black or white, could proclaim their political allegiance without immediate persecution. As late as 1948 Nelson Davis, the black Communist elected vice president of the nine-thousand-man Rouge foundry unit within Local 600, sold several hundred subscriptions to the *Daily Worker* every year. But even here, Communist influence among black workers rested on the party's identification with civil rights issues; indeed many blacks saw the party's foundry department "club" as little more than a militant race organization.[28]

With almost one hundred thousand black workers organized in the Detroit area, black union activists played a central role in the civil rights struggle. They demanded the hiring and promotion of black workers in metropolitan war plants, poured into the Detroit NAACP chapter, and mobilized thousands to defend black occupancy of the Sojourner Truth Homes, a federally funded project that became a violent center of conflict between white neighborhood groups and the housing-starved black community. In those efforts black activists encountered enormous resistance not only from plant management and the Detroit political elite but also from white workers, midlevel union leaders under direct pressure from white constituents, and conservatives in the black community. But as in the civil rights movement of the early 1960s, black militants held the political initiative, so that powerful white elites—the top officeholders in the UAW, company personnel officers, and the government officials who staffed the War Labor Board and War Manpower Commission—had to yield before this new wave of civil rights militancy.[29]

As in Winston-Salem, mass unionization transformed the character of the black community's traditional race advancement organizations. Under pressure from Local 600 leaders like Tappes, Horace Sheffield (his rival for leadership of the foundry), and the pro-union minister Charles Hill, the NAACP and the Urban League became more militant and activist. Black community leadership still came largely from traditional strata: lawyers, ministers, doctors, and teachers, but the union upsurge reshaped the protest agenda and opened the door to new forms of mass struggle. The NAACP itself underwent a remarkable transformation. In the successful effort to keep the Sojourner Truth housing project open to blacks, NAACP officials had for the first time worked closely with the UAW militants who organized the demonstrations and protests that forestalled city or federal capitulation to the white neighborhood groups that fought black occupancy. That mobilization in turn energized the local NAACP, as almost twenty thousand new members joined, making the Detroit branch by far the largest in the nation. Black workers poured in from the region's recently unionized foundries, tire plants, and converted auto/aircraft facilities, and from city government, streetcar lines, restaurants, and retail stores.[30]

By 1943 the Detroit NAACP was one of the most working-class chapters in the country. Its new labor committee, the largest and most active group in the branch, served as a forum for black workers to air their grievances and as a pressure group, urging companies and the government to advance black job rights. With UAW support, the labor committee sponsored an April 1943 march and rally that brought ten thousand to Cadillac Square to demand that managers open war industry jobs to thousands of still-unemployed black women in the region. Although the NAACP old guard repulsed a direct electoral challenge from UAW members and their sympathizers, the chapter added two unionists to its executive board and backed protest campaigns largely shaped by UAW militants: mass rallies, picket lines, and big lobbying delegations to city hall, Lansing, and Washington. By the end of the war the ministerial leadership of the black community was in eclipse. Horace White, a Congregational minister, admitted: "The CIO has usurped moral leadership in the [Negro] community."[31]

On the shop floor, black workers sought to break out of traditional job ghettos in the foundry and janitorial service, precipitating a series of explosive "hate" strikes as white workers walked off the job to stop the integration of black workers into formerly all-white departments. The strikes were almost always failures, however, not only because federal officials and UAW leaders quickly mobilized to cut them off but also because they failed to intimidate most black workers. During the war there were probably as many demonstrations and protest strikes led by black workers as racially inspired white walkouts.[32] For example, at Packard, scene of one of the most infamous hate strikes of the war, black workers eventually triumphed over white recalcitrance. A racialist personnel manager, a divided union leadership, and a heavily southern workforce heightened racial tensions and precipitated several white stoppages that culminated in June 1943 when more than twenty-five thousand whites quit work to prevent the transfer of three blacks into an all-white department. But black workers were also active. Under the leadership of foundryman Christopher Alston, a Young Communist League member, they had earlier shut down the foundry to demand that union leaders take more forceful action against recalcitrant whites; and in the months after the big wildcat hate strike, those same blacks conducted strikes and protests that kept the attention of federal officials and local union leaders focused on their problems. Their militancy paid off; by the end of 1943 about five hundred blacks had moved out of the Packard foundry and into heretofore all-white production jobs.[33]

Although newly assertive second-generation Poles and Hungarians had come to see their jobs and neighborhoods as under attack from the equally militant black community, top UAW officials championed civil rights during the war. In the aftermath of the great Detroit race riot of 1943, in which the police and roving bands of whites killed twenty-five blacks, the UAW stood out as the only predominantly white institution to defend the black community and denounce police brutality. During the hate strikes, UAW leaders often sought the protection of a War Labor Board back-to-work order in order to deflect white rank-and-file anger onto the government and away from themselves. But officials like UAW vice president Walter Reuther made it clear that "the UAW-CIO would tell any worker that refused to work with a colored worker that he could leave the plant because he did not belong there."[34]

Intraunion competition for black political support encouraged white UAW officials to put civil rights issues high on their agenda. During the 1940s black staffers and local union activists participated in an informal caucus that agitated for more black representatives in the union hierarchy and more effort to upgrade black workers in the auto shops. Initially chaired by Shelton Tappes of Local 600, the group was reorganized and strengthened by George Crockett, an FEPC lawyer the UAW hired to head its own Fair Employment Practices Committee in 1944. The overwhelming majority of UAW blacks, however, backed the caucus led by Secretary Treasurer George Addes and Vice President Richard Frankensteen, in which Communists played an influential role. The Addes-Frankensteen caucus endorsed the symbolically crucial demand for a Negro seat on the UAW executive board and generally supported black-white slates in local union elections. The other major UAW faction was led by Walter Reuther and a coterie of ex-socialists and Catholics, whose own internal union support came from workers in the General Motors plants (Flint and Western Michigan), in the South, and in the aircraft fabricating facilities of the East and Midwest. Support for Reuther's faction was particularly strong among the more assimilated Catholics and Appalachian whites in northern industry. Reuther denounced proposals for a black executive board seat as "reverse Jim Crow," but his group also advocated civil rights, not so much because they expected to win black political support, but because the rapid growth of a quasi-autonomous black movement had made militancy on civil rights the sine qua non of serious political leadership in the UAW.[35]

A MOMENT OF OPPORTUNITY

By the mid-1940s, civil rights issues had reached a level of national political salience that they would not regain for another fifteen years. Once the domain of Afro-American protest groups, leftist clergymen, and Communist-led unions and front organizations, civil rights advocacy was becoming a defining characteristic of urban liberalism. Thus ten states established fair employment practice commissions between 1945 and 1950, and four major cities— Chicago, Milwaukee, Minneapolis, and Philadelphia—enacted tough laws against job bias. Backed by the CIO, the Americans for Democratic Action spearheaded a successful effort to strengthen the Democratic Party's civil rights plank at the 1948 convention.[36]

In the South the labor movement seemed on the verge of a major breakthrough. *Fortune* magazine predicted that the CIO's "Operation Dixie" would soon organize key southern industries like textiles. Black workers proved exceptionally responsive to such union campaigns, especially in industries like lumber, furniture, and tobacco, where they were sometimes a majority of the workforce. Between 1944 and 1946 the CIO's political action apparatus helped elect liberal congressmen and senators in a few southern states, while organizations that promoted interracial cooperation, such as the Southern Conference for Human Welfare and Highlander Folk School, experienced their most rapid growth and greatest effectiveness in 1946 and 1947.[37]

The opportune moment soon passed. Thereafter, a decade-long decline in working-class black activism destroyed the organizational coherence and ideological élan of the labor-based civil rights movement. That defeat has been largely obscured by the brilliant legal victories won by civil rights lawyers in the 1940s and 1950s, and by the reemergence of a new mass movement in the next decade. But in Winston-Salem, Detroit, and other industrial regions, the time had passed when unionized black labor was in the vanguard of the freedom struggle. Three elements contributed to the decline. First, the employer offensive of the late 1940s put all labor on the defensive. Conservatives used the Communist issue to attack New Deal and Fair Deal reforms, a strategy that isolated Communist-oriented black leaders and helped destroy what was left of the Popular Front. The employers' campaign proved particularly effective against many recently organized CIO locals with disproportionate numbers of black members. Meanwhile, mechanization and decentralization of the most labor-intensive and heavily black production facilities sapped the self-confidence of the black working class and contributed to high rates of urban unemployment in the years after the Korean War.

Second, the most characteristic institutions of American liberalism, including the unions, race advancement organizations, and liberal advocacy organizations adopted a legal-administrative, if not a bureaucratic, approach to winning citizenship rights for blacks. The major legislative goal of the union-backed Leadership Conference on Civil Rights in the 1950s was revision of Senate Rule 22, to limit the use of the filibuster that had long blocked passage of a national FEPC and other civil rights legislation. The UAW and other big unions cooperated with the NAACP in the effort, but the work was slow and frustrating and the struggle far removed from the shop floor or the drugstore lunch counter.[38]

Finally, the routinization of the postwar industrial relations system precluded efforts by black workers to mobilize a constituency independent of the leadership. Focusing on incremental collective bargaining gains and committed to social change only if it was well controlled, the big unions became less responsive to the particular interests of their black members. By 1960 blacks had formed oppositional movements in several old CIO unions, but they now encountered resistance to their demands not only from much of the white rank and file but also from union leaders who presided over institutions that had accommodated themselves to much of the industrial status quo.[39]

POSTWAR REACTION: WINSTON-SALEM

Like most labor-intensive Southern employers, R. J. Reynolds never reached an accommodation with union labor, although it signed contracts with Local 22 in 1945 and 1946. Minimum wage laws and collective bargaining agreements had greatly increased costs of production, especially in the stemmeries, and the black women employed there were the heart and soul of the union. Soon after the war, the company began a mechanization campaign that eliminated several predominantly black departments. When the factories closed for Christmas in 1945 new stemming machines installed in one plant displaced over seven hundred black women. The union proposed a "share the work plan," but the company was determined to cut its workforce and change its racial composition by recruiting white workers from surrounding counties. The black proportion of the manufacturing labor force in Winston-Salem dropped from 44 to 36 percent between 1940 and 1960.[40]

The technological offensive undermined union strength, but by itself Reynolds could not destroy Local 22. When contract negotiations began in 1947, the company rejected union demands for a wage increase patterned after those won in steel, auto, and rubber earlier in the spring. Somewhat reluctantly, Local 22 called a strike on May 1. Black workers and virtually all of the Negro community solidly backed the union, which held out for thirty-eight days until a compromise settlement was reached. But, in a pattern replicated throughout industrial America in those years, Communist influence within the union became the key issue around which management and its allies mounted their attack. The *Winston-Salem Journal* soon denounced Local 22 as "captured . . . lock, stock, and barrel" by the Communist Party, warning readers that the strike would lead to "open rioting." This exposé brought Local 22 officers under the scrutiny of the House Committee on Un-American Activities (HUAC), which held a highly publicized hearing on the Winston-Salem situation in the summer of 1947.[41]

Communist Party members contributed to the volatility of the situation. In the late 1940s, Local 22 found itself politically vulnerable when foreign policy resolutions passed by the shop stewards' council followed Communist Party pronouncements. The Party's insistence on the promotion of blacks into public leadership positions sometimes put workers with little formal education into union leadership jobs they could not handle. Moreover, the party's obsession with "white chauvinism" backfired. After the 1947 strike, Local 22 made a concerted effort to recruit white workers. Some young veterans joined the local, although the union allowed most to pay their dues secretly.[42] The Party objected, remembered North Carolina leader Junius Scales. "'If they got any guts,' they would say, 'let them stand up and fight,' not realizing, as many black workers and union leaders realized, that for a white worker to just *belong* to a predominantly black union at that time was an act of great courage."[43]

With its workforce increasingly polarized along racial and political lines, Reynolds renewed its offensive in the spring of 1948. Black workers remained remarkably loyal to the union leadership, but the anti-Communist campaign had turned most white employees against the union and eroded support among blacks not directly involved in the conflict. The company refused to negotiate with Local 22 on the grounds that the union had not complied with the new Taft-Hartley Act. The law required union officers to sign an affidavit swearing they were not members of the Communist Party before a union could be certified as a bargaining agent by the NLRB. Initially, all the CIO internationals had refused to sign the affidavits, but by 1948 only Communist-oriented unions such as FTA still held out. When Reynolds proved intransigent, there was little the union could do. FTA had no standing with the NLRB, and it was too weak to win another strike.[44]

At the same time, Local 22 began to feel repercussions from the conflict within the CIO over the status of unions, like the FTA, that had rejected the Marshall Plan and endorsed Henry Wallace's Progressive Party presidential campaign in 1948. A rival CIO union, the United Transport Service Employees (UTSE), sent organizers into Winston-Salem to persuade black workers to abandon Local 22. In a March 1950 NLRB election, which the FTA requested after complying with the Taft-Hartley Act, UTSE joined Local 22 on the ballot. The FTA local retained solid support among its black constituency, who faithfully paid dues to their stewards even after the contract had expired and in the face of condemnation of their union—from the company, the CIO, and HUAC. Even the black community leader Alderman Williams asked workers to vote against the union and "send the Communists away for good." Yet Local 22 captured a plurality of all the votes cast, and in a runoff two weeks later it won outright. But when the NLRB accepted the ballots of lower-level white supervisors, the scales again tipped against the local.[45]

Local 22 disappeared from Winston-Salem's political and economic life, and a far more accommodative black community leadership filled the void left by the union's defeat. Beginning in the mid-1940s, a coalition of middle-class blacks and white business moderates had sought to counter the growing union influence within the black community. They requested a study of local race relations by the National Urban League's Community Relations Project (CRP). Largely financed by Hanes Hosiery president James G. Hanes, the CRP study appeared in late 1947 and called for improved health, education, and recreational facilities, but it made no mention of workplace issues. The Urban League foresaw a cautious, "step-by-step approach" and proposed that an advisory committee drawn from the black middle class discuss community issues with their white counterparts and help city officials and white philanthropists channel welfare services to the black community. The *Winston-Salem Journal* called the CRP's recommendations a "blueprint for better community relations" but one that would not alter "the framework of race relations."[46]

The Urban League's program helped make Winston-Salem a model of racial moderation. Blacks continued to register and vote in relatively high numbers and to elect a single black alderman. The city high school was integrated without incident in 1957, while Winston-Salem desegregated its libraries, golf course, coliseum, and the police and fire departments. But the dynamic and democratic quality of the black struggle in Winston-Salem would never be recaptured. NAACP membership declined to less than five hundred in the early 1950s, and decision making once again moved behind closed doors. When a grievance arose from the black community, a group of ministers met quietly with Hanes; a few phone calls by the white industrialist led to desegregation of the privately owned bus company in 1958.[47]

A similar story unfolded in the plants of the R. J. Reynolds Tobacco Company. After the destruction of Local 22, the company blacklisted several leading union activists, yet Reynolds continued to abide by many of the wage standards, benefit provisions, and seniority policies negotiated during the union era. The company reorganized its personnel department; rationalized procedures for hiring, firing, and evaluating employees; and upgraded its supervisory force by weeding out old-timers and replacing them with college-educated foremen. To forestall union activity, Reynolds kept its wages slightly ahead of the rates paid by its unionized competitors.[48]

In February 1960, when sit-ins began at segregated Winston-Salem lunch counters, the voices of black protest were again heard in the city's streets. But the generation of blacks who had sustained Local 22 played little role in the new mobilization. College and high school students predominated on the picket lines and in the new protest organizations that confronted white paternalism and challenged the black community's ministerial leadership. NAACP membership rose once again; more radical blacks organized a chapter of the Congress of Racial Equality (CORE). Public segregation soon collapsed.[49]

The subsequent trajectory of the freedom struggle in Winston-Salem was typical of that in many black communities. Heightened racial tensions set the stage for a 1967 riot and a burst of radicalism, followed by the demobilization of the protest movement and years of trench warfare in the city council. The political career of Larry Little, the son of Reynolds workers who had been members of Local 22, highlighted the contrasts between the two generations of black activists. Little moved from leadership of the North Carolina Black Panther Party in 1969 to city alderman in 1977, but despite the radicalism of his rhetoric, crucial issues of economic security

and workplace democracy were not restored to the political agenda in Winston-Salem. Because black activists of his generation confronted the city's
white elite without the organized backing of a lively, mass institution like
Local 22, their challenge proved more episodic and less effective than that
of the previous generation.[50]

THE LIMITS OF LIBERALISM IN POSTWAR DETROIT

A similar demobilization took place in Detroit after the war. There the
union, as well as the companies, helped undermine the independent
working-class base black activists had built in the six years since UAW organization of the Ford Motor Company. Racial issues were not of primary
importance in the factional conflict of 1946 and 1947 that brought Walter
Reuther to the presidency of the UAW. The victory of his caucus was based
both on rank-and-file endorsement of Reuther's bold social vision, especially exemplified in the General Motors strike of 1945–1946, and in the
Reuther group's anti-Communism, which struck an increasingly responsive
chord after passage of the Taft-Hartley Act.[51] Nevertheless, the Reuther victory greatly diminished black influence and independence within the UAW
and the liberal-labor community in which the union played such an important role. Reuther was as racially egalitarian as his opponents, but the political logic of his bitterly contested victory—he won less than 10 percent of
black delegate votes in 1946—meant that Reuther owed no organizational
debt to the growing proportion of union members who were black.

When the Reuther group consolidated their control of the union in
1947, there was a large turnover in the Negro UAW staff. Blacks with ties to
the opposition, such as John Conyers Sr. and William Hardin, two of the
first black staffers, and the articulate lawyer, George Crockett, the de facto
leader of the UAW's black caucus, were ousted from their posts. The young
dynamo, Coleman Young, lost his job with the Wayne County CIO council.
Tappes was hired as a UAW international representative in the early 1950s,
but only after he had broken with the Communists and lost his base of support in the Rouge plant.[52]

During the 1950s and 1960s, the Reuther group understood that civil
rights was a litmus test of labor liberalism. Reuther sat on the board of
directors of the NAACP, and the UAW probably contributed more funds to
that organization than all other trade unions combined. The UAW also
proved a ready source of emergency funds for the Montgomery Improvement Association, the Southern Christian Leadership Conference (SCLC),
and Students for a Democratic Society's early community organizing activities. Reuther was outraged that the AFL-CIO did not endorse the 1963
March on Washington; his union had provided much of the early funding,

and he would be the most prominent white to speak at the interracial gathering.[53]

Reuther also maintained a high profile on civil rights issues within the UAW. As president, he appointed himself codirector of the union's Fair Employment Practices Department and used the FEPD post to denounce racial discrimination and identify himself with postwar civil rights issues. Reuther pushed for a fair employment practices bill in Michigan and led the successful UAW effort to integrate the American Bowling Congress. During the crucial months after he had won the UAW presidency, but before his caucus had consolidated control of the union, such activism helped defuse black opposition; when Reuther was reelected in 1947 he won about half of all black delegate votes.[54]

Despite this public, and well-publicized, appearance, the emergence of a more stable postwar brand of unionism undermined civil rights activism in the UAW. As in many unions, the Reuther regime sought to eliminate or to coopt potentially dissident centers of political power. Local 600 was such a center of opposition, where black unionists still within the Communist orbit continued to play an influential, if somewhat muted, role well into the 1950s. Immediately after the 1952 HUAC hearings in Detroit, which publicized the continuing presence of Communists in Local 600, the UAW International Executive Board put the huge local under its direct administration. Six months later, tens of thousands of Rouge workers reelected their old officers, but the influence and independence of the giant local nevertheless waned in the next few years. Leaders of the UAW defused much of the local's oppositional character by appointing many of its key leaders, including Tappes and Sheffield, to the national union staff.

Equally important, Ford's postwar automation and decentralization slashed the Rouge workforce in half, eliminating the predominantly black production foundry. The same phenomenon was taking place in many of Detroit's other highly unionized production facilities, so that by the late 1960s a ring of relatively small and mainly white manufacturing facilities surrounded Detroit's million plus black population. Meanwhile, high levels of black unemployment became a permanent feature of the urban landscape after the 1957–1958 recession. Not unexpectedly, the size and social influence of the unionized black working class ceased to grow, although this stagnation was masked by the militance of inner-city minority youth late in the 1960s.[55]

The UAW's Fair Employment Practices Department also defused civil rights activism in the union. After 1946 the department was led by William Oliver, a black foundryman from Ford's Highland Park factory. Unlike the politicized blacks from the Rouge, Oliver had no large reservoir of political support in the UAW, nor did he attempt to build one. During Oliver's tenure, the FEPD had a dual role: it represented the UAW to the national

civil rights community, the NAACP, the Urban League, and the more liberal
federal agencies and congressmen; and it processed discrimination complaints as they percolated up from black workers in the locals. Rather than
serving as an organizing center for UAW blacks, the FEPD bureaucratized
the union's civil rights activities. "We are a fire station" admitted Tappes,
who served in the department during the 1950s and 1960s, "and when the
bell rings we run to put out the fire."[56]

A UAW retreat from civil rights militancy also became evident in politics. From 1937 to 1949, the UAW sought to reshape Detroit's formally
"nonpartisan" electoral politics along interracial class lines. Thus in 1945
and 1949 Richard Frankensteen and George Edwards, both former UAW
leaders, fought mayoral campaigns that helped move integrated housing
and police brutality to the center of local political debate. Both were
defeated by conservative incumbents, but their labor-oriented campaigns
nevertheless provided a focus around which civil rights forces could mobilize. However, after the CIO's "bitterest political defeat in the motor city,"
in 1949, the UAW ceased to expend its political capital in what many of its
leaders now considered fruitless campaigns to take over city hall. The UAW
continued to back the liberal governor G. Mennen Williams, but in the city
proper the union made peace with conservatives like Albert Cobo and Louis
Miriani, who had built much of their political base on segregationist homeowner movements.[57]

Neither the Communist Party nor the NAACP was able to fill the void
opened up by the UAW default. In the early 1950s many erstwhile leaders of
the union's black caucus joined the Detroit Negro Labor Council (NLC), a
Communist front organization. But the NLC faced relentless pressure from
the NAACP, HUAC, and the UAW, which denounced the council as a "Com-
munist-dominated, dual unionist organization which has as its sole objective
the disruption and wrecking of the American labor movement."[58] Both the
UAW and the NAACP made exclusion of Communists from civil rights coalition work a high priority in the early 1950s, and the NLC dissolved in 1956.
The NAACP, of course, maintained a cordial relationship with the UAW, but
it also declined in postwar Detroit. After reaching a wartime peak of twenty-
four thousand in 1944, membership dropped to six thousand in 1950, when
there was much discussion of the need to "rehabilitate" what had once been
the organization's largest unit. In the early 1950s national NAACP membership also fell to less than half its wartime level.[59]

When civil rights reemerged as a major issue in union and city politics in
the late 1950s, the Reuther leadership often found its interests counterposed
to the forces mobilized by the freedom movement of that era. By 1960
Detroit's population was about 30 percent black, and upwards of a quarter of
all autoworkers were Mexican or black. At the Rouge plant between 50 and
60 percent of production workers were nonwhite.[60]

Reuther's mode of civil rights advocacy seemed increasingly inadequate as the fears and conflicts of the early Cold War era receded. Two issues seemed particularly egregious. First, black participation in UAW skilled trades apprenticeship programs stood at minuscule levels, 1 percent or less. Second, no black sat on the UAW executive board, although blacks had been demanding that symbolically important post in UAW convention debates since the early 1940s. Failure to make progress on those problems genuinely embarrassed white UAW leaders, but Reuther and his colleagues were trapped by the regime over which they presided. Reuther hesitated to take on the militant and well-organized skilled trades, then in the midst of a long-simmering craft rebellion against the UAW's industrial unionism. Nor could a black be easily placed on the UAW executive board. In no UAW region did blacks command a majority of all workers; moreover, Reuther loyalists held all existing posts. Creating a new executive board slot seemed the only alternative, but that would dilute the power of existing board members and flatly repudiate Reuther's long-standing opposition to a specifically black seat on the executive board.[61]

In this context, and in the immediate aftermath of the Montgomery bus boycott, an independent black protest movement reemerged in Detroit politics with the founding of the Trade Union Leadership Council (TULC) in 1957. Initially TULC was little more than a caucus of UAW black staffers, but under the leadership of Horace Sheffield the organization challenged Reutherite hegemony. Despite the UAW's good reputation, Sheffield explained in 1960, a black-led organization was needed because "the liberal white trade unionists had long been 'mothballed,' . . . by the extensive growth of 'business unionism.' "[62] TULC opened a new chapter in Detroit politics in the 1961 mayoralty race. The incumbent mayor, Miriani, had the support of virtually all elements of the Detroit power structure, including the UAW, but he was hated by most blacks and not a few whites because of his defense of Detroit's increasingly brutal and racist police department. Sheffield used the mayoral campaign of Jerome Cavanagh, a young liberal lawyer, to establish his own network among Detroit's black trade union officials and make the TULC a mass organization of over seven thousand members in 1962 and 1963. Thereafter, a number of black activists whose political roots went back to the anti-Reuther forces of the 1940s won elective office, sometimes over bitter UAW protest. They included John Conyers Jr., who took Detroit's second black congressional seat in 1964; George Crockett, who won election as Recorders Court Judge in 1966 and later went on to Congress; and Coleman Young, who became mayor in 1973.[63]

TULC proved less successful in remolding UAW politics. The organization's mushroom growth, combined with the growth of the civil rights movement, forced the UAW to put a black on its executive board in 1962. But for this position the Reuther leadership chose none of the blacks prominently associated with TULC militancy, but instead the relatively little known Nelson Jack Edwards, a black staff representative. Although black appointments to the UAW staff increased markedly in the 1960s, TULC failed to generate a mass movement among rank-and-file black workers. TULC represented the generation of black activists politicized in the 1940s, but many had spent the intervening years on union staffs or in local office so they no longer enjoyed an organic link with the younger black militants who were flooding into Detroit's auto shops.[64]

When the Dodge Revolutionary Union Movement (DRUM) and other black insurgencies swept through the auto industry in the late 1960s, the new generation had come to see UAW liberalism as indistinguishable from corporate conservatism. They were mistaken, but in 1968, that year of great expectations and smashed hopes, such distinctions seemed beside the point. Many TULC veterans found DRUM's wholesale condemnation of the UAW irresponsible, while the young militants thought their elders merely a reformist wing of Reuther's union leadership. A reported exchange conveys DRUM members' impatience with TULC veterans' loyalty to the union. Shelton Tappes is said to have told a group of black Chrysler workers who had been fired for staging an outlaw strike and were picketing Solidarity House, the UAW's official home: "If the TULC had done what it was organized for there wouldn't be any such development as DRUM." And one of the young pickets reportedly answered, "And if Reuther and the other bureaucrats had done what the union was organized for, there wouldn't have been any need for TULC."[65]

CONCLUSION

E. P. Thompson once asserted that most social movements have a life cycle of about six years. And unless they make a decisive political impact in that time, that "window of opportunity," they will have little effect on the larger political structures they hope to transform.[66] For the black freedom struggle the mid-1940s offered such a time of opportunity, when a high-wage, high-employment economy, rapid unionization, and a pervasive federal presence gave the black working class remarkable self-confidence, which established the framework for the growth of an autonomous labor-oriented civil rights movement. The narrowing of public discourse in the early Cold War era contributed largely to the defeat and diffusion of that movement. The rise of anti-Communism shattered the Popular Front coalition on civil rights, while the retreat and containment of the union movement deprived black activists of the political and social space necessary to carry on an independent struggle.

The disintegration of the black movement in the late 1940s ensured that when the civil rights struggle of the 1960s emerged it would have a different social character and an alternative political agenda, which eventually proved inadequate to the immense social problems that lay before it. Like the movement of the 1940s, the protests of the 1960s mobilized a black community that was overwhelmingly working class. However, the key institutions of the new movement were not the trade unions, but the black church and independent protest organizations. Its community orientation and stirring championship of democratic values gave the modern civil rights movement a transcendent moral power that enabled a handful of organizers from groups like the Student Nonviolent Coordinating Committee, SCLC, and CORE to mobilize tens of thousands of Americans in a series of dramatic and crucial struggles. Yet even as this Second Reconstruction abolished legal segregation and discrimination, many movement activists, including Martin Luther King Jr., recognized the limits of their accomplishment. After 1965 they sought to raise issues of economic equality and working-class empowerment to the moral high ground earlier occupied by the assault against de jure segregation.[67] In retrospect, we can see how greatly they were handicapped by their inability to seize the opportunities a very different sort of civil rights movement found and lost twenty years before.

NOTES

The authors wish to thank Eileen Boris, William Chafe, Charles Eagles, Sara Evans, Jaquelyn Hall, Alice Kessler-Harris, Steven Lawson, Susan Levine, Leslie Rowland, Harvard Sitkoff, David Thelen, Seth Wigderson, and several readers for the *Journal of American History* for their helpful comments.

1. Richard M. Dalfiume, "The 'Forgotten Years' of the Negro Revolution," *Journal of American History* 55 (June 1968): 90–106; Steven Lawson, "The Second Front at Home: World War II and Black Americans," paper delivered at the Sixth Soviet-American Historians Colloquium, September 24–26, 1986, Washington (in Nelson Lichtenstein's possession). This view has recently been reinforced by the television documentary "Eyes on the Prize," which begins abruptly in 1954. Juan Williams, *Eyes on the Prize: America's Civil Rights Years, 1954–1965* (New York: Viking, 1986). However, a few sociologists have broken with the orthodox periodization: Aldon Morris, *The Origins of the Civil Rights Movement: Black Communities Organizing for Change* (New York: Free Press, 1984); and Jack Bloom, *Class, Race and the Civil Rights Movement* (Bloomington: Indiana University Press, 1987).

2. Harold M. Baron and Bennett Hymer, "The Negro in the Chicago Labor Market," in *The Negro in the American Labor Movement,* ed. Julius Jacobson (Garden City, N.Y.: Anchor Books, 1968), 188. See also Gavin Wright, *Old South, New South: Revolutions in the Southern Economy since the Civil War* (New York: BasicBooks, 1986), 239–57. For a discussion of black proletarianization, see Joe

William Trotter Jr., *Black Milwaukee: The Making of an Industrial Proletariat, 1915–1945* (Urbana: University of Illinois Press, 1985); Steven Lawson, *Black Ballots: Voting Rights in the South, 1944–1969* (New York: Columbia University Press, 1975), 134; Henry Lee Moon, *Balance of Power: The Negro Vote* (Garden City, N.Y.: Doubleday, 1949), 146–96; and Dalfiume " 'Forgotten Years,' " 99–100.

    3. Dalfiume, " 'Forgotten Years,' " 100; Harold Preece, "The South Stirs," *Crisis* 48 (October 1941): 318.

    4. James A. Gross, *The Reshaping of the National Labor Relation Board: National Labor Policy in Transition 1937–1947* (Albany: State University of New York Press, 1981), 5–41; Gary Gerstle, "The Politics of Patriotism: Americanization and the Formation of the CIO," *Dissent* 33 (Winter 1986): 84–92. Racist discrimination in hiring, promotion, and seniority were hardly eliminated by the new CIO unions; see Robert J. Norrell, "Caste in Steel: Jim Crow Careers in Birmingham, Alabama," *Journal of American History* 73 (December 1986): 669–701.

    5. Herbert R. Garfinkel, *When Negroes March: The March on Washington Movement in the Organizational Politics of FEPC* (Glencoe, Ill.: Free Press, 1959); Louis Kesselman, *The Social Politics of FEPC: A Study in Reform Pressure Movements* (Chapel Hill: University of North Carolina Press, 1948); William Harris, "Federal Intervention in Union Discrimination: FEPC and West Coast Shipyards during World War II," *Labor History* 22 (Summer 1981): 325–47.

    6. Horace Huntley, "Iron Ore Miners and Mine Mill in Alabama: 1933–1952" (Ph.D. diss., University of Pittsburgh, 1977); Michael Honey, "Labor and Civil Rights in the South: The Industrial Labor Movement and Black Workers in Memphis, 1929–1945" (Ph.D. diss., Northern Illinois University, 1987), 422–75; Nell Irvin Painter, *The Narrative of Hosea Hudson: His Life as a Negro Communist in the South* (Cambridge, Mass.: Harvard University Press, 1979); Rick Halpern, "Black and White, Unite and Fight: The United Packinghouse Workers' Struggle against Racism," paper delivered at the North American Labor History Conference, October 1985, Detroit (in Lichtenstein's possession); Dennis C. Dickerson, "Fighting on the Domestic Front: Black Steelworkers during World War II," in *Life and Labor: Dimensions of American Working-Class History*, ed. Charles Stephenson and Robert Asher (Albany: State University of New York Press, 1986), 224–36; Toni Gilpin, "Left by Themselves: A History of United Farm Equipment and Metal Workers, 1938–1955" (draft, Ph.D diss., Yale University, 1988) (in Toni Gilpin's possession).

    7. Nannie M. Tilley, *The Bright-Tobacco Industry, 1860–1929* (Chapel Hill: University of North Carolina Press, 1948); Nannie M. Tilley, *The R. J. Reynolds Tobacco Company* (Chapel Hill: University of North Carolina Press, 1985).

    8. Robert Korstad, "Those Who Were Not Afraid: Winston-Salem, 1943," in *Working Lives: The Southern Exposure History of Labor in the South*, ed. Marc Miller (New York: Pantheon Books, 1980), 184–99; and Robert Korstad, "Daybreak of Freedom: Tobacco Workers and the CIO, Winston-Salem, North Carolina, 1943–1950" (Ph.D. diss., University of North Carolina, Chapel Hill, 1987), 2–50; Tilley, *R. J. Reynolds Tobacco Company*, 373–414.

    9. *Winston-Salem Journal*, July 14, 1943, 6; ibid., July 25, 1943, 6; Horace R. Cayton and George S. Mitchell, *Black Workers and the New Unions* (Chapel Hill: University of North Carolina Press, 1939), 372–424.

10. *Winston-Salem Journal*, July 14, 1943, 6; ibid., July 16, 1943, 6; ibid., July 17, 1943, 6; ibid., July 25, 1943, 6.

11. Robert A. Levett to David C. Shaw, August 22, 1944, in R. J. Reynolds Tobacco Company, Case 5-C-1730 (1945), Formal and Informal Unfair Labor Practices and Representation Cases Files, 1935–48, National Labor Relations Board, RG 25 (National Archives); *Winston-Salem Journal*, November 17, 1943, 1.

12. "Directive Order, R. J. Reynolds Tobacco Company and the Tobacco Workers Organizing Committee," October 18, 1944, Case No. 111-7701-D, Regional War Labor Board for the Fourth Region, RG 202 (National Archives).

13. "Discussion Outline for Classes in Shop Steward Training," Highlander Folk School, n.d. (in Robert Korstad's possession); Velma Hopkins interview by Robert Korstad, March 5, 1986, ibid.

14. Ruby Jones interview by Korstad, April 20, 1979, ibid.

15. *Worker's Voice*, August 1944; ibid., January 1945, 2; ibid., April 1945, 2; Viola Brown interview by Korstad, August 7, 1981 (in Korstad's possession). The United Cannery, Agricultural, Packing and Allied Workers of America (UCAPAWA) changed its name to reflect the increasing number of tobacco locals within it.

16. Junius Scales interview by Korstad, April 28, 1987 (in Korstad's possession); Ann Matthews interview by Korstad, February 1986, ibid. See also Junius Irving Scales and Richard Nickson, *Cause at Heart: A Former Communist Remembers* (Atlanta: University of Georgia Press, 1987), 201–19; and Robin D. G. Kelley, "Hammer N' Hoe: Black Radicals and the Communist Party in Alabama, 1929–1941" (Ph.D. diss., University of California, Los Angeles, 1987), 296–311.

17. Roger Keeran, *The Communist Party and the Auto Workers Union* (Bloomington: Indiana University Press, 1980), 234; Painter, *Narrative of Hosea Hudson*, 306–12; Nat Ross, "Two Years of the Reconstituted Communist Party in the South," *Political Affairs* 26 (October 1947): 923–35; Wilson Record, *Race and Radicalism: The NAACP and the Communist Party in Conflict* (Ithaca, N.Y.: Cornell University Press, 1964), 84–168; Irving Howe and B. J. Widick, *The UAW and Walter Reuther* (New York: Random House, 1949), 223–25.

18. Saul Wellman interview by Lichtenstein, November 10, 1983 (in Lichtenstein's possession); Mark Naison, *The Communist Party in Harlem* (Urbana: University of Illinois Press, 1984), 23–34.

19. William H. Chafe, *Civilities and Civil Rights: Greensboro, North Carolina, and the Black Struggle for Freedom* (New York: Oxford University Press, 1980), 29–30; Lucille Black to Sarah March, March 28, 1945; Winston-Salem, 1945–55, file, box C140, National Association for the Advancement of Colored People Papers (Manuscripts Division, Library of Congress); Gloster Current to C. C. Kellum, November 19, 1947, ibid.; Memorandum, February 9, 1942, North Carolina State Conference file, box C141, ibid.; Membership Report, July 31, 1946, ibid.

20. *UCAPAWA News*, August 1, 1944, 2.; ibid., September 1, 1944, 5; *Worker's Voice*, October 1944, 3; ibid., March 1946, 4. For politics in the preunion era, see Bertha Hampton Miller, "Blacks in Winston-Salem, North Carolina, 1895–1920: Community Development in an Era of Benevolent Paternalism" (Ph.D. diss., Duke University, 1981), 6–74; *Worker's Voice*, October 1944, 3.

21. *Pittsburgh Courier*, June 3, 1944.

22. Board of Aldermen, Winston-Salem, North Carolina, Minutes, vol. 30, 278 (City Hall, Winston-Salem, N.C.); ibid., vol. 32, 555.

23. Herbert R. Northrup, *Organized Labor and the Negro* (New York: Harper & Brothers, 1944), 186–88; August Meier and Elliott Rudwick, *Black Detroit and the Rise of the UAW* (New York: Oxford University Press, 1979), 3–7.

24. Meier and Rudwick, *Black Detroit*, 8–22.

25. Ibid., 39–87.

26. Shelton Tappes interview by Herbert Hill, October 27, 1967, and February 10, 1968 (Archives of Labor History and Urban Affairs, Wayne State University, Detroit, Mich.).

27. Robert Robinson interview by Lichtenstein, October 9, 1983 (in Lichtenstein's possession), Ed Lock interview by Peter Friedlander, December 1976, ibid.; Walter Dorach interview by Lichtenstein, October 14, 1982, ibid.; Meier and Rudwick, *Black Detroit*, 106–107.

28. Wellman interview; Paul Boatin interview by Lichtenstein, October 12, 1982 (in Lichtenstein's possession); Keeran, *Communist Party and the Auto Workers Unions*, 33–67; U.S. Congress, House Committee on Un-American Activities, *Communism in the Detroit Area*, 82 Cong., 2d sess., March 10–11, 1952, 3036–45, 3117–35.

29. Meier and Rudwick, *Black Detroit*, 175–206; Alan Clive, *State of War: Michigan in World War II* (Ann Arbor: University of Michigan Press, 1979), 144–51.

30. "Twenty Thousand Members in 1943," *Crisis* 50 (May 1943), 140–41; Dominic J. Capeci, Jr., *Race Relations in Wartime Detroit: The Sojourner Truth Housing Controversy of 1942* (Philadelphia: Temple University Press, 1984), 75–99, 111–13.

31. "Twenty Thousand Members in 1943," 141; "All Out for Big Demonstration against Discrimination," file 1943, box C86, NAACP Papers; Meier and Rudwick, *Black Detroit*, 114–17; Howe and Widick, *UAW and Walter Reuther*, 103.

32. Meier and Rudwick, *Black Detroit*, 136–56.

33. Richard Deverall to Clarence Glick, "UAW-CIO Local 190 Wildcat Strike at Plant of Packard Motor Co.," Richard Deverall Notebooks (Catholic University of America, Washington); "Negro Workers Strike to Protest 'Hate Strike,'" *Michigan Chronicle*, November 18, 1944, Fair Employment Practices vertical file (Archives of Labor History and Urban Affairs); Meier and Rudwick, *Black Detroit*, 162–74.

34. Capeci, *Race Relations in Wartime Detroit*, 78–82, 164–70; Meier and Rudwick, *Black Detroit*, 164.

35. "Addes-Frankensteen to Support Proposal for UAW Board Member," September 25, 1943, *Michigan Chronicle*, Fair Employment Practices vertical file (Archives of Labor History and Urban Affairs); "[Reuther] Slaps Addes for Stand on Races Issues," October 2, 1943, ibid.; "UAW Leaders Assail 1,400 Hate Strikers," April 29, 1944, ibid.; "Split in Ranks of Officials Aid to Cause," September 16, 1944, ibid.; "Reuther Urges Support of NAACP Membership Campaign," *Detroit Tribune*, June 1, 1946, ibid.; George Crockett interview by Hill, March 2, 1968 (Archives of Labor History and Urban Affairs); William Dodds interview by Lichtenstein, June 12, 1987 (in Lichtenstein's possession); Martin Halpern, "The Politics of Auto Union Factionalism: The Michigan CIO in the Cold War Era," *Michigan Historical Review* 13 (fall 1987), 66–69.

36. Harvard Sitkoff, "Harry Truman and the Election of 1948: The Coming of Age of Civil Rights in American Politics," *Journal of Southern History* 37 (November 1971), 597–616. See also Peter J. Kellogg, "Civil Rights Consciousness in the 1940s," *Historian* 42 (November 1972): 18–41.

37. "Labor Drives South," *Fortune* 34 (October 1946): 237; *Wage Earner*, April 12, 1946, 3; *New York Times*, April 21, 1946, 46; *Final Proceedings of the Eighth Constitutional Convention of the Congress of Industrial Organizations, November 18, 19, 20, 21, 22, 1946, Atlantic City, New Jersey* (Washington, n.d.), 194; Barbara Sue Griffith, *The Crisis of American Labor: Operation Dixie and the Defeat of the CIO* (Philadelphia: Temple University Press, 1988).

38. Paul Sifton to Victor G. Reuther, "Revised Civil Rights Memorandum," June 13, 1958, Civil Rights Act of 1958 file, box 25, Joseph Rauh Collection (Library of Congress).

39. Sumner Rosen, "The CIO Era, 1935–55," in *The Negro in the American Labor Movement*, ed. Julius Jacobson (Garden City, N.Y.: Anchor Books, 1968), 188–208; Herbert Hill, "The Racial Practices of Organized Labor: The Contemporary Record," ibid., 286–357.

40. *Worker's Voice*, January 1947, 2; Tilley, *R. J. Reynold's Tobacco Company*, 485–488; Everett Carll Ladd, *Negro Political Leadership in the South* (Ithaca, N.Y.: Cornell University Press, 1966), 61. See also Howell John Harris, *The Right to Manage: Industrial Relations Policies of American Business in the 1940s* (Madison: University of Wisconsin Press, 1982), 96, 157.

41. *Winston-Salem Journal*, May 19, 1947, 1; Tilley, *R. J. Reynolds Tobacco Company*, 400–401; U.S. Congress, House Committee on Un-American Activities, *Hearings Regarding Communism in Labor Unions in the United States*, 78 Cong., 1 sess., July 11, 1947, 63–122; *Winston-Salem Journal*, July 12, 1947, 1.

42. Jack Fry interview by Korstad, October 16, 1981 (in Korstad's possession).

43. Harvey A. Levenstein, *Communism, Anticommunism, and the CIO* (Westport, Conn.: Greenwood Press, 1981), 286–87.

44. *Winston-Salem Journal*, July 15, 1947, 14; Robert Black interview by Korstad, March 4, 1985 (in Korstad's possession).

45. *Winston-Salem Journal*, March 18, 1950, 1; ibid., March 22, 1950, 1; ibid., March 25, 1950, 1; ibid. April 6, 1950, 1; Tilley, *R. J. Reynolds Tobacco Company*, 404–12.

46. Reginald Johnson to Lester Granger, memorandum, January 28, 1946, Community Relations Project, Winston-Salem, North Carolina, file, box 27, series 6, National Urban League Papers (Library of Congress); *Winston-Salem Journal*, November 16, 1947, sec. 3, 1.

47. Ladd, *Negro Political Leadership*, 121–27, 134–35; Black to March, January 25, 1950, 1946–55, file, box C140, NAACP Papers; Tilley, *R. J. Reynolds Tobacco Company*, 410; Aingred Ghislayne Dunston, "The Black Struggle for Equality in Winston-Salem, North Carolina: 1947–1977" (Ph.D. diss., Duke University, 1981), 59.

48. Tilley, *R. J. Reynolds Tobacco Company*, 412–14, 454–58, 463–71.

49. Dunston, "Black Struggle for Equality," 61–161.

50. Ibid., 270–71.

51. John Barnard, *Walter Reuther and the Rise of the Auto Workers* (Boston: Little, Brown, 1983), 101–70; Martin Halpern, "Taft-Hartley and the Defeat of the Progressive Alternative in the United Auto Workers," *Labor History* 27 (spring 1986): 204–26.

52. Crockett interview; Tappes interview; Studs Terkel, *Division Street, America* (New York: Pantheon, 1971), 328–30.

53. Walter Reuther, "The Negro Worker's Future," *Opportunity* 23 (fall 1945): 203–206; William Oliver to Roy Reuther, "Status of UAW Officers and NAACP Memberships," February 21, 1961, file 24, box 9, UAW Citizenship Department (Archives of Labor History and Urban Affairs); Herbert Hill interview by Lichtenstein, June 20, 1987 (in Lichtenstein's possession).

54. Martin Halpern, "The Disintegration of the Left-Center Coalition in the UAW, 1945–1950" (Ph.D. diss., University of Michigan, 1982), 237–40, 273–74, 433–37; Tappes interview.

55. William D. Andrew, "Factionalism and Anti-Communism: Ford Local 600," *Labor History* 20 (spring 1979): 227–36; Dorach interview. See also Nelson Lichtenstein, "Life at the Rouge: A Cycle of Workers' Control," in *Life and Labor*, ed. Stephenson and Asher, 237–59.

56. Tappes interview; Oliver to Roy Reuther, "Ford Plant, Indianapolis," December 20, 1957, file 29, box 8, UAW Citizenship Department (Archives of Labor History and Urban Affairs); Oliver to Walter Reuther, "Preliminary Analysis of Allegations Made Against UAW by the NAACP Labor Secretary Which Were Unfounded," November 1, 1962, file 10, box 90, Walter Reuther Collection, ibid.

57. Dudley W. Buffa, *Union Power and American Democracy: The UAW and the Democratic Party 1935–72* (Ann Arbor: University of Michigan Press, 1984), 133–73; B. J. Widick, *Detroit: City of Race and Class Violence* (Chicago: Quadrangle Press, 1972), 151–55.

58. *Proceedings, Fourteenth Constitutional Convention International Union United Automobile Aerospace and Agricultural Implement Workers of America (UAW) March 22–27, 1953, Atlantic City, New Jersey* (n.p. [1953]), 264; Philip Foner, *Organized Labor and the Black Worker* (New York: International Publishers, 1981), 295–309.

59. Herbert Hill to Roy Wilkins, December 23, 1949, Hill-1949 file, box C364, NAACP Papers; "Graphic Representation of Detroit Branch NAACP Campaigns, 1941 to 1948," Detroit file, box C89, ibid.; "Memorandum for Gloster Current on Rehabilitation of Detroit Branch," April 20, 1950, ibid.; Record, *Race and Radicalism*, 132–231; Lerone Bennett Jr., *Confrontation: Black and White* (Chicago: Johnson Publishing, 1965), 213.

60. Widick, *Detroit*, 138–40; "UAW Fair Practices Survey—1963," file 12, box 90, Reuther Collection; Robert Battle to James Brown, "RE: Civil Rights Hearing," December 13, 1960, file 13, box 50, ibid.

61. William Gould, *Black Workers in White Unions* (Ithaca, N.Y.: Cornell University Press, 1977), 371–88; Jack Stieber, *Governing the UAW* (New York: Wiley, 1962), 83–88; "UAW Fair Practices Survey—1963."

62. Horace Sheffield, "Bitter Frustration Gave Added Impetus to Trade Union Leadership Council," *Michigan Chronicle*, May 28, 1960, Horace Sheffield vertical

file (Archives of Labor History and Urban Affairs); B. J. Widick interview by Lichtenstein, August 6, 1986 (in Lichtenstein's possession).

63. Buffa, *Union Power*, 139–42; Widick, *Black Detroit*, 151–56. The UAW made an all-out, but ultimately unsuccessful, effort to stop George Crockett's reentry into mainstream political life. See Nadine Brown, "Crockett Supporters Charge Union 'Takeover' in First," *Detroit Courier*, October 6, 1966, George Crockett vertical file (Archives of Labor History and Urban Affairs); and Morgan O'Leary, "Hectic '49 Trial Haunts Crockett's Bid for Bench," *Detroit News*, October 7, 1966, ibid.

64. Nelson Jack Edwards and Willoughby Abner, "How a Negro Won Top UAW Post," *Detroit Courier*, April 4, 1964, vertical file, Trade Union Leadership Conference (Archives of Labor History and Urban Affairs); "Reuther Outlines UAW Position on Sheffield Assignment," file 9, box 157, Reuther Collection; Hill interview; Widick interview.

65. Foner, *Organized Labor and the Black Worker*, 423.

66. Notes on E. P. Thompson, speech in support of European peace movement, July 8, 1983, Berkeley, California (in Lichtenstein's possession). The notion that protest movements have a limited time frame in which to make their impact felt is also put forward by Frances Fox Piven and Richard A. Cloward, *Poor People's Movements: Why They Succeed, How They Fail* (New York: Pantheon Books, 1977), 14–34.

67. David Garrow, *Bearing the Cross: Martin Luther King Jr. and the Southern Christian Leadership Conference* (New York: W. Morrow, 1986), 431–624.

12

A. PHILIP RANDOLPH AND THE FOUNDATIONS OF BLACK SOCIALISM

MANNING MARABLE

Asa Philip Randolph was the most influential black trade unionist in American history. He may also have been, next to W. E. B. Du Bois, the most important Afro-American socialist of the twentieth century. His accomplishments in black union organizing, militant journalism, and political protest were unequaled for decades. His controversial newspaper, *The Messenger*, published from 1917 to 1928, was the first socialist journal to attract a widespread audience among black working- and middle-class people. In 1941 he led the Negro March on Washington Movement to protest racial discrimination in federal hiring policies, establishing a precedent which was to be revived over two decades later at the high point of the civil rights movement. Early in his career, Randolph earned the hatred and fear of the capitalist elite and federal government officials. President Woodrow Wilson referred to the black socialist leader as "the most dangerous Negro in America."

Later in his life, Randolph's contributions to the Afro-American freedom struggle were severely criticized. In the late 1960s, young black industrial workers condemned Randolph and other black trade union leaders for not representing their problems and vital interests. To the black activists in the League of Revolutionary Black Workers he came to repre-

From *Radical America* 14, no. 2 (March–April 1980): 7–32. Reprinted by permission of the author.

sent a modern Booker T. Washington, without the Tuskegee educator's skill at political compromise and power. In 1968 when blacks demanded greater decision-making authority in New York's public school system and charged the United Federation of Teachers with racism, Randolph heartily defended the AFT and its leader, Albert Shanker. In 1976 he lent his support to Daniel Patrick Moynihan, a conservative Democrat, when Moynihan was running for the U.S. Senate from New York. By then, Randolph's image as a radical socialist and militant trade unionist had been utterly erased. Upon his death in May 1979, Vice President Walter Mondale glorified the black leader, declaring that "America can speak out for human rights around the world, without hypocrisy, because of the faith A. Philip Randolph . . . showed in our country."

Thus we approach the great legacy of Randolph with some sadness and uncertainty. So many questions are left unanswered by the path of his brilliant and yet contradictory career. Some Marxists suggest that the "decisive break" in Randolph's career occurred in 1919, when he parted company with other black Socialists like Grace Campbell, Cyril V. Briggs, and Frank Crosswaith, who joined the fledgling Communist Party. "The issue was clear cut," argued Irwin Silber of the *Guardian*, "not support for socialism in general or in the abstract, but support for and defense of the Bolshevik revolution." Randolph's decision to choose "the path of social democracy" was "the decisive turning point in a political life devoted to preventing revolutionary forces from winning leadership of the Black liberation struggle."[1] As we shall observe, this split was not as decisive as Silber or others suggest. Randolph admired and supported the Russian revolution for many years. Throughout his early career, especially in the periods 1919–1922 and 1935–1940, he welcomed the support of Marxist-Leninists, although differing with them politically. In general, there is much greater continuity of political ideology and practice from the younger to the older Randolph than is usually thought.

This essay does not attempt to present a comprehensive view of Randolph's political life. (Numerous books and articles document his long and productive career, usually in a very positive light.[2]) Instead, this essay will examine Randolph's early career as a militant journalist, Socialist Party candidate, and trade unionist, from his arrival in New York in 1911 until the late 1920s. Many of Randolph's major accomplishments, such as founding the National Negro Congress during the Great Depression, the March on Washington Movement of 1941, and the civil disobedience campaign against military conscription in 1948, are discussed here only briefly, if at all. This is because, first, the fundamental outlines of Randolph's socialism and political activism were firmly established during an earlier period. The roots of his thought were in the chaotic experiences of World War I and its aftermath. Second, the foundations for subsequent black working-class activism and modern black nationalism were established in the twenties. The competing political forces in Harlem of the period—Garveyism, left black nationalism, militant integrationism, Marxism-Leninism—are themes which recur within the black movement today. The political decisions Randolph made during the 1920s, for better or worse, set much of the pattern of socialism and trade union work within the black community. The attempt here is to criticize Randolph's emergent theory of social transformation during his formative decade of political activism and to develop an understanding of the consequences of his sometimes eclectic political practice. The legacy of Randolph's politics and trade unionism which is carried on by his protégé Bayard Rustin will also be considered in this light.

A BLACK PROLETARIAT

The historical period of World War I and the immediate postwar years brought substantial changes to black Americans in general and to blacks in industrial labor in particular. For the first time in history, a substantial number of Southern, rural blacks were moving to the industrial North. Against the paternalistic advice of Booker T. Washington, almost half a million black men, women, and children left the South before and during World War I. Simultaneously, writes Philip Foner, "the first black industrial working class in the United States came into existence." The number of blacks employed in industry between 1910 to 1920 rose from 551,825 to 901,131. By 1920 about one-third of all Afro-American workers were employed in industry. However, only about 15 percent of those workers held skilled or semiskilled jobs. The great majority of black workers earned a living in the very lowest paying and most physically difficult jobs.[3]

As the political economy of black America took a decisive shift toward the industrial North, competing political interests began organizing, leading, and interacting with the new black labor force. Broadly conceived, four potential political forces presented alternative agendas to black industrial workers during this period. They were: (1) the old Booker T. Washington-capitalist alliance, which included conservative black ministers, businessmen, and journalists who preached cooperation with the capitalist class; (2) the American Federation of Labor, which in theory called for organizing black workers, but in practice upheld a strict Jim Crow bar; (3) the Marxist trade unionist in the Workers Party, later the Communist Party and many members of the Socialist Party, which advocated black-white labor unity; (4) independent all-black labor organizations, including black nationalist groups influenced by Marcus Garvey, which operated on the outside of the "House of Labor."

The success of Booker T. Washington in attracting white capital to his many enterprises, from the National Negro Business League to Tuskegee Institute, was dangerous for the new black working class in the North. Washington's Northern constituency, the aggressive but fragile black entrepreneurial elite, firmly supported a capitalist-Negro alliance against white labor. Washington had argued that blacks should appeal to white employers to hire black workers, since they were "not inclined to trade unionism" and not in favor of strikes. (Tuskegee scientist and inventor George Washington Carver was a friend of auto industrialist Henry Ford.) Thus, a major black newspaper such as the *Chicago Defender* supported Washington's strategy of alliance with the capitalist class. Many prominent black ministers, Republican politicians, and businessmen counseled black workers to reject unionism. Despite this influence, the overwhelming majority of new immigrants from the rural South saw this strategy for what it was, a "dead end" Jim Crow policy which only perpetuated low economic status for the black working class.

On paper, the American Federation of Labor sought to recruit the budding black proletariat to its cause; in actual practice it was scarcely less reactionary than the Ku Klux Klan. Between 1919 to 1927 the number of black locals in the AFL dropped from 161 to 21. Many unions had a long-established Jim Crow policy. Sometimes blacks were admitted to separate lodges, and then forced under the authority of a white local. The new president of the AFL, the United Mine Workers' former secretary-treasurer William Green, was not a friend of black workers. Green had tolerated Ku Klux Klan influence within the UMW, and had never taken a strong stand against racial segregation. Green's concern for black labor was only stimulated in the 1920s when it appeared that many Afro-American workers were moving toward Marxism and/or independent trade union activism.[4]

The only white groups which defended black workers' rights during this period were on the Left. Growing out of the militant tradition of the Industrial Workers of the World (IWW), thousands of socialist organizers of both races campaigned for worker unity against the issue of white racism. When the "Wobblies" split over the question of the Soviet revolution, many, such as William Z. Foster, joined the Communist Party. In 1920 Foster brought together a biracial coalition of Marxists and reformist trade union activists to create the Trade Union Educational League (TUEL). The TUEL advocated the building of a workers' and farmers' political party, greater racial egalitarianism inside the AFL, and the creation of militant unions for noncraft workers. In 1925 the CP was also active in the formation of the American Negro Labor Congress, an all-black labor group which advocated the building of "interracial labor committees" to promote the introduction of black workers into previously segregated crafts. As the Communists grew more influential in organizing black workers, the fears of AFL leaders mounted.[5]

Related to these developments in the labor Left was the rapid growth of independent black workers' organizations. As thousands of black laborers came to the North, the base for all-black, militant activism in labor increased dramatically. In 1915 a national organization of black railroad workers was created, the Railway Men's Benevolent Association. Within five years it had fifteen thousand members. In 1917 the Colored Employees of America was founded, one of the first of many groups which attempted to organize all black laborers. Two years later the National Brotherhood Workers of America was established, a coalition of black workers from almost every occupation, including blacksmiths, electricians, dock workers, porters, riveters, and waiters. Until its demise in 1921, it represented a potential alternative to the racist policies of the AFL. To the left of these organizations, black radicals and Marxists urged the development of independent socialist strategies for black labor.[6] Randolph's entire life must be viewed against this initial period of his activism, a time of tremendous growth and opportunities for black labor in the industrial North.

RANDOLPH'S SOCIALISM

Randolph's personal background conformed in most respects to that of other first-generation black immigrants from the South. Born in Crescent City, Florida, in 1889, he grew up in Jacksonville during the nadir of black-white relations. Inspired as a teenager by Du Bois's *Souls of Black Folk*, young Asa decided to leave the South and settle in New York City. Arriving in Harlem in the spring of 1911, Randolph first tried to become an actor. Failing at this, he drifted from one job to another. From 1912 to 1917 he attended courses at the City College of New York. A leftist philosophy professor, J. Salwyn Shapiro, acquainted Randolph with Marx's writings and other socialist literature. His discovery of socialism was so "exciting," he later reflected, that he studied "Marx as children read *Alice in Wonderland*."[7] He formed a group of radical "free thinkers" called the Independent Political Council, and began to follow the IWW closely. He began to identify himself with Harlem's premier black socialist and "leading street-corner orator," Hubert Harrison. He joined the Socialist Party at the end of 1916, and began to lecture on black history and political economy at the Socialist Party's Rand School. By the beginning of World War I, Randolph and his new black friend Chandler Owen, a fellow Socialist, had become "the most notorious street-corner radicals in Harlem, exceeding even Harrison in the boldness of their assault upon political and racial conditions in the country."[8]

Randolph and Owen became involved in a series of efforts to organize black workers in their community. After several weeks' work they won the support of six hundred black elevator operators for starting the United Brotherhood of Elevator and Switchboard Operators. The new union's demands included a minimum wage of $13 a week, and an eight-hour day. Receiving a federal charter from the AFL, the short-lived organization tried, and failed, to organize a strike to force recognition. Randolph and Owen were also active in the Headwaiters and Side Waiters Society as editors of the union's journal, the *Hotel Messenger*. After a dispute with the Society's president, William White, the young Socialists were fired. Within two months they organized their own monthly magazine, the *Messenger*, with the critical financial support provided by Randolph's wife, Lucille, who earned a living as a popular and successful Harlem hairdresser. Over the next months, the new publication acquired the enthusiastic support of older radicals like Harrison and younger militants like Jamaican Socialist W. A. Domingo.[9] Between 1917 and 1918 the journal received the support of a wide variety of Harlem radicals and liberal black intellectuals of various shades: William Pickens, a field secretary of the NAACP; Robert W. Bagnall, NAACP director of branches; Wallace Thurman, Harlem Renaissance author; essayist George S. Schuyler, a Socialist who evolved into a right-wing, Goldwater Republican.

The theoretical basis for Randolph's socialism in his early years, between 1914 to 1920, was an uneven combination of traditional religious reformism, economic determinism, fervent internationalism, and Karl Marx. His father, the Reverend James Randolph, was a pastor in the African Methodist Episcopal Church. Upon his move to Harlem, the first organization he joined was the Epworth League, a social club whose principle activity was Bible study and prayer. Later friends recalled that Randolph was the outstanding participant in all Epworth forums. Throughout Randolph's youth his father regarded him "as a fine prospect for the AME ministry."[10] Randolph rejected the orthodoxy of the cloth, but not the meaning of black spirituality in his politics. The language of the Old Testament would inform many of his speeches, as he deliberately used religious principles of brotherhood and humanism in organizing black workers. Even at the high point of their radicalism, Randolph and Owen spoke at black churches and worked closely with progressive clergy. "There are some Negro ministers," the *Messenger* declared in March 1920, "who have vision, intelligence, and courage. There [are] some upon whose souls the Republican Party has no mortgage."[11] Randolph continued to believe that the black church was "the most powerful and cohesive institution in Negro life." Like his friend Norman Thomas, Randolph's socialism was never rooted in an atheistic outlook.[12]

Like many other Socialists of the day, especially those influenced by the intellectual debates between Eduard Bernstein and Karl Kautsky of German Social Democracy, Randolph believed that socialism was a series of economic reforms taking place between management and labor. Through the vehicle of the trade union, the working class seized an increasingly greater share of the decision-making power within the means of production. The expression of working-class politics was, of course, the Socialist Party. The revolution against capital would be a revolt of the majority against the selfish interests of a tiny, isolated elite. Randolph's definition of socialism limited all of his subsequent work. If the Socialist Party was, as Randolph believed, the highest expression of working-class consciousness, and if blacks were profoundly working class, then no other political formation could address blacks' interests as well as the party. Race and ethnicity played no role in the "scientific evolution" of class contradictions; class was an economic category without cultural or social forms. Randolph increasingly viewed any form of black nationalism as a major obstacle between white and black workers in the struggle toward socialist democracy.

The outbreak of World War I deepened Randolph's commitment of militant pacifism and "revolutionary socialism." Like Debs, Randolph and Owen opposed World War I on the principle that "wars of contending national groups of capitalists are not the concern of the workers." The *Messenger*'s first issue denounced the "capitalist origins" of the conflict in a fiery essay, "Who Shall Pay for the War?" The editors told black men that they should not serve when drafted, and charged that the Wilson administration's claim that it was "making the world safe for democracy [was] a sham, a mockery, a rape on decency, and a travesty on common justice."[13] In 1918 Randolph and Owen participated in a Socialist Party antiwar speaking tour. On August 4, 1918, the two were arrested by federal agents after a mass rally in Cleveland and charged with violating the Espionage Act. Freed with a warning, the young men continued their lecture tour, visiting Chicago, Milwaukee, Washington, D.C., and Boston, where black radical Monroe Trotter joined their mass antiwar rally. In mid-August, Postmaster General Albert Burleson denied second-class mailing privileges to the *Messenger*. Owen was drafted and sent to a Jim Crow army base in the South. Only the armistice kept Randolph out of the draft.[14]

The Bolshevik Revolution inspired Harlem's radicals, seeming to vindicate their faith in revolutionary socialism. "Lenin and Trotsky . . . are sagacious, statesmanlike, and courageous leaders," the *Messenger* proclaimed in January 1918. "They are calling upon the people of every country to follow the lead of Russia; to throw off their exploiting rulers, to administer public utilities for the public welfare, to disgorge the exploiters and the profiteers."[15] For several years, Randolph argued that the Communist revolution meant the "triumph of democracy in Russia." He praised the Soviet Army's defeat of the White Russians in 1920, stating that the capitalist opponents of socialism "had not reckoned with the indomitable courage and the cold resolution born of the unconquerable love for liberty."[16] Randolph boldly predicted that Bela Kun's Hungarian Communists would eventually defeat the Social Democrats and send the aristocracy "to that oblivion and obscurity from which they ought never to emerge";[17] he also believed that British capitalism was on the brink of "an impending financial revolution."[18] Domestically, Randolph participated eagerly in the Socialist Party's activities. In 1917, the *Messenger* campaigned for Morris Hillquit, Socialist Party candidate for mayor. In 1920 Randolph ran as the party's candidate for state comptroller and polled 202,361 votes, only 1,000 less than Socialist presidential candidate Eugene V. Debs in the state! In 1921 he ran another unsuccessful campaign for secretary of state. Despite these failures, Randolph's belief in a democratic socialist revolution remained uncompromised.[19]

CONFLICT WITH DU BOIS

Randolph's strong antiwar position led to a decisive break with Du Bois— the major black leader of the NAACP and Randolph's intellectual mentor— in 1918, when the editor of the *Crisis* urged black Americans to support the war effort.[20] Up to this point, the *Messenger* had praised Du Bois as a race leader and opponent of "disfranchisement," condemning only his attitude on labor. "One has not seen where the doctor ever recognized the necessity of the Negro as a scab," Owen wrote, "allaying thereby the ill feeling against him by the working white men."[21] Now Du Bois's advocacy of the war crystallized Randolph's and Owen's opposition to his entire political line—from the "Talented Tenth" theory—the idea, used in *The Souls of Black Folk*, of a black intellectual leadership which would act as a vanguard for the black masses—to his views on segregation. By July 1918, Randolph condemned almost every major essay or book that Du Bois had ever written. Du Bois was a "political opportunist," simply representing "a good transition from Booker Washington's compromise methods to the era of the new Negro."[22]

Never one to avoid a fight, Du Bois defended his anti-Socialist Party, anti-trade unionist, anti-Bolshevik, and prowar positions head on. As early as January 1912, when he was a member of the Socialist Party, Du Bois complained about racism within the organization. He left the party to endorse the election of Woodrow Wilson later that year.[23] His opposition to trade unionism was well established.[24] Du Bois's position on the war evolved from examination of the colonial and racist origins of the conflict. The destruction of the German empire, Du Bois reasoned, might have resulted in the possibility of greater African self-determination.[25] Meanwhile, black Americans would be regarded for their loyalty to America's war effort against Germany.[26]

About Russian Socialism Du Bois was profoundly skeptical. After the "February Revolution" in early 1917, Du Bois suggested to his *Crisis* readers that the event "makes us wonder whether the German menace is to be followed by a Russian menace or not."[27] Although he criticized Alexander Kerensky's "blood and iron methods" in governing Russia, he said nothing about the Bolshevik's' rise to power.[28] When radical Harlem Renaissance writer Claude McKay questioned why Du Bois "seemed to neglect or sneer at the Russian Revolution," he replied curtly that he had "heard things which [were] frighten[ing]" about the upheaval. I am "not prepared to dogmatize with Marx or Lenin."[29]

For the new Negro generation, these opinions relegated "the Doctor" to the status of "the old, me-too-Boss, hat-in-hand Negro generally represented by Robert Russa Moton of Tuskegee."[30] Randolph declared that Du Bois was "comparatively ignorant of the world problems of sociological and economic significance."[31] In 1920, the *Messenger* charged that the *Crisis* had an editorial policy of "viciousness, petty meanness" and "suppression [of] facts pertaining to the NAACP." It attacked Du Bois's associates, especially field secretary William Pickens, as advocates of "sheer 'claptrap.' "[32] It laughed at Du Bois's provincial liberalism and staid social conformity. By the end of Wilson's administration, the Justice Department reported that the *Messenger* was "by long odds the most dangerous of all the Negro publications." Throughout Harlem, Randolph and Owen became known as "Lenin and Trotsky," the most revolutionary black Bolsheviks on the scene. Their political break from Du Bois seemed complete.[33]

RANDOLPH AND GARVEY

Having declared war against Du Bois and the NAACP leadership, Randolph and Owen sought the support of other black activists in Harlem. They needed support because, by their own admission, Du Bois remained "the most distinguished Negro in the United States today."[34] Marcus Garvey seemed a likely addition to their struggle against the *Crisis*'s editor. Born in Jamaica, Garvey had established his Universal Negro Improvement Association (UNIA) in 1914. Inspired by the racial "self-help" slogans of Booker T. Washington, the young black nationalist eventually settled in New York City in 1916. Randolph claimed the distinction of having been the first prominent black radical to invite Garvey to Harlem. He recalled years later that "when he finished speaking . . . I could tell from watching him then that he was one of the greatest propagandists of his time."[35] Garvey was attracted to Harrison, who by 1917 had left the Socialist Party to form his own Left black nationalist movement, the Afro-American Liberty League. Although Garvey was one of the main speakers at the league's first rally on June 12, 1917, he quickly established separate UNIA offices near the *Messenger* on 135th Street. Randolph and Garvey worked together in the International League of Darker Peoples, an organization which demanded that the

African territories and colonized nations be represented at the Versailles peace conference. Some Garveyites began to assist Randolph's efforts. Domingo, who was editor of Garvey's *Negro World*, worked as a contributing editor on the *Messenger*.[36] Randolph certainly welcomed Garvey's public attacks on Du Bois as an "antebellum Negro."[37]

The first major disagreement between the black nationalists and Randolph probably occurred over the creation of the Liberty Party, an all-black political coalition of former Socialists, Republicans, and Democrats, in late 1920. The stated slogan of the party was "Race First"; it advocated running a black presidential candidate and independent candidates at local levels. Randolph condemned the notion on all conceivable grounds. First, the Negro party was criticized because it had no prospects for support from white workers. "A party that has no hope of becoming a majority has no justification for independent action; for it can never hope to be of positive benefit to its supporters." Second, the party had no economic platform. Third, the proposition of a Negro president was "tragically inane, senseless, foolish, absurd, and preposterous. It is inconceivable that alleged intelligent, young colored men could take such obvious, stupendous political folly seriously." Last, the Liberty Party consisted of "opportunists, discredited political failures who are now trying to capitalize race prejudice of the Negro." The basis for this vituperative attack was Randolph's view that it was in the interests of "Negro workers to join and vote for the Socialist Party."[38]

It is probable that Harrison's Liberty League supported the new party. Another more menacing factor, of course, was Garvey, who had long been a proponent of an all-black political party.[39] J. W. H. Easton, the UNIA leader for U.S. blacks, was the party's nominee for president.[40] The idea of a separate, race-conscious, political organization, rather than the Liberty Party per se, was the real issue. Randolph and Owen had begun to view black nationalism as being even more dangerous than the threat presented by Du Bois and his *Crisis*.

The *Messenger* began to challenge the Garvey movement for hegemony within Harlem's black working-class population. In December 1920, Randolph issued an editorial, "The Garvey Movement: A Promise or a Menace," which argued that "the class-struggle nature of the Negro problem" was missing from the UNIA's work. Revolutionary black nationalism "invites an unspeakably violent revulsion of hostile opposition from whites against blacks." In Randolph's view, any all-black organization could "only misdirect the political power of the Negro. All party platforms are chiefly concerned with economic questions" and not with race. Therefore, the *Messenger* concluded, Garvey's entire program "deserves the condemnation and repudiation of all Negroes."[41] Relations with Garveyites swiftly worsened. Randolph insisted that Garvey's advocacy of an independent Africa for the Africans was unrealistic, because the Africans do not possess "the ability . . . to assume the responsibilities and duties of a sovereign nation."[42] By mid-1922 the *Messenger* concentrated on opposition to Garvey. "Here's notice that the *Messenger* is firing the opening gun in a campaign to drive Garvey and Garveyism in all its sinister viciousness from the American soil."[43]

Nowhere in the black press of the time was the anti-Garvey campaign expressed so bluntly, and with such anti-West Indian sentiments, as in the *Messenger*. Every significant aspect of Garvey's program was denounced as "foolish," "vicious," "without brains," or "sheer folly." The UNIA's proposal for a Booker T. Washington University will have "neither students nor teachers" since the former "will not trust it to give out knowledge" and the latter "will not trust it to give out pay." Garvey's wildest claim, that the UNIA had 4.5 million dues-paying members, proved that he was "a consummate liar or a notorious crook." But Randolph failed to explain the reasons for Garvey's massive popularity among black workers in Harlem, and ignored the hard evidence of the UNIA's progressive positions on African and international affairs.[44]

RANDOLPH BREAKS WITH BOLSHEVISM

As the Bolshevik Revolution forced the creation of a Third International, Randolph felt himself pulled gradually toward the Right. For the first time in several years he was no longer "the first voice of radical, revolutionary, economic, and political action among Negroes in America."[45] Revolutionary black activists outside both UNIA and *Messenger* factions were making political waves across Harlem. In the fall of 1917 Cyril V. Briggs founded the African Blood Brotherhood (ABB), a leftist and black nationalist group. A native of the Dutch West Indies and a former editorial writer for the *New York Amsterdam News*, Briggs began to edit his own nationalist journal, the *Crusader*. Many members of the ABB, which included Lovett Fort-Whiteman, Richard B. Moore, and Otto Huiswood, were quickly recruited into the newly formed Workers, or Communist, Party. (Harrison did not go over to the Communists, according to Harold Cruse, but he did "assist" them in certain situations.[46]) By 1922, the Communists had begun "to assail Garvey's program as reactionary, escapist, and utopian" while simultaneously trying "to influence, collaborate with, or undermine his movement."[47] As Marxists-Leninists, the ABB also attacked Randolph's firm ties with the Socialist Party, his reformist and quasi-religious theories for social transformation, his bitter hostility toward black nationalism, and growing tendency toward political and economic conservatism.[48]

The *Messenger* turned on its former Left friends almost as viciously as it had turned against Garvey. Declaring all black Communists "a menace to the workers, themselves, and the race," Randolph judged their policies "utterly senseless, unsound, unscientific, dangerous, and ridiculous." Black Marxist "extremists" were hopelessly out of touch with the mentality of Negro laborers, since the latter had not "even grasped the fundamentals and necessity of simple trade and industrial unionism!" As further proof that "Communism can be of no earthly benefit to either white or Negro workers," Randolph pointed out that the Soviet Union's new economic policy of "state capitalism" had replaced the radical socialist economics of the war Communist years.[49]

Opposition to "Communists boring into Negro labor" united Randolph and Du Bois.[50] Their joint opposition to Garvey's success was even stronger, and drove them back into some collaboration. There was no indication that Du Bois had changed his views on any of the major points that had separated him from Randolph during the war. If anything, Du Bois's opposition to "state socialism" and the "class struggle," and his advocacy of black "capital accumulation to effectively fight racism," placed him to the economic right of many Garveyites, and perhaps even Garvey himself at this time.[51] But the distance that had separated Randolph and Du Bois had now narrowed due to Garvey's gospel of black nationalism. The *Crisis* and the *Messenger* concurred in opposition to all forms of racial separatism and distrust of Garvey's business methods and honesty.

Working closely with the NAACP's assistant secretary, Walter White, Randolph coordinated an elaborate campaign against Garvey, which included the distribution of anti-Garvey handbills throughout Harlem. In January 1923, Randolph, Owen, Pickens, and several other black leaders drafted a memorandum to Attorney General Harry M. Daugherty asking for the conviction of Marcus Garvey on charges of mail fraud, various criminal activities, and "racial bigotry." Garvey was eventually convicted of mail fraud, and imprisoned in February 1925. By the late 1920s the UNIA had virtually collapsed, partially due to Randolph's anti-Garvey activities. The irony of this entire episode was that Randolph, a would-be leader of the black working class, had participated in the destruction of the largest black workers' and peasants' organization in American history.

THE BROTHERHOOD OF SLEEPING CAR PORTERS

Unlike Garvey, Randolph at first met with little success in his efforts to organize black workers. Randolph and Owen created the Friends of Negro Freedom in 1920, a biracial group which promoted black entrance into trade unions and held lectures on economic and political issues. Friends of Negro Freedom included Domingo, Baltimore *Afro-American* newspaper editor Carl Murphy, and black intellectual Archibald Grimké. In 1923 Randolph attempted unsuccessfully to establish a United Negro Trades organization to bring black workers into independent trade unions. Finally, in August 1925, a few Pullman porters asked Randolph to help them establish the Brotherhood of Sleeping Car Porters. Despite the fact that several black Pullman employees such as W. H. Des Verney and Ashley Totten had been more instrumental in organizing rank-and-file support for the Brotherhood, Randolph was named president. The initial prospects for this union's success looked just as dim as all the other groups that Randolph had led, however. The eleven thousand black porters working on Pullman cars faced the united opposition of the federal government, the Pullman Company, and its black conservative allies.

Given Randolph's early inability to build a successful and popular mass organization of black workers, it is not surprising that he began to reassess his overall theoretical outlook and political practice. Gradually, socialism was given less emphasis in his writings; by 1923 the *Messenger* had succeeded in attracting several black businessmen and merchants to advertise in its pages. Articles by Emmett J. Scott, the former secretary of Booker T. Washington, and even Robert Russa Moton, of Tuskegee, began appearing in the journal.[52] Quietly, editorial policies began to change. In January 1925, Randolph declared that "Negro businessmen are rapidly rising to the high mark of responsibility." Many black entrepreneurs were "splendid, courteous," and a "*delight* to deal with."[53] Randolph's blanket condemnation of the AFL and his earlier critical descriptions of Gompers—a "conservative, reactionary, and chief strikebreaker"—mellowed into fawning praise. The AFL was no longer a "machine for the propagation of race prejudice," but a progressive and democratic force. Randolph banned articles critical of William Green, the newly elected AFL leader.[54]

The editors endorsed Hampton and Tuskegee Institutes five-million-dollar fund drive by defending Washington's position on industrial education against Du Bois's Talented Tenth ideal. "Dr. Du Bois has probably been responsible for a great deal of misunderstanding about industrial education in America," they argued. "We need more brick masons, carpenters, plasterers, plumbers, than we do physicians; more cooks than lawyers; more tailors and dressmakers than pupils."[55] Yet there were only 40,000 black secondary and elementary teachers, 3,200 black physicians, and 900 black lawyers in the United States at this time. Only 50 percent of black children between the ages of five and twenty were enrolled in school: 25 percent of all adult blacks in the South were illiterate.[56] Randolph had moved toward a defense of private property and capitalism—a posture which he would never relinquish.

Thus Randolph persuaded the Brotherhood to apply for an international charter from the AFL in 1928, after it had spent several years as an independent, all-black union. The AFL rejected the application for equal membership, and instead proposed a "compromise" of "federal union" status inside the organization. Despite criticism from leftists, black workers, and some journalists, Randolph agreed to these terms. Both parties got something in the deal: Green and the AFL acquired a major black union, silencing their Marxist and black critics like Du Bois; Randolph received the promise of assistance from organized white labor in his growing struggle with the Pullman Company.

Randolph built the Brotherhood with characteristic enthusiasm. Appeals to porters to join were made in racial and religious terms. "Ye shall know the truth, and the truth shall set you free," was the slogan on Brotherhood stationary. In language reminiscent of some Garveyites, the Brotherhood's literature declared its faith in God and the Negro race: "Fight on brave souls! Long live the Brotherhood! Stand upon thy feet and the God of Truth and Justice and Victory will speak unto thee!"[57] Randolph's efforts to organize the porters received a boost in 1926, when the Garland Fund, administered by the American Civil Liberties Union, donated $10,000 to the Brotherhood. The money allowed Randolph to hire Frank W. Crosswaith, a West Indian Socialist and graduate of the Party's Rand School in New York City, as a professional organizer and executive secretary of the Brotherhood.[58] Randolph also benefited from many intelligent and creative leaders among the porters: Morris "Dad" Moore and C. L. Dellums of Oakland; T. T. Patterson of New York City; Des Verney, and Totten. Chief among them was Milton Webster. Two years Randolph's senior, he had been fired by Pullman because of his militancy. In the twenties he became a bailiff and was one of Chicago's influential black Republican leaders. As assistant general organizer of the Brotherhood and chief organizer for the Chicago area, next only to Randolph, the aggressive yet politically conservative Webster became the major spokesperson for the porters.[59]

Randolph's leadership was soon tested against the Pullman Company.[60] After the Board of Mediation, established by the Railway Labor Act of 1926, ruled the following year that the parties could not reach an agreement and recommended voluntary arbitration, Randolph's only alternative was to call a strike to force the Pullman Company into collective bargaining. The strike was set for June 8, 1928.[61]

Across the country, porters were excited at the prospect of a confrontation between themselves and the Pullman Company. Despite red-baiting against Randolph, random firings, and veiled threats, the porters backed the Brotherhood leadership almost unanimously. The strike vote, 6,053 to 17, astonished even Randolph. Some porters made plans for a long siege, even blocking the use of strikebreakers. Ashley Totten and his associates in Kansas City began collecting "sawed-off shotguns, railroad iron taps, boxes of matches, knives, and billy clubs" and storing them in a local black-owned building. Facing the prospect of an extensive and probably violent strike which would disrupt Pullman railroad service nationwide,

Randolph began to have doubts. Could an all-black workers' strike succeed without some measure of white trade-union and working-class support? Three hours before the scheduled strike, Green sent Randolph a telegram stating that "conditions were not favorable" for a strike. He suggested that the Brotherhood engage in "a campaign of education and public enlightenment regarding the justice of your cause." Randolph called the strike off.[62]

It is difficult to know whether the strike would have been successful. Throughout the remainder of his life, Randolph insisted that the possibilities were nil. The historical evidence points in the opposite direction, however. William H. Harris's research on Brotherhood correspondence suggests that Webster had a great deal of difficulty in convincing his local members not to strike by themselves. "Aside from disruption of peak travel, what could be more damaging to interstate commerce than to tie up the rails during the time when both national political parties were holding conventions in such remote cities as Houston and Kansas City?" Harris asked. "Even the Pullman Company recognized this as a potential danger."[63] The union was "in shambles after the abortive strike." The *Messenger* was forced to halt production; porters lost confidence in the Brotherhood and stopped paying their regular dues. Black newspapers like the *New York Argus* attacked the leadership of "A. Piffle Randolph."[64] The Communists accused him of "betraying Negro workers in the interest of the labor fakers."[65] The American Negro Labor Congress charged that Randolph had "forsaken the policy of militant struggle in the interest of the workers for the policy of class collaboration with the bosses and bluffing with the strike." Within four years, the Brotherhood's membership declined from almost 7,000 to only 771 in 1932.[66]

It was only in April 1937 that the Pullman Company agreed to bargain seriously with the Brotherhood. On August 25 of that same year Pullman agreed to reduce the porters' monthly workload from 400 to 240 hours, and provide a substantial pay increase. But many of his critics, black and white, suggested that these and other accomplishments would have been achieved much sooner if A. Philip Randolph had had a little less faith in the system and a little more confidence in the militancy of the black working class.

NATIONAL CIVIL RIGHTS STRUGGLES

In the Depression, Randolph again exhibited courage and some of his former political independence. Contrary to Du Bois, Randolph charged that "the New Deal is no remedy" to black people's problems. It did not "change the profit system," nor "place human rights above property rights." Assisted by Alain Locke, Ralph Bunche, and other Left-oriented black intellectuals, Randolph initiated the National Negro Congress in February 1936.

Hundreds of black trade unionists, radical civic reformers, and Communists participated in a black united front in blunt opposition both to Roosevelt's "welfare capitalism" and to the do-nothing acquiescence of the NAACP. Despite the breakup of the Congress in the early 1940s over the issue of "Communist control," the organization represented one of the most advanced coalitions of black activists ever assembled.[67]

With the onset of World War II in Europe, the Roosevelt administration began expanding production in defense industries. Prior to America's direct involvement in the war, thousands of new jobs were created in industrial, clerical, and technical fields related to wartime production. Black workers were largely kept out of these positions because of a tacit policy of Jim Crow followed by white labor, big business, and the federal government. Although Congress had forbidden racial discrimination in the appropriation of funds for defense training, the law was essentially a dead letter. With Randolph's resignation from the National Negro Congress in 1940, he turned his energies toward the issue of black employment in defense industries with federal contracts. Working again with Walter White, Randolph sought to influence Roosevelt to initiate action against white racism.

By January 1941, Randolph was prepared to take what was, for that time, radical action. Randolph urged blacks to organize a militant march in Washington, D.C., on July 1 to protest the discrimination against black workers. The idea of a "March on Washington Movement" seized the imagination of the black working class, the unemployed, and even the petty bourgeoisie. The Brotherhood of Sleeping Car Porters was the central force behind the campaign. Hundreds of March-on-Washington-Movement meetings were held in black churches, union halls, and community centers. With able support, Randolph succeeded in committing over one hundred thousand black people to the march. Foner observes that the "March on Washington Movement represented the first occasion in American history when a black labor organization assumed leadership of the struggle of the Negro masses on a national scale and became the spokesman for all black Americans, conservative and radical alike." Neither Garvey, Washington, nor Du Bois had ever succeeded in forming a popular coalition of the black business and professional elites, the working class, and rural blacks toward a single, progressive cause.

The driving force behind the 1941 March on Washington was black nationalism. Taking another page from Garvey's book, Randolph insisted that only blacks participate in the march. It was important for blacks to show white America that they were able to build an effective, militant, national organization without white assistance. C. L. Dellums explained that the Brotherhood informed its "white friends over the country why this had to be a Negro march. It had to be for the inspiration of Negroes yet unborn." White progressives and trade unionists were asked to offer "moral support, to stand on the sidelines and cheer us on."[68]

The demand for an end to discrimination in defense plants appealed to the typical black industrial worker who, like porters in the 1920s, was on the verge of class consciousness. But its expression among blacks was nationalism, a force involving religious, cultural, and ethnic qualities which Randolph was forced to deal with in a concrete manner. Randolph's biographer [Jervis Anderson] emphasizes that "a certain strain of black nationalism . . . ran through his social and religious heritage." Not surprisingly, "when the chips were down," Randolph had to return to his own origins to find the means to understand his own constituency and to articulate their aspirations. Anderson writes, "It is a wonder that black nationalism did not become the central activating force and principle of Randolph's political life."[69]

Roosevelt used his considerable power to force the organizers to stop the march. As black workers in Harlem, Washington, D.C., Chicago, and every major city prepared for the confrontation, Roosevelt finally agreed to sign an executive order prohibiting the "discrimination in the employment of workers in defense industries because of race, creed, color, or national origin." The Democratic administration promised to create the Fair Employment Practices Committee (FEPC), a commission which would supervise the compliance of federal contractors with the executive order. Although this was not everything that the March on Washington Movement had asked for, Randolph and other leaders agreed to call off the demonstration on June 24.[70]

Historians August Meier and Elliott Rudwick point to the March on Washington Movement as the real foundation for the civil rights movement of the 1950s and 1960s. "Though its career was brief, the former organization prefigured things to come in three ways," they note. It was, first, "an avowedly all-Negro movement"; second, it involved the direct "action of the black masses"; third, "it concerned itself with the economic problems of the urban slum-dwellers."[71] Two additional points can be made. The FEPC was the beginning of today's Federal Office of Contracts Compliance Programs, the Department of Labor's affirmative-action watchdog. The principle of equal opportunity for black people in employment was, for the first time, considered a civil right. Randolph's ideology behind the march also "prefigures" the 1950–1960s because of the impact of Gandhi's approach to social change. In an address before the March-on-Washington associates given in Detroit in September 1942, Randolph called attention to "the strategy and maneuver of the people of India with mass civil disobedience and noncooperation." Huge, nonviolent demonstrations "in theaters, hotels, restaurants, and amusement places" could be a potential means to gain full equality. Years before Martin Luther King Jr., Randolph envisioned the basic principles of *satyagraha* applied to the fight against Jim Crow.

Yet for all his foresight and commitment to the ideals of black struggle, Randolph's subsequent political behavior did little to promote the creation of a permanent organization. The March-on-Washington Movement's last major conference was in October 1946, and it lapsed completely the next year. Randolph's ongoing fights with AFL officials still produced meager results. As in the past, Randolph's failure to carry out the threat of militant action compromised the pursuit of his long-range goals. Even at the peak of his influence throughout black America, during the March-on-Washington Movement of 1940–1941, Randolph failed to establish a mass-based, permanent force which promoted his rhetorical commitment to democratic socialism and black economic equality. Again and again, especially later in his career, he failed to trust the deep militancy of the black working-class masses, relying instead upon tactical agreements with white presidents, corporate executives, and labor bureaucrats. Curiously, like Booker T. Washington, Randolph always preferred class compromise to class struggle.

With the end of World War II and the beginning of the Cold War, Randolph's creative contributions to the struggle for black freedom had largely ended. Like other labor leaders and socialists such as Norman Thomas, Randolph capitulated to the posture of extreme anti-Communism. Randolph and Thomas traveled to the Far East lecturing against the evils of radical trade unionism, for instance, under what later was revealed to be the auspices of the CIA. Randolph became an acknowledged "elder statesman" during the civil rights movement of the 1950s. Making his peace with those black leaders he had formerly opposed in the NAACP and Urban League, he had little to offer in the way of guidance or political theory to a new generation of black radicals, the rebels of SNCC (Student Non-Violent Coordinating Committee), CORE (Congress of Racial Equality), and the SCLC (Southern Christian Leadership Conference). Ironically, it was during this period that Du Bois, now in his eighties, moved toward a thoroughly radical condemnation of America's political economy. The old so-called political opportunist had become the active proponent of world peace and international liberation, while his "Young Turk" critic had become a defender of the conservative status quo.

Since the 1960s, Randolph's role in the AFL-CIO hierarchy has been filled by his trusted assistant, Bayard Rustin. Like his mentor, Rustin is a socialist and pacifist with a long history of principled and at times even courageous struggle. As a participant in CORE's "Journey of Reconciliation" campaign of 1946, he tested local Jim Crow laws by sitting in white sections on interstate buses in the South. With other early "freedom riders" he received a thirty-day jail term on a North Carolina chain gang. Rustin was one of the major organizers of the 1963 March on Washington, and inspired a generation of younger black activists like SNCC's Stokeley Carmichael and Phil Hutchings. But when he became head of the A. Philip Randolph Institute, founded by George Meany and the AFL-CIO in 1965, he acquired the language and outlook of white labor's elites. Rustin bitterly denounced Malcolm X as a "racist,"[72] and condemned the Black Power movement as "antiwhite" and "inconsistent." Rustin and Randolph defended the Vietnam War and criticized King for linking domestic civil rights with America's involvement in Southeast Asia.

In the 1970s Rustin's position within the black movement drifted increasingly toward the Right. At the September 1972 convention of the International Association of Machinists, he attacked black rank-and-file activists and defended the AFL-CIO's shabby record on integration. The next year he was critical of the creation of the Coalition of Black Trade Unionists, arguing that the Randolph Institute should be viewed as the "catalyst" for black advancement in union leadership positions. On the international front, at the time of Randolph's death in 1979, Rustin participated in a "Freedom House" delegation to Zimbabwe which declared that the white minority regime's fraudulent elections were democratic. Cruse analyzed him best in 1968, observing that "Rustin's problem is that in thirty years he has learned nothing new. He has done nothing creative in radical theory in American terms. . . ."[73] Put another way, Rustin is a victim of what Marx postulated in "The Eighteenth Brumaire of Louis Bonaparte"; that "all great personages occur, as it were, twice—the first time as tragedy, the second as farce." Rustin's life is tragic, because of his greatness and yet untapped potential. Rustin's is a caricature, in another historical period, of that lost greatness.

Despite Randolph's changes and shifting images certain consistencies remain. Throughout his career, Randolph perceived union organizing as a "top-down" rather than a mass-based strategy. Although he was not a porter, he asked for, and received, the presidency of the Brotherhood in 1925; he left the presidency of the National Negro Congress after realizing that he could no longer control the leftists in it. He consistently preferred compromise and gradual reform to confrontation and class/race struggle. The capitulation of the Brotherhood's 1928 strike and the 1941 March on Washington were the most outstanding instances, but not the only ones. He made a similar compromise in December 1965, after the establishment of the Randolph Institute. After years of criticizing the racial policies of the AFL-CIO, Randolph reversed himself at the San Francisco national convention by announcing that racism had virtually disappeared from organized labor.

Another of Randolph's central characteristics was his inability to appreciate the relationship between black nationalism, black culture, and the struggle for socialism. Randolph's and Owen's editorials in the *Messenger* declared that "unions are not based upon race lines, but upon class lines," and that "the history of the labor movement in America proves that the employing class recognizes no race lines." This crude and historically false oversimplification led Randolph into pragmatic alliances not only with the white Marxists, but also with the AFL after 1923, and later the Kennedy and Johnson administrations. His successes in winning higher wages and shorter working hours for the Brotherhood were achieved at the expense of building an autonomous, all-black protest movement which was critical of both racism and capitalism. The *Messenger's* vicious attacks against Garvey did not stop hundreds of thousands of rural and urban black workers from defending black nationalism. Randolph was ill equipped to understand the rank-and-file revolt of black industrial workers in the past two decades who were influenced by Malcolm X, Franz Fanon, and their Black Power disciples.

Cruse's comments on the entire generation of Harlem radicals, both in politics and the arts, are an appropriate critique of Randolph as well. Because "the Negro intellectuals of the Harlem Renaissance could not see the implications of cultural revolution as a political demand," Cruse notes, "they failed to grasp the radical potential of their own movement." Like the renaissance poets and novelists, Randolph was hesitant to place black culture, ethnicity, and nationalism on the same agenda with other social and political concerns. "Having no cultural philosophy of their own, they remained under the tutelage of irrelevant white radical ideas."[74]

This same assessment was also made by Du Bois in 1933. He criticized the literary renaissance as "literature written for the benefit of white readers, and starting primarily from the white point of view. It never had a real Negro constituency and it did not grow out of the inmost heart and frank experience of Negroes. . . ."[75] Similarly, Randolph's economic determinism, his political pattern of compromise and reconciliation, his narrow definitions of class and culture, proved harmful throughout his entire career. In the first Negro March on Washington when he did turn to the black workers with an avowedly nationalistic style and a program for political confrontation of the segregationist status quo, he was dramatically successful. When he overcame his Socialist Party training and used the language of the black church and Southern black political protest traditions to appeal to his Brotherhood's rank and file, he reached a potentially revolutionary force. But his ambiguous hostility toward the Negro's nationalism negated the full potential of his efforts.

Randolph's contribution to the ongoing struggle for black self-determination was unique and important. His activities in creating the Brotherhood of Sleeping Car Porters, the National Negro Congress, and the March on Washington Movement of 1940–1941 were necessary preconditions for the black activism of the 1950s and 1960s. Harold Cruse is correct that "not a single Negro publication in existence today matches the depth of the old *Messenger*." Randolph was the first great leader of the black urban working class. But unlike Du Bois, he was unable to reevaluate himself and his movement dialectically; ultimately he became a prisoner of his own limited vision for black America.

In the next stage of history, black working people and activists must transcend Randolph's contradictions. If they succeed, as they must, they will begin to realize the possibilities of socialism within the means and relations of production. In doing so, they will carry out the legacy of Randolph that he was unable to achieve for himself and his own generation.

NOTES

1. Irwin Silber, "Randolph: What Was His Role?" *Guardian*, May 1979.

2. Jervis Anderson's biography, *A. Philip Randolph: A Biographical Portrait* (New York: Harcourt Brace Jovanovich, 1972), examines the black Socialist's personal and political life. There are two excellent sources on the Brotherhood of Sleeping Car Porters: William H. Harris's recent study, *Keeping the Faith: A. Philip Randolph, Milton P. Webster, and the Brotherhood of Sleeping Car Porters* (Urbana: University of Illinois Press, 1977), and Brailsford R. Brazael, *The Brotherhood of Sleeping Car Porters: Its Origin and Development* (New York: Harper & Brothers, 1946). Theodore Kornweibel's, "The *Messenger* Magazine, 1917–1928" (Ph.D. diss., Yale University, 1971) examines Randolph's early years as a political activist.

The list of popular and scholarly articles published about Randolph or his role in the black movement are almost endless. See, for example, L. W. Thomas, "Three Negroes Receive 1964 Presidential Freedom Medal," *Negro History Bulletin* (December 1964): 58–59; M. Kempton, "A. Philip Randolph," *New Republic* (July 6, 1963): 15–17; Arna Bontemps, "Most Dangerous Negro in America," *Negro Digest* (September 1961): 3–8; John Henrik Clarke, "Portrait of an Afro-American Radical," *Negro Digest* (March 1967): 16–23; A. Morrison, "A. Philip Randolph: Dean of Negro Leaders," *Ebony* (November 1958): 103–104.

3. Philip S. Foner, *Organized Labor and the Black Worker, 1619–1973* (New York: Praeger, 1974), 129–35.

4. Ibid., 169–72.

5. Ibid., 164–66, 171–72.

6. Ibid., 147–60.

7. Anderson, *A. Philip Randolph*, 32, 50, 51, 52.

8. Ibid., 76–77; Harris, *Keeping the Faith*, 28–29. In 1944 Randolph commented that his "extensive reading of Socialist literature" was one of the "fundamental forces that had shaped his life." The Socialist Party theorists and authors he named included Morris Hillquit, Algernon Lee, Norman Thomas, Frank Crosswaith, and Eugene V. Debs. Until 1964, when he voted for Lyndon Johnson, he had consistently endorsed the Socialist Party ticket. Anderson, *A. Philip Randolph*, 343.

9. Anderson, *A. Philip Randolph*, 79–82.

10. Ibid., 48, 59.

11. Editorial, "Some Negro Ministers," *Messenger*, March 1920, 3.

12. Anderson, *A. Philip Randolph*, 25. Randolph stopped attending church within a year after his arrival in Harlem in 1911. But in December 1957, the Reverend Richard Allen Hildebrad, an AME minister in Harlem, received a request from Randolph to become a member of his church. Randolph seldom attended, if ever;

nevertheless, he probably rested somewhat easier with the spiritual knowledge that he was a member.

13. Anderson, *A. Philip Randolph*, 97–98.

14. Ibid., 107–109.

15. "The Bolsheviki," *Messenger*, January 1918, 7.

16. "The Russian Triumph," *Messenger*, March 1920, 3–4. Randolph's mechanistic, economic determinism is evident in his faulty commentary on the Bolsheviks and the coming American revolution. "The Government of the United States . . . is located in Wall Street. When the large combinations of wealth—the trusts, monopolies, and cartels are broken up . . . a new government will then spring forth just as the Soviet Government was an inevitable consequence of the breaking up of the great estates of Russia and assigning the land to the peasants, and the factories to the workers. It is as impossible to have a political machine which does not reflect the economic organization of a country, as it is to make a sewing machine grind flour." "The Negro Radicals," *Messenger*, October 1919, 17.

17. Editorial, *Messenger*, September 1919, 9–10.

18. Anderson, *A. Philip Randolph*, 92–96.

19. "When British Capitalism Falls," *Messenger*, March 1920, 3.

20. One of Du Bois's most controversial prowar editorials was "Close Ranks," published in the July 1918 issue of the *Crisis*. He argued, "Let us, while this war lasts, forget our social grievances and close our ranks shoulder to shoulder with our white fellow citizens and the allied nations that are fighting for democracy."

21. Chandler Owen, "The Failure of the Negro Leaders," *Messenger*, January 1918, 23.

22. Randolph, "W. E. B. Du Bois," *Messenger*, July 1918, 27–28; editorial, *Messenger*, March 1919, 21–22.

23. W. E. B. Du Bois, "Socialism Is Too Narrow for Negroes," *Socialist Call*, January 21, 1912; Du Bois, "A Field for Socialists," *New Review* (January 11, 1913): 54–57; Du Bois, "Socialism and the Negro Problem," *New Review* (February 1, 1913): 138–41. This does not mean that Du Bois disavowed socialism. In May 1914, Du Bois joined the editorial board of the Socialist Party's journal, *New Review*. His criticisms of some socialists' explicitly racist platforms in the South did not lessen his intellectual commitment to socialist economic goals.

24. W. E. B. Du Bois, "The Black Man and the Unions," *Crisis* (March 1918).

25. W. E. B. Du Bois, "The African Roots of the War," *Atlantic Monthly* (May 1915): 707–14.

26. W. E. B. Du Bois, "The Reward," *Crisis* (September 1918).

27. W. E. B. Du Bois, "The World Last Month," *Crisis* (March 1917).

28. W. E. B. Du Bois, *Crisis* (September 1917): 215.

29. W. E. B. Du Bois, "The Negro and Radical Thought," *Crisis* (July 1921). Du Bois's attitude toward the Bolshevik Revolution warms as Randolph's attitude wanes. See Du Bois's "Opinion" on Russia, *Crisis* (April 1922): 247–52, and his essay, "The Black Man and Labor," *Crisis* (December 1925), where he states, "We should stand before the astounding effort of Soviet Russia to reorganize the industrial world with an open mind and listening ears."

30. "The Crisis of the *Crisis*," *Messenger*, July 1919, 10.

31. Anderson, *A. Philip Randolph*, 100–101, 110.

32. "A Record of the Darker Races," *Messenger,* September 1920, 84–85; Owen, "The Failure of the Negro Leaders," 23.

33. Anderson, *A. Philip Randolph*, 115–19.

34. "W. E. B. Du Bois," *Messenger*, July 1918, 27.

35. Anderson, *A. Philip Randolph*, 122.

36. Ibid., 122–23; Tony Martin, *Race First: The Ideological and Organizational Struggles of Marcus Garvey and the Universal Negro Improvement Association* (Westport, Conn.: Greenwood Press, 1976), 9–10. On the Garvey Movement, also see Amy Jacques-Garvey, ed., *The Philosophy and Opinions of Marcus Garvey*, vols. 1 and 2 (1923; reprint, New York: Atheneum, 1977).

37. Martin, *Race First*, 320. After Harrison's newspaper, *The Voice*, closed in 1919, Garvey offered him a position on the *Negro World*. During 1920–1921 Harrison was "joint editor" of the paper. Martin, *Race First*, 92.

38. "A Negro Party," *Messenger*, November 1920, 130–31.

39. Martin, *Race First*, 320.

40. "The Garvey Movement: A Promise or a Menace," *Messenger*, December 1920, 171. Throughout the entire history of the *Messenger* one finds an antinationalistic bias. Randolph and Owen even took the extreme position that the greatest danger to American socialism and the trade union movement was not the racist, conservative white worker, but the Negro! "Negroes must learn to differentiate between white capitalists and white workers," the editors declared. Since they do not, "this makes the Negro both a menace to the radicals and the capitalists. For inasmuch as he thinks that all white men are his enemies, he is as inclined to direct his hate at white employers as he is to direct it at white workers." In the *Messenger's* opinion, the only hope was for organized labor to "harness the discontent of Negroes and direct it into the working-class channels for working-class emancipation." "The Negro—A Menace to Radicalism," *Messenger*, May–June 1919, 20.

41. Ibid., 170–72.

42. Editorial, *Messenger*, November 1992, 523.

43. Editorial, *Messenger*, July 1922, 437.

44. A. Philip Randolph, "The Only Way to Redeem Africa," *Messenger*, January 1923, 568–70, and February 1923, 612–14. Du Bois's comments against the Garvey organization were provocative. He defended the *Negro World* against Attorney General Palmer's attacks during the Red Summer of 1919, and in late 1920 described Garvey as "an honest and sincere man with a tremendous vision, great dynamic force, stubborn determination, and unselfish desire to serve." In 1921, he admitted that the "main lines" of the UNIA's activities "are perfectly feasible." It was only in 1922 and 1923, when Garvey began to consider the Ku Klux Klan as a potential ally to the black liberation movement, that Du Bois registered his strongest denunciations. See "Radicals," *Crisis*, December 1919; "Marcus Garvey," a two-part essay in *Crisis*, December 1920 and January 1921; "Back to Africa," *Century Magazine*, February 1923, 539–48.

45. Anderson, *A. Philip Randolph*, 82.

46. Harold Cruse, *The Crisis of the Negro Intellectual* (New York: Morrow, 1967), 45, 75. At its peak in 1921, the ABB had 2,500 members in fifty-six chapters

throughout the country. It demanded the right for black self-defense, "absolute race equality," a "free Africa," and political suffrage. In many respects, its platform was strikingly similar to the agendas of Malcolm X's Organization of Afro-American Unity, over forty years later. See "Cyril Briggs and the African Blood Brotherhood," WPA Writers' Project No. 1, Schombert Collection, New York Public Library.

47. Ibid., 46.

48. The final break between the black Marxist-Leninists and Social Democrats does not come in early 1919, as many have suggested, but much later. As late as mid-1920 Briggs was a participant in Randolph's Friends of Negro Freedom. Martin, *Race First*, 320.

49. "The Menace of Negro Communists," *Messenger*, August 1923, 784. The division between black Socialists and Communists tended to be along ethnic as well as political lines. Cruse observes that "after 1919, the split among Negro Socialists tended to take a more or less American Negro vs. West Indian Negro character. The Americans, led by Randolph, refused to join the Communists, while the West Indians—Moore, Briggs, and Huiswoud—did." There were several exceptions; Fort-Whiteman, an American, joined the Communists. It is interesting to note that Cruse does not fully discuss the fate of Harrison, a revolutionary Socialist who abandoned the Socialist Party because of its racism and never joined the Marxist-Leninists; a black nationalist who nevertheless did not wholeheartedly embrace the Garvey phenomenon. His primary concerns were generating independent black political activity and developing a greater race-consciousness among all Socialists. See H. Cruse, *The Crisis of the Negro Intellectual*, 118.

50. Du Bois, "Communists Boring into Negro Labor," *New York Times*, January 17, 1926, 1–2.

51. Du Bois, "Socialism and the Negro," *Crisis*, October 1921, 245; Du Bois, "The Class Struggle," *Crisis*, August 1921, 151.

52. Emmett J. Scott, "The Business Side of a University," *Messenger*, November 1923, 864. Early in its career, the *Messenger* was not reticent in its denunciations of Moton. "Moton has neither the courage, education, or the opportunity to do anything fundamental in the interest of the Negro," Randolph declared in 1919. "He counsels satisfaction, not intelligent discontent: he is ignorant of the fact that progress has taken place among any people in proportion as they have become discontented with their position. . . ." "Robert Russa Moton," *Messenger*, July 1919, 31.

53. "High Types of Negro Business Men," *Messenger*, January 1925, 21.

54. "Samuel Gompers," *Messenger*, March 1919, 22; "Why Negroes Should Join the I.W.W.," *Messenger*, July 1919, 8; and "Unionizing of Negro Workers," *Messenger*, October 1919, 8–10.

55. "The Knowledge Trust," *Messenger*, March 1925, 197–209.

56. "Black Persons in Selected Professional Occupations, 1890–1970," "Percent of Persons Five to Twenty Years Old Enrolled in School," and "Illiteracy in the Population Fourteen Years Old and Over for Selected Years," in U.S. Department of Commerce, Bureau of the Census, *The Social and Economic Status of the Black Population in the United States: An Historical View, 1790–1978* (Washington, D.C.: Government Printing Office, 1979), 76, 89, 91.

57. Brazeal, *The Brotherhood of Sleeping Car Porters*, 40. At this time Randolph also began a modest effort within the AFL to drum up support for the Brotherhood's position against Pullman. See Randolph, "Case of the Pullman Porter," *American Federationist*, November 1926, 1334–39.

58. Ibid., 18; Anderson, *A. Philip Randolph*, 140. Crosswaith eventually became a member of New York City's Housing Authority, appointed by Mayor Fiorello LaGuardia in the early forties. Earlier, he had been a leading political opponent of Marcus Garvey, and revolutionary Socialist Party theorist.

59. Anderson, *A. Philip Randolph*, 171–74; Harris, *Keeping the Faith*, 76, 78–79, 91. It is significant to note that Du Bois had anticipated Randolph's interest in the porters by at least a decade. In a brief essay for the *New York Times*, Du Bois suggested that the porters should organize as a union and strike for higher wages and better working conditions. See Du Bois, "The Pullman Porter," *New York Times*, March 16, 1914, 5.

60. Robert L. Vann, conservative black editor of the *Pittsburgh Courier*, argued that "the company will not deal with [Randolph] because of his history as a socialist. It is known that American capital will not negotiate with socialists." *Courier*, April 14, 1927. A more fundamental reason was provided by one lower-level Pullman boss to his black employees: "Remember, this is a white man's country, white people run it, will keep on running it, and this company will never sit down around the same table with Randolph as long as he's black." Anderson, *A. Philip Randolph*, 181.

61. Harris, *Keeping the Faith*, 110; Foner, *Organized Labor and the Black Worker*, 183–84.

62. Harris, *Keeping the Faith*, 111; Foner, *Organized Labor and the Black Worker*, 185.

63. Harris, *Keeping the Faith*, 112.

64. Ibid., 113, 114.

65. Foner, *Organized Labor and the Black Worker*, 184.

66. Anderson, *A. Philip Randolph*, 204–205. It should be noted as well that after 1928 Randolph remained "the dominant figure" in the Brotherhood, but no longer wielded "absolute power." Webster demanded and won the right to have all major union decisions made within the Brotherhood's Policy Committee, which he chaired. Historian William H. Harris describes Randolph as the union's "national black leader," whereas Webster was "a union organizer. Randolph thought in wider terms; he saw the problem of blacks in the totality of American society, whereas Webster thought mainly of the porters and of finding ways to improve their conditions at Pullman."

67. Ralph J. Bunche, "A Critical Analysis of the Tactics and Programs of Minority Groups," *Journal of Negro Education* (1935): 308–20; Ralph J. Bunche, "The Programs of Organization Devoted to the Improvement of the Status of the American Negro," *Journal of Negro Education* (1939): 539–50; A. Philip Randolph, "The Trade Union Movement and the Negro," *Journal of Negro Education* (1936): 54–58; Walter Green Daniel, "A National Negro Congress," *Journal of Negro Education* (1936); A. Philip Randolph, "Why I Would Not Stand for Re-Election as President of the National Negro Congress," *American Federationist*, July 1940, 24–25.

68. Anderson, *A. Philip Randolph*, 254.

69. Ibid., 254–55.

70. Ibid., 241–61.

71. August Meier and Elliott Rudwick, *From Plantation to Ghetto*, rev. ed. (New York: Hill and Wang, 1970).

72. On the question of Malcolm, we confront again the inconsistencies of Randolph's views on black nationalism. According to one source, Randolph was "a friend and admirer of Malcolm" even during his years as minister of Harlem's Temple Number Seven of the Nation of Islam. In 1962, Randolph invited him to serve on the Committee on Social and Economic Unity, a multiethnic coalition in Harlem. Several conservative black ministers threatened to leave when Malcolm arrived. Randolph replied that he would leave immediately if Malcolm was denied a voice on the committee. See Anderson, *A. Philip Randolph*, 13–14.

73. Harold Cruse, *Rebellion or Revolution* (New York: Morrow, 1968).

74. Harold Cruse, *The Crisis of the Negro Intellectual*, 65.

75. W. E. B. Du Bois, "The Field and Function of the Negro College," in Herbert Aptheker, ed., *The Education of Black People, Ten Critiques, 1906–1960* (Amherst: University of Massachusetts Press, 1973), 95–96.

Part 4

AFFLUENCE, POSSIBILITIES, AND PROBLEMS

In surveying the hard times that befell radical labor activists after World War II, many scholars and insurgents alike have argued that consumerism was a significant factor in weakening working-class consciousness in the United States. Lizabeth Cohen investigates the ways that consumer culture transformed workers' identities and expectations while failing to alter their underlying economic insecurity. Cohen sketches out the ways that the federal government, corporations, and workers themselves helped build the institutions of a "consumer's republic" that was mostly for whites: relatively strong unions, affordable higher education, and racially exclusive suburban bedroom communities and shopping districts. The result was an institutional framework that encouraged white men to develop family and race-centered identities in the community while simultaneously retaining working-class perspectives at the workplace. While the economic basis for working-class consumerism has been weakening for two decades, Cohen suggests that many workers refuse to abandon their middle-class identities and aspirations.

Mark McColloch suggests that unionization enabled steelworkers to achieve "industrial citizenship" in the consumer republic described by Cohen. Consistent with Cohen's approach is McColloch's observation that the modicum of comfort and dignity that workers had achieved did not afford them industrial democracy, that is fundamental control over corporations. McColloch appears to differ from Cohen in that he finds while steel-workers in the 1970s enjoyed a modest middle-class standard of living, this was the result of several decades of struggle and hardship. Well into the early 1960s, many steelworkers found it difficult to afford to retire and had to rely on the aid of children, spouses, and their own part-time work. While McColloch does not investigate workers' aspirations, he suggests that in economic terms, industrial workers' "middle-class standards of living" is largely a myth which enabled corporations to shift the blame for deindus-trialization from themselves to unionized workers.

While most industrial workers were deradicalized in the post–World War II "boom," Ed Mann was not. In "We *Are* the Union," Mann offers his life story of work and political struggle in the Youngstown area. In Mann's expe-rience, fat paychecks were tempered by frequent layoffs, and the benefits of unionism were limited by its undemocratic leadership and their tolerance of favoritism and racism in the workplace. After years of persistent struggle, Mann became a leader in his local and a force in the movement to democ-ratize the United Steel Workers and stop the shuttering of the steel industry.

John Hinshaw examines another struggle for democracy led by indus-trial workers in the postwar period in "Black Working-Class Protest in Pitts-burgh: The Struggle for Civil Rights, 1937–1975." Because black workers never realized the equality of opportunity that unionization promised, they continued to struggle against institutionalized racism in their unions, work-places, and in the wider economy. Although deeply aware of the limitations of business unionism, black workers' tactics and critique of postwar America were deeply influenced by their experiences as unionists. In many ways, they sought to make unionism live up to its ideals and spread its ben-efits throughout society as a whole.

13

WORKING-CLASS LIVES/ WORKING CLASS STUDIES

A Historian's Perspective [1]

LIZABETH COHEN

A s we come together to discuss the state of "Working-Class Lives/ Working-Class Studies" in the late twentieth century, I would like to share a clipping from the *New York Times*. An advertising column in the business section was devoted to a newly launched multimedia campaign to promote *Martha Stewart Living*, the extraordinarily fast-growing magazine published by Martha Stewart, a woman the article alternately describes as "the doyenne of decoupage," "the diva of domesticity," and, quoting one of her critics, "a control-freakish middlebrow taste maker." Martha Stewart's story is filled with social-class ambiguities; she who markets herself as the blue-chip, WASPy hostess from Westport actually was born Martha Kostyra, the oldest daughter of six children in a Polish Catholic family from ethnic, lower-middle-class Nutley, New Jersey. Likewise, the landed aristocrat who guides 5.3 million viewers a week through her country estate via a half-hour syndicated TV show confused the world several years ago by signing an exclusive merchandising deal with KMart. Last week's *New York Times* article celebrates the most recent "deliciously incongruous twist," that the "creative boutique" (i.e., ad agency) in New York developing the campaign to promote her four-year-old magazine is named "Working Class Inc." "She likes that," David Metcalf, president of Working Class, said of Ms. Stewart, laughing. "The name comes from the fact we work our butts off," he added. "And she works like crazy, too; she never bloody stops."[2]

I present the case of Martha Stewart not to amuse you, but to suggest how complicated social-class definitions and identities have become in contemporary America, a condition rooted, I would argue, in the specific circumstances of the post–World War II United States. The main message I want to convey today is the importance of historically grounding the definitions of working class that inform our thinking about "Working-Class Lives/Working-Class Studies." Moreover, those definitions must take into account both social structure—the lived experience of class—and social identity—the way people understand their place in the social order. If the Martha Stewart story has anything to teach us it is that class categories in postwar America are slippery and need to be handled with as much dexterity as possible. We are not living in a simple world when working-class and lower-middle-class customers—who may not identify as such—are making a wealthy woman out of one of their own who passes as an upper-class member of-the-manor-born, who teaches them how to "pass" as well, and who allows her media empire to be promoted by a firm calling itself Working Class Inc., intentionally substituting associations with "hard-working" and "classy" for the traditional connotations of working class.

Now one *could* say that the Martha Stewart case is the old story of American exceptionalism, of Americans believing in individual social mobility and the ideology of opportunity. In this rather ahistorical view, even when Americans live a reality of class stratification, they display an ingrained cultural propensity to deny class as a social category of differentiation. My own research in twentieth-century United States history, however, refutes this generalization and suggests that class as a conjuncture of experience and identity is much more historically contingent. I would insist that for any particular historical moment we must investigate carefully the complex way that workers' place in the social structure, and their social identity, interrelate.

In my first book, *Making a New Deal: Industrial Workers in Chicago, 1919–1939*, I set out to examine the character and ramifications of workers' class identity during the 1920s and 1930s, an era when, according to popular historical perceptions, the consumer society revolutionized social and cultural life in the United States, integrating people of all social classes into a depoliticized, classless mass culture. Looking carefully at the lives of working-class people in Chicago, I concluded that working-class identity survived the twenties, as the expansion of mass culture and mass consumption was mediated through ethnic and working-class institutions such as corner stores, neighborhood movie theaters and local, grassroots radio stations. Even as the disseminators of mass culture consolidated over time, they helped create a new kind of pan-working-class culture free of ethnic provinciality, which unified and mobilized working-class Chicagoans politically when they faced the ravages of the Great Depression. Through supporting CIO unions and FDR's national Democratic Party and New Deal state, working people felt they were endorsing a self-consciously working-class vision of equity and opportunity, what I call a "moral capitalism." In the interwar period, then, American exceptionalism did not prevail. Mass culture did not destroy working-class culture, and working-class people did not seek to deny their class origins by embracing a new culture and lifestyle coded as middle class.

My new research project has taken me into the post–World War II period, and here I am encountering a different, historically specific conjuncture of working-class experience and identity that may help us understand the Martha Stewart phenomenon. During the period 1945 to 1970, the American economy was built around what *Time* magazine in 1965 called a "nonvicious circle" of mass production and mass consumption where "spending created more production, production created wealth, wealth created more spending." Expanded mass consumption capacity became the nourishment required for sustaining a healthy economy. In concrete terms this meant that keeping people employed required empowering as many people as possible as consumers. Although it would prove to be more of a delimited era than participants expected, organized labor prevailed in more segments of the economy than ever before, and increasingly became more inclusive of women and minorities. Meanwhile, the structure of the economy was shifting in the postwar era so that white-collar service-sector jobs grew for men and women. Both phenomena—a unionized blue-collar sector and an expanding white-collar sector—helped put more spending money in American pockets, whatever their relative size.

This reorientation to consumption as the motor of economic growth proved to have important repercussions in American political culture, including encouraging postwar Americans to identify more as consumers than they had before. Although people's identity as producers in no way disappeared, a constellation of changes that accompanied the rise of a mass consumer economy made consumer identity—as purchaser of goods, as homeowner, as taxpayer—more formative than what one did to earn a living. Although the language of working-class identity was most explicitly tied to workers' production relations as employees and union members, growing identification as consumers did not by definition have to undermine class identity. After all, my research for *Making a New Deal* revealed that during the 1920s and 1930s workers' consumer experiences helped foster class identity and created new springboards for working-class assertiveness. Yet when we look closely at what happened to working-class people over the period from 1945 to 1970 in an area like Northern New Jersey—where a quintessential consumer-oriented postwar society developed—we can begin to see the consequences of the mass consumption economy for working-class experience and identity.

I'm going to focus on two key building blocks of the postwar mass consumer order—the GI Bill and the shift in marketplace from downtown to shopping center. On June 22, 1944, President Franklin Roosevelt signed the "Servicemen's Readjustment Act of 1944," better known as the "GI Bill of Rights." The two main provisions of the act most influential in reshaping postwar America were educational benefits for veterans and mortgage loans and guarantees to help them purchase homes with little or no downpayment. Although the GI Bill was publicly defended as the fulfillment of the nation's obligation to its servicemen and women, in reality it was designed to ease the transition from wartime to peacetime, thereby avoiding the severe economic recession that followed World War I. The educational benefits would stave off unemployment and unrest among veterans, keeping them occupied until reconversion created new jobs, and the VA loan-guarantee program would jump-start the economy through encouraging much-needed housing construction and making returning vets suburban homeowners and good credit risks for futher borrowing and purchasing of consumer durables. Class differences were not erased by the GI Bill; labor unions charged, for example, that it was much easier for college- and graduate-school-bound vets to take advantage of the act than those seeking secondary-level or vocational education, and evidence repeatedly showed that the more education a vet had before service, the more likely he or she was to take advantage of the educational benefit afterwards. Likewise, some veterans complained that the home-loan program, administered as it was through private banks, discriminated against those who did not qualify as good credit risks in traditional terms.

Nonetheless, working-class veterans did expand their career possibilities thanks to the GI Bill. A preliminary comparison of the Rutgers University class of 1942 and 1949 found the latter to be much more plebian than the former. A census bureau study of the early 1960s showed that nationally the average male veteran completed more than twelve years of school while the average nonveteran completed a little less than nine. And the GI Bill also made working-class veterans into homeowners. Between the end of World War II and 1966, one out of every five single-family residences built were financed by the GI loan program for either World War II or Korean War veterans. Overwhelmingly those homes were in newly developed suburban areas, as the VA mortgage regulations, like those of the FHA, favored new construction and racially homogeneous, residential communities.[3]

Most important for the shape of the postwar world, however, were those excluded from the beneficence of the GI Bill: women and African Americans. Most women, of course, were excluded by virtue of not having served in the armed forces, since less than 3 percent of military personnel in World War II were female. But even among those who did serve, overwhelming evidence indicates that they took much less advantage of their GI benefits, for reasons including the male connotations of veteran status and women's lack of integration into the influential veterans organizations. Hence, one of the most transformative pieces of legislation ever passed by Congress, empowering the state to subsidize the two most important routes to social mobility—education and property ownership—favored men over women and thereby reinforced a patriarchal family structure that the Great Depression and the war had begun to unravel.

Similarly, although African American GIs were theoretically eligible for benefits for their service in segregated military units, the segregated character of American postwar society kept them from fully utilizing them. Educational institutions of all sorts discriminated against blacks who sought to use their GI benefits to enroll. They had the same problems utilizing the VA home-loan program. When the NAACP complained to the Veterans Administration in 1955 that blacks were not getting their due, a sympathetic administrator agreed that although racial figures were not kept, his own educated guess was that out of the almost four million home loans guaranteed to date, less than thirty thousand went to "colored veterans," an "unfavorably disproportionare participation," he acknowledged. Discrimination from banks and other lending agencies made it difficult for blacks to qualify for VA loan guarantees and even when they did, restrictive covenants and other exclusionary tactics kept them out of the suburban areas favored by the VA mortgage provisions.[4] Homeownership in newly developed suburbs of single-family tract homes, made possible through VA mortgages and educational benefits that expanded earning and purchasing power, became an advantage enjoyed primarily by whites, whether of working-class or middle-class origin and occupation. The postwar residential landscape that resulted became increasingly differentiated between black-urban renter and white-suburban homeowner, even as open-housing legislation and court decisions broke down the legal defenses of residential segregation. While Martha Stewart was growing up in Nutley in the 1940s and 1950s, Northern New Jersey was fast becoming a patchwork quilt in black and white, with the old industrial cities of Newark, Paterson, and Passaic becoming increasingly black and nearby suburban communities remaining white, except for the handful of communities becoming known as black suburbs. Nutley itself was 98.4 percent white in 1960, while Newark was less than two-thirds and losing white population steadily every year. By the late 1970s, Newark's population had become 70 percent nonwhite.

The racial segmentation of the postwar metropolitan landscape was reinforced by the restructuring of the consumer marketplace beginning in the 1950s from downtown commercial centers to suburban shopping centers. Between 1947 and 1953, America's suburban population increased by 43 percent, in contrast to a general population increase of 11 percent. Moreover, the buying power of these suburbanites was even greater than their numbers suggested; they had higher median incomes and homeownership rates, and more children fourteen and under, than the rest of the metropolitan population, all indicators of high consumption. Gradually, merchandisers recognized the enormous profitability of serving these growing numbers of people living at some distance from urban centers. By the mid-1950s a new kind of marketplace—the regional shopping center—emerged, aimed at satisfying suburbanites' consumption and community needs. Here was the "new city" of the postwar era, a utopian vision of how community space should be constructed in a political economy and society built on mass consumption. In Paramus, New Jersey, a postwar suburb seven miles from the George Washington Bridge that sprouted virtually overnight in the vegetable fields of Bergen County, two centers—the Bergen Mall and the Garden State Plaza—opened within six months of each other at the intersection of three major highways. By the end of 1957, Paramus became the home of the largest shopping complex in the country.

When planners and shopping center developers envisioned this new kind of community center in the 1950s, they set out to *perfect* the concept of downtown, not to *obliterate* it, even though projects like the Paramus mall directly challenged the viability of existing commercial centers like Newark, Paterson, and Hackensack, the neighboring political and commercial seat of Bergen County. The ideal was still the creation of centrally located public space that brought together commercial and civic activity; moreover, in appearance these early shopping centers idealized—even romanticized—the physical plan of the traditional downtown shopping street, with stores lining both sides of an open-air pedestrian walkway that was landscaped and equipped with benches. And these shopping centers were more than places to shop. A full range of services, recreational facilities, and programming for entertainment and education legitimized these malls as true community centers. Although these new "shopping towns," as visionary shopping center developer Victor Gruen called them, brought many of the best qualities of urban life to the suburbs, they nonetheless offered the opportunity to improve on (in Gruen's words) "the anarchy and ugliness" characteristic of many American cities. A centrally owned and managed Garden State Plaza or Bergen Mall offered an alternative model to the inefficiencies, visual chaos, and provinciality of traditional downtown districts. A centralized administration made possible the perfect mix and "scientific" placement of stores, so that customers' needs were met while store owners' profits were maximized. Management kept control visually by standardizing all architectural and graphic design and politically by requiring all tenants to participate in the tenants' association. Common complaints of downtown shoppers were directly addressed: parking was plentiful, safety was insured by hired security guards, delivery tunnels and loading courts kept automotive traffic away from shoppers, canopied walks and air-conditioned stores made shopping comfortable year around, piped in background music replaced the cacophony of the street.

When developers and store owners set out to make the shopping center a perfection of downtown, they aimed to exclude from this public space unwanted urban elements, such as vagrants, prostitutes, racial minorities, and poor people. Market segmentation became the guiding principle of this mix of commercial and civic activity, as the shopping center sought both to legitimize itself as a true community center and to define that community in exclusionary socioeconomic and racial terms. Much the way we have seen that homeownership and residential suburbanization extended racial segregation in the postwar era, so too did the development of suburban shopping centers. As Baltimore's Planning Council lamented, "Greater numbers of low-income, Negro shoppers in Central Business District stores [with the migration north of Southern blacks in the 1950s], coming at the same time as middle- and upper-income white shoppers are given alternatives in . . . segregated suburban centers, has had unfortunate implications [for downtown shopping]." A survey of consumer expenditures in Northern New Jersey in 1960–61 revealed that while 79 percent of all families owned cars, fewer than one-third of those with incomes below $3,000 did, and that low-income population included a higher percentage of nonwhite families than the average for the whole sample. Although bus service to the Paramus shopping centers was available for shoppers without cars, routes were carefully planned to serve nondriving customers—particularly women—from neighboring towns, not low-income and nonwhite customers from cities like Paterson and Newark. While individual department stores had long targeted particular markets by class and race, such as selling to "the carriage trade" at the upper end, when that segmentation was carried out on the scale of a downtown, it pushed it to an entirely new level. In promoting an idealized downtown, shopping centers like Garden State Plaza and Bergen Mall not only tried to filter out the inefficiencies and inconveniences of the city, but also what many felt were the "dangerous classes" who lived there. Furthermore, those urban populations suffered even more by the 1970s when the downtown stores they depended on closed because of the outflow of consumer dollars to suburban stores. Newark saw every one of its major department stores close between 1964 and 1992 and most of its retail space remain abandoned, prompting residents like Raymond Mungin to wonder, "I don't have a car to drive out to the malls. What can I do?" Much the way postwar residential patterns incorporated workers into the category of white suburban homeowner, postwar retail developments integrated them into commercial centers that also enforced the color line.

We next need to ask specifically how this postwar metropolitan landscape constructed around a norm of homeowning and consumption-oriented community space affected class identity, particularly the identities of those whose occupations defined them as working class. Although it is always more difficult to pin down attitudes than economic structures or behaviors, studies of postwar American workers suggest that the achievement or accessibility of these consumption goals encouraged working people to orient their ambitions toward them and when achieved, to identify them as the markings of a mainstream middle-class status. Ely Chinoy's classic study of 1955, "Automobile Workers and the American Dream," documented how workers were increasingly marking advancement by, in his words, "the progressive accumulation of things as well as the increasing capacity to consume." As one nonskilled maintenace worker who had been in the plant for fourteen years commented, "If I can just increase the value of my possessions as the years go by instead of just breaking even or falling behind and losing, if I can keep adding possessions and property—personal property too—and put some money away for when I can't work, if I happen to own two or three houses like this one . . . and have five thousand dollars put away in the bank, I'll figure I got ahead quite a lot." It was homeownership particularly that Chinoy found to matter. A thirty-nine-year-old welder said it all: "We're all working for one purpose, to get ahead. I don't think a person should be satisfied. My next step is a nice little modern house of my own. That's what I mean by bettering yourself—or getting ahead."[5]

Twenty-five years later, when sociologist David Halle studied a group of chemical workers employed in Northern New Jersey, he found them so ensconced in an elaborated suburban homeowning, consumer culture that he argued for a split between their awareness of a class hierarchy at work and their more middle-class identities in the domestic setting. Almost all of the workers at Imperium Oil and Chemicals (a pseudonym) were homeowners, which conformed to the national pattern where by 1975, three-quarters of all AFL-CIO members owned houses. He found, moreover, that most did not inhabit "working-class suburbs," and even more crucially, that they did not define the communities in which they lived as "working class," but rather as occupationally mixed with notably less variation in income, given the good pay of many blue-collar workers. The "other" for these workers were very exclusive places where "the rich" live or areas with high proportions of black or Hispanic residents. In fact, Halle concluded that it was division by race, into black and white areas, that dominated workers' residential mapmaking far more than division by occupation. When six workers moved to Clark, New Jersey, from communities closer to inner-city ghettos, one explained, "Why do I live in Clark: Well, there are no niggers in Clark" (26). Moreover, ethnographic investigation into the leisure and family lives of Imperium workers deepened Halle's argument that they seldom viewed their lives outside the workplace as distinctly "working class." He contended that they viewed the class structure as having some fluidity in its middle range, even though at work they were more aware of their fixed place in the occupational hierarchy. The class hierarchy most workers embraced distinguished three levels: at the top were "the million-aires" or "the upper class"; in the middle was the "middle class"; and at the bottom were "the poor" or "people who can't [or won't] make it," who were assumed to be predominantly black and Hispanic. As they identified them-selves as "middle class," they pointed to income level, lifestyle, material possessions, and the quality of residence and neighborhood as the deter-mining factors. I should add that Halle concludes his study with a strong injunction that readers not interpret his analysis as grist for the mill of those like Herbert Marcuse, John Alt, and Ferdynand Zweig who argue for the narcotizing implications of the shift from the primacy of labor to the primacy of consumption. Rather he claims that entrenchment in a middle-class consumer culture outside of work did not distract these Imperium workers from experiencing class conflict at the workplace, and that the realm of consumer goods gave them a way to advance in both an absolute and relative manner, given the ceiling on mobility in the automated chem-ical plant. Halle did not want his analysis to be too simply dismissed as evi-dence of working-class "embourgeoisement."

At this point let's return to Martha Stewart and see if we can make any more sense of what seemed to be confusing class signals in her story. When I decided to begin my talk today with that *New York Times* article on the marketing of *Martha Stewart Living*, I thought it was only responsible of me to go out and buy the current issue at the newstand to know of what I was speaking. The June 1995 issue served as a perfect text to analyze, although I suspect that any issue would do as well. To begin with, in Martha's own column entitled "Remembering" not only did she not bury or distort her modest origins—as I might have expected her to do before undertaking this analysis—but she flaunted them. She recalls that as soon as her family moved to Elm Place in Nutley, New Jersey, when she was three, her father planted an extensive garden, "so that we would always have fresh flowers in our small three-bedroom house." She goes on to recount her own entry at age ten into a local flower show, acknowledging that she identified herself as "M. Kostyra" and used an old teapot of her mother's as her container. Winning a blue ribbon, she became the official family flower arranger: "My father and mother deferred to me in all the flower arrangements we made for the house, modest though they were." Rather than suppress her modest origins, then, Stewart seems to use them to connect with her readers, who, a close examination of the magazine sug-gests, span a wide spectrum of the self-identified middle-class market. Despite the glossy elegance of the magazine's presentation, articles instructing readers how to use a caterer for the first time, or how to paint a room yourself so that it looks professional, or how to repair broken glass, indicate that Stewart has not strayed so far from her KMart merchandising strategy. Here, too, she seems to be helping working-class and lower-middle-class homeowning suburbanites (including the likes of Halle's chemical workers) learn how to live middle class, much as she did.

Martha Stewart's instruction in living a middle-class lifestyle tells us something about the fragility of this postwar pan-middle-class status. Lurking not far from the surface for newcomers like Halle's workers is an anxiety about fulfilling and sustaining that status. If the middle range of the social structure is fluid, movement down is just as possible as movement up; worries about the proximity of undesirables—geographical as well as economic—repeatedly bubble to the surface, particularly as the relative prosperity of the mass consumer economy of the 1945 to 1970 period has faltered with deindustrialization, corporate downsizing, and union decline. For the last twenty years, the ladder that many workers climbed to middle-class status—homeowning, suburban living, consuming—has become shakier, yet abandoning middle-class identity has become almost inconceivable after a generation. In some ways, the marketplace has accommodated growing diversity within the middle class; increasingly over the postwar period, for example, so-called middle class shopping centers have become segmented and aimed at distinctive income markets ranging from lower-middle to upscale. Yet it remains a task for future historians to interpret the social-class configuration of the last quarter of the twentieth century, when not only did white workers' economic security of the previous quarter century erode but also African Americans increasingly entered, and identified with, the middle class as well.

All this discussion is perhaps a long way of arguing for the importance of investigating the way working-class experience and identity are historically constructed in any particular era, and not of assuming that timeless definitions of social class necessarily hold. "Working-Class Lives/Working-Class Studies" should above all be a call to root class analysis in concrete historical contexts, the present included, of course. To do so both recognizes the structural constraints that shape people's class experiences, as well as the agency involved when they give their own meanings to those experiences.

NOTES

1. Keynote Address, Working-Class Lives/Working-Class Studies Conference, Youngstown State University, June 9, 1995.

2. Stuart Elliott, "Advertising: A Tongue-in-Cheek Campaign for *Martha Stewart Living* Pokes Fun at the Magazine's Guiding Spirit," *New York Times*, June 2, 1995, D4; Barbara Lippert, "Our Martha, Ourselves," *New York*, May 15, 1995, 27–35.

3. "History of the GI Bill," publication of the Dept. of Veterans Affairs on the 50th Anniversary of the GI Bill, 1994; "Conference on Labor and the Veteran spon-

sored by the New Jersey State Industrial Union Council," March 3 and 4, 1945, New Jersey "Q" File, Newark Public Library, 34–35; "GI Bill's Birthday Tomorrow," *Newark News*, June 21, 1964; Kurt Piehler, Rutgers Oral History Archives of World War II.

4. NAACP Papers, II, G 11, files "GI Benefits, 1945–June 1946," "GI Benefits, July 1946–1949"; II, A 657, "Veterans' Housing, 1945–55"; II, B 78, "Housing, NJ, General, 1949–50."

5. Ely Chinoy, *Automobile Workers and the American Dream* (1955; reprint, Boston: Beacon Press, 1965), 126.

14

MODEST BUT ADEQUATE

*Standard of Living for Mon Valley Steelworkers
in the Union Era*

Mark McColloch

D uring the forty-five years that followed the loss of the Homestead
Strike, basic steelworkers in the United States lived and worked in
an atmosphere of slightly qualified industrial tyranny. In few places was this
tyranny more complete than in the Monongahela Valley, in the line of
plants that ran from Monessen to Pittsburgh's Southside. Hours of work
were incredibly long, wages very low, and health and safety conditions poor.
Workers had little power on the shop floor or in their communities. As one
steelworker told pioneering sociologist Margaret Byington in 1906, "If you
want to talk about the union in Homestead, you have to talk to yourself."[1]

The unionization of the Mon Valley basic steel plants (all the major
plants were owned by either US Steel or Jones and Laughlin, both of which
signed contracts with the United Steel Workers of America [USWA] in
1937) dealt a heavy blow to the old industrial tyranny. By 1945, as I have
outlined elsewhere,[2] the outlines of a new polity, industrial citizenship, had
been consolidated. Over the next twenty-five years, this new status for
workers was buttressed and solidified. There were major improvements in
shop-floor working conditions and in what David Brody has called the
"workplace rule of law."[3] Workers and unions gained a greater say in their
community life and there was a significant rise in standard of living. On the
other hand, industrial citizenship was a qualified and limited status for
workers. Management retained the initiative or upper hand in many areas

of industrial relations, and there were many other crucial decisions, such as investment choices, over which management ceded no power at all. Furthermore, there were serious limitations on many of the gains won by workers. Industrial citizenship was not the same as industrial equality or industrial democracy.

One important arena of change in the lives of steelworkers in the era of industrial citizenship was a rise in the standard of living which they enjoyed. Unionization did bring real, very important gains in standard of living for hundreds of thousands of people. These gains lifted steelworkers out of the poverty in which they had lived in the era of industrial tyranny. On the other hand, the gains came very slowly and were won only by protracted struggles. Furthermore the starting point was a miserably low one, and there were big variations among workers in what was won. The final irony is that just when most steelworkers had finally achieved a decent standard of living, management drastically restructured the industry, destroying most of the jobs and the newly won gains. Let us examine the changes in standard of living from 1940 to 1980 in more detail.

From the Steel Workers' Organizing Committee's (SWOC) formation in 1936, through 1940, the union was preoccupied with organizing the basic steel firms and with holding onto its contracts during the renewed depression of 1937–39, which brought with it an antiunion counterattack. Not until World War II brought prosperity to the steel firms was the union able to go forward at all on standard of living.[4]

The union won contractual gains on wages in 1941 and, through or despite the intervention of the War Labor Board, won rate hikes in 1942, 1943, and 1944. Average hourly wage rates rose 13 percent faster than inflation from 1940–44. Because of the longer hours in the war (the War Production Board mandated a forty-eight-hour week in steel), real weekly earnings rose much more rapidly, increasing by 36 percent over the same period, to a level that would not again be equaled until the early 1950s. Because, however, of brief periods of joblessness due to conversion, reconversion, and shortages, real annual earnings rose by a more modest 26 percent for 1940–45.[5] The war years also brought greater equality of earnings within the steel workforce, due to the USWA's policy of seeking across-the-board wage increases rather than percentage hikes. Thus, hourly wage rates rose 50 percent during the war for the lowest labor grade and by only 20 percent for the highest.[6]

Important as these gains were, we need to keep in mind the continuing poverty or near poverty of most steelworkers. In early 1942, the average worker in basic steel earned less than 80 percent of the money required for a family of four to subsist on the spartan Heller Budget, developed by the famous economist. Even at the 1944 peak of real weekly earnings the metal workers still did not have an average weekly wage equal to the Heller budget.[7]

The end of the war and the second half of the 1940s brought almost no progress in standard of living for steelworkers, and by some measures there was actually a deterioration. Just staying roughly even, however, took a fight, in the midst of the high inflation of the postwar period. The union fought one of its longest and most important strikes in 1946, with wages at the center of the battle, and wage increases were won, after protracted negotiations, in 1947 and 1948.[8] Despite these gains, average hourly earnings *fell* by 4.5 percent from 1945–48, after inflation is taken into account. This figure seriously understates the actual dimensions of the problem. The drying up of overtime and the reappearance of unemployment meant that average weekly wages plunged more rapidly. The average workweek fell from a 1944 high of 47.4 to 37.1 in 1946 (exclusive of the strike period), and remained at about 39 for the rest of the decade. This meant that real weekly earnings in 1946 were 21 percent below those of 1944. As late as 1949, they were still 12 percent under the wartime high.[9]

What did these figures mean in terms of the lifestyle lived by steelworkers? In the late 1940s, the Bureau of Labor Statistics began providing figures for the income needed for a "minimum" budget. This budget envisioned a family of four, living in a rented apartment, consisting of a kitchen, bath, and three other rooms. The family had hot running water and owned a washing machine. On the budget "it should be possible to serve meat for dinner several times a week, if the cheaper cuts are served." Each child could have a bottle of pop every other day, and one beer a week could be consumed. Three shirts and two pairs of pants could be purchased each year for the growing boy. The family did not own a car and there was no money in the budget for any vacations but every three weeks the family could afford a movie, if they bought no food at the theater. The average steelworker did not earn enough money to enjoy even this harsh standard of living in the 1940s! In March 1946, $2,761 was required for the minimum budget. Average earnings, including premium pay, were $1.28 an hour for 1946. Even if a worker had toiled forty hours a week for all fifty-two weeks of the year, he or she would have made $100 less than the budget. In fact, if we look at annual earnings, the average steelworker made only $2,471 in 1946. By June 1947, a Pittsburgh family needed $3,291 for the "minimum" budget. Even with the longer average hours of 1947, workers fell 7 percent below the minimum, on average.[10]

By 1949, the situation had worsened, due to the recession. Average annual earnings fell by over 10 percent, to just $3,064, while prices fell by just 1 percent that year. At the end of the decade, despite fourteen years of union struggle that had brought some real gains, the typical steelworker did not yet earn enough money to lift a family from poverty.[11]

We should also note that there were important variations within the ranks of the USWA on standard of living. The wage increases of 1947 and

1948, as would be the case in almost all USWA contracts from that time on, were composed of two elements. The first was an across-the-board increase of 12.5¢ in 1947 and 9.5¢ in 1948. The second was money applied to widening the differentials between each of the thirty-two labor grades. In each of 1947 and 1948 an additional half cent was added to the differential for each of the thirty-two labor grades. The result was that a worker in the Labor Grade 1 got a 12.5¢ raise in 1947, while a worker in LG 32 was hiked 28¢. Similar figures for 1948 were 9.5¢ and 25¢ an hour, very slightly widening the percentage pay gap.[12] Under the 1948 contract, a worker in LG 1 made $1.18 1/2 an hour. That meant a projected full-employment annual wage of $2,465 or dire poverty for a family. (Of course, LG 1 workers were also likely to have very low seniority and thus suffer more unemployment.) An LG 32 worker, however, would have a comparable figure of $5,366 a year, enough to comfortably support a family.[13]

Milan Y. was a drill press operator at McKeesport's National Tube. In 1946, at age fifty-nine, he earned $2,278, over 20 percent below the Department of Labor's minimum budget. In 1947 he made $3,596, about 10 percent above the budget, but in 1948 earnings stagnated at $3,514 and fell to only $3,292 in the recession year of 1949, back below the minimum budget level.[14]

The 1950s brought important, if limited, gains to steelworkers. The 1949 negotiations, strike, and resulting contract were the opening round of these gains. The central issue in this battle was the demand by the USWA for the payment by the company of a pension and other fringe benefits. We must begin by understanding just how unbelievably bad the situation was in 1949. Under the company plan in effect in 1949, extremely long-service retirees received a company pension averaging $5.30 a month. Combined with the average Social Security payment of $41 a month to a steelworker and spouse, this left an elderly couple a pitiful $100 a month short of what the Social Security Administration called "the minimum needed for existence for an aged couple." No wonder that 72 percent of all the retirees surveyed by the USWA had nearly exhausted their savings and 31 percent admitted to being primarily supported by relatives.[15]

In the 1949 strike the USWA won a noncontributory pension plan from the company. The new pension plan was an enormous step forward. Workers with twenty-five years' seniority could now retire at sixty-five, with a minimum monthly pension of $100, including Social Security. This was scaled down to a minimum of $60 for those retiring at sixty-five with fifteen years of continuous service. The most highly paid quarter or so of the workforce would receive modestly higher pensions. Even though most of the $100 came not from the company, but from Social Security, the companies were forced to substantially increase their payments to the fund and an important principle had been established.[16]

Still, unless a retiree had substantial savings or other income, the 1949 pensions represented a level below that of mere survival, even with the $12 Social Security spouse allowance added in. The union was not able to win any increases in pensions at all until 1954. The Social Security hikes of those years brought almost no gains to workers, since the company simply reduced their own contributions to the level needed to maintain the combined $100 a month minimum. For the thirty-thousand steelworkers who retired under the 1949 pension plan, the inflation of over 15 percent from 1950–54, actually eroded the modest value of their retirement plans.[17]

In 1954, however, the USWA did succeed in squeezing out an important increase in the pension plan for new retirees. Under the 1954 contract, the new minimum pension, still combined with Social Security, was $140 for a worker with thirty years' service retiring at sixty-five, and $130 for a worker with twenty-five years' service. Furthermore, in a very important gain, any future rises in Social Security payments would not be offset by corresponding reductions in company payments.[18] Milan Y., who retired in 1955 with an awesome forty-eight years' of service, received a pension of $151 per month, including Social Security. Thomas W., a relatively well-paid first helper, who retired in 1958, received a monthly pension of $219. Duane W., however, who retired the same year, had fewer years' service and had made less money as a shipping clerk. His pension was only $117 a month, including Social Security.

Pensions were not the only breakthrough on fringe benefits won by the 1949 USWA strike. Prior to that point, steelworkers had no company-paid health insurance at all. That was at a time when the American Medical Association itself estimated that an income of $5,000 a year was needed to afford even "average medical care."[19] Under the new contract, the company and workers would each pay 2.5¢ an hour into a social insurance fund. The fund provided for basic hospitalization costs for steelworkers and their families. It also gave, for the first time, sickness and accident benefits, after a one-week waiting period, of $26 a week for up to twenty-six weeks, for non-work-related health problems. Steelworkers also received modest life insurance policies, equal to about a year's wages.[20]

The social impact of these programs was very large. During the first year, over 2.48 million persons came under the coverage of the plan. About 263,000 people used the hospitalization benefits, receiving an average payment of about $110. A roughly equal amount was paid out in life insurance and sick benefits.[21]

In August 1951, the major companies agreed to add Blue Shield surgical benefits to the coverage of the plan.[22] The 1954 contract brought more modest gains. The contributions of both parties were now upped to 4.5¢ per hour. The duration of payments for hospital stays was greatly lengthened and sick benefits were increased to $40 a week. For accidents on the job, any difference between worker comp payments and the $40 would be made up.[23]

The early 1950s were also years of important gains for workers on the wage front. The union won wage increases in every year from 1950 through 1955. Combined with the low inflation rate in every year except 1951, real hourly wage rates rose by 20 percent from 1950 through 1954.[24] Once again, the contracts followed the pattern of providing for a general increase, coupled with modest increases on the spread between labor grades. The result was that the steel industry continued to have a very wide range of earnings among its workers. In January 1951, average hourly pay in the industry was $1.79. One-quarter of the workers, however, earned less than $1.50, while 25 percent earned more than $2.00.[25] The gap between the wages of Milan Y. and Thomas W. fluctuated in the early 1950s, from a 1952 low of a 25 percent spread, to a 1954 high of 46 percent.

Despite the gains of the period, steelworkers still had a long way to go to achieve a comfortable standard of living. The Bureau of Labor Statistics (BLS) estimated that in November 1951 weekly earnings of $79.46 were needed for a typical family to achieve a modest standard of living. Steelworkers at the bottom of the scale had a weekly wage of only $52.40. About 60 percent of the workforce fell below the modest standard figure, even during a week when they worked forty hours.[26]

Progress was made over the next few years. The negotiated wage increases, combined with the high employment levels of the Korean War years (1953 was the highest employment total of the unionized era), brought big gains in annual earnings. In 1953, average annual earnings reached $4,542, at a time when about $4,256 was needed to reach the BLS modest budget. For the first time, the average steelworker was no longer at a poverty level of income. The next year, however, brought problems. Employment levels fell by about 12 percent, overtime dried up, and average annual earnings fell to $3,947, almost 10 percent below the modest level.[27] Milan Y.'s wages fell from $5,376 in 1953 to $4,647 the next year.

The second half of the 1950s brought some more important steps forward, but, once again, many steelworkers could not enjoy these, due to economic downturns. From 1955 to 1960 the average hourly wage outstripped inflation by 34 percent. Gains negotiated under the 1955 wage reopener and under the three-year contract that followed the 1956 strike were the key to these rapidly rising wages. By 1958, a worker in the lowest wage classification in basic steel, who worked full-time year-round, would have earned $4,245, or about $400 short of what was needed for the modest budget. A similar worker in Labor Grade 6, would have reached the modest budget figure. It would seem that the era of a decent standard of living for most steelworkers had finally arrived.[28]

Alas, this was not the case, due to unemployment. The number of wage workers in the industry fell from 513,000 in 1955 to 412,000 in 1958 and 400,000 in 1959. Even for those who had not totally lost their jobs, shorter layoffs were common in the late 1950s. In 1955, 26 percent lost at least a week due to this problem. In 1956, all workers lost four weeks due to the strike, and 24 percent were off for longer than that. The worst came in 1958, when 46 percent of all steelworkers were laid off for at least a week and one-third for over five weeks. The average work week fell from 38.6 hours to just 34.3 from the first half of 1957 to the first half of 1958. Then, in 1959, sixteen weeks were lost due to the strike that year. The result was that annual earnings in this period were much lower than we might expect.[29]

In 1955 average annual earnings reached $5,021, well above the modest budget, but slipped back to $4,926 in 1956. They rebounded to a comfortable average of $5,350 in 1957, but the next two years were bad ones. In 1958 the average employed steelworker made just $4,840, or 3 percent above the modest budget, and slipped back further in 1959 to $4,837, only 2 percent above the spartan level. Of course, this does not include the over one hundred thousand workers whose jobs disappeared in this period.[30]

For those still on the payroll there were big variations in annual earnings. The 1950s had brought a modest compression of wage rates as across-the-board increases and the cost-of-living clause negotiated in 1956 offset the additional money paid on the increments. The lowest labor grade rose by 73 percent over the decade, while that of the highest labor grade increased by 60 percent. Usually, however, low labor grade and low seniority went hand in hand. The result was that while the percentage of workers earning over $6,000 a year remained relatively stable at 30 percent in 1957 and 28 percent in the bad year of 1958, things were much more volatile at the low end. In 1957, just 9 percent of the employed workers made less than $3,600, but the figure grew to 22 percent in 1958. Such earnings did not even reach the level of family subsistence.[31] Hugh Z., a National Tube craneman with four children, saw his earnings reach $6,031 in 1957, but fall to $5,598 in 1958 and to only $5,202 in the strike year of 1959. For Lloyd W., a McKeesport steelworker with one child, earnings plateaued in the $5,200s in 1957–1958, before falling to $4,086 in 1959. Skilled worker Thomas W.'s earnings fell from $7,207 in 1956 to $6,166 the next year. For John W., 1957 was the peak at $4,935, dipping to $4,317 in the recession year and to only $3,877 in 1959. John was, however, a widower with no children, so while his earnings could not buy a modest standard of living for a family, it was close to it for an individual.

The high unemployment in steel in the late 1950s was cushioned, somewhat, by the introduction of Supplementary Unemployment Benefits (SUB) in the 1956 contract. This major negotiating breakthrough had produced a company-financed plan that, combined with state unemployment compensation (UC) benefits, was designed to pay a laid-off worker 65 percent of his or her former income. During the recession of the late 1950s, however, this plan had severe limitations. Only those workers with two years of continuous service were eligible for the payments. This meant that the workers who bore the heaviest brunt of the layoffs received no payments. (Almost 20 percent of workers had below two years' seniority.) The SUB payments were capped at a maximum size of $33, so that any worker who had made above about $2.50 an hour would not receive the 65 percent figure. Furthermore, as the fund became depleted, and it was severely depleted in 1958, payments were drastically reduced. In the Donora mill, for example, where 1,100 workers were laid off, only about one-third were receiving SUB payments of any amount, and of course, SUB did not affect the other 2,800 Donora workers on a short workweek. Typical was widower Frank Roman, who had formerly made about $125 a week, to support himself and his two children. Bumped down to a lower-paid job before being totally laid off, he now received only $53.38 a week from SUB and UC.[32]

The late 1950s did bring important gains in other fringe benefits. Pensions were increased under the 1956 contract. Effective in November 1957, the minimum pension for a worker retiring with twenty-five years' service at age sixty-five was $62.50 plus Social Security. The minimum company payments for workers who had retired under the 1949 and 1954 plans were also raised to $50 and $56.25, respectively. Under the new pension plan a typical retiree and wife could expect a combined income of about $235 a month from the company and Social Security, in other words, just above dire poverty, but, for the first time, just above it.[33]

Sick benefits were also raised from the former $40 a week to a range of $42–57. Hospitalization benefits now included partial payment for a private room and diagnostic procedures, such as X rays. The joint contributions to the fund were raised to about $9.50 a month for each worker.[34]

Both the workers and management responded to the tough times of the late 1950s with toughened stances at the bargaining table. The result was the long strike of 1959, and continuation of late 1950s conditions for many steelworkers, through the early Kennedy years.

The new contract, reached after the use of a Taft-Hartley injunction by the Eisenhower administration damaged the union's positions, brought no wage increase until December 1960, followed by another modest hike in October 1961, with a severe 3¢ a year cap on the COLA (Cost of Living Allowance). The 1962 contract also contained no wage hike in its first year. The wage reopener in 1963 brought no general increase either.[35] The result was that average hourly straight-time earnings and actual earnings only crept up in this period, rising by about 8 percent from 1960–65, *before* inflation.[36]

Unemployment worsened the picture, as usual. The decade began well enough. In late 1959 and early 1960, employment regained over half the losses of the late 1950s. It was not to last. Over 20 percent of steel jobs were lost in late 1960. By 1961, employment was back down to about 401,000 workers and it remained at this level for the Kennedy years. Even in prosperous 1960, average annual income for steelworkers was $5,427. In the fall of 1959, the BLS issued a revised budget plan for a "modest but adequate" standard of living. The family of four still rented, drove an old used car, could buy a TV every eighteen years, and so on. This lifestyle required an income of $6,199, about 12 percent more than a typical steelworker made.[37]

By 1963, when average hourly earnings were $3.36, a worker employed year-round would gross $6,789, or just above the modest but adequate budget. Average weekly earnings, however, which take layoffs into account, were still below the modest budget figure. The experience was much worse in 1961 and 1962, when average annual earnings fell several hundred dollars short of the modest budget.[38]

Once again, the SUB fund proved inadequate. The restrictions of the 1956 contract still prevailed and the fund again ran short in early 1961, cutting payments. The 1962 contract did bring improvements. Company payments to the SUB fund were virtually doubled, insuring more regular payments, and weekly benefits were raised.[39]

There were also some slight improvements in pensions in these years. The 1960 contract effectively raised the pensions of the better-paid third of the workforce by $20 a month. Full pensions were granted to workers at fifty-five with twenty years' service whose jobs were lost due to plant or departmental shutdowns. By 1961, there were about 76,000 retirees alive, receiving an average company payment of $80.63. Sick benefits were also raised, lifting weekly payments to a range of $53–68.[40]

Health-care benefits were also improved. Most importantly, the social insurance program was made noncontributory in 1960. For those with at least two years' seniority, hospitalization was continued for six months if they were laid off.[41]

Only in the mid-1960s did the combination of low unemployment and improved contracts lift steelworkers above the lean years that had lasted since the mid-1950s. Employment in basic steel turned up in 1964, reaching a high of 459,000 in 1965, and did not slip back to the levels of the late 1950s until 1970.[42]

The union, now operating in an atmosphere of low unemployment, won wage hikes in 1965 and 1967 under the 1965 contract and in 1968 through 1970 under the 1968 three-year pact. By August 1969, straight-time pay scales ranged from $2.77 per hour to $5.34 in the highest labor grade. Furthermore, 85 percent of all steelworkers were now under an incentive plan that boosted rates somewhat.[43]

Nonetheless, the lean years were not quickly overcome. The BLS issued a new moderate budget figure in 1966. This budget, which, incidentally, allowed absolutely no money for savings or for educational expenses for the children, required an annual income of $9,191. A worker on straight time, employed full-time year-round, would have to be in LG 29, near the top of the scale, to earn this figure in 1966. Workers in LG 16, the middle of the scale, even with incentive pay added in, fell substantially below this level and most workers were in LGs below 16. In 1967, average hourly earnings, with incentive, but without overtime, were $3.42. About $4.54 an hour was needed to attain the modest budget, if employed year-round.[44]

In fact, weekly earnings were below that. In 1965 the average employed steelworker actually made about $7,181 and the figure slipped back a bit in 1966. By 1969 it had risen to $8,238, still chasing the modest budget for a family of four.[45] Andy Y., an expanding machine operator with one child, saw his earnings rise from just $6,613 in 1964 to $8,796 in 1967 and a 1960s high of $10,031 in 1968, before suffering a heart attack in 1970, going on extended disability, and retiring in 1971 on a company pension of $346 a month.

The SUB payments were improved in the 1965 contract and a Quarterly Earnings Benefit Fund was established to pay those who lost their jobs due to technological change 85 percent of their earnings for one year.[46]

There were major improvements on the pension front in the late 1960s. Effective in August 1966, minimum monthly company payments were raised to $5 a month, times the years of service, for workers who had reached sixty-five. In addition, workers could retire with full pension at any age once they had thirty years of service. By 1969, this had been pushed up to $6.50 a month. For the first time, spouses received 50 percent of the pension payments once their partner died. Combined with a Social Security payment, a retired couple could now afford the Social Security Administration's modest budget of about $3,200 for a retired duo. The pensions of those who had retired earlier were raised by $15 a month in 1966, but many of them remained at a poverty level.[47]

Health-care benefits were improved in the late 1960s. Sick benefits were raised to $80 a week in 1967 and extended for up to a year, versus the old six months. Hospitalization now covered actual doctors' fees instead of an old, outdated schedule and coverage was extended to children up to the age of twenty-five, if they were in college. In 1968 the major medical plan was further updated.[48]

The 1970s were a mixed picture in terms of standard of living. Those steelworkers who remained on the job chased and often outstripped the raging inflation of the decade. On the other hand, employment levels fell substantially from the already low 415,000 of 1969. By 1972, one out of every eight workers employed in 1969 no longer had a job. Things recovered a bit in 1973–74, but by 1975 a new low of 340,000 production workers had been reached, falling to 291,000 in 1980. In other words, 30 percent of the workforce in steel lost their jobs in the "prosperous" 1970s.[49]

For those steelworkers who held on to their jobs, however, the 1970s brought standard of living gains. The USWA won wage increases in 1971 and 1972 and the restoration of a good COLA. Then, in 1973, the Experimental Negotiating Agreement (ENA) was signed. The ENA gave wage hikes of 3 percent a year and a COLA that covered about 70 percent of inflation. The ENA was renewed in 1976.[50]

By 1975, average hourly earnings had reached $7.12, enough to achieve the level of the new BLS intermediate budget, if a worker were employed forty hours a week year-round. Unfortunately, 1975 was also a year of severe unemployment, so average annual earnings fell well short of this figure. By 1980, average hourly earnings had risen to $11.84, enough to exceed the intermediate budget by about $3,000. Average weekly earnings were just about at the intermediate budget level.[51]

There was also a continuation of the trend toward contraction of the earnings range among steelworkers. General wage increases, the importance of the COLA and the fact that incentive increases tended to affect all labor grades meant that wages rose faster at the low end of the scale in the 1970s than at the high. In 1972 a typical LG 32 worker made 80 percent more than one in LG 1, but by 1980 this had fallen to 44 percent.[52]

The 1970s also brought major gains in pension payments, SUB, and health-care benefits. New retirement benefits more than kept pace with inflation, but the rapid rise in cost of living dealt heavy blows to retirees under the older plans, despite a few updates. Company payments for the health insurance were also brought sharply upwards, in order to maintain benefits in an era of sky-rocketing medical profiteering.[53]

One of the functions and indicators of rising standard of living was the changing residency patterns of steelworkers. There is a general sense that over the union era, steelworkers moved from the crowded mill towns out into the suburbs, as their incomes rose. John Hoerr, for example, has argued that during the 1940s and 1950s the prosperous of McKeesport moved "to suburban retreats, followed first by their more affluent middle class and later many working-class families."[54] He argues that the same pattern was followed in Duquesne, Braddock, Homestead, and Clairton.[55]

The timing and extent of this phenomena, as well as variations from mill to mill, remain to be studied in the necessary detail. I will venture some preliminary conclusions, however, based on fragmentary data from the Mon Valley.

I examined census data for eight Mon Valley towns, in which major mills were located: Braddock, Clairton, Donora, Duquesne, Homestead, McKeesport, Monessen, and Munhall. In all cases, except that of Munhall, population fell precipitously in the union era. In the extreme cases of Braddock and Homestead, population was only one-fourth the 1930 levels by 1980. Donora, Duquesne, and Monessen lost about half their population, while the loss in McKeesport was about 35 percent and in Clairton about 25 percent. The timing of this depopulation varies, but the trend is toward a late exodus from the steel towns, rather than an early one. Raw population loss was greatest in the 1960s for five of the eight towns, and for the 1970s in the case of Monessen. Only Homestead, which lost almost half its population in the major mill expansion of the 1940s, and Braddock, which lost slightly more people in the 1950s than in any other decade, defied this trend. Monessen actually grew in the 1950s. In percentage terms, the trend toward late departure was even more clear. In four towns the percentage loss was greatest in the 1960s, while in three cases, the biggest declines did not come until the 1970s. Only Homestead defied the trend.[56]

Perhaps another measure of the exodus of better-paid steelworkers from the mill towns might be the growing percentage of their populations who were African Americans. In seven of the eight cases, the black percentage of the population rose in these towns from 1930 to 1980, usually dramatically. Only Munhall, where very few blacks ever lived, was different. In six of the eight cases, the absolute number of African American residents actually rose in this period, despite the fact that the towns were in the midst of depopulation. In percentage terms, the 1950s saw the biggest rise in black population in Donora, Duquesne, and McKeesport; the 1960s in the cases of Braddock, Clairton, and Homestead; and the 1970s in the case of Monessen.[57]

Officer lists for the Mon Valley locals from 1957 and 1960 provide some more hints on residency. In most cases, in 1957, the delegates elected to a district conference still lived very near to their mills. Eight of ten delegates from the Edgar Thomson mill lived in Braddock or contiguous North Braddock or East Pittsburgh. Only two lived in semisuburban East McKeesport. At Rankin's Carrie Furnace, seven of ten delegates lived in Rankin or Swissvale, which adjoined it. Eight of ten delegates from the Duquesne mill lived in that town. At the Homestead works, nine out of ten dwelled in the four contiguous mill boroughs of Homestead, Munhall, West Homestead, and Whitaker, with half in Homestead itself. Similarly, eight of ten delegates from National Tube lived in McKeesport. At the Clairton works, seven of ten lived in that mill town, while two of the remainder were from nearby McKeesport.[58]

Lists of officers for 1960 show a somewhat similar pattern, but with a bit more dispersion. Six of thirteen officers at Carrie Furnace were from Rankin or Swissvale. At the Duquesne works, twenty-six of forty officers still resided in that town, and nine others hailed from the mill towns of Homestead or McKeesport. At the Edgar Thomson works all but six of eighteen officers lived in the narrow Braddock-North Braddock-Rankin-Swissvale corridor that ran along the Monongahela. Thirteen of the nineteen officers from Clairton lived in that mill town. At the Homestead mill ten of nineteen lived in the mill complex of Homestead-Munhall-Whitaker-West Homestead.[59]

Of course, it may very well be that, to a degree, union activists disproportionately chose to remain in the mill towns or that those who remained behind disproportionately became union activists. Still, the trend toward continued residence in the factory towns is so strong for this group in the 1957–60 period that it reenforces the perception that suburbanization came late for most steelworkers.

In a very small sample of workers who retired from National Tube in McKeesport during the 1960s, all continued to live in McKeesport itself. These were, of course, all older men, and were perhaps less likely than younger men to move outward.[60]

An additional piece of evidence supports this trend. I examined residency at the time they went on the payroll for a sample of five hundred workers at the J&L plants in Pittsburgh's Hazelwood and South Side, from 1936–69. During the 1930s, 76 percent lived in Pittsburgh, almost all on the Southside, Hazelwood, Greenfield, or the Hill District, all close at hand to the mill. Only 11 percent could, under the most generous interpretation, be classified as suburban livers and most of these were probably from mining camps. During the 1940s, the trend held up totally among the much larger number employed. Fully 85 percent of the new hires lived in Pittsburgh, overwhelmingly in the same neighborhoods.[61]

The 1950s, that stereotypical decade of suburbanization, did not see a strong move outward among those hired at the J&L mills, where 79 percent still lived in Pittsburgh. Even within the limits of the Steel City, the four close-in neighborhoods still strongly predominated. The 1960s brought the most change. The percentage from Pittsburgh fell to 62 percent. There was more dispersion within Pittsburgh itself and true suburbs, such as Allison Park and West Mifflin, show up more frequently.[62] This sample may understate the extent of suburbanization, since workers may have only moved out, once they landed a mill job. On the other hand, some workers may have moved closer to work once hired. Nonetheless, it is clear that suburbanization among these steelworkers is very much a post-1960 phenomenon.

One final piece of evidence supports the trend toward limited and late suburbanization. Using an address list for the 4,900 blue-collar workers at the Homestead mill in 1980, I sampled 1,500. In that year, about 35 percent of the workforce still lived in the Whitaker-Munhall-Homestead-West Homestead corridor, with 27 percent of the total residing in Homestead itself.[63]

We should not, however, think that the other 65 percent were suburbanites. Far from it. In fact, the largest single place of residence was nearby Pittsburgh proper, where 34 percent of the factory's workers were located. Another 7 percent lived in other nearby Mon Valley mill towns, chiefly Braddock, Clairton, Duquesne, and McKeesport.[64]

By the broadest definition, only 25 percent lived in suburban bedroom communities. West Mifflin, which adjoins the Homestead mill-town complex, was by far the most important of these, at 16 percent of the total.[65] In the case of Homestead, at least, the image of a general exodus of prosperous steel-workers to the suburbs does not hold up to close scrutiny.

Much more work is required on the question of standard of living in the union era. In particular, we need to know more about the family economy, particularly household size, composition, and multiple wage earners. Larger and more diverse samples are needed for residency patterns. We can, how-ever, draw some general conclusions from this preliminary research. Union-ization and continuing collective bargaining struggles did bring some real gains for steelworkers. By the mid-1950s, a frugal, but decent standard of living seemed at hand. The tough times of the 1957–63 period then undercut these gains for many steelworkers and slowed further progress for others. From the mid-1960s on substantial gains were made for those steelworkers who were still employed. Not until the end of the 1970s, however, could an average steelworker's annual earnings actually bring a family a modestly com-fortable lifestyle. True prosperity for most steelworkers was brief, sandwiched between the poverty of the nonunion and early union years on the one hand and the downsizing of the industry in the 1970s and, to a much greater degree, the early 1980s, on the other. The image of the typical steelworker as prosperous, nearly wealthy, and full of outrageous demands which were always about to bankrupt the industry, and finally did so, is, like so many other manufactured myths about American workers, a profoundly false one.

NOTES

1. Margaret F. Byington, *Homestead: The Households of a Mill Town* (University of Pittsburgh, 1974), 175; David Brody, *Steelworkers in America, the Nonunion Era* (New York: Harper & Row, 1969). A shortened version of this paper was presented at the Homestead Centennial Conference, Homestead, Penn., July 1992.

2. Mark McColloch, "Consolidating Industrial Citizenship," in *Forging a Union of Steel*, ed. Ronald Filippelli and Peter Gottlieb (Ithaca, N.Y.: Cornell ILR Press, 1988).

3. David Brody, see comments in *Workers in Industrial America: Essays on the Twentieth Century Struggles* (New York: Oxford University Press, 1980).

4. Walter Galenson, *The CIO Challenge to the AFL: A History of the American Labor Movement, 1935–41* (Cambridge, Mass.: Harvard University Press, 1960), 873.

5. Companies' Presentation before Special Panel, Wage Stabilization Board, Steel Industry Case, D-18-C, 1952, vol. 1, 88; Paul A. Tiffany, *The Decline of American Steel* (New York: Oxford University Press, 1988), 36; McColloch, "Consolidating Industrial Citizenship," 62.

6. McColloch, "Consolidating Industrial Citizenship," 64.

7. Ibid., 63; Tiffany, *The Decline of American Steel*, 36; 1952 Steel Case Companies Presentation, 88. Family size and earnings by other family members of course greatly affect standard of living. Average family size was clearly less than the

statistical model "family of four." In 1943, the USWA argued that family size aver-
aged 3.44, while US Steel, utilizing somewhat unreliable W-4 tax forms, claimed a
family size of 3.0. The firm argued that, in 1941, about one-third of steelworker
family income came from the nonprimary wage earner. In its 1943 survey, the
USWA found that only 32 percent of steelworkers had two or more dependents and
earned 90 percent or more of family income. Still, the fundamental point remains,
a typical steelworker did not earn enough to be the sole support of a spouse and two
children at a modest standard of living.

8. McColloch, "Consolidating Industrial Citizenship," 63; William T. Hogan,
The Economic History of the Iron and Steel Industry in the United States, vol. 4
(Lexington, Mass.: D.C. Heath), 1616, 1618.

9. Steel Case Companies Presentation, 87; Tiffany, *The Decline of American
Steel*, 36.

10. *Charting Steel's Progress* (American Iron and Steel Institute, 1954), 50;
Hogan, *Economic Trends in the Iron and Steel Industry*, 6; *Monthly Labor Review*
(February 1948): 125.

11. Tiffany, *The Decline of American Steel*, 36; *Economic Trends*, 87.

12. Hogan, *Economic History*, 1616, 1618.

13. *Steel Labor*, August 1948, 2.

14. National Tube, United States Steel records, Box 976, UE Labor Archives,
University of Pittsburgh.

15. *Steel Labor*, August 1949, 8; *Steel Labor*, September 1949, 15.

16. *Economic History*, 1619; *Monthly Labor Review*, December 1949, 676.

17. Tiffany, *The Decline of American Steel*, 36; *Steel Labor*, November 1953, 2.

18. *Monthly Labor Review* (August, 1954): 907; National Tube, Box 976.

19. *Steel Labor*, September 1949, 15.

20. *Monthly Labor Review* (October 1950), 474.

21. Hogan, *Economic History*, 1621.

22. *Steel Labor*, August 1951, 1; *Monthly Labor Review* (September 1951): 319.

23. *Monthly Labor Review* (August 1954): 907; *Monthly Labor Review* (March
1956): 319.

24. Tiffany, *The Decline of American Steel*, 36; Hogan, *Economic History*,
1622–33.

25. *Monthly Labor Review* (February 1952): 158; National Tube, Box 976.

26. *Steel Labor*, February 1952, 5.

27. *Steel's Competitive Challenge* (AISI, 1961), 41; National Tube, Box 976;
Tiffany, *The Decline of American Steel*, 36.

28. *Steel Labor*, January 1959, 16; *Economic Trends in the Iron and Steel
Industry* (AISI, 1960), 31; Tiffany, *The Decline of American Steel*, 36.

29. *Competitive Challenge*, 40; *AISI Annual Report* 1975 (AISI, 1976), 21;
Annual Statistical Report, American Iron and Steel Institute, 1960 (AISI, 1961),
28–29.

30. *Competitive Challenge*, 41; Tiffany, *The Decline of American Steel*, 21. The
high joblessness and lack of new hiring in the late 1950s is reflected in the low
number of young workers employed. In 1960, only 6 percent of the steel workforce
was under twenty-five, and only 29 percent was under thirty-five. This was a sig-

nificantly lower percentage than for the early 1950s or the 1965–75 period. *Annual Statistical Report, 1960*, 32.

31. *Monthly Labor Review* (October 1959): 1092, 1094; National Tube, Box 976.

32. *Steel Labor*, June 1957, 13; *Monthly Labor Review* (September 1956): 1070; *Steel Labor*, January 1958, 8.

33. *Monthly Labor Review* (September 1956): 1071; *Steel Labor*, November 1956, 12.

34. *Monthly Labor Review* (November 1957): 1364.

35. Hogan, *Economic History*, 1641; *Monthly Labor Review* (February 1965): 178; *Monthly Labor Review* (February 1960): 161.

36. *AISI Annual*, 1975, 22.

37. Ibid., 21; *Monthly Labor Review* (August 1960): 787; *Competitive Challenge*, 41; *AISI Annual Report, 1960*, 28–29.

38. *Handbook of Labor Statistics 1975*, ref. ed. (U.S. Government Printing Office, 1975); *AISI Annual, 1975*, 22; *Steel Labor*, January 1967, 3.

39. *Steel Labor*, March 1961, 3; *Monthly Labor Review* (February 1965): 178.

40. *Steel Labor*, June 1961, 10; *Monthly Labor Review* (October 1960): 1077; Hogan, *Economic History*, 1641.

41. *Monthly Labor Review* (December 1960): 1074; Hogan, *Economic History*, 1637, 1641. The 3¢ a year cap on the COLA could also be applied instead to financing the social insurance fund, if it went broke. That is what actually occurred.

42. *AISI Annual, 1975*, 21.

43. Hogan, *Economic History*, 1643–44; *Steel Labor*, August 1968, 2; *Steel Labor*, August 1969, 11.

44. *Steel Labor*, December 1967, 4; *Monthly Labor Review* (August 1968): 51.

45. *Labor Statistics*, 255; National Tube, Box 976.

46. Hogan, *Economic History*, 1644; *Steel Labor*, September 1969, 9.

47. *Steel Labor*, April 1967, 11; *Steel Labor*, September 1965, 3; Hogan, *Economic History*, 1643–44.

48. *Steel Labor*, September 1965, 2; Hogan, *Economic History*, 1644.

49. *AISI Annual, 1975*, 31; *AISI Annual, 1989* (AISI, 1990), 15.

50. William T. Hogan, *The 1970s: Critical Years for Steel* (Lexington, Mass.: Lexington Books, 1972), 73; Robert W. Crandall, *The United States Steel Industry in Recurrent Crisis* (Brookings Institution, 1981), 35.

51. *Monthly Labor Review* (June 1975): 42; *Monthly Labor Review* (August 1980): 29; Crandall, *The United States Steel Industry in Recurrent Crisis*, 37.

52. *Monthly Labor Review* (December 1980): 62.

53. Hogan, *The 1970s*, 73; *Steel Labor*, August 1970, 8.

54. John Hoerr, *And the Wolf Finally Came: The Decline of the American Steel Industry* (University of Pittsburgh Press, 1988), 177.

55. Ibid.

56. Census of the United States. I used the 1940 through 1980 editions.

57. Ibid. It should also be noted from this data that these eight towns all went from predominantly male to predominantly female during this same period.

58. Delegates to District Conference, October 18, 1957, District 15 Files, USWA Archives, Pennsylvania State University.

59. Lists of Officers, 1960, District 15 Files, USWA Archives.

60. National Tube, Box 976.

61. Ibid.

62. Ibid.

63. A copy of this list, which I obtained from Mike Stout, one of the last officers of USWA Local 1397, is in my possession. I received valuable advice on statistical sampling from Dr. John Bryant of the Mathematics Department of the University of Pittsburgh.

64. Ibid.

65. Ibid.

15

WE *ARE* THE UNION

ED MANN

TREATING PEOPLE FAIRLY

I was born in 1928 in Toledo, Ohio. My mother was raised there. My father grew up in Hackensack, New Jersey. He was a salesman. In the late 1920s he went to Toledo and met my mother. My father's parents lived in New Jersey. My grandfather had franchises to open up a string of beautiful, old-style movie theaters, where you had balconies and loges. I don't know whether he owned them or managed them or what. He was from Hungary.

My grandfather on my mother's side was a custom tailor. He came from

The text is drawn from interviews with Ed Mann that were tape-recorded by Pat Rosenthal, Bruce Nelson, and Alice and Staughton Lynd. A draft of the text was read aloud to the Workers' Solidarity Club of Youngstown, to which Ed Mann has belonged since 1981. Ed and others made corrections and suggested changes.

Ed Mann often asked why the Youngstown-area public schools do not teach labor history. Ed took his grandchildren to picket lines so that they can learn about this part of their heritage. This chapter is dedicated to Ed Mann's grandchildren, Rodney and Jed.

Ed Mann's speech of January 28, 1980, which led to the occupation of the US Steel administration building in Youngstown, was tape-recorded by Eric Davin and is reproduced from Staughton Lynd, *The Fight Against Shutdowns: Youngstown's Steel Mill Closings, 1977–1980* (Singlejack Books: San Pedro, 1983), by permission of the author. That book and a Workers' Solidarity Club pamphlet, *The Trumbull Hospital Strike*, were used to supplement the interview material.

what was Prussia at that time. He left there because he didn't want to fight for the kaiser. He came over in about the 1880s. He enlisted in the army for the Spanish-American War and never went overseas, but he got his citizenship through that. He married and took the name of Berman.

My father opened up Richman Brothers clothing stores, so he always had a job. One of the stores he had to open up was in Youngstown. We moved to Youngstown during the Depression. I remember starting school here at Sheridan School on the South Side. We lived on Florida Street.

In 1939, my mother and father were divorced and my mother and I moved back to Toledo. We had some very progressive teachers at that time in Toledo, teachers who had been through college during the Depression. They seemed to stress social justice. They thought reading and discussing what you read was very important. They gave you a lot of insight into what was going on in the world around you.

My mother was a fair and decent person. Treating people fairly was the undercurrent in our family. There were a lot of people we would call "homeless" today. In those days they were called "on the bum," and my mother always had something to share at mealtime if they came around. We didn't have a lot but we shared. I had a strong family community. There were cousins and aunts and uncles. My grandfather on my mother's side lived with us. He had been all over the world.

I remember how when I was a kid the old-timers in the neighborhood would come to our house on Sunday afternoons and sit around and discuss current events. There was no TV to watch. There was no tag football out in the yard. The kids sat and listened and the oldtimers talked. I can remember folks coming around recruiting for the Spanish Civil War. I don't think it was a structured Socialist group. I think there was a Socialist tendency, which probably came out of the 1848 period in Germany. I got this without having any input, but just listening.

It was primarily a Jewish neighborhood and all the kids were raised Jewish—Orthodox, Conservative, and Reform. I went to a Reform temple, which is probably about as liberal as you can get in the Hebrew tradition. I never felt the religious side of it was a big thing in my life. It was important to my mother but it wasn't very important to me. Some of the traditions I still feel very comfortable with. I like Jewish food. Jews are always called People of the Book. Reading was a very important part of my life. I saw some anti-Semitism as I was growing up. Toledo had a large Polish population. The kids would get in fights. I don't think there was any burning of synagogues. During World War II we were very much aware of the Holocaust. We had a rabbi who was very literate and very concerned. But it was a case of, "What could you do?" I felt the attitude was, "Don't make waves. We don't want to create any more anti-Semitism than there is already."

First Jobs

I had an uncle who was somewhat of a hustler. He helped me to get eggs and I had an egg route. I could keep 5¢ a dozen. I had to fight to keep the boys in the neighborhood from breaking my eggs. Then I got a job in a butcher shop for $1.50 a week. After that I got a job for $4.00 a week in a kosher butcher shop. I would feed the chickens, and clean the cases and the steam table where the hot corned beef was cut. They had barrels of corned beef, dill pickles, and dill tomatoes in the basement. When anybody wanted some I would go down in the basement, and I could taste some. I worked there every day after school. They were closed Saturday and Sunday.

During the Second World War, I worked for Willys Jeep. They would contract with a gang of four or five high school kids to unload railroad cars for $22 a car. We were unloading wood. They used it to make crates to ship the jeeps overseas. When the crates were disassembled they could use the wood to make barracks. When I was fifteen or so I worked for a General Tire recapping plant vulcanizing truck tires. It was a dirty miserable job. They couldn't get anybody to do it so they hired kids. We had to dismount truck tires by hand.

When I was about sixteen years old, I left home and went to California. The day school let out, a friend of mine and myself hitchhiked out and stayed there for the summer. Our parents didn't know where we were. Whenever we'd leave a town, we'd send them a postcard from that place. We came back when school started. It was the top of my junior year.

The Marines

I never finished high school. When I was seventeen, I enlisted in the Marines and spent two years there, 1945–1947. That was the first time I was in the service. I didn't get overseas. I was stationed in Paris Island, Quantico, Camp LeJeune, Cherry Point, in a place called Bowdoin Field, and in Washington, D.C.

When they discharged us, they were pretty tricky. They said, "We've signed everybody up in the Reserves but if you want to hang around until Monday [this was Friday] we'll change the paperwork." Hell, nobody wanted to hang around until Monday and there was never going to be another war—the old bullshit—so here I'd been enlisted in the Reserves for six years in 1947. That was as long as they could put you in. I didn't pay any attention to it, never went to any meetings. It was inactive reserve.

THINGS LIKE THAT POLITICIZE PEOPLE

I went back to Toledo to get my high school diploma. I had taken a GED test when I was in the service but they wouldn't recognize it for a high school diploma where I went to high school. They said, "Nothing doing. You got to go back to school." So I went back to school and worked in a slaughterhouse. It was called Star Packing. I worked midnights, dragging cows off railroad cars, and I went to school stinking from work. That didn't last too long.

I enjoyed reading and I think I retained some of what I read. In those days, we had a library right handy to where we lived. I can remember reading the Jack London stories, Steinbeck's *Grapes of Wrath*, books by some of the muckrakers like *The Octopus* and Upton Sinclair's *The Jungle*.

In Toledo, much as in many other places, they had a black YMCA and a white YMCA. After getting out of the service in 1947 I got a six-month membership in the YMCA. I'd always been interested in Golden Gloves boxing. I never participated but it was a sport I liked to watch. I had this membership in the Y and I met this black fellow. I don't even know how I met him. His name was Bell. He was going to box and he said to me, "Ed, I've got to take off four or five pounds" to get in a certain weight class. I said, "I've got this membership in the Y. Let's go down. They have a steam room." Never giving a thought that there's a white Y and a black Y. It just never entered my mind.

So we go down there. Here I am, a returned veteran from the Second World War, black fellow with me, and I went up to the desk and I said, "I want a guest pass." They looked at me like I was crazy! They said, "You better talk to the manager." So I went in and I said, "Hey, I want a pass for my buddy here. We want to work out." Just a week or so before they had given me this membership and told me all the benefits I had. It was still fresh in my mind. They said, "Look, don't cause any trouble. He's got his YMCA and this is yours."

I think it's things like that that politicize people. I was at an age where I was like a sponge, wanting to participate in society. Then I found out what society was like where I was living at that point in time.

Youngstown 1948–1950

When I went into the service I met some folks from Youngstown. They said, if you want to earn good money and go to school you can do both in Youngstown. The steel mills were paying well and the university would take anybody on the GI Bill. That's what brought me to Youngstown. I arrived on Valentine's Day, 1948. My Dad lived on Winona Drive. He was remarried by this time. I took the trolley down Federal Street to the Brier Hill Works and made out an application. Then I went to the Erie roundhouse and filed an application. I walked across the Division Street bridge to the Ohio Works and applied there. Then I took the trolley home.

By the time I got home the roundhouse had called, so I took the job on the railroad as a fireman. It was a steam engine. I had never done that kind of work but I thought it would be interesting. They gave me a ten-minute orientation. I learned how to signal at night with a lantern. The engineer couldn't stand a greenhorn so he fired up himself. At Westlake crossing he said to me, "Come over here. I want to show you something." Just then something sheered off the side of the engine where I'd been standing. A railroad car had been sticking out onto the track. There was an investigation. I was not fired, didn't even get any time off. I came back out and learned the job. Six months later they went to diesel and that was the end of the steam-engine job.

It was so easy to get jobs in Youngstown at that time. I had eleven different jobs in one year and never got fired from one of them. I worked at Receiving Hospital. I worked in different steel mills, mostly fabricating plants, and in aluminum extrusion. They were decent-paying jobs. The reason I quit was because the conditions were horrendous. They were all union jobs but unions were just starting to feel their oats. There was not much union activity during the war, just the organizing efforts. They were still building the union. They really hadn't settled into job descriptions and bonus systems and crew sizes.

John Barbero

Youngstown State University was a college at that time. When I applied for entrance to YSU I still had no high school diploma. I said, "I'll take an entrance exam. If I pass, let me go to school on the GI Bill." They said, "You don't have to." And they signed me up. I got a job in the cafeteria at the university. I was batching it and I wanted meals. The woman who ran the place liked the boys who worked there. We ate good. That's where I met John Barbero.

John came from a family that had steel mills in their blood. His dad and mother were strongly involved in the 1937 Little Steel Strike. His dad worked at Republic. He was one of the folks that was blackballed at Republic during 1937 and one of the I don't know how many that got their jobs back through the Supreme Court. John was a very literate guy. He'd been in the Marine Corps during the Second World War. He was an interpreter. He learned to speak Japanese and married a Japanese woman. He felt strongly about what happened with the atomic bomb. He was sympathetic to many different ideas.

John Barbero and I belonged to the United Labor Party. The United Labor Party was founded in Akron at the end of World War II, and ran candidates for local office until about 1950. I really liked the people there: Marie Wagner, Lee Heilman. I liked the intermingling of groups. It was a tough, strong outfit at that time.

There was a multiracial organization at the university called the Inter-Group Good Will Council, or something like that. John and I were pretty active in it. Their attitude was not to start a crusade where you were going to get blacks integrated and do things *for* blacks. We cooperated with folks that wanted to change things. In the early 1950s, blacks wanted to integrate the North Side pool. They lived near there. We helped them on that. We demonstrated there. It wasn't a popular position to take but the pools are integrated now.

We also picketed against the Ku Klux Klan. The Ku Klux Klan was burning a cross between here and Akron. They were trying to recruit in the area. They had some redneck farmer who let them use his farm to have their demonstrations. We went up. There was a black minister, Lonnie Simon. We couldn't get a rabbi. We couldn't get a priest. There were some blacks and some union guys, including John Conroy. We went there with about twenty people. Deputy sheriffs were in the middle of the road. We were on one side and the Klan was on the other. We were young then. We wanted to mix it up.

Folks like John Barbero said to me, "Why don't you go in the mill now the railroad's shut down?" One of our fellow students was an employment personnel guy. I went to apply at Brier Hill and he was taking the applications. He said, "Sure, you got a job!" So I got hired at Brier Hill for the first time. This was in 1948. John started there a year or so ahead of me. After a while I quit to go back to college. I spent all the time I had accrued on the GI Bill at YSU, seven years. I'm about thirty-three hours short of a degree.

Merlin Luce and Others

There was also a group of Trotskyists at US Steel's Ohio Works. They had a core of maybe ten people who belonged to the Socialist Workers Party. They also had a meeting place on East Federal Street in downtown Youngstown, over a bar. I went to some of their meetings. I was political, but my role for many years was passive. I went to demonstrations. I didn't understand much of the speeches. I never read Marx. I felt strongly about peace and freedom, and I felt very comfortable with socialism. I knew about the Socialist Workers Party and the Communist Party, but I wasn't a joiner. I did know that they were decent people. These guys talked sense, in my estimation. They had ideas. They did things. I felt comfortable with them. They built a strong union at the Ohio Works. There were blacks and whites. They had a good literate newspaper. Ted Dostal was editor, I think. They had job descriptions. They ran the local like it was supposed to be run.

In the 1950s the Socialist Workers Party started splitting. It was like the Protestant Church. When there are splits and you don't understand why, you become disillusioned. It gave some of them the opportunity to get out and become respectable. They became staff men for the international union. Ted Dostal didn't.

Another member of that group was Merlin Luce. He was raised on a farm. He worked his ass off just to eat. He had some bad experiences in the service, and got pneumonia. I like being around Merlin. He's not a know-it-all kind of guy who jumps in and creates more problems than there were before. He's really calm. I like the way he treats people.

BETTY LOOKED A LOT NICER

In the summer of 1949 I went back to Toledo for the summer. I went to summer school at Toledo University. Betty lived in an apartment with one or two other women and I was dating one of the other women that lived there. I saw Betty and I said, Betty looks a lot nicer. We started going out. We were married in Youngstown. Betty came to Youngstown on the B&O Railroad carrying all her belongings. She was wrapped up in a babushka. We were married in an evangelical church. There were probably eight or ten people there, just friends of mine.

The Marines Again

We lived in a trailer on Four Mile Run Road. The Korean War started and in October 1950 I got a telegram: "Be in Philadelphia Navy Yard in ten days." I had a wife and a baby. I was going to college, had a job and no money. I had to quit school and quit my job. Betty's dad came down and took the trailer up to Michigan. We went to Toledo to see my mother and my uncle gave us $1,000. Ned was six months old. We had a United Labor Party meeting at John's house about that time. An FBI informer was there. He took pictures of everyone, including Ned.

I was in the service one year that time. In January or February 1951, we got word that we were going overseas. Most of the fellows in my squad were married and had kids and weren't too happy about being back in the service. We knew when our troopship was leaving. They wouldn't give any-body a leave so we got a weekend pass for thirty miles. Everybody headed for home! Some of the fellows went to Boston, another fellow went to Eliz-abeth, New Jersey. One fellow was from Chicago and there was a fellow there from Youngstown. Betty was in Upper Michigan and I went up there to see her and Ned.

I got back just as the outfit was leaving to board the troopship. I got a flight out of Detroit to Washington. When I got off the Navy plane, the Shore Patrol was there checking everybody's passes. My pass said thirty miles and it had expired about a week before. So they put cuffs on us, put us on a military bus, and took us back to Camp LeJeune. The captain knew the situation. He was in the Reserves, too. He didn't want to go. The captain said, "I sympathize with you because I did the same thing." He said, "I just got back. But I got to put you on the report." So they took us aboard ship in irons, put us in the brig, and let us out when we got to Gibraltar. It was an interesting trip, bread and water. Didn't hurt, though. At least you didn't have to chip any paint!

We went to Greece. Greece was having a civil war. NATO was getting organized and they sent a group of Marines in there with the Greek army. We were trying to stay out of sight. We'd been in the Marine Corps before and we weren't interested in getting shot or anything like that. Most of the fellows couldn't have cared less whether it was Communist or Hindu or Baptist. They just wanted to get the hell out. We went to France. We went to Italy. We went to Sardinia. We were on Malta and Crete.

Brier Hill for Good

When I got out—I think it was December 7, 1951—Betty's Dad said there was a good job in the Upper Michigan Highway Patrol. "Why don't you go see about it?" he said. I went up and I put in an application. I was a quarter of an inch too short.

I said, "I've got a job in Youngstown at Hines Steel." I had gotten that job just before I was called back into the service. "I've got so many days to claim it. I'm going." I had only worked at Hines Steel about six weeks. It was a small fabricating plant. I went there and I said, "I want my job back." They said, "We have no record of you ever working here." I said, "Well, I've got a paystub." (I don't know why I had saved it.) They wouldn't give me the time of day!

So I went to the VA. I knew the fellow there because I had been to college with him. He called them and said, "If you don't want a lawsuit, you better put this guy back to work." So I went back to work. They put me on the job I was entitled to, as a craneman. As soon as I got a pay I sent it to Betty and Betty came down. Hines Steel was going to put on an apprentice program for machinists. That's what I wanted if I could get it but they kept putting me off.

A friend of mine worked in the machine shop at Brier Hill. He said, "They're going to put on some more apprentices at Brier Hill." John Barbero was working at Brier Hill and I'd worked there back in 1948 for a summer, so I knew the guys there. I went to the employment office. I said, "I want to be a machinist in the apprenticeship program." He said, "They're going to give the test this month. I'll put you in there as a rigger helper." I said, "Fine."

You got a thirty-day probationary period. So in that thirty days I took the apprenticeship test. The fellow who gave the test said, "I can tell right now seeing the answers to the test that you passed it." After they graded it, he said, "You got the highest score in the company." In the meantime, the guys in the shop got me appointed as steward. Nobody else wanted the job. Going through the job descriptions, I found that a machinist working in the shop gets paid one rate, and when you're out in the mill you're supposed to get a nickel an hour more. I filed a grievance for all the machinists. I won the grievance! And I never heard a thing about the apprentice program after that.

I got hired at Brier Hill in 1952. The first twelve years I worked there I didn't have a full year's pay because of the layoffs. Steel was real cyclical. Nineteen fifty-three was almost a year layoff. Nineteen fifty-four was a good year. Nineteen fifty-five was the most prosperous year in steel that I can recall. I think I made $5,000. We thought we were living! One year I was laid off eleven months. Another layoff was for thirteen months.

John Barbero and I went to the auto plantz in Twinsburg. They said to me, "We need a quality control inspector. Can you tell quality steel?" I said, "Yeah!" "Can you read blueprints?" "Yeah!" "Can you read micrometers?" "Yeah!" They made me an inspector. We lived in a twenty-seven-foot trailer in Girard. We lived in it seven years, with two kids. In 1954 we bought property. We built the garage and put the trailer next to it. Beth was born in 1956. Then we started on the house. Timmy was born in January 1958. We moved into the house two weeks before. Nothing was finished. That year we lived on $39 a week.

I REALLY LIKED THAT OPEN HEARTH

When I started at Brier Hill it was a big plant. It was an integrated plant in the sense that they started out with iron ore and made a finished product, electric weld pipe. In that plant there were three local unions. Local 1462 was the biggest, with about 3,300 members when I started there.

John Barbero worked in the open hearth. A fellow by the name of Dominic Perry with whom I'd gone to college said, "Look, if you want to make some money, come on up in the open hearth and get all the overtime you want." They did pay well. So I went up to the open hearth. (A week later they put on two new apprentices in the machine shop.)

I really liked that open hearth. I think the first three months I was there, they must have had ten wildcat strikes. The guys wanted better working conditions. We'd say, "We want rubber-tired wheelbarrows!" because the ones they had been using were steel-tired. They'd hit a rail, it would twist, and guys would get hurt. "We want a relief man!" "We want potable drinking water!" "We want cold water!" The refrigerator system would break down and the superintendent was too cheap to buy ice. We needed safety jackets and safety masks for wearing near the furnaces. "We need safety masks today! Hey, somebody got burned. We want safety jackets or we aren't going to work on those furnaces!" "We want black in the gun so it's not too hard to shovel!"

The grievance procedure wasn't working. That's why we had wildcat strikes. We weren't going to get tied up in paperwork. The wildcats didn't last long: a day, two days at the most, maybe eight hours. The ones I led came later. I was just learning the ropes.

Local 1462

It was the first place I worked that had even the facade of a big union. We had a real dictator as president and he was making all kinds of deals. So the rank and file had to apply pressure to get things changed. We had some strong young people with ideals. We believed in what the union was supposed to be like.

Before the local was organized, a lot of Italians lived in the vicinity of the plant. They were discriminated against as much as blacks were discriminated against. They got the lousiest jobs. They were track labor. They were helpers in the mason gang. They could not aspire to the jobs in the shops that the Germans or the English had. Most of the Italians were of limited formal education. They couldn't express themselves as well as those that they called "Johnny Bulls," the English, Irish, and Scotch. They got a young guy who was very literate. His name was Danny Thomas. He was tough. If a foreman was mistreating an old Italian guy, he'd grab the foreman by the shirt and say, "Leave that old guy alone!" So he got a lot of respect in the Italian community.

Danny Thomas was president of Local 1462 from the late 1940s until the early 1960s, when he became a staff man for the international union. The Thomas machine was led by Mafia types. The way the Mafia operated was to say, "Hey, I'll lend you twenty bucks. You give me thirty back on payday. If you don't, I'll break both your legs." They did favors for people. They'd fix you up with a little overtime, or maybe get your kid a job in the summer. The boss let them use the phone so they did the boss favors.

I remember local union meetings. We used to meet on the second floor of this old house. We were at a confrontation at a union meeting there back in the late 1950s. We were going up the stairs and our guys were carrying mostly jack handles. The guys that were in power, the Mafia types, were going down to get their guns out of their cars. It was exciting! We all met on the stairway. We won. When they went out to get their guns, we took over the union hall. They called the police.

We had the most dishonest elections you can imagine. One time they had a bottomless ballot box and they set it over a cold air return in this old house. As you vote you put your ballot in the ballot box. It would drop down into the cellar. There were two people down there. "This one's okay." They'd put it aside. "This one's no good." They'd throw it in the furnace. (We heard this after these guys retired, years later.) We'd wonder, "We had three thousand people vote but we only got eight votes? There's more of us than that!" Once we had an election where everybody in the plant voted, the way the ballots came out, and that's impossible. That was the game that was played. Really, if you don't have the power to count the votes, you don't have the power to win. We learned that early on.

Rank and File

We knew we had two battles to fight, with the company and the union. We weren't interested in breaking away or destroying the union. But we felt that the union had to be more responsive to what the members needed. The union thought what was good for the company was good for the union. I don't agree. I think the union should look out for its members. The company can look after itself. I got involved with the union because I thought it was the best way to be represented. You're on an equal footing with management. I always thought you had to demand your rights. You had to fight for them.

We spoke up in favor of union officers working at least one year in four in the mill; that no official should take more than the wages of the highest-paid member he or she represents; that staff be elected, not appointed. One of our main issues was, "We want to elect our stewards." Back then the local union president appointed all the stewards. In a 3,300-person plant, Danny Thomas had over one hundred paid people, like precinct committeemen. They had control over overtime and days off. We wanted stewards to be responsible to people who elected them.

We won that issue many times on the floor. We would bring a group of people to the union hall and we'd vote for electing them instead of appointing them. Next meeting, our people didn't show up, he had a majority, he'd vote it down. This went on for years until we took office in 1973.

There was an increase in dues in the late 1950s. And there was a real upsurge of rank-and-file people that resented the international union asking for more money. We don't have the right to strike, so why build up a big strike and defense fund for the international union when local problems are not being taken care of? A fellow by the name of [Donald] Rarick took the lead in opposing this at the international convention and he built

up a slate of candidates to run against the international officers. He was a
local union president, a likable person, and an average guy. He got quite a
following here in Youngstown for his Dues Protest Committee. The Dues
Protest was a fight that united everybody. We had membership cards and
petitions. It was as if it was payday. You might have been a laborer and
black, and I might have been a first helper making $40 a day, and hey, we
were buddies.

Then there was the Organization for Membership Rights. It was very
small: eight or ten people at Brier Hill including John Barbero, Bill Litch,
Ken Doran, and Bob Lewis. We tried to make sure everybody was being represented fairly. The Organization for Membership Rights became the Rank-
and-File Team.

Rarick had a heart attack and died. Bill Litch from our local tried to run
for president of the international union. I think there were about 3,500
locals at that time. You had to have 150 or 200 locals nominate you. There
was no physical way we could contact every local. We tried by mailing to
every local union secretary a request to nominate the Rank-and-File Team.
We got hardly any response because most local unions are run by the staff
man. The international had staff men in each local who were on the payroll.
If they are not run by him, the officers generally support the international
because most presidents would like a staff job. Bill didn't get on the ballot.

When I. W. Abel ran against David McDonald for president of the international union in 1964, and defeated him, we supported I. W. Abel. We
always had hope for people that said the right thing. How do you know
when people aren't going to do what they say they are going to do?

WE HAD SOME TOUGH BLACKS WHO STAYED

It was maybe the first five years I was in the mill that they started moving
blacks up on jobs. In the open hearth where I worked most of the time,
there were blacks in the pit (that's behind the furnace where they pour the
steel). But on the floor where the first, second, and third helpers and the
melters were, it was white until the early 1950s. John Barbero and I helped
to bring blacks in there.

If you wanted to work on a furnace that meant you had to be able to
take the heat. There were five doors on these furnaces. Let's say a black guy
was going to go up there and try to learn that job, shoveling into the furnace. The first helper would pull the door all the way up when the black guy
would come near and the flame would shoot out twenty or thirty feet. If he
had common sense, he wouldn't want to work there. These are the games
that were played.

We had some tough black guys who stayed, took it, got the job, and moved up. They weren't in the majority by any means, but there were some black fellows who worked there who could do their job and the jobs of the guys on either side of them. There were some that were easily discouraged. Hell, there were white guys who wouldn't do it, but for different reasons. It was a hard job.

Blacks Got the Worst Jobs

Blacks got the worst jobs. They worked in the coke plants, blast furnaces, track labor, plate mill, scarfing yard. There were very few blacks in the skilled trades (we called it trade and craft). The only blacks I can recall in a skilled trade during my early years in the mill were bricklayers. There were none in the shops. No electricians. Maybe a few millwrights and motor inspectors but not many. Even in the black departments, the top job was usually held by a white man.

Blacks did not get the jobs where there was a chance to promote. Maybe he became the truck driver, but he could never become the roller. Maybe he could become the craneman but he could never become the charging machine man. There should be a line of progression so that he can get to the top job somehow.

Blacks had been brought in as scabs in 1919 and 1937. Not all blacks were brought in as scabs. There might have been twenty, thirty, fifty. But this gave any white racist an excuse to say, "The blacks are going to take your jobs. They are scabs. They'll work for less." And it's an excuse, because many of the blacks, when they found out they were being used as scabs, came out of those mills. This isn't what we hear about.

Blacks had their place and whites had their place. Nothing was done to discourage this by the managers or by the unions. It reflected the community, a very ethnic community. There was always a hidden resentment of blacks. Sort of a, "Watch out for that fellow, he's different" attitude. It's the propaganda that we're fed all our lives. We're a pretty racist society.

I look at a black person and say, "What does he want out of life?" Probably no more than any white person wants. If a black man wants to work and make a living and support his family and have the things that people want for their families, why shouldn't he be free to obtain that if he can without blacks and whites interfering with each other? You don't blame the victim. You work together. You better the workplace and make the job better for each other.

The union was not aggressive in upgrading blacks. They'd give them a meeting and let them blow off steam. I would say that under Danny Thomas, the union used them insidiously by giving certain blacks positions in the local that were (I don't like to use the term) Uncle Tom positions. And the people in those positions liked that role of being a veneer. They were as rotten as any white guys we had down there. They were not interested in black progress, as far as I could see. They wanted a piece of the action. That's the type of black leadership we had from the Danny Thomas group. He knew there were votes there. As illegally as he did things with his voting procedure, he still wanted blacks voting for him.

There were some very literate blacks. Oliver Montgomery and Jimmy Davis are two that stick in my mind. It was the younger ones who came back after the Second World War and the Korean War that showed positive leadership. We had one friend, Archie Nelson. He was a black guy in the conditioning yard. The conditioning yard worked as a gang. They scarf the steel, burn the impurities off slabs: a hard, hot job. In those kinds of jobs you develop leadership. He was the leader of the blacks. He controlled that department. They knew how much they had to do. They did that much. They didn't work their heads off. They all had white supervisors. All the blacks had to do was just fold their arms and there would have been nothing done. So they let him run the crew. Then they were going to put some new foreman on and they said to Archie, "If you don't take the foreman job, we are going to hire a black guy off the street." So he took the job. But he didn't become a company man. He had principles.

The Consent Decree

There were certain practices that were started with the Danny Thomas regime and they didn't just disappear. There was no revolution in the local. You had to pick away, pick away at these various practices. We helped integrate the open hearth. We supported the blacks to press the issue. Don't get the impression that I did it, or John did it. It was a group effort. The people in the mill knew it was the right thing to do. They may have been racist but they knew it was the right thing to do.

Most of the people in the labor pool were black because the coke plant, which was almost a wholly black department, was shut down. Willie Aikens, a black man who later became chairperson of the local's civil rights committee, was in the labor pool for a long time. So was I. He spent a lot of time on layoff and while he was on layoff white guys were being hired off the street in some departments. That happened to me. That was serious. Things would slip. We weren't in office then.

Everybody that was laid off was in the pool. You were placed on jobs that were below job class 5 according to your seniority in this layoff pool. Let's say that in the blooming mill a job class 3 job comes open. Before they can hire anybody off the street, they have to take the oldest person in the labor pool and put him on that job. The weakness of the labor pool agreement was that labor pool people could not get into a job above job class 5. If there was nobody to fill the job from the department, they could hire right off the street! We tried to open up all the jobs to people in the labor pool. We had a tough time. We raised it maybe an increment a time over a number of years, but by then it didn't matter any more because things were slowing down so much.

In the open hearth, where John Barbero was chairman and where I came from, we did get an agreement with the superintendent that he would open up all jobs to the people in the pool. But we're talking about half a dozen jobs at the most. The furnace jobs, the big money jobs, started at job class 6. After everybody got their forty hours, you could promote somebody from the labor pool to those class 6 jobs. Nothing higher than that ever came open anyway. We made a breakthrough but it didn't last because they kept taking furnaces off.

There was almost turn seniority at times. If you worked a certain turn, say, day turn, you had seniority in that little group. We tried to broaden that. By the time the mill shut down we had plantwide seniority. Assuming everything was booming, it was a good idea, but we were losing jobs. So you were fighting over the few jobs that were left.

There were people that agitated over the consent decree, how unfair it was. "We've been here all these years and these blacks are coming in. They don't know how to do this and they don't know how to do that." Well, everybody has to learn. The guy that's got the top job didn't come in off the street a genius on how to make steel. Somebody had to teach him.

In the department where Willie Aikens worked there was a lot of hand-eye coordination. It was a department of very young people. They had a lot of young white hustlers in there who could work their asses off, and make good bonus. Now you're bringing in some black folks who have not been exposed to jobs with a lot of hand-eye coordination, who are older, and who also come in feeling, "Nobody likes me here," because they are moving up and taking the white guys' jobs. It was a problem. Nobody would show them what to do.

The company wanted production, and didn't really care whether there was a black or a white guy. It was the responsibility of the foremen to train a new worker. They said, "He's got to have the *ability* to do the job." Well, who determines the ability? The company. And who's supposed to train them? The company. The company wouldn't train the black guys or wouldn't train them properly.

Many blacks had the feeling, "I've caught hell all these years. I've got a lot of seniority now. I'm going in and get Looey's job!" But that wasn't the case. He could get Looey's job, but it had to be in a period when there was an increase in production and they open up the bidding. They'd say, "Hey, how come I'm not getting that job?" There were rules. There had to be an opening. If he was entitled to the job, we fought to see that he got the job. If he wasn't, you had to tell him straight out, "Look, you're not going to get that job until it's posted or until there's a vacancy or until they put on more turns." I did see it make a lot more equity if you had some basis of determining who gets the job. Seniority, in my estimation, has got to stay. It's the only fair way and it's the only way the company can't wheel and deal with people.

Some blacks *lost* because of the consent decree. You never hear that! Those were odd cases. We had two brothers. They were both white, hillbillies from Kentucky. One brother was advantaged and one was disadvantaged by the consent decree. One worked very closely with me in the open hearth. He was a second helper. The consent decree came along with plantwide seniority. The brother that worked with me had been in the labor gang in another department in the early years, then transferred to the open hearth. Now he could bring that seniority with him. He moved up to first helper in the open hearth, which is a much better job, because he had plant seniority.

The other brother was a railroad engineer on the narrow gauge railroad. He had been in that department since he got hired and worked his way up to engineer. When they shut the coke plant, which was primarily black, a lot of blacks moved into the railroad department as brakemen. When the mill went to plantwide seniority they were able to bring their coke plant seniority with them, which didn't cut any mustard before that. They bumped those white engineers. And there was a lot of friction: nothing physical, but a lot of hot language in their own groups.

In a growth-type time it would have been much better, but we were losing jobs. If there was a cutback in operation everybody was bumped back. Then another turn went on or another furnace went on and, under the consent decree, the black promoted because of his plant seniority. The white stayed at the lesser job where in prior years he would have moved back up.

They didn't come in and knock him off his job. It was an up-and-down level of operations. When the new promotion came he didn't get it. He had to go by plant seniority. When you are talking about leveling off at a lower level of operations and seniority becomes the main criterion for promotion, that's where it hurt. That's where the consent decree took effect. It wasn't perfect but it was fair. Yet you're in a dying plant in a dying industry and that was the unfairness of it. There weren't the promotional opportunities.

The sad part was that the union was as guilty as the company or there wouldn't have been a consent decree directed against both. If the union had done its job in the early years when the union was being formed, it would have been a different story. The words were beautiful: We are all brothers. But the international union just lived off the organizing days. It didn't keep its promises. Then it had to reap the harvest: the consent decree.

We felt that the consent decree was as fair as it could be at that time and we followed it to the letter. We helped some people. We hurt some people. Generally, it helped a lot of blacks and Hispanics who had been discriminated against. Women started coming in in the early 1970s. They didn't come in with any seniority. Everything was being cut back. So they had the bottom jobs. They gradually moved up in the departments as people retired or quit.

I think that the people who were racist stayed racist. The people who thought integration was the only fair way stayed that way. I don't sense that there was any physical retaliation. There were people who were going to harass a black, whether it was the 1950s or the 1960s or the 1970s. But basically, people were there to do a job. They needed the money. They did their work. I know there were different things going on in auto and in other places. But in the steel plant that I worked in, I did not see any big changes. The activity to upgrade blacks was ongoing at Brier Hill. It wasn't easy. But now and then we'd get some victories.

I BELIEVE IN DIRECT ACTION

I think we've got too much contract. You hate to be the guy who talks about the good old days, but I think the IWW had a darn good idea when they said, "Well, we'll settle these things as they arise." I believe in direct action. Once a problem is put on paper and gets into the grievance procedure, you might as well kiss that paper good-bye. When the corporations started recognizing unions, they saw this. They coopted the unions with the grievance procedure and the dues checkoff. They quit dealing with the rank and file and started dealing with the people who wanted to be bosses like them, the union bosses.

We were the troublemakers. We'd have a wildcat strike. The international would say, "Either you get back to work or you're fired." It wasn't the company saying this. It was the union.

The Dolomite Gun and the Bonus System

One strike we led, they had a dolomite gun they used to spray the furnaces after the heat was tapped out. Prior to them getting this piece of equipment we used to have to shovel in the dolomite. It was in the summertime and the superintendent wouldn't use the gun. It was real hot. So we just stayed on the floor or went to the office and said, "We're not going to do any shoveling until you put that gun on the floor to give us some relief." We got help like that. Most of the superintendents in that time had come up through the ranks and they knew the conditions of the job. They knew you weren't kidding.

But in a production department, say like where Archie Nelson was where people were scarfing, if they slowed down it affected production. Sometimes the stuff was needed at the next point of operations on a certain timetable. The further a piece of metal gets down through the operation, the more costly it becomes. So the further down the line you make your move or your action, it becomes more costly to the company. If you're at the finish where they are going to ship the pipe and you refuse to load it, because it's gone through all these steps that piece of pipe is worth X number of dollars where when it was in the furnace as molten metal it was worth only pennies.

In the open hearth, you worked on a big furnace that held two hundred tons of molten metal. If you slowed down the operation, you'd burn the furnace up. The furnace would melt. And then you had a lot of physical hard work repairing the furnace, shoveling and so on: backbreaking work. The idea was to get the heat out as quick as you could; make your steel, get it out of that furnace so it wouldn't tear the furnace up, and you made a little bit of bonus.

The people who could slow down the procedure were the people who charged the furnaces, who put in the scrap and molten iron. These were the charging-machine men and cranemen. They had a little control over how the operation went. If your first helper wanted two boxes of raw lime and a box of ore in the furnace to make the steel up to specifications, the charging-machine man could give them a little extra or not enough and screw up everything.

The longer you keep molten steel in a furnace the more likely you are to tear up the production equipment. You tap the steel into a ladle. You got to get it out of that ladle and into the molds or it's going to freeze up on the ladle. We're talking about two hundred tons of steel in one big chunk. There's the labor of putting new brick in and of the boilermaker doing patchwork. And if you don't get the steel to the blooming mill in a certain period of time it's going to get too cold and they will have to reheat it, which costs money, and it will change the makeup of the steel. You got to hit them where it hurts.

Once they were going to change the bonus system. They were going to give the first helper and the second helper an increase in bonus and cut the third helpers. In other words, they were just moving the money around. Third helpers refused to go out on the job. Second helpers stuck with them. Then there was nobody out there to help the first helpers so they agreed to go out with us. It was a wildcat.

Well, we were out that night. The midnight turn comes out and finds out about this. We are all sitting in the washroom. The company comes out with the president of the local, Danny Thomas. "What's the problem here?" There's the plant manager and the local union president and so on. I'm sitting there. As spokesman for the group I said, "They're cutting our bonus. We don't want to hear it."

Danny Thomas says to the superintendent, "You get rid of that guy and your troubles are over." And the whole open hearth gang is sitting there. This doesn't hurt me politically at all. It got the guys hotter. They didn't care about getting rid of me. They didn't want to lose our bonus! The superintendent was crying, "What am I going to do with this steel?" I said, "Tap it out on the ground. I don't care what you do with it." He said, "The blast furnace is ready to tap. We got to move that iron." "Dump it on the ground," I said. "We want our bonus." They agreed.

"Now who's going to get paid? Are we going to get paid for the time we've been docked here?" [The supervisor said,] "Oh, we can't do that. You guys didn't do any work." We said, "The furnace did the work. We want pay or we're going home right now." And it worked. You wonder why Danny Thomas and I didn't get along? He tells the superintendent that if he gets rid of me his troubles are over!

The Wildcat Over Tony's Death

This was the first experience I had that showed that *people* can really be involved. At the time I was recording secretary of the local, and John and I were both stewards in the open hearth. We filed a grievance with the superintendent about thirty-three different safety violations. One of the items was, we wanted vehicles to have back-up signals. They used big heavy trucks in the pit. There was a lot of noise. It was hard to hear. We wanted a warning horn on the back so when a truck was going to back up the people working there could hear it.

The company rejected the grievance out of hand. They weren't going to discuss any of the thirty-three demands. Shortly after the grievance was rejected, a man who was going to retire in about seven days was run over by one of these trucks. He was crushed. He was a well-liked person who had worked there a long time and was about to retire. This happened on day turn, about one o'clock in the afternoon.

I was working afternoon turn that day, three to eleven. I came out to work and somebody said, "Tony got killed." "How did he get killed?" "You remember that grievance you filed asking for back-up signals on the truck? The truck backed over him and crushed him." So I get up on the bench in the washroom and I say to the guys coming to work: "What are we going to do about this? Are we going to work under these lousy conditions? Who's next? Who's going to get killed next? Don't we give a damn about Tony?" The guys agreed to go out.

Now some didn't agree to go out. "What's the matter with you guys? Here you are. A union brother murdered. We had a grievance in and it was rejected. Are you going to let the company pull this shit?" We actually had to drag some people out because we had all kinds of people. "That's not my problem. I don't work down there. I run a crane." "Let's get out! Let's go!"

We went up to the union hall. We were the afternoon turn that was supposed to go to work. Day turn has finished working, they've tapped the heats out, and the people working day turn now come up to the union hall. We've got two turns there. We tell them the situation. They agree, "Shut her down!" The guys called their buddies on the midnight turn from the union hall, "Don't come out to work tonight." John was out of town that weekend. They were looking to me for leadership. I said, "Here's what we'll do. Rather than get the stewards fired, let's appoint a committee for each area and let's start listing our demands on safety," bypassing the union structure. It worked. Every area—pit, cranes, floor—was represented.

In the meantime Lefty DeLarco, who was departmental chairman of the open hearth at that time, was working day turn. He calls over to the union hall on the company phone and says, "Hey Ed, what's going on? Why aren't these guys coming to work?" I'm sure the phone is bugged. I could have been fired for leading the strike. I say, "Why don't you come up here, Lefty, and find out?"

The company called the international union rep. "What's going on here?" "There's nothing going on until these grievances are resolved." "What grievances?" We didn't just say, "Goddamn it, Tony got killed and we're shutting it down." We said, "This is what we want. Get a meeting with the company. We'll meet at any time they want." They set up a meeting for that night, about nine o'clock. They had to get the plant manager from wherever he was. The company said, "We're only going to deal with the departmental chairman." I said, "Then you're not going to deal with anybody because this is the committee." I said, "The only reason you want to deal with Lefty is that you want to fire him," which wasn't the case but it got Lefty off the hook. He wouldn't have to tell the people to go back to work.

We refused even to have the superintendent in the office because it was he who rejected the grievance. We said, "We're not going to deal with him if he can't answer. We want to talk to somebody that has more authority." They brought in the division manager. We met late in the night with the company and all the next day. They agreed to everything. They wanted this committee to meet with the company on a regular basis on safety conditions, bypassing the safety committee because this was an immediate issue, whereas the safety committee worked on things month by month—a meeting this month to correct this light bulb burned out, next month they come back and say, we didn't have any light bulbs.

So next day we have a meeting at the union hall to explain what happened, what we gained and all that. We're discussing whether we're going back to work or not and I'm saying to the guys, "Look, if there's anything else you want, let's hear it." Then the Youngstown newspaper comes out. It reports the accident and the strike and it says, "Tony got killed because of his own negligence." The company sent out that statement. The guys got furious. "We want that statement retracted in tomorrow's paper." Not just a phone call or a letter. They wanted it in the paper, retracted. The paper doesn't come out for another twenty-four hours. The guys stayed out another day. And in the next day's paper they retracted that statement and the guys went back to work.

They reprimanded everybody in the open hearth that went out and they gave me three days off. We said, "Wait a minute, take the reprimands away." And they did take them off everybody else. I said, "Hey, I don't care. You guys go back to work." Other departments didn't go out on strike in sympathy, but there was just no work for them. We made the steel. That cost the company a lot of profits. Everything cost, measured as trainloads of material coming in or scrap half loaded. That's a feeling of power. And it isn't something you're doing as an individual. You're doing it as a group.

If you're not going to *do* something, then you're not going to be a leader, are you? I had credibility. I'd just gotten elected recording secretary. I got more votes out of the open hearth than the president got. The grievance was rejected. The members knew that the grievance was rejected. The guy was going to retire. It was an emotional issue. He was a guy everybody liked. It wasn't prepared timing. It fell into place. You've got to recognize those situations. Be there when there are credible steps to take. Some people, it never happens in their lives. I was lucky.

The Wildcat About the Stool Cleaners

Grievances were backlogged sometimes two and three years. You got to settle these things right at the point of production, and RIGHT NOW! For example, we had a group of engineers and brakemen who would take the ingots to the blooming mill on a narrow gauge railroad. The ingots were poured, the molds were removed, and the ingots remained on what they call "stools." They were taken to the blooming mill, then brought back, and somebody had to clean the gravel or cinders or scrap off the stools. That job usually went to an old-timer. All he had to do was to spray those molds with an air gun and then splash on some lime. It was a good job for an old guy who was going to retire.

The company said, "We're going to eliminate that job and the brakemen are going to do that." A crew would be two brakemen, an engineer, and a stool cleaner. That's four men on a turn. It's a twenty-four-hour operation. Four times four turns, because there was always a turn off: sixteen guys, maybe seventeen with an extra guy. But if they don't work, those ingots don't come out of the open hearth and go to the blooming mill. It has to be on a timed basis so that they don't get too cold or they crack. This is high-priced steel.

So at 3:00 A.M., here comes the whole midnight crew knocking at the door of my house. "What's the problem?" "They want to eliminate the stool cleaner's job and we're not going to do that." "Okay," I said, "it's the middle of the night." I said, "Why don't you guys just bunk here and in the morning we'll go down to the gate and when the superintendent comes in, we'll talk to him.'" "Okay." So they slept on the couch and the floor or whatever. The company knew these guys had walked off so I didn't have to call anybody. We got up early, got down to the gate, waiting for the superintendent, and day turn is coming to work. They say, "What's happening?" I said, "They eliminated the stool cleaner's job." "Bullshit!" So now we got two turns at the gate. Here comes the superintendent. This was a new superintendent. He was a fair person. The people who made this decision were the foremen, thinking, We can eliminate this job, put a feather in our hats, cut costs. He said, "Look, Ed, I don't know anything about this. Let me see what I can find out." "Okay, Bob," I said, "but these guys aren't going to work." He said, "I wish they would." I said, "No. The job's been eliminated. No." He said, "What time do you want to meet?" I said, "You let me know. I'll be at the union hall with these guys. You can call."

So I got a call about ten o'clock in the morning and he said, "We want to meet with you guys at three o'clock." They'd had some general foreman stay over to do the job. They got the job done. But they were running into trouble because these bosses don't like to work either! At three o'clock we met him at the gate. Here is the head of industrial relations, the superintendent of the open hearth, and all his foremen. It's a small office. There's a desk in there, a couple of chairs, file cabinets. All these guys are coming in. The only people we don't have now is the turn that is off. People who are working 3:00 to 11:00 are there at the gate.

The industrial relations guy said, "Wait a minute, Ed. We only want the representatives in here." I said, "I just made all these guys representatives. I can appoint all committees. These guys are Dinky Skinner's committee." These were the old guys, all broken down and worn out, that were going to be displaced. So he said, "All right, bring them in." The guys are all standing around, really intimidating the supervisory folks.

The industrial relations guy, a young guy, says to me, "Ed, you got three options." I said, "Time out. You got one option. Put these guys back on the job or that steel is not going to the blooming mill because the open hearth is walking out and also the blooming mill. The word is out. You are not eliminating these guys' jobs." He said, "Let me talk to these guys for fifteen minutes," meaning his foremen.

So we go out. Everybody is hot. They're feeling pretty good. We are milling around in the hallway. They can hear us saying, "They can't do this!" Fifteen minutes later he said, "We're putting them back on." I said, "We got one other thing to discuss. We want pay for these three turns that have been down. Because the steel got to the blooming mill. Somebody did it, and we're entitled to pay."

"We don't pay for people going out on strike!"

"Let's go, fellows."

"Wait a minute!"

We got them paid. No big deal. But that's how these things happen. Sure, we could say, "You guys can't strike. You better get back on the job and file a grievance." But that won't get the problem resolved. If workers don't sympathize, they won't engage in direct action. That's their own way of saying it's not a good grievance.

YOU GOT TO PUT DOWN ROOTS

I participated in the March on Washington in 1963. I was also against the Vietnam War and went to Washington from the beginning on that. It was usually John Barbero and myself and other folks who felt the same way. When we went to the first anti–Vietnam War demonstration that I can recall, we hardly had enough people to march around the White House. And before it was all over, there were millions of people.

It's so much easier to go somewhere else and demonstrate than to demonstrate in your own hometown. I can remember that in Youngstown we could only get together about five or seven of us to march down Wick Avenue to the square and protest against the war. Mostly people ignored us.

When we integrated the better jobs in the open hearth, it wasn't a popular position to take. It was a correct position but not a popular position. To be anti–Vietnam War, anti–Kent State, wasn't a popular position. I was red-baited. But I found that the people didn't really care what my politics were as long as I won grievances, did my job as a union officer. They didn't care what kind of cockeyed ideas I had. Their question was, Does he produce as a union representative?

I had one leaflet I put out that said, "I am a radical." Gerry Dickey wrote it. It had a picture of me on the front. It said, yes, I am a radical and these are some of the things I stand for. I was probably known as a communist because I don't think people can differentiate. I didn't go around with a bullhorn saying, "I'm Ed Mann, your local socialist." I think my actions spoke.

In a steel mill the work wasn't like in an auto plant where you were hitting a press for eight hours and as soon as the bell rings you want to get the hell out of there and get a drink or get home or do whatever you got to do. The type of work we were involved in was gang-type work. You couldn't do the job yourself. You had to help the guy in the next furnace. He helped you. You didn't have to like him but you knew, to get the job done and not die, you had to help each other.

So then you start talking. "How's the kids?" "What kind of car do you got?" Everyday stuff. And before you know it, "Come on over and have a beer. We're going to have a party. Why don't you bring your wife?" Before you know it you're friends. And then the politics started talking. That's what I experienced.

You go to the union meetings and speak your piece. Somebody says, "Hey, I don't know him but that's the way I feel." So you go over and say, "Hey, I'm Ed and I work in the open hearth. Do you come to these meetings very often?" That sort of thing. If you're going to be a socialist, you got to be sociable.

We were communicative. We would talk to people. We could express ourselves. We weren't afraid of the boss. We were always thought of, "Hey, look at these radicals, look at these reds." But we would do our job. You got a job, you did it. You are not a slacker. You didn't do any extra. You helped your fellow worker. Over the years you develop a certain credibility.

Every time you get knocked down you either get the hell out or you say, "Hey, I'm going to stay." Some stay. We saw many people come into the Brier Hill plant, real hotshots, every shade of the rainbow as far as radicals went, from fiery communist to whatever, but they couldn't stay! They could run off at the mouth pretty good, write manifestos, but they couldn't stay and do the job. For me to have gone out to the gate and pass out the Socialist Workers Party newspaper, and not know anybody there, and expect to recruit thirty people by the end of the month, would have been insane! You got to put down roots if you want to change anything. You can't be like a damn butterfly, flitting around all over.

President of Local 1462

It was always a part of our strategy to run people for local union office because we figured you had to have a base. We were trying to build a union in the plant, not worldwide. I ran for office many times. In 1961, I ran against Danny Thomas for president. I didn't get very many votes because we didn't have the power to count the votes. When Thomas was elevated to staff man, his vice president, Don Bernard, inherited the office. In 1964, Don Bernard had to stand for election. I ran against him and I lost.

In 1967, we ran Frank Leseganich for president and I ran for recording secretary on the slate and we won. Leseganich was by no means a radical yet he was a popular guy. He acted democratically in the local by letting us have a newspaper, elected stewards, committees that functioned, and so on. We thought this guy would make one hell of a district director. We ran him for district director and we won. He never looked back. He became a tool of the international. He was totally lost. That was our fault. We misread his actions as being democratic.

Once we had a local that functioned as a local, without all the petty bullshit, we reached out to other locals. We had a district conference one year in the late 1960s. We had about twenty-five resolutions that we wanted passed for our next Steelworkers contract. There were about two hundred locals in the district at that time. You had to present your resolutions ahead of time to the executive board of the district.

The international union recommended that these resolutions not be passed. And we defeated the international union on every one of those issues, by caucusing and leafletizing and setting examples. They said, "We will not accept these resolutions." We reversed that. This was an unheard-of defeat for the international union. Not that they did anything with the resolutions, but publicity-wise and through the minutes, it showed that they had lost control of the district.

In 1970, I ran against Augie Naples, who was Leseganich's vice president, and I lost by about one hundred votes. It was an honest election. Steward elections were held a month after the president was elected. I was elected steward in the department. In 1973, I ran for president and defeated Augie Naples. I ran two more times after that and won. The last time I ran unopposed.

You got 10 percent of the folks in the union that are company and 10 percent that are real union folks. The rest pay their dues and go home. People only came to union meetings when *they* had a problem. It's contract time? Okay. Are we going out on strike? Everybody's there and wants to know. Or in one department, something may happen that brings everybody together. But no continuity. People weren't die-hard dedicated. People had other interests.

We knew we couldn't get them to a union meeting so we mailed a newspaper to every member. If a guy doesn't want to come to meetings, he's still entitled to information and their wives can read about it, too. Gerald Dickey, the recording secretary, had taken a course in journalism. He had a good union-oriented attitude and he became the editor. We'd all contribute articles. We put articles in from anybody who wanted to submit them. It was controversial as hell. The international filed charges against us for what we printed. And we'd print those charges, so the members could see. Then we'd have a local union meeting and say, "What do you want to do about it?" They'd say, "Just keep doing what you're doing. It's the members' paper." We told the international that we'd give them equal time if they wanted it.

When the mills were shutting down, we made an issue of the international not knowing what to do. But we didn't just attack the international. Mostly we attacked the company and explained the right position to take on a lot of stuff. We would also put in letters to the editor if somebody disagreed with us. We got all kinds of awards for best article or best editorial, from the Labor Press Association and the Ohio Labor Press Association, and even a few from the Steelworkers Press Association.

We gave them democracy in the local. Once we had elected stewards for a couple of years you couldn't appoint a steward, because the guys would jump all over your ass. "We don't want that son of a bitch. Here's the guy we want." That made it easier for me as president, too. I didn't have to accept the heat for somebody I appointed. "You guys elected him. If he's no good, get him the hell out of here."

Guys who didn't get elected could be appointed to committees. We had committees like workers' comp, unemployment, pensions, hospitalization, that did their jobs. We had one guy who wasn't a good union steward. We made him head of the blood bank. It was a noncontroversial job. He loved it. It gave him a role in the local.

We Are *the Union*

We had assumed the mill would always be there. In October 1978 we learned otherwise. The Brier Hill works were shut down as the result of a merger between the Lykes conglomerate, owner of the Youngstown Sheet & Tube Steel Company, and the Ling Temco Vought (LTV) conglomerate, owner of Jones & Laughlin (J&L) Steel. The first notice to the local union was in a prospectus concerning the proposed merger that Lykes and LTV mailed to their stockholders. The prospectus described phasing out Brier Hill as one of the "anticipated benefits" of the merger.

We organized a picket line at the mill. About two hundred steelworkers carried signs reading "Keep Brier Hill Open," "People First, Profits Second," "Impeach Griffin Bell" (a reference to Attorney General Bell's approval of the Lykes-LTV merger), "Youngstown: Victim of Corporate Rape," and "Save Our Valley." This was the first direct action taken by steelworkers in response to the Youngstown shutdowns.

On January 22, 1979, Local 1462 held a meeting at the union hall. By coincidence, Gordon Allen, Sheet & Tube's superintendent, was speaking that same evening at the Mahoning Country Club not far away. At the meeting I mentioned the fact that Allen was speaking nearby. I said that I still had the signs from the picket line in the back of my pickup truck. People began moving toward the door. We drove to the Country Club and set up a picket line outside the front door. Ken Doran moved up and down the line. He kept saying, "Let's go inside." Finally, Doran opened the door, and John Barbero led the group through. In the lobby we set up a chant, "Where's Gordon Allen?" It was a way of saying, will we ever get to talk to somebody who can make a decision to save our plant?

The management of the country club called the Girard police. The police arranged themselves inconspicuously and made no attempt to interfere. Roger Slater, J&L's Youngstown district manager and Gary Wuslich, superintendent of industrial relations, pleaded with me to keep the demonstrators outside. After a heated discussion, I agreed to hold people in the lobby until Allen came out. We waited ten or fifteen minutes. When Allen approached he paused and said to me, "Now, Ed, you know we are handling this through the union." I and several others responded in one voice, "We *are* the union!"

We made the best fight we could. I think John Barbero and I had different attitudes. John thought we should fight to the end to keep the mill open. I felt that was unrealistic. You had to cut the best deal you could in the real situation that existed. We had people who were close to retirement, people who had very little seniority, and people in the middle group. I figured I was elected to represent everyone.

We bargained for Trade Readjustment Allowance (TRA). The company said, If you promise not to destroy the mill (they were paranoid as hell), we'll agree that we are shutting down because of foreign imports (which was a lie). I said, "I guarantee you the guys won't tear the mills down." It was a sure bet. The agreement included Campbell, Brier Hill, Rod and Wire, everybody from the plant manager down. It came to about $15,000 per employee.

I'M GOING DOWN THAT HILL

In November 1979, U.S. Steel announced that it was closing all its mills in the Youngstown area. Another 3,500 workers would lose their jobs. Later that month about three hundred Youngstown steelworkers together with Pittsburgh supporters occupied the first two floors of U.S. Steel's national headquarters in Pittsburgh. The occupation lasted several hours. Then on January 28, 1980, there was a rally at the hall of Local 1330, USWA, in Youngstown. The hall was just up a hill from U.S. Steel's Youngstown administration building. The politicians came and made their speeches. They didn't say anything. I think the crowd thought they were there to get votes.

I began my speech by saying: "You know we've heard a lot about benefits this morning but I thought we were here to save jobs." I went on:

> I think we've got a job to do today. And that job is to let U.S. Steel know that this is the end of the line. No more jobs are going to be shut down in Youngstown. You've got men here, you've got women here, you've got children here, and we're here for one purpose. Not to be talked to about what's going to happen in Congress two years from now. What's going to happen in Youngstown today?
>
> There's a building two blocks from here. That's the U.S. Steel headquarters. You know the whole country is looking at the voters, the citizens. What are you going to do? Are you going to make an action, or are you going to sit and be talked to? The action is today. We're going down that hill, and we're going to let the politicians know, we're going to let U. S. Steel

know, we're going to let the whole country know that steelworkers in Youngstown got guts and we want to fight for our jobs. We're not going to fight for welfare! [Cheers]

In 1919 the fight was on for the eight-hour day and they lost that struggle and they burned down East Youngstown, which is Campbell. Now I'm not saying burn anything down but you got the eight-hour day.

In 1937 you wanted a union and people got shot in Youngstown because they wanted a union. And everything hasn't been that great since you got a union. Every day you put your life on the line when you went into that iron house. Every day you sucked up the dirt and took a chance on breaking your legs or breaking your back. And anyone who's worked in there knows what I'm talking about.

Then I said:

Now, I don't like to read to people but in 1857 Frederick Douglass said something that I think you ought to listen to:

"Those who profess to favor freedom and yet discourage agitation are men who want crops without plowing up the ground. They want rain without thunder and lightning. They want the ocean without the awful roar of its waters. This struggle may be a moral one [and you've heard a lot about that] or it may be a physical one [and you're going to hear about that] but it must be a struggle. Power concedes nothing without a demand. It never did and it never will. Find out what people will submit to and you will find out the exact measure of injustice and wrong which will be imposed upon them. And these will be continued until they are resisted in either words or blows or with both. The limits of tyrants are prescribed by the endurance of those they oppress."

This was said in 1857 and things haven't changed. U.S. Steel is going to see how much they can put on you. And when I say "you" I mean "Youngstown," you know. We've got lists. We've got an obituary of plants that were shut down in the last twenty years. When are we going to make a stand?

Now, I'm going down that hill and I'm going into that building. And anyone that doesn't want to come along doesn't have to but I'm sure there are those who'll want to.

People liked the idea! At least seven hundred people were involved. When we got to the U.S. Steel building we told the property protection people to step aside, and they did. We took over the building. On the top floor we found an executive game room no one ever knew about. My daughter, Beth, changed her baby's diaper on the executives' pool table. Some supported by picketing outside. That's okay. Everybody has different roles. You don't want people in a position that they can't handle. But they did something! And for most of them, it was the only thing they did in their lives that wasn't in compliance with what the establishment would like. People were proud.

At the end of the afternoon Bob Vasquez, president of Local 1330, decided to end the occupation. But if we had it to do again, I know that he, and I, and everyone I know who was there, would have stayed in that building for as long as it took.

I THINK THERE'S A BETTER WAY

I retired in March of 1980. In 1981 the Workers' Solidarity Club of Youngstown was organized. It's a pretty freewheeling organization. We don't have membership lists. We don't have dues. I think the makeup of the club is exciting: people from different unions, unemployed folks, retirees, people from all walks of life. We do a lot of support work for people on strike. We make an effort to organize the unorganized. I joined the Industrial Workers of the World (IWW) about 1984. And in 1986, after LTV filed for bankruptcy, I became active in an organization of LTV retirees called Solidarity USA.

Trumbull Memorial Hospital

In July 1982, the service and maintenance workers in an AFSCME local union at Trumbull Memorial Hospital in Warren, Ohio, went out on strike. The hospital began to hire strikebreakers early in the strike. The Solidarity Club put out a leaflet. It appealed to scabs: "THINK before you cross a picket line. Think before you take your neighbor's job." It also called for demonstrations at the hospital every Wednesday in support of the strike.

The Wednesday afternoon rallies grew larger and larger. Unionists came with banners and homemade signs. The crowd chanted slogans like: "Warren is a union town, we won't let you tear it down." On Wednesday, October 13, we met at the hospital and decided to go to a street called Country Club Lane, to try to present a petition to several hospital trustees who lived there. The walk down Country Club Lane was intended to be a peaceful demonstration. We wanted to walk down the street with our banners and our signs and our chanting, to walk down and walk back.

When the door was not answered at the first trustee's home, Jean Maurice wrote our message on the door with lipstick. She was arrested. When the rest of us surrounded the police car and sat down, the police waded in with their clubs. Someone suggested that we should go back to the hospital. I drove with Nancy Wilson. We parked the car and started picketing again. The police arrived quickly. There were at least twenty to thirty policemen in full riot gear. They read something about how we were violating the law and to leave the area within so many minutes.

We saw the lineup of police across the street. We didn't have a hundred people. Ken Porter and I said to each other, "Look, we don't have that many people here. Let's get out of here." The cops came after me. I wasn't going to turn my back on them. One of them took his club and held it against my neck. I got a bruise on my shoulder and a brush burn on my neck. Another came at me and struck me with a nightstick, breaking my rib. I passed out. Then, when I was being dragged, I came out of it. A lot of other labor people were arrested. Danny Thomas Jr. represented them. He told them all to cop a plea, plead to a lesser charge, pay their fifty bucks. Only the three of us from the Club—Ken Porter, Greg Yarwick, and myself—plead not guilty.

I was charged with inciting to riot and resisting arrest, was tried and found guilty. So were Ken and Greg. We were all found not guilty on appeal. I had to appeal to the Ohio Supreme Court. The ACLU represented me in the case. The ACLU in Youngstown was the second chapter to be organized nationwide. It was called the Workers' Defense League then. It was organized around 1919 because of the attacks on the IWW, socialists, and anarchists, and the way workers were treated during the Palmer Raids. I have belonged to the ACLU in Youngstown for many years.

I found that the case had a very devastating effect. I didn't do very much for four years. If it had been resolved early on, I might have done other things. For four years I think I was intimidated. You're not getting any younger. Your juices don't flow as they did the year before. There's always this thing hanging over you. You don't really mind getting involved yourself but you're dragging other people in, creating a problem for others.

Still, the union at Trumbull Hospital survived. In December 1982 strikers ratified a contract that included a timetable for recall of the strikers over a thirty-month period. In 1989 the strikers received a huge settlement as the result of an NLRB charge.

The IWW

The IWW is a lot like the Solidarity Club. Whoever wants to do their thing at the moment, does it. If you want to participate, you participate, and if you don't, you don't. The AFL-CIO is afraid of getting fined for violation of a contract, but if you don't have a treasury, what the hell good is it going to do to fine you?

I like the Wobblies' history: the Sacco-Vanzetti thing, the Bill Haywood stuff, the Ludlow mine. They actually won some clean bunks. Pretty basic stuff! I like their music. I like the things they were active in. They were against the First World War. A lot of folks went to jail. A lot of people were deported. Out west they had laws that you couldn't stand out in the middle of the street and give a speech. Somebody would get up on a soapbox and start talking. The cops would take him away. Somebody else would get up.

Sometimes they'd put out a call to members of the IWW, and they'd all converge on that town, and just fill up the jail until they got the right to speak.

These folks believed that workers should exercise some power, instead of handing it over to bureaucrats they elect, and letting them make the decisions. The people have to live with the decisions. If you make a decision that's bad, and you have to live with it, you can't blame somebody else. But what happens when a bureaucrat makes a decision and you have to live with it?

A lot of our folks belong to established unions and they don't want to attack the AFL-CIO because they feel that by doing that you're attacking the union movement. I don't sense that there's any movement there at all. We have people who are sensitive about attacking the AFL-CIO for not doing its job. But it's not going to do its job. It's not structured to do its job. I don't regard the AFL-CIO as "the union." I think the union's in the people. Don't forget, there's only 13 million workers organized in the AFL-CIO, but there're probably 100 million workers, or close to it. As long as people work they are going to have grievances. Now, who is going to handle those grievances? Some kind of organization: that is, people together. Bureaucrats aren't going to solve our problems.

It's very unpredictable. If we read our history, we know that back in [Eugene] Debs's time the railroads were one of the biggest industries in the country. They had a lot of shops: people worked as blacksmiths, as machinists, whatever. The company cut their pay so much a day. They didn't do anything about it. Six months later the company cut their pay again, quite a bit. They didn't do anything about it. Then the company came up with a pay cut that was infinitesimal. That was enough! The whole country went down. It was like a general strike. They burned the railroad yards in Pittsburgh and in many other places. Who knows what is going to make the workers say, "This is enough?" But the point is, somebody has to be there when they say, "This is enough!" Maybe the CIO has run its course. Maybe there will be unions but they won't be structured as we see them today. The Solidarity Club is a very small step toward that.

The companies say they want workers to participate in the work process, in management. But they're not giving away any decision making. The company's rights are very clear-cut and defined. You may be able to discuss how many parking places there will be in the parking lot, or what kind of pop will be in the pop machine. But when it comes to hiring, firing, disciplining, the rules of production, and so on, you're not involved. They talk about "work teams." This is garbage. A work team tends to say, "Hey, this guy isn't keeping up, let's get rid of him."

The Wobblies say, "Do away with the wage system." For a lot of people that's pretty hard to take. What the Wobblies mean is, you'll have what you need. The wage system has destroyed us. If I work hard I'll get ahead, but if I'm stronger than Jim over here, maybe I'll get the better job and Jim will be sweeping floors. But maybe Jim has four kids. The wage system is a very divisive thing. It's the only thing we have now, but it's very divisive.

Maybe I'm just dreaming but I think there's a better way.

16

BLACK WORKERS' STRUGGLES FOR JOBS AND CIVIL RIGHTS IN TWENTIETH-CENTURY PITTSBURGH

JOHN HINSHAW

INTRODUCTION

At the beginning of the twentieth century, African Americans had been residents of Pittsburgh for over one hundred years, but had been denied access to the full range of jobs available in this industrial region. The major corporations in Pittsburgh's leading industries such as railroads, machine-building, and electrical-equipment manufacturing hired very few blacks and relegated them to menial positions such as janitor. Almost no African American men were employed as skilled craftsmen, professionals, or clerical workers and most black women labored as domestics or laundresses. Most black industrial workers were employed in the steel industry, and these corporations concentrated them in hot, dirty, and man-killing jobs in the blast furnaces, open hearths, or coke ovens.

While blacks were initially a relatively small part of the industrial workforce, institutionalized racism was central to corporations' management of the industrial economy. In addition to corporations' spies, blacklists, and armies of private police, employers sought to derail the mobilization of workers as a class by encouraging individual workers (or even unions) to pursue their gains within an industrial order deeply stratified along ethnic and racial lines. In short, at the beginning of the century, the "carrot" of racism was dangled beneath the club of repression. However, once industrial unions had been formed in the 1930s, the club of repression was withdrawn, but racism remained and severely deformed the strategy and practice of workers' organizations.

The struggles throughout the twentieth century to widen African Americans' access to economic opportunity should be seen as a significant part of the civil rights movement.[1] (There were other dimensions to the struggle in Pittsburgh, including campaigns to desegregate housing, education, and public facilities, but this essay will focus the efforts to widen blacks' access to jobs, primarily in the steel industry, because of its importance to African Americans and the class struggle in general.) Those militants who struggled for black jobs and civil rights were clearly part of what Paul Le Blanc terms the vanguard of the workers' movement, even if many civil rights militants did not think of themselves as leftists.[2] Sometimes these campaigns were organized by "uplift" organizations, radical parties, or within unions, but just as often it was the result of "ordinary" workers in a mill or neighborhood.

Whatever their organizational affiliation, activists' fight against institutionalized racism was affected by the general level of workers' organization or disorganization. For instance, as Robert Korstad and Nelson Lichtenstein show in "Opportunities Found and Lost" [see chapter 11 in this book], when conservatives drove radicals out of leadership positions in unions at the onset of the Cold War, the struggle for civil rights was set back and the labor movement itself suffered.[3] The Cold War clearly weakened the effectiveness of workers' struggles against racism, but it did not end them. While black workers had to fight against conservative *unions* to realize gains, black *unionists* were frequently in the forefront of struggle, both before and after the civil rights laws of the 1960s. By 1970, Pittsburgh's labor market seemed on the road toward desegregation but many white workers saw this not as a step forward for the workers' movement but as a loss of traditional privileges. Thus many white unionists embraced conservatism even though this movement also set as its goal the dismantling of unions and of the social welfare system in general.

Thus racism and antiracism have been an important part of Pittsburgh's industrial development and class struggle. While black workers have had an immediate interest in fighting segregation, some whites refused to buy into a system that pitted worker against worker. Workers' defense or assault on white privilege was only partly the result of skin color; it was also a test of workers' political loyalties. Just as not all black workers were willing to directly challenge racism, there were always some radical whites who participated in these struggles. Even though antiracist workers' struggles were opposed by many conservative trade unionists, antiracists have made important contributions to the labor movement and their legacy deserves to be recognized and expanded on by the next generation of working-class organizers.

THE ROOTS OF A RACIAL DIVISION OF LABOR IN STEEL AND PITTSBURGH: 1880s–1937

Pittsburgh's racial division of labor was profoundly influenced by the region's history of industrialization and class struggle in the nineteenth century. Iron and steel companies were the region's largest employers and the resolution of their labor-management conflicts helped to establish a stratified division of labor that for men was based on race and ethnicity. In the mid-nineteenth century, Pittsburgh was already an important manufacturing center dominated by small, family-owned businesses that were labor, rather than capital, intensive. For instance, iron manufacturers relied on the skill of puddlers to make small batches of iron and on rollers to fashion the finished product.[4] As a result, highly skilled workers, most of them native-born whites or immigrants from northwestern Europe, enjoyed a high standard of living and workplace autonomy.[5] The emergence of large-scale, capital-intensive industry in the 1880s led to conflicts between workers and managers over who would control the pace of production, culminating in the 1892 lockout of workers at Andrew Carnegie's Homestead Works. Despite a heroic struggle, workers were defeated and craft unions decimated.[6] Pittsburgh's working class had been temporarily defeated, and it was about to be permanently remade.

The rising industrial empires of the steel barons caused Pittsburgh's economy and population to expand rapidly. By 1894, the mills in Allegheny County produced 43 percent of the steel in the United States.[7] Allegheny County grew from a population of 262,204 in 1870 to 1,018,463 in 1910 and to 1,374,410 in 1930. However, it was the confluence of industrialists' desire for a heterogeneous labor force and the aspirations of immigrants that caused the Pittsburgh region to become racially and ethnically diverse. African Americans comprised 3 percent of the region's population in 1890 but made up 6.1 percent of the population of Allegheny County in 1930. During the late nineteenth and early twentieth centuries, foreign-born whites or their children made up nearly 30 percent of Pittsburgh's population before dropping to 16 percent of the population in 1930. The children of immigrants comprised slightly more than a third of the region's population for the entire period between 1890 and 1940.[8]

Workers' attempts to unionize steel mills in the 1880s and 1890s floundered in part because employers successfully manipulated the racial and ethnic divisions among mill workers. Native-born and northern European rollers and puddlers had built up a union tradition based on their technical skills and sense of white manliness. From the perspective of these unionists, even native-born laborers possessed neither the requisite technical skill, nor the proper social identity to join their unions. In the late nineteenth century, the social distance between skilled and unskilled worker widened considerably as employers increasingly hired laborers from eastern and southern Europe and black skilled workers. Despite the ethnic chauvinism of many unionists, eastern European immigrants and some blacks supported Homestead's skilled workers during the 1892 lockout.[9]

After 1892, steel companies made an ethnic rapprochement with native-born skilled steelworkers.[10] Their union smashed, these workers received privileges such as subsidized housing, promotions, bonuses, pensions, and steady work all of which reinforced the view that they were "white" and unskilled eastern European immigrants were "hunkies."[11] Employers didn't take their white employees' loyalty for granted but hired an extensive network of spies. When workers in Homestead attempted to reform the union in 1899, "the company let the newly made union men know that it was cognizant of every move that had been made." Little wonder that men believed that "if you want to talk in Homestead, you talk to yourself."[12] Employers increasingly recruited eastern European immigrants to work as unskilled labor and these men received few benefits beyond a job. By 1910, nearly half of all steelworkers were from eastern or southern Europe.[13] The racial and ethnic stratification of the steel industry was replicated by other industrialists and provided incentives for some workers to support the system that produced enormous profits for monopolists.

Blacks' place in working-class stratification was significantly different from that of European immigrant workers. Blacks' chief obstacle was entering industry. In the late nineteenth century, the relatively small numbers of black steelworkers were generally skilled workers many of whom had worked in mills in Virginia. However, as early as 1875, white unionists barred African Americans from their unions, and many blacks were forced to enter the industry as strikebreakers. In 1881, the Amalgamated Association of Iron, Steel and Tin Workers attempted to stem the flow of African American strikebreakers by inviting blacks to join a Jim Crow local—subsequent relations between white and black unionists remained tense. Although some African Americans supported the union in the 1892 Homestead lockout, others crossed the picket line. Racial (and ethnic) tensions would remain a barrier to steelworkers' unity for years to come. In the 1901 Amalgamated strike against U. S. Steel, black strikers at the Lafayette Lodge sought temporary work at another union mill; white workers refused to work alongside the black men.[14]

Despite most black workers' justified antipathy toward craft unionism, between 1892 and the early 1910s employers preferred eastern European immigrants as laborers. Employers such as Andrew Carnegie continued to employ small numbers of skilled black workers as an implicit threat to white workers not to take their relative privileges for granted.[15] During World War I, steel companies began to recruit Southern blacks as unskilled laborers in their mills, dramatically increasing the size of black Pittsburgh's industrial working class. Although European migrants slowly moved into semiskilled positions, most blacks were stuck in the hottest, heaviest, and most dangerous positions in the mill.[16]

In 1919, another effort was made by craft unionists to organize the steel industry. The decisive moment came when skilled whites and skilled and unskilled African Americans crossed the picket lines. (Many "American" workers had gone on strike in their hometown but traveled to a nearby steel mill to scab.[17]) Employers also relied on their "Cossacks," the Coal and Iron Police and the Pennsylvania State Police, who brutalized unionists while a corporate-controlled press relentlessly red-baited the union. Most industrialists (and workers) believed that black workers, and not skilled whites, defeated the strike.[18] In a testimony to the crude racism of the day, the strike has been remembered as the "hunky strike." The tension between "100 percent Americans," blacks, and "foreigners" remained a potent division into the 1930s.[19]

Outside of the steel industry, blacks' relationship to the trade union movement was also troubled. In the 1920s, although there were a couple of hundred blacks in the hod carriers and laborers unions, most craft unions, such as those in the skilled construction trades, blocked blacks from membership. This severely limited the opportunities for black electricians, plumbers, or bricklayers. Even if black tradesmen went into business, conservative unions' refusal to work with "scabs" prevented black contractors from receiving lucrative contracts.[20]

Similarly, although there were numerous black coal miners, the United Mine Workers' traditions of interracial organization coexisted with a great deal of racial animosity. Although some white unionists treated black workers fairly, many allowed or encouraged the marginalization of black miners. In one strike, formerly unionized black coal miners waved their union cards at white workers; as blacks crossed picket lines they yelled, "You would not work with me before the strike. Now I have your job and I am going to keep it."[21] Similarly, even within the Communist Party (CP), which emphasized antiracism, there were serious problems with what the Party termed "white chauvinism." Harry Heywood, a black Communist organizer recalled that in 1931 although the CP's National Miners Union had several black leaders (they were sometimes the only workers in the mines who spoke English), many white unionists "seemed to expect that black miners should forget about racist incidents that occurred during the last strike, [or] job discrimination in the mines."[22] Throughout the 1920s, many employers viewed black workers as reliably antiunion.

Although Pittsburgh's steel industry continued to expand in the period between 1900 and 1930, newer facilities in Detroit, Cleveland, and Chicago grabbed old and new markets such as the lucrative automobile trade.[23] By

1934, U.S. Steel's numerous Pittsburgh-area mills were operating at only 30 percent of capacity while similar mills in Chicago were operating at 50 percent and mills in Detroit were working at 100 percent.[24] The advantages of Pittsburgh's cheap coal became less important as thoroughly modern, and therefore less expensive, mills opened in Chicago, far closer to midwestern markets. If the early 1930s created problems for Pittsburgh's giant corporations, it was an unmitigated disaster for the region's workers. In 1929, the income of steelworkers at U.S. Steel's Duquesne Works was about $1,350 but by 1934, most steelworkers earned about $423.[25] Harvey O'Connor, a radical journalist in Pittsburgh, observed that "now many homes are bare of the furnishings for which the workers sacrificed so much. Vans have pulled up in front of the squalid homes and taken away living room and bedroom furniture that represented the savings of a decade."[26]

The crisis of the Great Depression helped to undermine corporations' control over their workers. By the early 1930s, a liberal state government, pushed by trade unions, radicals, and communists, outlawed private police forces such as the Coal and Iron Police.[27] At U.S. Steel, the spy system remained in place but discontent among workers reached all-time highs. By 1934, only 20 to 35 percent of steelworkers worked full time and favoritism ran rampant.[28] Among black steelworkers, unionism gained ground in large part because steel companies openly favored white workers during layoffs and recalls in the Great Depression.[29] With little or no help from the national leadership of the union, steelworkers formed their own Amalgamated locals, in which national membership surged from about 3,000 to at least 80,000. John Fitch, a longtime observer of the steelworkers noted that U.S. Steel executives said "a few years ago we would have fired them like that," but that "times have changed" as managers refused to confront the federal government over the issue.[30]

Throughout the late 1920s and early 1930s, the CP attempted to build their own unions in coal and steel. While these efforts failed, the Communists' emphasis on interethnic and interracial unity would be widely replicated. Some radicalized blacks joined immigrant workers in agitating for unions, such as the Amalgamated and later the Steel Workers Organizing Committee (SWOC). Some "rank and filers" as William Sprang, the white president of the local at the Duquesne Works, were particularly concerned about destroying racism: "My sole idea in going into the movement," he said, "was to get white and colored people together whom capitalists have tried to keep apart."[31] Building on the rank and filers' efforts, the CIO union carefully articulated a philosophy of ethnic and racial egalitarianism. By 1937, U.S. Steel and Jones and Laughlin (J&L) had signed union contracts and most large steel locals had elected several black officers.[32]

NEW RELATIONSHIPS AND NEW POSSIBILITIES, 1937–1948

However, once SWOC was established, it failed to carry through on its egalitarian philosophy. Although the union had several dozen available positions for organizers and staffmen in the Pittsburgh area alone, SWOC hired just one black. Even more importantly, the union incorporated industrialists' racial division of labor into its seniority system. SWOC contracts did not allow plantwide seniority; instead, workers gained job and departmental seniority. Workers were not able to apply their seniority to any job in the mill; instead, workers' seniority was effective only within lines of progression that often locked whites and blacks into racially exclusive job lines and departments. Once hired into a "black job line," a worker would have to lose all his seniority to move into a better line—assuming managers allowed him to transfer. Since many white unionists were at best indifferent to blacks' seniority rights, most African American unionists remained frozen out of white jobs. John Hughey, a black unionist, summarized the situation: "Even if you got to be as old as Methuselah, you couldn't get out of the room" where your job line was located.[33]

Nonetheless, the formation of SWOC was a step forward for black workers who now had a relatively secure base from which to fight racial discrimination. Many black industrial workers credited the union for improving their lives. Harry Gregg, a Monongahela (Mon) Valley black unionist at the American Brake Shoe and Foundry, observed that blacks never would have become cranemen or molders if not for the union.[34] M. Truitt, a black furnaceman, praised SWOC as the "boon, if not the salvation" of African American steelworkers.[35] Yet blacks' occupational advances came after they had forced the federal government to create the Fair Employment Practices Committee (FEPC) that prohibited discrimination among defense contractors. Some black steelworkers cynically observed that the only time black workers advanced was when a FEPC officer got directly involved in their case.[36]

Despite the FEPC and wartime labor shortages, industrialists continued to reserve the best jobs in the mills for whites. In 1943, one Manpower Commissioner reported that "the available manpower in the Homestead area has been scraped clean."[37] Consequently, many whites worried "that a mass migration of 1,000 colored workers were to be brought in to work in the local mills." However, U.S. Steel assured its workers that local white women and not blacks would be hired into the Homestead Works.[38] Steel companies hired white women for skilled and clerical positions that managers had told black men for years they were unqualified for. One black worker admitted that "I got a little bitter for a while. When you see women move in on jobs that you thought you would have a chance to get, and they would actually put [women] on better jobs than the [black] men that had been there for years."[39] It is probable that companies favored white women because supervisors knew that white women would eventually be forced to leave the mill and black men would not. Thus, managers protected a racist and sexist division of labor in the mill that could have been upset had black males been allowed to move into jobs reserved for white men.[40]

Despite the limitations of actually existing trade unionism, during World War II, black workers adopted unionist tactics in their attack on steel's racial division of labor. Black workers ran for union office, engaged in strikes, and petitioned the government in order to improve their situation. Black steelworkers led numerous strikes to force their employers to promote employees on the basis of seniority or to pay black workers the same rate of pay as that of whites. For instance, on February 25, 1944, over fifty black workers at the Clairton Works refused to maintain the equipment that generated fuel for the furnaces, claiming they "were being steadily barred from any of the higher jobs they had once held." Managers were frantic because if the equipment was unattended for several hours, the extreme heat would ruin the machinery and the subsequent loss of power would force the shutdown of all of U.S. Steel's furnaces at several mills. The men went back to work with the promise that seniority would guide future promotions, but the fact that black steelworkers at Clairton continued to strike suggests those promises were not kept.[41] Blacks' protests over their limited upward mobility led one FEPC case officer to observe that in terms of racial conflict, Pittsburgh was the "touchiest and most tense" city in America.[42] In addition to black workers' strikes, there were scattered "hate strikes" where white workers refused to work with African Americans.[43] While the interracial philosophy of many CIO unions helped to keep the number of hate strikes low, so did the fact that the advancement of blacks into white jobs was limited.[44]

Despite the elimination of the federal FEPC in 1945, in the early postwar years it seemed possible to build interracial coalitions to press for racial justice at the workplace. At J&L's Hazelwood mill, infuriated black steelworkers watched as whites moved into departments that were supposedly not hiring and the only decent jobs in "black departments" went to native-born white friends of the foremen. The heaters of the coke ovens, a highly skilled job, were classified in a separate line from heater helpers, who did the hot and dirty work under these men. One man observed, "They've taken those jobs out and given 'em to white men. That's the way they're doin' all the time." In August 1946, 250 black and white steelworkers staged a sitdown strike at J&L's coke ovens, the fifth strike since 1941. The leaders of the strike were two African American brothers, Charles and Harold Winbush, who compared the "slow strangulation of Negroes on the job in Pennsylvania to [a recent] lynching in Georgia."[45]

The J&L strikers had limited faith in their union. Bypassing official channels, the wildcatters demanded that Boyd Wilson, the United Steel Workers of America (USWA) only black official, attend their negotiations with J&L. (SWOC had changed its name in 1942.) When told by their white district director that Wilson was out of town, the strikers said that they, and the entire mill, would wait until he returned. He was quickly produced. The men went back to work in return for a promise of a "full-scale investigation."[46] In the end, the 1946 wildcat strike led nowhere. Black heater helpers would not be able to become heaters, instead white cranemen would continue to move into that plum job. One striker explained that "the whole thing in a nutshell is that our local union and local grievance man put up no fight at all."[47] In 1947, another wildcat broke out. This time, the USWA enforced its recent no-strike pledge and the company fired twenty black workers. Black observers noted that this "nasty situation" could have been avoided had the international supported the workers.[48] A black unionist at J&L caustically reviewed the union's recruitment of black workers, "You know as well as I do that the union didn't bring us in because they wanted us. They needed us to protect themselves."[49] Discrimination at this plant was a continuing issue until the 1970s.[50]

In the period after World War II, black steelworkers' power within their union declined. Postwar layoffs (and the growing strength of union bureaucracies) made "wildcat" or illegal strikes riskier. The ease of steelworkers' success in their national strike in 1946 (steel companies did not mount a serious "back to work" movement) apparently convinced many white workers that black workers would not ever be called on to cross picket lines—thereby removing an important reason to accommodate black workers. Furthermore, beginning in 1948, the union movement began to purge Communists from leadership positions, and the loss of articulate advocates for civil rights further undermined blacks' position in steel. Furthermore, the red scare drove many blacks out of the union because conservative unionists assumed any black worker attending a union meeting was a Communist. Whatever the cause, the number of black officials within the union fell.[51]

A few black unionists doggedly attempted to make the USWA live up to its racially egalitarian rhetoric but their "successes" indicated how little the USWA's Cold War liberals cared for black workers. In 1948, African Americans from Pittsburgh and Chicago proposed that the USWA form a Civil Rights Committee or CRC, headed by Boyd Wilson, which would safeguard and improve the status of racial minorities in the steel industry.[52] Instead, Philip Murray, the president of the USWA, proposed an entirely white CRC whose central purpose was to promote civil rights legislation.[53] The CRC had a largely symbolic presence in the USWA and even its symbolism was questionable. Murray appointed a pair of white brothers, Thomas and

Francis Shane, as chair and executive director of this committee.[54] Instead of a permanent staff, the CRC had a few international and district staff representatives who met four times a year and recommended courses of action to the president.[55] When confronted with a recalcitrant company or union local, the CRC could only use moral suasion.[56] The CRC spent most of its time cultivating a liberal image in the community by providing staff support and contributions to the Pittsburgh Urban League (PUL), the NAACP, and other groups.[57] Figures are not available for all years, but the union donated thousands of dollars annually to civil rights organizations.[58] Although the USWA's support of black organizations strengthened Pittsburgh's middle-class civil rights organizations, it did little to aid black steelworkers.

THE STRUGGLE WIDENS, THEN FRAGMENTS

In the late 1940s, black community organizations, strengthened by their relationship with liberal unions, sought to desegregate downtown Pittsburgh's department stores. Since the 1930s, blacks in Pittsburgh (sometimes in conjunction with leftists) had organized sporadic "buy rights" campaigns. As in Harlem, where blacks led a "don't shop where you can't work" campaign, blacks in Pittsburgh were frustrated that their patronage of downtown merchants did not result in a large black sales staff.[59] Employers feared that if blacks were hired, sales to whites would collapse. As a result, blacks were only half as likely as whites to find jobs in retail, and most of their jobs were in menial positions such as elevator operator and janitor. In 1947, the black community led by PUL, NAACP, black churches, and the Negro Elks, massed pickets in front of downtown department stores in an attempt to force the hiring of African Americans; the Retail Merchants Association quickly signed an agreement.[60] (While some unions supported the effort, the steelworkers' union opposed it, ostensibly because they felt it would hamper the chances to establish a state FEPC.[61])

As soon as the ink was dry on these agreements, however, white businessmen pressured the PUL to fire their executive director, K. Leroy Irvis. White businessmen fumed, "Is this the reason we finance the Urban League, so you can send young people downtown and embarrass us?"[62] Like many organizations funded by their opponents, the PUL moderated its approach. In 1950, the PUL observed that "Negro salespersons are no longer rarities."[63] By other accounts, however, progress in the retail sector remained slow. During the 1950s, Pittsburgh's FEPC (which had been established with unions' support) received three times as many complaints about retailers as it did about the entire manufacturing sector. In 1955, the Pittsburgh FEPC observed that "it is a simple fact that most retail stores do not employ Negro salesmen or saleswomen."[64] As late as 1960, the *Pitts-*

burgh Courier reported that black sales staff remained a rarity, even during the Christmas rush.[65]

The persistence of occupational segregation and the conciliatory approach of the PUL prompted the formation of the Greater Pittsburgh Improvement League (GPIL) in 1949. Headed by a group of friends who operated out of a barbershop, the GPIL sought to "gain employment for Negroes where it never existed" by leading boycotts and picketing companies that refused to hire blacks.[66] The GPIL frequently targeted retailers who were particularly vulnerable to these tactics. In 1951, the GPIL led a "buy rights" campaign in Homewood, focusing on forcing department stores and banks to hire black sales staff and clerks.[67] In 1954, Edgar Rideout became the first black driver for a milk delivery company as a result of the GPIL's efforts.[68] Beverage companies, such as Coca-Cola and Duquesne Brewing Company, also succumbed to community pressure.[69] Although most businesses still refused to hire or promote black men and women, the GPIL's efforts indicated that many blacks supported a direct assault on the economic underpinnings of Jim Crow. Relations between the PUL and the GPIL remained tense because the PUL refused to help protesters, preferring a more nonconfrontational approach.[70]

The unionization of black workers in the 1930s was a significant turning point in the history of black workers. Although many white workers continued to support institutionalized racism, black workers were able to protest more effectively than before. Black unionists led several wildcat strikes and petitioned the government to upgrade or hire black workers. Black organizations were beginning to build mass support for opening up employment opportunities in sectors of the economy previously closed to African Americans. These efforts were cut short by the retreat of the federal government and unions from the principles of fair employment that only grew more pronounced with the onset of the Cold War. Beginning in the late 1940s, Pittsburgh's ideological climate and economy both began to deteriorate and both factors would complicate the efficacy of black protest for the next decade.

RETRENCHMENT AND DECLINE: 1948–1959

After World War II, Pittsburgh's industries experienced a long period of stagnation and decline. Even the Korean War boom and government subsidies of capital investment in heavy industry could not overcome the downward spiral in employment. Whatever new investment occurred was aimed at eliminating jobs and thus automation and disinvestment resulted in partially closed mills or reduced crews in the remaining plants. At the end of the Korean War, the steel industry employed 160,000 people and 848,000 nonagricultural workers lived in the Pittsburgh metropolitan area. By 1959, only 119,000 people worked for steel companies and the total number of jobs in Pittsburgh's economy had declined by 84,000.[71] The regional recession continued until the late 1960s.

The population of the Pittsburgh region peaked at 2,400,000 people in 1960 and then began to decline. Although the region's black population continued to grow throughout the 1950s, reaching 163,000 in 1960, Pittsburgh's African American community grew at only half the rate of all Northern American cities.[72] Furthermore, the lengthy regional recession intensified the resistance of unions and employers to African Americans' demands to desegregate Pittsburgh's job markets.

CONSTRUCTION AND THE CRAFT UNIONS

The struggles within the construction industry were particularly frustrating for black activists. Although construction had always been an important sector of the economy for black men, employers and unions succeeded in blocking African Americans from more desirable jobs. In the 1930s and 1940s, proportionally more black men than white men worked in construction, although most African Americans worked as laborers or as marginalized independent contractors.[73] After World War II, blacks began to lose ground in construction as the number of unskilled jobs fell and as contractors and unionists prevented blacks from moving into skilled jobs. In 1956, Henry W. Davis, a veteran black construction worker, observed that "unless something is done to break this economical caste system, our futures in the trades are dim."[74]

Pittsburgh's FEPC proved too weak to help black workers desegregate construction unions. In the late 1940s, Paul Leach, an African American electrician, was barred from membership by the International Brotherhood of Electrical Workers (IBEW) Local 5. Local 5 told him that "there wasn't enough work for their own members . . . besides, the contractors wouldn't give him work." In the early 1960s, despite the intervention of the FEPC, the union was making similar excuses to Leach.[75] As Lain Lee, a black electrical worker observed, "They have so many doors to keep Negroes out of the craft unions, they might as well be using steel bars."[76] One black observed that skilled black tradesmen have "found it almost impossible to join trade unions . . . because of 'buck-passing' between contractors and tradesmen."[77] Although by 1963, seven craft unions, among them IBEW Local 5 and Iron Workers Local 3, *agreed* to let blacks join them, it was years before blacks *actually* became members.[78]

The PUL, which had been attempting to improve blacks' position in construction since the 1920s, fared little better in Cold War Pittsburgh than it had thirty years before. In 1963, the PUL helped three black bricklayers find temporary work when black residents threatened demonstrations at a housing project if some blacks were not hired.[79] That same year, the PUL claimed to have placed 120 black craftsmen in the building trades and even to have obtained some union cards.[80] Notwithstanding the claims of the PUL, most unions in construction did not have any black members and the position of black workers in the trades continued to deteriorate.[81] In 1963, Plumbers Local 29 agreed to open its apprenticeship program to blacks, but as of September 1967, none had been accepted in the union.[82] In fact, the first report of the Equal Employment Opportunity Commission reported only sixteen black skilled construction workers in 1967.[83] The refusal of construction unions to allow blacks to join their unions effectively blocked blacks from that sector of the job market.

BLACK STEELWORKERS REORGANIZE AND DEMAND "FAIR SHARE"

Black steelworkers faced a different kind of racist union than did black construction workers. The USWA did not attempt to block blacks from membership, it simply refused to carry out its civil rights mission. Jesse Walker, a black unionist, caustically recalled that his union's civil rights organization was "a laugh."[84] Furthermore, the close relationship between the USWA, the NAACP, and the PUL complicated black steelworkers' attempts to use these agencies to move the USWA to take a more aggressive stand against discrimination. The PUL concentrated its efforts on construction and white-collar workers while the NAACP viewed problems in the steel industry as a matter best handled by the USWA. Consequently, black activists within the USWA could not rely upon civil rights organizations for legal or logistical aid.[85]

Black steelworkers relied on each other (and some whites) to advance. By teaching workers how to defend their jobs or advance into previously all-white positions, skilled black men played a key role in breaking down institutionalized racism in the 1950s. George Henderson remembered how he helped the men on his crew: "They'd-a quit long time ago if it wasn't for me. I made 'em stay. . . . See you can't run from place to place hunting jobs. You stay in one place and protect the job you got. That's all you got to do. So they all got to sticking."[86] After surreptitiously watching the incumbent white worker for a year, one black man at the Duquesne Works was able to move into that "white job." (Radical white unionists, or whites who were retiring, also helped train black workers.) In his view, getting a skilled position was the first step in allowing other blacks to move ahead. After he became the incumbent, he gathered together an all-black crew.[87]

What made this method of advancement so slow was the extreme resistance of white foremen to blacks' movement into white jobs. John Hughey, an active trade unionist at the Carrie Furnaces, recalled how Ralph Johnson became the first black cranemen in the 1950s: "The test that Ralph Johnson had to go through, he should-a been driving a rocketship. Because they put a little bucket down there, a little teapot there. Put him up on the crane and give him one try to come down with the boom and put it in the bucket. One try. But Ralph was lucky. He came down the first time and didn't that damn thing go in the bucket. Right in the bucket it went and they almost dropped over."[88] By 1960, in spite of such heroic efforts, there were only 276 black cranemen in all of Pittsburgh's factories (compared to 8,736 white cranemen).[89]

The union, especially locals, played a key role in racial discrimination. In 1957, twenty years after the union had been established, no black had ever been elected to union office at the Homestead Works. Blacks felt the union conspired with management to deny them access to decent jobs. Albert "Sweet Lucy" Everett charged that Al Duch, his grievance man, and George Urban, president of Homestead Local 1397, manipulated the seniority system so that whites advanced into skilled jobs while blacks languished. Everett claimed that "Duchy fixes it so white boys can move up and colored can stick with pick and shovel."[90]

In 1957, long-simmering resentment burst into the open. Led by members of a black protest organization, Fair Share, blacks battled to retain Everett, who had been appointed the union's first black assistant grievanceman. Duch had appointed Everett, then fired him when he pressed too hard for change. When blacks packed a meeting of the local union, Pete Jackson, a black USWA representative, urged Everett to "exhaust your union remedies." The two men fought, Everett saying that Jackson was "one of the fellows that has been holding us back" while Jackson called Everett a liar.[91] (Relatively few blacks held positions in the union bureaucracy, and men like Jackson were generally the product of black unionists' protests within the union. However, while black union reps also aided civil rights protests, black officials were frequently under pressure from their higher-ups to head off further black mobilization at the grassroots.[92])

In March, the Homestead local voted whether to acquit Duch of the charge of racism. Only eighteen blacks attended the meeting, and were voted down by twenty-five whites. Although the conservative whites had won this round, they were particularly angry with the four white unionists who had voted with the blacks.[93] Given the conservative political culture of this local, it was a small miracle that these four "race traitors" held their ground.

Despite the pervasive racism of the Homestead Works, the protest died out. Because they were a minority within the union, blacks were simply voted down.[94] Furthermore, shortly after Fair Share began its protests, the

FBI had begun investigating alleged Communist involvement in Fair Share.[95] Within a couple of weeks, rank-and-file black unionists from Homestead were denying any ties to Fair Share.[96] Battered but not destroyed, Fair Share activists continued to agitate. Later in 1957, George Backer became the first black to be elected in Local 1397; as the local president had openly backed another candidate, this was an especially sweet victory for black workers.[97] In order to show black unionists that some progress was being made, the union helped a black transfer into the machine shop, one man became a millwright helper, and others were tested for cranemen's jobs.[98]

Black trade unionists began to consolidate local gains into a regionwide network of activists. In September 1960, twenty-seven black union activists met in Homestead to form a "permanent organization for action," because they were "sick and tired of getting promises that are never filled." "Groups and factions" of veteran trade unionists "which had been opposed to each other over the years" were united by the formation of the Negro American Labor Council (NALC).[99] In May 1960, one thousand black officials from unions in a variety of industries, including steel, auto, and rubber, joined together to pressure the house of labor to end its tolerance of racial discrimination. The NALC was led by former Socialist A. Philip Randolph, the head of the Brotherhood of Sleeping Car Porters and a veteran of AFL-CIO infighting.[100]

Although the NALC never fulfilled its promise as an national civil rights vehicle that linked black unionists and community organizations, in Pittsburgh, black unionists brought new life to the local struggle.[101] One of the NALC's first targets was the Civic Arena which, although located in the predominantly black Hill District, hired just eight blacks out of a workforce of several hundred. The NALC and the NAACP staged a mass picket as the "awakening event" for Pittsburgh's black community.[102] The demonstrators won the promise of jobs for black men and sparked numerous other demonstrations that united the activists within unions and the community in a quest for equal employment opportunities.[103] Throughout the 1960s, black trade unionists would play a crucial role in mobilizing community pressure to break down occupational discrimination.

BLACK UNEMPLOYMENT, BLACK PROTEST: 1960–1975

The radicalization of black protest occurred as the economic situation of blacks grew more desperate. By the early 1960s, Pittsburgh had not yet recovered from the recession begun in the late 1950s. Many observers estimated that the unemployment rate for white men was about 10 percent while the comparable rate for black men ranged between 20 percent and 40 percent.[104] Although Detroit had a higher rate of black unemployment, Pittsburgh's unemployment was more remarkable in that it occurred without a massive influx of recent migrants.[105]

As in other northern cities, blacks' anger became focused on the economic apartheid practiced by large corporations. Pittsburgh major companies still believed that African Americans were fine for janitorial and production work, but strangely ill-suited for white-collar positions. All of Pittsburgh's corporations, including Gulf, Koppers, and Duquesne Light, claimed that they would hire any "qualified Negro," but in fact hired few blacks. In 1963, the *Pittsburgh Courier* found that Alcoa and U.S. Steel each employed just two black secretaries at their downtown headquarters.[106] In 1966, U.S. Steel told *Business Week* that it had tried to hire more black women as clerical workers, but "few qualified"; only fifteen blacks worked among the fifteen hundred employees at U.S. Steel's Monroeville research laboratories.[107] Koppers, which proudly made their board room available for civil rights meetings, had only three African American non-janitorial employees; the corporation explained that its "hiring standards" required it.[108]

Black trade unionists formed an important part of the black protest movement. In 1963, James McCoy, a black staff member of the USWA, revitalized the NAACP's moribund Labor and Industry Committee, shaping it into the United Negro Protest Committee (UNPC). The UNPC first targeted Duquesne Light which employed 3,900 whites and thirty blacks.[109] After two thousand demonstrators gathered outside its headquarters, Duquesne Light agreed to hire more blacks, and four years later, it had ninety-seven black employees.[110] (In response to the UNPC, the Pittsburgh police developed the infamous "tactical squad" who massed at each demonstration to intimidate pickets.[111]) The UNPC also wrested agreements to hire more blacks from companies as diverse as the Penn Sheraton, Gimbals, and Bell Telephone.[112] The passage of the 1964 Civil Rights Act strengthened the UNPC's hand. Instead of using boycotts and community pressure, they could "ask the federal government to look into violations of the Civil Rights Act" at U.S. Steel, Dravo, and Alcoa, in order to "cut off those big money contracts many of the companies are holding."[113] Indeed, the threat of lawsuits strengthened black protests and slightly widened the economic opportunities for black workers.

BLACK POWER AND THE PITTSBURGH PLAN

The small but significant successes won by the UNPC encouraged civil rights organizations to attempt to desegregate the construction industry which remained a visible bastion of white privilege. In 1968 and 1969, Pittsburgh experienced a massive building boom as corporations such as U.S. Steel spent $200 million to expand their office space and the city of Pittsburgh built a new stadium for the Steelers and the Pirates. Although most of the new structures were within sight of black ghettos, few African Americans worked on the construction sites. Having heard for years that the unions would allow blacks into their midst when there was work for all their members, it was galling to many to see that many white construction workers had been brought in from out of state. A few blacks were visible "lifting or wheeling or carrying but not . . . doing any skilled work other than a token here and there."[114] In 1969, eighteen community and civil rights groups formed the Black Construction Coalition (BCC) and led mass demonstrations at construction sites throughout downtown Pittsburgh in order to pressure unions and contractors to train and hire black workers. At one of the first demonstrations, white construction workers pelted BCC demonstrators with rocks.[115]

Although the BCC, the city, and the police agreed to coordinate future demonstrations in an effort to avoid violence, the police themselves turned violent. On August 25, 1969, or "Black Monday" as activists called it, thousands of demonstrators—black and white—chanting "Jobs now" and "Shut it down" marched past contested downtown construction sites, which the city had closed in an effort to prevent racial clashes. As the protesters approached the job site at the Three Rivers Stadium, the infamous tactical squad brutalized the marchers.[116] One marcher, Aurelia Diggs, watched helplessly as a "burly sadist bigot garbed in a policeman's uniform straddled a young black woman and beat her like an animal."[117] Although the BCC, contractors, unions, and the city agreed to a five-day moratorium on demonstrations and building, angry white construction workers stormed the mayor's office demanding that he reopen work sites and compensate them for lost time. The city eventually paid the workers.[118]

As white resistance escalated, the BCC countered by attempting to freeze federal aid for building projects until blacks were hired. As a result of this mounting pressure, local unions and contractors negotiated the controversial "Pittsburgh Plan" with some members of the BCC.[119] Under the plan, federal moneys would be used to train blacks for construction jobs; contractors and unions promised that by 1973, twelve hundred blacks would have both jobs and union cards.[120] Because there were no guarantees, several member organizations of the BCC refused to ratify the agreement. The *Pittsburgh Courier* and the NAACP were critical of the Pittsburgh Plan from the start. Especially troublesome was the fact that some of the black administrators of the Pittsburgh Plan were also the contractors responsible for training black construction workers.[121] As early as 1971, the *Pittsburgh Post-Gazette* detailed that much of the money going to train construction workers was being paid to nonexistent companies run by black administrators of the Pittsburgh Plan.[122] In 1972, only 158 blacks had obtained union jobs, far below the 1971 target of 314 jobs, and the *Courier*'s editor disputed even that low figure.[123] The U. S. Department of Labor's Office of Federal Contract Compliance found that fully one-half of the unions were not complying with the plan's goals and therefore faced a three-year ban on working on federal contracts, but no union or contractor was *ever* denied a federal contract. Indeed, the black members of the Pittsburgh Plan urged the release of federal funds.[124] Nonetheless, the Pittsburgh Plan was hailed by the Nixon administration, construction unions, and contractors as a success.[125]

THE CONSENT DECREE IN STEEL

The BCC's demonstrations represented the high-water mark of mass protest in Pittsburgh. White elites were clearly threatened by mass mobilizations of African Americans that threatened to become urban insurrections. While the ability of the Pittsburgh Plan to actually improve the status of black construction workers was limited, black steelworkers won a more substantial victory. In the 1960s, black steelworkers joined with the NAACP in suing the USWA and steel companies in an effort to force the end of racial discrimination in steel. Black unionists used their local Civil Rights Committees and lawsuits based on violations of Title VII to pressure the USWA and steel firms to promote black workers.[126] At the Homestead Works, John Turner, the head of the CRC, became disgusted with the glacial pace of change within his union and instituted a class action lawsuit against both the company and the union.[127] Turner was joined by other steelworkers in Fairfield, Alabama; Lackawanna, New York; Baltimore, Maryland; and Youngstown, Ohio.[128] The hundreds of lawsuits finally compelled the steel industry to take action.

In 1973, as discontent mounted within the union, the steelworkers' union and several companies, including J&L and U.S. Steel, capitulated and signed a consent decree that required steel companies to pay $31 million in damages to African American, Hispanic, and women workers.[129] The decree also stipulated that workers could bid on jobs based on plant seniority and that 20 percent of new hires would have to be women or racial minorities. The victory was only partial, as the USWA and steel companies never admitted to violating the civil rights of their black and Latino members, and by cooperating, both were allowed to administer the implementation of the consent decree.[130] Many men felt that their compensation, no more than a few hundred dollars, was an insult and refused to cash the checks from their companies. Although flawed, the consent decree finally allowed black men to use their seniority to transfer into decent jobs. The Valley Machine Shop, or the Big Shop in the Homestead Works had traditionally been off-limits to blacks. By 1982, ninety-two of its 474 employees were minorities, and many were moving into decent jobs.[131]

BACKLASH

Since the late 1960s, the increasing militancy and victories of the civil rights movement helped to generate a backlash among white workers. Many white unionists were angered that their seniority rights had been sold out without allowing them to vote and accused the USWA's leadership of "dictatorship." Within days of the news of the consent decree, three hundred unionists picketed the USWA headquarters complaining of reverse discrimination. Some of their motives were crassly economic. One white unionist noted that before the consent decree, "after twenty years in the mills, I was making $15,000 a year." After the consent decree, "I'm making $10,000. How am I supposed to take that?"[132] Conservative white steelworkers, including the majority of presidents of local unions in the Mon Valley, organized Steel Workers for Justice (SWFJ) in order to challenge the legality of the consent decree.[133]

Steel companies adroitly used the consent decree to manipulate racial and gender tensions among workers. Typically, managers promoted a woman over the heads of qualified black and white men. In response, one of the founders of the SWFJ filed a reverse discrimination complaint with the Equal Employment Opportunity Commission. Michael Bonn, an assistant grievance committeeman at the Irvin Works, said he was passed over to become a motor inspector apprentice because of his "race (white) and sex (male)."[134] Bonn was upset because he had been waiting for years to enter an apprenticeship program and he was passed over by a nineteen-year-old black woman. Bonn argued he was not a bigot, but believed that since he had been waiting for years to get an apprenticeship, she should have to "wait her turn."[135] (Bonn neglected to mention that the Irvin Works had previously only hired a handful of black men as janitors.) Numerous black unionists such as Ray Henderson at the Duquesne Works were indignant that local union presidents spent their locals' moneys to fight the consent decree, but had never fought to protect blacks from discrimination.[136] The turmoil over the consent decree helped to divide unionists at a time when steel firms were not maintaining their steel plants. By the early 1980s, the Homestead, Southside, and Duquesne Works were totally shuttered and substantial parts of the Clairton, ET, and Irvin Works were also closed, throwing tens of thousands of unionists like Bonn and Henderson onto the streets.

The backlash against civil rights was also influenced by the physical and social deterioration of the mill towns. By the early 1970s, it was clear that the mill towns of the Mon Valley were dying. Duquesne had half as many people in 1970 as it had in 1940, Homestead, less than one-third.[137] Ironically, the good wages of the steel industry, about 25 percent above the average manufacturing wage, allowed white steelworkers to move from gritty mill towns such as Homestead, Duquesne, or Braddock to predominantly white blue-collar suburbs such as Munhall, West Mifflin, or Swissvale. By contrast, Homestead, Braddock, and Duquesne were increasingly populated by African American steelworkers, retirees, and the poor.[138] Most black steelworkers were unable to buy the modest brick bungalows in the new bedroom communities. Black steelworkers' wages were usually too low to follow their white fellows, but the prejudice of realtors, bankers, and white residents were powerful barriers to those African Americans who had the money and desire to move to the suburbs.[139]

Ironically, the suburbanization of the Mon Valley's white population made deteriorating mill towns such as Homestead appear to whites to be increasingly *dominated* by blacks. Although the numbers of blacks remained roughly constant, the belief in a "black influx" grew, which fueled many whites' desire to move out of mill towns. The proportion of blacks in Homestead grew from 18 percent in 1960 to 28 percent in 1970. By 1980, 37 percent of Homestead was black. According to one former Homestead steelworker who was interviewed in the mid-1970s, "With the influx of laborers, colored people, it's changed. This used to be a nice spot. We had no problems."[140] One white woman recalled that she did not remember blacks drinking at the tavern her husband owned, only "workers": "Men would come from work and come in. The town was beautiful when I came."[141]

Although blacks received much of the blame for the physical deterioration of the Mon Valley, it is clear that the erosion of jobs in the mill and the suburbanization of the middle class and the white working class were at the root of the mill towns' problems. As early as the 1960s, the declining employment opportunities in the steel industry helped to drive between 20 percent to 30 percent of men and women in their twenties from the region.[142] As suburban shopping malls, such as Century III, opened, retail trade in mill towns plummeted. Ironically, Century III was owned by U.S. Steel's real estate division.[143] Braddock was one of the first mill towns to decline. Documentary filmmaker Tony Buba portrayed downtown Braddock, vibrant as recently as the 1950s, lined with boarded-up storefronts in 1974.[144] Unfortunately, the victories of the civil rights movement, coinciding with the physical deterioration of the mill towns, provided the raw materials for a racist narrative of deindustrialization that blamed the decline of steel and the Mon Valley on black workers. As Steve Vravel, a worker at the Homestead Works, remembered, before the 1960s, Homestead "didn't have any black problems . . . they were too busy working to go out parading and carrying on trying to destroy the system."[145]

INTERPRETING DEINDUSTRIALIZATION

In the aftermath of civil rights protests and a conservative backlash, the region's mills grew increasingly aged. The region never quite recovered from the layoffs in the mid-1970s, but many refused to believe the mills would really close. Pittsburgh was an epicenter of the wave of plant closings in the late 1970s and early 1980s that destroyed well-paid blue-collar "life-time jobs." In 1953, there were 160,000 steelworkers in Pittsburgh; in 1979 there were just under 100,000. By 1983, however, there were only 40,000; by 1987 just 24,000 remained (many of them employed in corporate head-quarters) and the number continues to fall. The impact on the region has been enormous. Many of the former steel towns are bankrupt; one of the region's biggest exports is now its young people. Pittsburgh has the urban oldest population (outside of Florida) in the country, and the population of the Pittsburgh metropolitan area is still falling. Despite the rumors of a high-tech economic renaissance, the living standards of those workers who remain are far lower than they were ten years ago.[146]

The causes of deindustrialization are as political as they are economic. Most steel companies in the world receive direct subsidies, a point that American steel executives never tired of explaining. The high interest rates of Paul Volcker made it next to impossible for steel firms to borrow money to purchase new capital stock or even to maintain existing furnaces or machines. However, deindustrialization cannot simply be understood as a question of the profitability of specific facilities—indeed, the Duquesne Works was profitable when U.S. Steel closed it. In 1982, after receiving concessions from steelworkers and the federal government, U.S. Steel took this windfall and purchased Marathon Oil, thus continuing its policies of diversifying its holdings. Shortly thereafter, the company changed its name to USX.[147]

Popular interpretations of deindustrialization are also political. The mass media emphasizes that low-wage producers abroad "inevitably" undercut the profitability of American firms forced to pay high wages and meet stringent environmental standards. By implication, workers are encouraged to accept not only the blame for their downward mobility, but low-wage jobs as well. Radical interpretations of deindustrialization stress the mismanagement of American companies and their shift from investment in domestic steel production to real estate or even steelmaking abroad. Many white ex-steelworkers and residents of the Mon Valley, borrowing from both mass media and radical interpretations, articulate a *race-based* narrative of plant closings. While frequently acknowledging the critical role that high wages and U.S. Steel's disinvestment in steel played in shutting down local mills, many whites emphasize the "fact" that the Mon Valley was beautiful until blacks moved into their neighborhoods and the steel industry was profitable prior to affirmative action. Thus, collective action along class lines is discouraged even as efforts to roll back affirmative action and "welfare" are applauded. This racist narrative is simply the latest chapter in the long history of a racial division of labor in industrial cities such as Pittsburgh. What is interesting is that many black unionists also saw a racial dimension to deindustrialization, but emphasize the irony of losing their jobs just as they were finally making progress.

CONCLUSION

Beginning in the 1930s, the collective struggle of black industrial workers helped to move the civil rights movement toward improving the economic opportunities of African Americans more generally. In the 1940s, activists experimented with direct-action tactics, but the hostile white reaction, particularly by industrialists, caused many organizations to choose less confrontational methods. Until the late 1950s, black protest was splintered into a variety of different organizations and strategies. By the early 1960s, the increasing rate of black unemployment, combined with new levels of organization and solidarity among black industrial workers, sparked a return to the mass pickets, boycotts, and publicity campaigns of the late 1940s. The NAACP and black unionists began to work closely together and took advantage of new legislation to win some important victories such as the consent decree. However, questions of the union's overall political culture or acceptance to the dictates of capital were left unresolved. The civil rights movement was hamstrung by the weakness of radical organizations which might have provided leadership, alternative networks, and institutional memory necessary to generate the widespread involvement of workers. Furthermore, the gains of black workers and professionals in the 1970s coincided with a worsening economic situation that helped to spark a white backlash that still dominates the political landscape and historical memory.

Although outside the scope of this essay, the decades of slow, painful gains made by blue-collar workers were largely undone in the late 1970s and early 1980s as heavy industry corporations abandoned the region. Deindustrialization also devastated white workers, but as in earlier hard times, black workers shouldered a disproportionate amount of the region's unemployment.[148] Rather than make common cause with black workers, many whites chose to embrace the growing conservative movement which blamed affirmative action and social programs for the hard times confronting working and middle-class Americans.

As Pittsburgh confronts the harsh realities of "postindustrial" capitalism, the problems confronting the black community are greater than ever. As corporations, governments, and universities downsize, the rate of unemployment and occupational marginalization among African Americans grows. In the face of an increasingly hostile ideological climate, it is doubtful whether the black community alone will be able to mobilize sufficient pressure to force governmental intervention to combat the continuing crisis of unemployment and underemployment in its neighborhoods. Without a vigorous labor movement able to fight for the interests of the entire class, the civil rights struggle appears doomed to struggle on as the ground erodes beneath its feet.

NOTES

1. Historians generally interpret the civil rights movement as an attempt by African Americans in the 1950s and 1960s to realize their *political* and *social* rights as American citizens. As with King himself, scholars' attention to the economic dimensions of Jim Crow and the northern struggle have been relatively late in coming. An excellent overview of the literature on civil rights is Adam Fairclough's "Historians and the Civil Rights Movement," *Journal of American Studies* 21 (December 1990): 210–22. See also *New Directions in Civil Rights Studies*, ed. Armstead L. Robinson and Patricia Sullivan (Charlottesville: University Press of Virginia, 1991). Steven F. Lawson, "Freedom Then, Freedom Now: The Historiography of the Civil Rights Movement," *American Historical Review* 96 (April 1991): 456–71. One account of the North during the 1960s is James A. Gershwender's *Class, Race, and Worker Insurgency: The League of Revolutionary Black Workers* (New York: Cambridge University Press, 1977). For an account of the 1930s and 1940s, see August Meier and Elliot Rudwick, *Black Detroit and the Rise of the UAW* (New York: Oxford University Press, 1979). An excellent treatment of a Southern city in this time period is Michael K. Honey's *Southern Labor and Black Civil Rights: Organizing Memphis Workers* (Urbana: University of Illinois Press, 1993).

2. Paul Le Blanc, "Revolutionary Vanguards in the United States in the 1930s," *U.S. Labor in the Twentieth Century: Studies in Working-Class Struggles and Insurgency*, ed. John Hinshaw and Paul Le Blanc (Amherst, N.Y.: Humanity Books, 2000).

3. Robert Korstad and Nelson Lichtenstein, "Opportunities Found and Lost: Labor, Radicals, and the Early Civil Rights Movement," *Journal of American History* 75 (December 1988): 786–811. See also James Green, *The World of the Worker: Labor in Twentieth-Century America* (New York: Hill and Wang, 1980).

Increasingly historians, influenced scholars of "black proletarianization" such as Joe Trotter, Robin D. G. Kelley, and Earl Lewis, view black workers as well as movement or union leaders as crucial historical actors. Yet most studies of black proletarianization focus on the period between 1915 and 1945, few studies have examined the struggles of black workers within unions and industry after World War II. Joe William

Trotter Jr., *Black Milwaukee: The Making of an Industrial Proletariat* (Urbana: University of Illinois Press, 1985); Robin D. G. Kelley, *Hammer and Hoe: Alabama Communists During the Great Depression* (Chapel Hill: University of North Carolina Press, 1990); Earl Lewis, *In Their Own Interests: Race, Class, and Power in Twentieth-Century Norfolk, Virginia* (Berkeley: University of California Press, 1991). One of the few accounts of black unionists' travails during the cold war period is Dennis Dickerson's *Out of the Crucible*, which analyzes black steelworkers struggles within the United Steel Workers (USWA). Dennis Dickerson, *Out of the Crucible: Black Steelworkers in Western Pennsylvania, 1875–1980* (Albany: State University of New York Press, 1986), 1. Another study of black workers within the USW is Philip W. Nyden's, "Evolution of Black Political Influence in American Trade Unions," *Journal of Black Studies* 13 (June 1983): 379–98. See also James E. Jones and Herbert Hill, *Race in America: The Struggle for Equality* (Madison: University of Wisconsin Press, 1993).

4. William T. Hogan, *Economic History of the Iron and Steel Industry of the United States*, vol. 3 (Lexington, Mass.: Lexington Books, 1971), 813.

5. Francis G. Couvares, *The Remaking of Pittsburgh: Class and Culture in an Industrializing City, 1877–1919* (Albany: State University of New York Press, 1984), 9–13; Richard Oestreicher, "Working-Class Formation, Development, and Consciousness in Pittsburgh, 1790–1960," in *City at the Point: Essays on the Social History of Pittsburgh*, ed. Samuel P. Hays (Pittsburgh: University of Pittsburgh Press, 1989), 116, 129–30.

6. Paul Krause, *The Battle for Homestead, 1880–1892: Politics, Culture and Steel* (Pittsburgh: University of Pittsburgh Press, 1992), 284–314; David Brody, *Steelworkers in America: The Nonunion Era* (New York: Harper and Row, 1969), 58–60; David Montgomery, *The Fall of the House of Labor: The Workplace, the State and American Labor Activism, 1865–1925* (Cambridge: Cambridge University Press, 1987), 36–43; Arthur G. Burgoyne, *The Homestead Strike of 1892* (1893; reprint, Pittsburgh: University of Pittsburgh Press, 1979).

7. David B. Houston, "A Brief History of the Process of the Capital Accumulation in Pittsburgh: A Marxist Interpretation," in *Pittsburgh-Sheffield Sister Cities: Proceedings of the Pittsburgh-Sheffield Symposium on Industrial Cities*, ed. Joel Tarr (Pittsburgh: Carnegie Mellon University, 1986), 38. By 1907, Allegheny County produced 30 percent of all rolled steel in the United States, see Kenneth Warren, *The American Steel Industry, 1850–1970: A Geographical Interpretation* (Pittsburgh: University of Pittsburgh Press, 1973), 197.

8. Source: Roy Lubove, *Twentieth-Century Pittsburgh: Government, Business and Environmental Change* (New York: John Wiley and Sons, 1969), 267; John Bodnar, Roger Simon, and Michael P. Weber, *Lives of Their Own: Blacks, Italians and Poles in Pittsburgh, 1900–1960* (Urbana: University of Illinois Press, 1982), 30.

9. Krause, *Battle for Homestead*, 215–26; Montgomery, *Fall of the House*, 14–28.

10. Brody, *Steelworkers in America*, 99, 136, 265–67; Horace R. Cayton and George S. Mitchell, *Black Workers and the New Unions* (Durham: University of North Carolina Press, 1939), 73–87; see also Dickerson, *Out of the Crucible*, passim.

11. Cayton and Mitchell, *Black Workers and the New Unions*, 134–36; Brody, *Steelworkers in America*, 90–91.

12. Brody, *Steelworkers in America*, 82–84.

13. Montgomery, *Fall of the House*, 42.

14. Cayton and Mitchell, *Black Workers and the New Unions*, 73–87; Sterling D. Spero and Abram L. Harris, *The Black Worker: The Negro and the Labor Movement* (New York: Columbia University Press, 1931), 249–54; Peter Gottlieb, *Making Their Own Way: Southern Blacks' Migration to Pittsburgh, 1916–1930* (Urbana: University of Illinois Press, 1987), 152–64.

15. Cayton and Mitchell, *Black Workers and the New Unions*, 73–87; Spero and Harris, *The Black Worker*, 249–54; Gottlieb, *Making Their Own Way*, 152–64.

16. Gottlieb, *Making Their Own Way*, 92.

17. Brody, *Steelworkers in America*, 118–21, 259–61.

18. Cayton and Mitchell, *Black Workers and the New Unions*, 73–87; Brody, *Steelworkers in America*, 258–61.

19. Cayton and Mitchell, *Black Workers and the New Unions*, 134–36.

20. National Urban League, *Negro Membership in American Labor Unions* (New York: Negro University Press, 1969), 138–39; "Worker's Institute," n.d. (1940) box 3, file 155, Pittsburgh Urban League Papers (PUL), Archives of Industrial Society, University of Pittsburgh (AIS).

21. Gottlieb, *Making Their Own Way*, 147–54, 174.

22. Harry Haywood, *Black Bolshevik: Autobiography of an Afro-American Communist* (Chicago: Lake View Press, 1978), 366.

23. Lubove, *Twentieth-Century Pittsburgh*, 5.

24. Warren, *American Steel Industry*, 209.

25. Harvey O'Connor, *Steel—Dictator* (New York: John Day Company, 1935), 5.

26. Ibid., 7.

27. "Hold Hunger March as Coal Cops Lose Power," June 30, 1931, in box 27, folder "Coal and Iron Police," in Harvey O'Connor Papers, Archives of Labor and Urban Affairs, Wayne State University.

28. Philip Klein et al., *A Social Study of Pittsburgh: Community Problems and Social Services of Allegheny County* (New York: Columbia University Press, 1938), 160.

29. Augustine, Thomas, "The Negro Steelworkers of Pittsburgh and the Unions" (master's thesis, University of Pittsburgh, 1948).

30. John Fitch, "A Man Can Talk in Homestead," *Survey Graphic* 25, no. 2 (February 1936): 75.

31. Cayton and Mitchell, *Black Workers*, 162.

32. Thomas Augustine, "The Negro Steelworkers of Pittsburgh and the Unions" (master's thesis, University of Pittsburgh, 1948), 20–22; Cayton and Mitchell, *Black Workers*, 162–63.

33. John Hughey and Jesse Larrington, interview by Ray Henderson and Tony Buba, summer 1992, tape recording.

34. Harold Keith, "Who's Who in Labor," *Pittsburgh Courier*, February 11, 1947, 2; Harold Keith, "Who's Who in Labor," *Pittsburgh Courier*, March 29, 1947, 34.

35. Ernestine Holt, "Status of Steelworkers: Negroes Refused Supervisory Jobs," *Pittsburgh Courier*, August 24, 1946, 16.

36. Ralph E. Kroger, "When J&L Workers Got Off the Job, Management

Decided to Get 'On the Ball,'" *Pittsburgh Courier*, August 3, 1946, and "See 'Unfair' J&L Decision," *Pittsburgh Courier*, September 20, 1947, 1, 13.

37. "District Labor Pool Exhausted WMC Announces," *Homestead Daily Messenger*, November 27, 1943, 1.

38. "Steel Works Officers Deny Worker Migration," *Homestead Daily Messenger*, May 27, 1943, 1.

39. Bodnar, Simon, and Weber, *Lives of Their Own*, 239.

40. See John Hinshaw, "Dialectic of Division: Race and Power Among Western Pennsylvania Steelworkers" (Ph.D. diss., Carnegie Mellon University, 1995), 52–110.

41. Milo Manly to G. James Fleming, "Memorandum," March 7, 1944; see also, "Strikes Occuring Over Racial Issues," file "Strike Data," box 404, Records of the FEPC (RG 228), National Archives.

42. John P. Davis to Joy P. Davis, May 16, 1944, file "Tension Data," box 404, RG 228, National Archives.

43. On November 19, 1943, seven white grinders refused to train three African American "learners." The union refused to back the white men, and the black learners were put on the machines, see November 19, "Strike or Work Stoppage Report No. 15," in box 28, S-5 (A), file "Strike Reports 1946–1952," U.S. Steel Duquesne Works Papers, AIS.

44. K. H. M. to W. C. O., December 27, 1944, regarding "strikes," in box 18, S-5 (A), file "Strikes (General Correspondence), USX Duquesne Works Papers, AIS.

45. Kroger, "When J&L Workers Got Off the Job," 1, 5; R. L. Prattis, "Labor Everywhere," *Pittsburgh Courier*, August 10, 1946, 14.

46. Kroger, "When J&L Workers Got Off the Job," 1, 5.

47. Kroger, "'Unfair' J&L Decision," 1, 13.

48. Harold Keith, "Who's Who in Labor," *Pittsburgh Courier*, May 14, 1947, 20.

49. Augustine, "Negro Steelworkers of Pittsburgh," 43.

50. For evidence that discrimination at this mill was a continuing problem, see: Minutes of the September 12, 1956 USWA Committee on Civil Rights, 3, box 6, file 5, "Civil Rights Committee, 1953–56"; Hague Papers, USW Archives; "Committee on Civil Rights Participation in USWA District Conferences, 1966," 3, box 11, file 32, "Committee on Civil Rights, 1965–66," Civil Rights Department Papers, USWA Archives.

51. Keith, "Who's Who in Labor," *Pittsburgh Courier*, February 22, 1947, 6. Edward McNary, shop steward at Local 1272, J&L's Southside Works, noted that fifteen hundred blacks worked at that mill, but only ten to twenty-five regularly attend meetings, and only eight are actively involved in the union, see Keith, "Who's Who in Labor," *Pittsburgh Courier*, April 5, 1947, 16; Keith, "Who's Who in Labor," *Pittsburgh Courier*, March 29, 1947, 34.

52. Phyl Garland, "From the Soil to the Shop," June 11, 1960, *Pittsburgh Courier*, Magazine Section; Boyd Wilson interview, in Dickerson, *Out of the Crucible*, 180–81.

53. Minutes of CRC, February 3, 1959, 1, Hague Papers, box 6, file 7, "Civil Rights Committee, 1959," USW Archives.

54. Garland, "From the Soil to the Shop," June 11, 1960, *Pittsburgh Courier*, Magazine Section; Dickerson, *Out of the Crucible*, 180–81.

55. Sam Everett, quoted in Minutes of Regular Quarterly Meeting, August 27, 1957, 7, box 9, file 5, "USA Committee on Civil Rights, Correspondence, 1957," Civil Rights Department Papers, USWA Archives.

56. A black was not appointed to the CRC until 1952, and Wilson was left off of it until 1958. Dickerson, *Out of the Crucible*, 195.

57. In 1952, Alexander J. Allen, the executive director of the Pittsburgh Urban League, observed that the USWA shared with the UL and the NAACP the distinction of being one of a handful of organizations in the state of Pennsylvania that sought to eliminate the color line in employment. "The Negro in Labor and Industry: Urban League Roundup," *Pittsburgh Courier*, September 14, 1954, Special Section, 10. See also, "FEPC Review," October, 1954, 1, box 10, file 5, NAACP Records, AIS.

58. Francis Shane to members of the CRC, April 17, 1961, box 6, file 9, "Civil Rights Committee, 1961," Hague Papers, USWA Archives. United Steelworkers of America, *Proceedings of the Tenth Constitutional Convention of the United Steelworkers of America* (Pittsburgh: United Steelworkers of America, 1960), 349. The CRC donated $400,000 over three years to civil rights groups.

59. "Report of Department of Industrial Relations," January and February 1933, box 3, file 133, PUL, AIS. Mark Naison, *Communists in Harlem During the Depression* (Urbana: University of Illinois Press, 1983).

60. Arthur J. Edmunds, *Daybreakers: The Story of the Urban League of Pittsburgh, the First Sixty-Five Years* (Pittsburgh: Pittsburgh Urban League, 1983), 114–15. *Pittsburgh Courier*, February 1, 1947, 2. See also *Inside Facts* 2, no. 2, January 25, 1947, series 13, box 23, file "Printed Material, Pittsburgh, 1947–1949," National Urban League Records, Library of Congress. See K. Leroy Irvis, "Summary Report on the Campaign to Secure a Non-Discrimination Hiring Policy in the Major Pittsburgh Department Stores," series 13, box 23, file "Printed Material, Pittsburgh, 1947–1949," NUL Records, Library of Congress. See also James Hackshaw, "The Committee for Fair Employment in Pittsburgh Department Stores: A Study of the Methods and Techniques Used by the Committee in Their Campaign to Secure a Non-Discriminatory Hiring Policy in the Department Stores of Pittsburgh" (master's thesis, Department of Social Work, University of Pittsburgh, 1949).

61. Hackshaw, "Committee for Fair Employment," 38.

62. Edmunds, *Daybreakers*, 114–15.

63. "Highlights of 1956," *Balance Sheet* 8, no. 1, series 13, box 24, file "Printed Matter, Pittsburgh, 1956–1958," NUL Records, Library of Congress.

64. *Second Annual Report: Discovered Patterns*, Pittsburgh Fair Employment Practices Commission, March 25, 1955, 15–16, box 11, file 5, "Fair Employment Practices Commission, 1955–1958," NAACP Records, AIS.

65. *Pittsburgh Courier*, December 10, 1960, 7.

66. May 13, 1961, Minutes of the Executive Board Meeting, part 2, series 2, box 18, file "Pittsburgh, 1960–1961," NUL Records, Library of Congress.

67. *Pittsburgh Courier*, December 10, 1960, 2.

68. *Pittsburgh Courier*, May 29, 1954, 5.

69. Minutes of the Executive Board Meeting, October 20, 1960, 3–4, part 2, series 2, box 18, file "Pittsburgh, 1960–1961," NUL Records, Library of Congress.

70. Minutes of the Executive Board Meeting, October 20, 1960, 3–4, part 2, series 2, box 18, file "Pittsburgh, 1960–1961," NUL Records, Library of Congress.

71. U.S. Department of Labor, Bureau of Labor Statistics, *Employment, Hours and Earnings: States and Areas, 1939–1974*, Bulletin 1370-11 (Washington, D.C.: U.S. Government Printing Office, 1975), 631–32.

72. Morton Grodzins, *The Metropolitan Area as a Racial Problem* (Pittsburgh: University of Pittsburgh Press, 1958), 2.

73. Department of Research and Investigation of the National Urban League, *Negro Membership in American Labor Unions* (New York: Negro University Press, 1969), 138–39.

74. *Pittsburgh Courier*, June 30, 1956, section 2, 19.

75. Arthur J. Edmunds (executive director, PUL) to Patrick Fagan, president Pittsburgh city council, January 3, 1963, part 2, series 4, box 67, file "Pittsburgh, 1962–1963," NUL, Library of Congress. See also Industrial Relations Department (IRD), "Program Prospects for 1950," May 15, 1950, series 13, box 24, file "Pittsburgh, 1950–1951," NUL, Library of Congress; "Year-End Summary" of the IRD, June 25, 1951, series 13, box 24, file "Pittsburgh, 1950–1951," NUL Records, Library of Congress.

76. *Pittsburgh Courier*, July 13, 1963, 1.

77. Monthly Report February 1961, February 2, 1961, box 38, NUL, Library of Congress.

78. *Pittsburgh Courier*, June 13, 1963, 1; *Pittsburgh Courier*, October 26, 1963, 1. See also PA HRC, "Human Relations Reports" (Pennsylvania Human Relations Commission), September 1963, 12, box 44, file "Commission on Human Relations," NAACP Records, AIS.

79. Quarterly Report, "October–December 1963," January 29, 1964, part 2, series 4, box 67, file "Pittsburgh, 1963–April 1964," NUL Records, Library of Congress.

80. Second Quarterly Report, April–June 1963, part 2, series 4, box 67, file "Pittsburgh, PA, 1963–April 1964," NUL Records, Library of Congress.

81. "Proposal from the Urban League of Pittsburgh to the Commission on Human Relations," April 23, 1963, part 2, series 4, box 67, Program Department, file "Pittsburgh, PA, 1963–1964," NUL, Library of Congress.

82. Human Relations Report, July–September, 1967, 7–8, box 15, file 4, "Pennsylvania Human Rights Commission, 1967," Civil Rights Department, USWA Archives.

83. Equal Employment Opportunity Commission, *Minority Group Employment by Occupation and Sex for Selected Industries*, Bulletin 1-889, 646.

84. Jesse Walker, interview by Henderson and Buba, summer 1992, tape recording.

85. John Hughey, interview by author, August 5, 1993, tape recording.

86. George Henderson, interview by Henderson and Buba, summer 1992, tape recording.

87. Anonymous, interview by Henderson and Buba, summer 1992, tape recording.

88. John Hughey, interview by Henderson and Buba, summer 1992, tape recording.

89. U.S. Department of Commerce, Bureau of the Census, *Population*

Census: 1960 (Washington, D.C.: U.S. Government Printing Office, 1961), 40-752-4.

90. Harold Keith, "Workers Defend Albert Everett," *Pittsburgh Courier*, January 12, 1957, 2.

91. Harold Keith, "Sparks Fly at Steel Union Parley," *Pittsburgh Courier*, January 5, 1957, 3.

92. Hinshaw, "Dialectic of Division," 361–73.

93. "Acquittal of John Duch Irks Negro Members of Steel Union," *Pittsburgh Courier*, March 2, 1957, 3.

94. Ibid.

95. John Hughey and Jesse Larrington, interview by Henderson and Buba, summer 1992, tape recording. John Hughey with author, August 5, 1993, tape recording.

96. Harold Keith, "Clobbering Jim Crow," *Pittsburgh Courier*, February 16, 1957, section 2, 6.

97. Harold Keith, "Who's Who in Labor: Backer Sets Precedent, Wins Post in USW Local," *Pittsburgh Courier*, August 31, 1957, section 2, 1.

98. Keith, "Clobbering Jim Crow."

99. Harold Keith, "Negro Steelworkers Show Unrest as Big Convention Opens," *Pittsburgh Courier*, September 24, 1960, section 2, 3. The *Pittsburgh Courier* praised the NALC's formation, see "Negro Labor's Giant Step," *Pittsburgh Courier*, June 11, 1960, 13.

100. Kim Moody, *An Injury to All: The Decline of American Unionism* (New York: Verso Press, 1988), 74–75.

101. "Labor Group Meets, Plans for Future," *Pittsburgh Courier*, August 26, 1961, 11.

102. October 16, 1961, "News Release," box 38, file "News Release—Courier, 1961," NAACP Records, AIS.

103. "Courier, NAACP, NALC Mass Protest Wins: Arena to Improve Job-Hiring Policy," *Pittsburgh Courier*, October 28, 1961, 2.

104. U.S. Department of Labor, Bureau of Labor Statistics, *Employment, Hours and Earnings: States and Areas, 1939–1974*, Bulletin 1370-11 (Washington, D.C.: U.S. Government Printing Office, 1975), 631–32; "The Urban Leaguer," vol. 1, no. 1, February 1962, part 2, series 8, box 11, file "Printed Matter, Pittsburgh, 1961–1965," NUL Records, Library of Congress; Alvin Rosensweet in *Pittsburgh Post Gazette*, September 12, 1963.

105. *Pittsburgh Post Gazette*, November 1, 1964; the number of blacks rose from 163,000 in 1960 to 175,000 in 1980. "Pittsburgh Off Course During 1950–62 Exodus," *Pittsburgh Courier*, October 30, 1965, 3. The 1970 census reinforced the black community's pessimism: only twenty-six thousand or one-quarter of Pittsburgh's black population had been born in the South and fully two-thirds of them had been born *before* 1925. Most Southern-born blacks in Pittsburgh had almost certainly come to work during WWII or the Great Migration period of 1916–1931, see U.S. Department of Commerce, Bureau of the Census, *Population Census: Detailed Characteristics* (Washington, D.C.: U.S. Government Printing Office, 1971), 40-749-50.

106. Alvin Rosensweet, "The Negro in Pittsburgh: Joblessness a Basic Problem Here," *Pittsburgh Post-Gazette*, September 12, 1963, 1, 8.

107. "Negroes Zero in on Steel Industry," *Business Week*, December 10, 1966, 156.

108. "Vicious Prejudice Seen as Roadblock to the Employment of Skilled Negroes," *Pittsburgh Courier*, December 12, 1959, 5. Consequently, blacks were three times as likely as whites to work as domestics, unskilled laborers, or service workers. Forty-five percent of black men and 60 percent of black women held these jobs.

109. *Pittsburgh Courier*, August 17, 1963, 1.

110. *Pittsburgh Post-Gazette*, September 15, 1967.

111. Ed Wintermantel, "Craig Credits Police Five-Year Plan With Keeping Riots Here Bloodless," *Pittsburgh Press*, April 14, 1968, section 3, 1; Nick Ludington, "Hotel Here Okays Hiring More Negroes," *Pittsburgh Press*, May 26, 1964, 4.

112. *Pittsburgh Press*, May 26, 1964; *Pittsburgh Post-Gazette*, April 25, 1966; *Pittsburgh Post-Gazette*, September 7, 1967; *Pittsburgh Post-Gazette*, September 15, 1967.

113. "No Black Executives at ALCOA, Dravo, WABCO," *Pittsburgh Courier*, August 16, 1969, 1. Carl Morris, "Comment: Blacks Need United in Quest for More and Better Jobs," *Pittsburgh Courier*, July 19, 1969, 13; Carl Morris, "Comment: Demonstration Post-Mortem," *Pittsburgh Courier*, May 6, 1967, 5.

114. Charles Owen Rice, "Bias in Building," *Pittsburgh Courier*, August 23, 1969, 13.

115. Diane Perry, "Violence Erupts at North Side Stadium Site," *Pittsburgh Courier*, August 16, 1969, 1. The BCC would serve as a model for community organizing in cities from Chicago to Boston; see Philip S. Foner, *Organized Labor and the Black Worker, 1619–1981* (New York: Praeger, 1981), 408–409.

116. Diane Perry, "Golden Triangle Is Hit with Cop Brutality, Mass Arrests," *Pittsburgh Courier*, August 30, 1969, 1, 15; "Police Lost Respect at Demonstration," *Pittsburgh Courier*, September 8, 1969, 12; Diane Perry, "Mass March, Boycott Started," *Pittsburgh Courier*, September 13, 1969, 1; "Job Tensions at New High: Black Coalition Won't Back Down," *Pittsburgh Courier*, September 27, 1969, 1.

117. Aurelia H. Diggs, "Became Black After Seeing Brutality," *Pittsburgh Courier*, September 6, 1969, 13.

118. "Blacks Agree to 'Holiday' for Parleys," *Pittsburgh Press*, August 28, 1969, 1, 4; John P. Moody, "City's Protesters Taking a Break Over Labor Day," *Pittsburgh Post-Gazette*, August 30, 1969, 1, 3; "Construction Workers Get 'Lost' Pay," *Pittsburgh Post-Gazette*, September 12, 1969.

119. Edward Verlich, "Builders, Coalition Race July 1 Deadline: $300 Million in U.S. Funds at Stake," *Pittsburgh Press*, June 21, 1970; Lawrence Walsh, "Construction Ban Awaits Black Jobs," *Pittsburgh Press*, February 8, 1970, 1, 12; "Call Pittsburgh Plan Totally Worthless," *Pittsburgh Courier*, December 12, 1970. They threatened to do so again, see "May 'Freeze' Pittsburgh Plan Projects," *Pittsburgh Courier*, September 18, 1971, 1, 4.

120. The *Pittsburgh Courier* was highly critical of the Pittsburgh Plan. Byrd Brown, a prominent civil rights leader and attorney, claimed that he never even saw the agreement; see "BCC Never Ratified the Pittsburgh Plan," *Pittsburgh Courier*,

November 7, 1970, 1; for the promise of twelve hundred jobs, see "The Pittsburgh Plan," *Pittsburgh Courier*, February 12, 1972, 8.

121. "Near Riot Over Black Union Members: Iron Workers Admit Five Despite Furor," *Pittsburgh Courier*, July 25, 1970, 1; "IBEW Accepts First Negro," *Pittsburgh Courier*, February 27, 1971, 1; "Leaders Rap Pittsburgh Plan: Trainees Take Case to D.C.," *Pittsburgh Courier*, May 8, 1971, 1, 4; Barbara White Stack, "Minorities Shut Down Hill Job," *Pittsburgh Post-Gazette*, January 12, 1983, 4; Virginia Linn, "Black Coalition Moves to Gain Minority Work on Airport," *Pittsburgh Post-Gazette*, April 18, 1987, 5.

122. Ralph Z. Hallow, "War on Poverty Costs Plenty, Goes Nowhere," *Pittsburgh Post-Gazette*, September 21, 1971, 1–2. Diane Perry, "Black Construction Coalition Backs Pittsburgh Plan Trainees," *Pittsburgh Courier*, May 22, 1971, 1, 5; "Pittsburgh Plan Trainees Still Out of Work," *Pittsburgh Courier*, June 5, 1971, 1, 5.

123. "The Pittsburgh Plan," *Pittsburgh Courier*, February 12, 1972, 8.

124. "U.S. Says Unions Not Complying," *Pittsburgh Courier*, June 12, 1971, 1; Woody L. Taylor, "Pittsburgh Plan Asks to Place Seventeen Unions 'in Compliance,' " *Pittsburgh Courier*, July 3, 1971, 5.

125. In December 1971, the *Pittsburgh Press* reported that "most unions (are) opening to blacks"; see Edward Verlich, "Most Unions Opening to Blacks, Study Shows," *Pittsburgh Press*, December 12, 1971, A3; Roger Stuart, "Once-Hostile Blacks, Unions Unite on Job," *Pittsburgh Press*, September 9, 1973, A17.

126. Robert E. Nelson to Alex Fuller, March 7, 1966, box 10, file 9, "Clifford, Ernest L., 1966," CRD, USWA Archives; Robert R. Hobson to Charlie Hampton, January 9, 1969, box 21, file folder 17, "U.S. Department of Labor, General, 1966, 1969," CRD, USWA Archives; "Clarence Gunther," Homestead Local 1397 Records, box 44, (unorganized), Homestead Local 1397 Records, Indiana University of Pennsylvania (IUP).

127. "District 15 Parley Hears Civil Rights Problems Discussed by Members," *Steel Labor*, March 1971, 14; Delegate Dorothy Kelley, Local 6057, District 15, see USWA, *Proceedings*, 1972, 311; "Negroes Push to Rise Higher in Unionism," *Business Week*, June 29, 1968, 125–26.

128. Staughton Lynd remarks at Working Class History Seminar at University of Pittsburgh, winter 1992. See also Robert Lewis, "Origins of the Seniority System in Steel" (seminar paper, University of Pittsburgh, 1977), 84, 93.

129. Philip Shabacoff, "Steel and Union Adopt a Plan on Job Equality," *New York Times*, April 14, 1974, 1; Shabacoff, "Steel and Union Accept Job Plan," *New York Times*, April 16, 1974, 64.

130. "Audit Committee Guides Rights Decree Implementation," *Steel Labor*, June 1974, 5.

131. Incumbency roster, Valley Machine Shop, April 23, 1982, box 31, file 3, Homestead Local 1397 Records, Indiana University of Pennsylvania.

132. William Wesser, "Steelworkers Picket 'Union Dictatorship,' " *Pittsburgh Press*, June 17, 1975, 7.

133. John Hughey, interview by author, August 5, 1993, tape recording; Edward Verlich, "Steelworkers Here Map Fight Over Minority Decree," *Pittsburgh Press*, October 4, 1974, 2.

134. *McKeesport Daily News*, July 1977, no box, file "Consent Decree," Steffie Domike Papers, AIS.

135. Mike Bonn denied that race was a factor in this organization; see Michael Bonn, interview by author, September 3, 1993, tape recording. Resentment was fueled by anxiety over jobs. Between 1970 and 1980, thirty thousand workers lost their jobs in Pittsburgh mills, see U.S. Commerce Department, U.S. Bureau of the Census, *Census of Population: 1970*, 40-404; U.S. Commerce Department, U.S. Bureau of the Census, *Census of Population: 1980*, 40-920-2. Denise Weinbrenner Edwards, interview by author, June 15, 1992, tape recording. John P. Moody, "Civil Rights Panel Costs USW Officers Here," *Pittsburgh Post Gazette*, October 28, 1974, 21.

136. Ray Henderson, conversation with author, December 2, 1993, notes.

137. Beckman, Yoder and Associates, Inc., *Steel Valley Area Regional Development Plan* (Pittsburgh, n.d., probably 1974), 22. Mill towns were still quite polluted; see Lubove, *Twentieth-Century Pittsburgh*, 119.

138. John Hoerr, *And the Wolf Finally Came: The Decline of the American Steel Industry* (Pittsburgh: University of Pittsburgh Press, 1988), 177–78; Beckman, Yoder and Associates, Inc., *Steel Valley*, 25, 69–71.

139. "Housing Discrimination?" *Pittsburgh Courier*, February 12, 1955, 1; George Barbour, "Barbour Can't Rent Apartment in White Neighborhood Even If a U.S. Serviceman," December 6, 1959, 3; "Black Family Under Constant Harassment in Hazelwood Home," *Pittsburgh Courier*, December 30, 1972, 1; see also, Ray Henderson, interview by author, August 6, 1993, tape recording.

140. Mel Rutter, interview, May 11, 1976, transcript, Homestead Oral History Project, AIS.

141. Jane Stophel, interview, May 11, 1965, transcript, Homestead Oral History Project, AIS.

142. Beckman, Yoder and Associates, Inc., *Steel Valley*, 28.

143. Ibid., 71.

144. Tony Buba, *J Roy's New and Used Furniture*, in *Braddock Chronicles I* videorecording (Braddock: Braddock Films, 1994); Beckman, Yoder and Associates, Inc., *Steel Valley*, 71–74.

145. Steve Vravel, interview, May 28, 1976, transcript, Homestead Oral History Project, AIS.

146. Steve Massey, "Economy Leaves Blacks Behind," *Pittsburgh Post-Gazette*, October 18, 1994, 1, 8; United States Department of Commerce, *Statistical Abstract of the United States, 1992* (Washington, D.C.: U.S. Government Printing Office, 1992), 30–32; U.S. Department of Labor, Bureau of Labor Statistics, *Employment, Hours and Earnings, States and Areas, 1939–1975* (Washington, D.C.: U.S. Government Printing Office, 1975), Bulletin 1370-12, 631–37; U.S. Department of Labor, Bureau of Labor Statistics, *Employment, Hours and Earnings, States and Areas, 1972–1987* (Washington, D.C.: U.S. Government Printing Office), Bulletin 2320, 1431–33.

147. Dale A. Hathaway, *Can Workers Have a Voice? The Politics of Deindustrialization in Pittsburgh* (University Park: Pennsylvania State University Press, 1993).

148. Steve Massey, "Economy Leaves Blacks Behind," *Pittsburgh Post-Gazette*, October 18, 1994, 1, 8.

Part 5

APPLYING THE LESSONS OF THE PAST

In the final section of this book, practitioners who are active in labor education and struggles analyze labor's recent history with an eye toward the possibilities for its renewal.

In "Why Unions Matter," Elaine Bernard argues that unions are fundamental to making societies more democratic because they place limits on the vast economic and political powers of employers. This point receives concrete illustration in Irwin Marcus's hundred-year overview of Homestead, Pennsylvania. However, labor's weakness has not only resulted from the strength of corporations but from the organizational form of "business unionism." In this system, union workers' dues have traditionally supported a bureaucracy which provides services to members—but whose agenda and vision generally does not extend to the working class as a whole. However, even on its own terms, business unionism isn't working. Furthermore, business unionism's lack of democracy breeds passivity among unionists whose vigilance and struggle has traditionally been the prerequisite for labor's victories.

James Matles helped to build the social unionism of the 1930s and 1940s. He fought hard to keep the radical spirit of the early Congress of Industrial Organizations alive during the Cold War. Matles looked ahead, with remarkable clarity, to the crisis of the 1970s and 1980s when the New Deal economic and political order would come asunder. His philosophy and tactics for how to rebuild labor's political and economic organization remains timely.

There are signs that a more class-conscious model of unionism is developing. Peter Rachleff argues that the labor movement could be on the verge of a monumental upsurge of militancy. Over the course of the 1980s and 1990s, rank-and-file unionists built innovative organizations and impressive solidarity networks. These new forms of "solidarity unionism" could be the building blocks of the future development of the labor movement.

Many scholars and activists have long looked to Detroit for clues to the future of American workplaces and cities. General Baker analyzes how autoworkers who were once at the center of the American economy have been made redundant by computerized robots. These workers still need homes and food, and their demands for the basic necessities of life could prove a potent new form of labor organizing.

While it is possible that organized labor could continue to decline in numbers and economic or political influence, there are signs that the labor movement is beginning to be revitalized. New organizations in the workplace, community, and political spheres may forge solidarity out of diversity.

17

WHY UNIONS MATTER

Elaine Bernard

W ith the election of a new leadership committed to putting the "movement" back into the "labor movement," now is an important time for reflection on the role of organized labor in our society. We need to bring into open discussion questions that many in the progressive community have been asking: Do unions really matter anymore? And if they do, what should be their mission? Specifically, shall we build a movement simply to represent our own members, or does this movement have a wider role in society as a whole? And does the fate of the labor movement and workers' rights in the workplace concern more than just the ranks of organized labor?

THE WORKPLACE AS AN IMPORTANT SITE FOR ORGANIZING

For too long, there has been an irrational and self-defeating division of duties among progressives in the United States in which unions organize workplaces, while other groups, the so-called social movements and identity groups, organize in the community. Even the term "labor movement" has come to mean simply trade unions, which are supposed to focus on narrowly defined bread-and-butter workplace issues—wages and benefits. This topical and organizational division of turf misleadingly implies that there is an easy division between workplace issues and other social struggles. And that wages and benefits are somehow unifying and other social issues are divisive. These separate spheres of influence have resulted in the sad fact that U.S. progressives often march in solidarity with labor movements and workers around the world, but rarely give a thought to the plight of the working majority here at home.

For activists striving for social and economic justice, the workplace is a crucial environment for organizing. Indeed, it is often already organized, and not only when it is unionized; even nonunion employees tend to share common hours, lunches, and breaks, and most still go every day to a common location. By definition, everyone at the workplace is earning money, so it's a resource-rich community in comparison to many other locations. Much of the production of goods and services occurs there. Decisions of great importance are made and acted upon. It is a place where global capital puts it foot down. And anywhere capital puts its foot down, there is an opportunity for people to act upon it and influence it. For all of these reasons, the workplace is an important location for organizing—and not just for immediate bread-and-butter issues, important as they may be.

DEMOCRACY AND THE RIGHT TO PARTICIPATE VERSUS BENEVOLENT DICTATORSHIP

The work site is also a place where workers learn that they actually have few rights to participate in decisions about events of great consequences to their lives. As power is presently distributed, workplaces are factories of authoritarianism polluting our democracy. Citizens cannot spend eight or more hours a day obeying orders and accepting that they have no rights, legal or otherwise, to participate in important decisions that affect them, and then be expected to engage in robust, critical dialogue about the structure of our society. Eventually the strain of being deferential servants from nine to five diminishes our after-hours liberty and sense of civic entitlement and responsibility.

Thus, the existing hierarchy of employment relations undermines democracy. This is not to suggest that all workers are unhappy, or that all workplaces are hellish. Rather, they are unique locations where we have come to accept that we are not entitled to the rights and privileges we normally enjoy as citizens. Consider how normal it seems that employers, even very progressive employers, when asked how they would feel if "their" employees were to form a union, respond that they would view such an act as a personal rebuke, a signal that they had failed, and a rejection of their management. Consider for a moment, why are such paternalistic attitudes which would be quickly recognized as such in politics, widely accepted in employment relations?

But is the workplace really so autocratic? Why such an extreme characterization? Consider some illustrations of the unique environment, in which the normal rules of our legal system simply do not apply. Citizens are transformed into employees who learn to leave their rights at the door.

Take, for example, a fundamental assumption in our legal system—the presumption of innocence. In the workplace, this presumption is turned on its head. The rule of the workplace is that management dictates and workers obey. If a worker is accused of a transgression by management, there is no presumption of innocence. Even in organized workplaces the rule remains: work first, grieve later. Organized workers protected by a collective agreement with a contractual grievance procedure can at least grieve an unjust practice (or more specifically, one that violates the rights won through collective bargaining). Unorganized workers, on the other hand, are left with appealing to their superiors' benevolence or entering the unemployment line. The implied voluntary labor contract—undertaken by workers when they agree to employment—gives management almost total control of the work relationship. "Free labor" entails no rights other than the freedom to quit without penalty. That's one step up from indentured servitude, but still a long distance from democracy.

There is not even protection in our system against arbitrary and capricious actions by management. There is no right to employment security and no prohibition against unjust dismissal in the private sector such as exists in most other advanced industrial countries. The law of the U.S. workplace is governed by the doctrine of "employment at will." There is some protection to ensure that an employee may not be dismissed for clearly discriminatory reasons of race, gender, disability, or age. But that same employee can be black, female, older, and all or none of the above, and as long as the employer dismisses her for "no reason," the dismissal is legal. Most Americans believe that there is a law that protects them from being fired for "no cause." But that's simply not the case.

CONSTITUTIONAL GUARANTEE OF FREE SPEECH FOR BOSSES BUT NOT FOR WORKERS

The asymmetric application of the First Amendment provides one last illustration of the perverse nature of the workplace regime. Often celebrated as one of the most cherished rights of citizens, freedom of speech does not extend to the workplace, or at least not to workers. A careful reading of the Bill of Rights reveals that First Amendment freedom applies only to the encroachment by government on citizen's speech. It does not protect workers' speech, nor does it forbid the "private" denial of freedom of speech. Moreover, in a ruling that further tilted the balance of power (against workers) in the workplace, the Supreme Court held that corporations are "persons" and therefore must be afforded the protection of the Bill of Rights. So, legislation such as the National Labor Relations Act, or government agencies such as the National Labor Relations Board that seek to restrict a corporate "person's" freedom of speech, is unacceptable. Employers' First Amendment rights mean that they are entitled to hold "captured audience meetings"—compulsory sessions in which management lectures employees on the employers' views of unions. Neither employees nor their unions have the right of response.

Almost as if the work site is not a part of the United States, workers "voluntarily" relinquish their rights when they enter into an employment relationship. So, workers can be disciplined by management (with no presumption of innocence) and they can be denied freedom of speech by their employer. The First Amendment only protects persons (including transnational corporations designated as persons) against the infringement of their rights by government—but not the infringement of rights of real persons (workers) by the private concentration of power and wealth, corporations.

Such limitations on workers' rights are incompatible with the requirements of a democracy. In comparison to European countries, the legal rights of workers in the United States are remarkably limited. For a country that prides itself on individual rights, how can we permit the wholesale denial of those rights for tens of million of American workers?

INDUSTRIAL DEMOCRACY OR AN END TO WORKPLACE CONFLICT?

Few people today remember that when the National Labor Relations Act (NLRA), the cornerstone of U.S. labor law, was adopted by Congress in 1935, its purpose was not simply to provide a procedural mechanism to end industrial strife in the workplace. Rather, this monumental piece of New Deal legislation had a far more ambitious mission: to promote industrial democracy. To achieve this extension of democracy into the workplace, the NLRA instituted "free collective bargaining" between workers and employers. Unions were to be encouraged, as it was understood that workers could not engage in meaningful collective bargaining without collective representation.

Needless to say, it has been a long time since we've heard any president or administration, much less Congress, talk about promoting industrial democracy. In fact, the very term "industrial democracy" seems like a contradiction in terms. While we might not expect politicians to lead the charge for democracy in the workplace and the right of workers to fully participate in workplace decisions, what about organized labor? Has labor been on the defensive so long that they have lost sight of this long-term goal?

While the occasional union document makes a passing reference to "workplace democracy," beyond this brief salute to the cause, there has been little effort by labor in recent years to draw the connection between worker rights in the workplace and the overall struggle of working people for democracy in the United States. Rather than relegating workplace democracy to an abstract long-term goal, labor today needs to tap this source of wider appeal for unions by placing the extension of democracy into the workplace front and center in its vision of a new labor movement and its role in the changing workplace. Fighting for democracy in the workplace, and not simply the right to form unions, is vital to restore the social mission of labor and to return unions to their social-movement heritage. While unions remain a necessary instrument in our society to actualize workplace rights, it is important for unions to lead the charge on the whole antidemocratic workplace regime.

Viewing labor rights as part of a wider struggle for democracy is essential for the growth of the labor movement today. With organized labor down to only 15 percent of the total workforce, and a dismal 11 percent in the private sector, the vast majority of today's workers have no direct experience with unions. But as citizens, they have a concept of democracy and the rights of citizens. Unfortunately, however, American workers are schooled every day at work to believe that democracy stops at the factory or office door. But democracy is not an extracurricular activity that can be relegated to evenings and weekends. The labor movement is the natural vehicle to lead the struggle for basic democratic rights in the workplace.

ASSUMPTION of the NATURAL STATE OF the WORKPLACE—UNION-FREE

Organized labor, of course, has long sought to restore some balance to U.S. labor law, which is currently so stacked against workers that unionization is very difficult everywhere, and almost impossible in some sectors of the economy. Supreme Court decisions rolling back union and worker rights, as well as management-inspired amendments to labor law, have tied the hands of union organizers while freeing management to penalize workers who attempt to exercise their rights.

While the battle to restore "fairness" in labor law is important, even a victory in this campaign would simply bring us back to 1935. We should instead question the basic assumption of U.S. labor law that the natural state of the workplace is union-free with workers having no rights. We need to reestablish among a new generation of workers that one of the key purposes of a union is to bring democratic rights of participation, enjoyed in the rest of society, into the workplace.

In a truly democratic society, all workers would have rights, and collective decision making would be the norm. If workers wished to give up their rights in the workplace, they should be required to demonstrate that they are doing so of their own free will. Yet most of our laws operate in a completely opposite manner. U.S. labor law is largely a series of barriers over which workers must climb to gain elementary rights. And each year these barriers are getting higher and higher. Management can, of course, voluntarily recognize unions or permit workers to participate in decision making, but this is nothing more than a form of benevolence, the granting of privileges which can be retracted at any time—not to be confused with rights which cannot be arbitrarily taken away. Why is the assumption of the law that workers have no rights to participate in workplace decisions? In a democracy would it not make more sense to assume such rights and to apply strict scrutiny to those workers who relinquish their rights rather than those who exercise them?

Seen in this light, even the much-touted right to collectively bargain is a very limited right. Like a hunting license, it does not guarantee anything but an opportunity which may or may not yield results. It should not be confused with actually conferring rights on workers, though it does help workers create a power which can win them rights. With the winning of bargaining rights, workers, through their union, have the right to collectively bargain with the employer, who has a duty to bargain in good faith; however, the employer is under no obligation to come to a settlement.

The authoritarianism of the workplace in the United States diminishes our standing as a democracy. Indeed, in the latter part of this century, instead of the democratization of the American workplace, the hierarchical corporate workplace model is coming to dominate the rest of society.

BEYOND "BREAD-AND-BUTTER" UNIONISM

Unions, as the self-organization of working people for social and economic justice, must play a crucial role in the fight to extend democracy into the workplace. But unions have many roles to play. One crucial function of unions has always been to achieve decent wages and working conditions for their members. With the United States reporting the highest levels of inequality in the advanced industrial world, and the majority of U.S. workers experiencing declining real wages for twenty years, we might be tempted to think that the problems of democracy in the workplace should be put on the back burner for more settled times and that the labor movement should focus only on this growing economic inequality. Yet, the two are linked. Democracy and workers' rights in the workplace are crucial issues for organizing. And without greater levels of organization, inequality is unlikely to decline.

If the aims of unions are, as stated by the AFL-CIO, to "achieve decent wages and conditions, democracy in the workplace, a full voice for working people in society, and the more equitable sharing of the wealth of the nation," then unions must be more than service organizations for their members. Yet, unions cannot meet these admirable goals if they are simply a type of business—"Contracts R Us"—or if they operate merely as a non-profit insurance company seeking to protect its clients/members from unexpected trouble.

There has always been a tension within unions between servicing members and fulfilling the wider social mission of labor to serve the needs of all working people, whether they are organized or not. It is becoming increasingly clear in today's political environment that unions need to do both. Unions, like any organization, will not survive if they do not serve the needs of their members. But unions will not survive and grow if they only serve the needs of their members.

The experience of organized labor in the United States demonstrates that simply delivering for their own members is not sufficient in the long run. Measured in the narrowest sense of delivering for members, U.S. trade unions have been the most "successful" labor movement in the world. Unions won for their members a social wage (benefits such as pensions, health care, paid vacations) that working people in other advanced industrial countries were only able to win through political as well as industrial action. In addition, U.S. trade unionists enjoy the highest wage premium of unionists in any country—that is the difference in pay and benefits between organized workers and the unorganized workers in the same sector.

Thus, if serving the membership was the key to building unions, then the United States should have the highest rate of unionization in the world, not one of the lowest. The low levels of unionization underline the fact that there is a downside to labor's achievement for its members: The higher the wage premium, the greater the employer resistance to unionization. The sad lesson for labor is that by failing to extend the gains made by unions to the rest of working people, these gains have come to be threatened. By comparison, in Canada, where unions have been more successful in socializing the gains first achieved through collective bargaining, from health care to vacation pay, rates of organization are double what they are in the United States. Management resistance to unionization in Canada is less vigorous than in the United States. If management busts a union in Canada, it cannot take away Canadian workers' health care because this benefit has been socialized and is an entitlement of all Canadian residents. By winning benefits first through collective agreements and then extending them to all working people through political action, labor in Canada has not only assisted all working people, but has made its own victory that much more secure.

A second problem for unions in winning benefits only for their own members is that over time this approach has lead to the isolation of unionists from other working people. Unionists are left with little sense of a broad class movement, that includes all workers, organized and unorganized. Unions come to see themselves and their members see them as businesses narrowly servicing members' needs (McDonald's unionism—"We do it all for you"). These attitudes replace a sense of solidarity among members ("An injury to one is an injury to all") with a sense of entitlement ("What's in it for me?"). Members see joining the union as purchasing a service, not participating in a movement for social change.

Thus, this business approach weakens unions and reinforces antiunion, individualistic ideology. And unions eventually lose their ability to mobilize members in their own defense. Ultimately, this approach depoliticizes working people, including union members who start to see unions as simply another "special interest" rather than organizations representing the interests of the vast majority of people—workers.

UNIONS and POLITICS: the PROCESS of CONSTRUCTING the POSSIBLE

For unions to succeed they need to have a wider social vision. Pure and simply, trade unionism is not possible. Most unionists recognize that politics is important to the labor movement and that there is nothing that labor can win at the bargaining table that cannot be taking away by regulation, legislation, or political decision making. It's therefore urgent for organized labor and working people in general to organize on two fronts—politically in the community through political parties and social movements, and industrially in the workplace through unions. Unionists cannot leave politics alone, because politics will not leave unions alone.

To operate effectively in the contemporary political context, the labor movement must understand the challenge that the New Right presents for unions and the rights of working people. At fourteen million members, the labor movement remains the largest multiracial, multi-issue membership organization in the country. As such, it is a prime target of the New Right's assault on working people's rights, both in and out of the workplace.

Politics has always been fundamentally a contest of ideas. Political scientist Robert Dahl has defined politics as "the art of the possible," but for the working person today, it might be more useful to see politics as the process of constructing the possible. In essence, it is the process of deciding which issues warrant a societal response and which are best left to the individual.

The recent debate over health-care reform exemplified this process in politics. The question was whether we should leave this critical service to individuals seeking private solutions through a maze of various insurance plans or whether society as a whole should organize a system of insurance coverage to assure universal comprehensive, affordable, quality coverage for all. The Canadian single-payer system was held up as an example of how the provision of insurance could be socialized, while leaving the practice of medicine private, and assuring complete freedom of choice of doctors. Although we have already socialized health insurance for the elderly through Medicare, many Americans seemed to balk at the prospect of socialized medicine for all. Yet in U.S. history we have often done precisely this—socialized a service—transforming it from an individual responsibility to a community-provided right of all.

The fire department and fire service throughout this country at the turn of the century were private; fire service was an individual responsibility. Those who could afford it, and those who had the most to lose in case of fire, financed private fire companies in their communities. The companies gave their patrons iron plaques which they could post on the outside of their buildings, to assure that in case of fire, that the local fire service would know they were insured and act promptly.

Of course, fire does not confine itself to purchasers of fire service. And while the uninsured could engage in expedited negotiations with the fire service over fees when fire struck, fire spreads easily from the uninsured to the insured, and so it gradually dawned on the insured that the only protection for anyone in the community was to insure everyone. So, the insured sought to socialize the service, that is, extend fire service to everyone—through a universal, single-payer, high-quality, public system. Taxes, rather than private insurance fees, financed the universal system. And the universal system was cheaper and more efficient. The quality was assured because rich and poor alike were covered by the system. Everyone could access the system as needed and everyone paid into the system through their taxes to the community. No doubt, the cynics of the day argued that the poor would take advantage of this social service, or that people would simply not be able to appreciate what they had unless they paid for it.

Through the political process, the problem of fires was moved from the realm of individual concern to collective responsibility. Today, the need for universal fire service seems obvious. Interestingly, the need for health care is still not regarded as a societal right. But that is the essence of the political challenge—to construct what is possible.

THE NEW RIGHT AND THE SUBSTITUTION OF MARKETS FOR SOCIAL DECISION MAKING

Clearly understanding this point, the New Right has a program to construct a new political consensus. In the United States and elsewhere, this program designates virtually all problems as the responsibility of the individual, whose fate is left to the mercy of the market. Former British prime minister Margaret Thatcher summarized this approach succinctly: "There is no such thing as society, only individuals and their families." If there is no such thing as society, then there is clearly no role for government, or indeed collective institution of any sort—including unions. We are thus left with only individuals and their families, working in isolation, making decisions within the narrow context of the market, thinking only of themselves. This program seeks nothing less than the destruction of civil society, without which there can be no democracy.

The market must not be permitted to replace social decision making. Markets have their uses, but they are not to be confused with democratic institutions. Markets, for example, might be useful in determining the price of goods, but they should not be mechanisms for determining our values as a community. Markets are oblivious to morals and promote only the value of profit. To take an example from our own history, a slave market thrived on this continent for over three hundred years. Nor did this market collapse on its own. It took political intervention and armed resistance—in a communal assertion of values—to abolish slavery. Markets are no substitute for the democratic process.

In a democracy, it's "one person, one vote." But in the marketplace, it's "one dollar, one vote," which, despite an appearance of neutrality, is an inherently unjust equation that privileges the rich at the expense of the poor. In such statements as "let the market decide," promoted as principle by the New Right, the market disguises human agency while serving the demands of the wealthy whose dollars shape the rules of the market. According to "free-market" ideology, government intervention is futile at best, and disruptive of the natural order at worst, and always unwelcome (though in practice the New Right uses government shamelessly for its own purposes, e.g., corporate welfare).

The elevation of markets as the sole arbitrator of value deprives people of a sense of belonging to a community. Instead, people feel isolated, which in turn leads to demoralization. If each of us is on our own, none of us can change very much, so we should just accept things as they are. No single individual can answer the big questions in our society. An individual can't opt for single-payer health care, or rapid transit, or address the problems in our public schools. So by default these problems become "unsolvable."

This frightening worldview forces people to seek individual solutions and pits people against one another, reducing social responsibility and cohesion. If there is no such thing as society, then government is a waste, and redistributive programs are robbery. Anything that goes from my pockets into the community is a scam. Worse yet, anything that goes from my pocket makes it just that much harder for me and my family to survive. This is a zero-sum view of society where your gain is my loss, and an injury to one is his problem. And this is the view that will ultimately prevail if the New Right succeeds in its attempt to eviscerate democratic institutions from government to communities to unions.

UNIONS AND CIVIL SOCIETY

By destroying all collective institutions and making government regulation and actions appear to be illegitimate and infringements of individual rights, the New Right is destroying the last vestiges of social solidarity. They are, in essence, expanding the undemocratic regime in the workplace into all aspects of civil society, thus their determination to end entitlement programs and destroy unions.

The labor movement builds communities—that's what unions do. By bringing together workers, who have few rights, who are isolated as individuals and often competing against each other, unions forge a community in the workplace. They help workers understand that they have rights, and they provide a collective vehicle for exercising those rights. Beyond the defense and promotion of individual union members' rights, unions also provide a collective voice for workers. They provide a powerful check to the almost total power of management in the workplace. And they fight for the right of workers to participate in decision making in the workplace.

But labor movements and other communities of common interest don't just happen. They have to be consciously constructed, with a lot of hard work, discussion, and engagement. Constructing democratic communities is an ongoing process, rather like democracy. And like democracy, it's a process that can be rolled back or reversed.

The cause of unions in the twenty-first-century United States reaches far beyond their own survival. Because we have not yet succeeded in extending democracy to the workplace, democracy and civil society themselves are threatened. The labor movement cannot be seen in isolation from the political environment, and any revitalization of unions will require an effective response to that environment. While the New Right tries to reduce everything to an individual responsibility, we must create democratic communities in the workplace and beyond.

18

A CENTURY OF STRUGGLE IN HOMESTEAD

Working-Class Responses to Corporate Power

IRWIN M. MARCUS

In the late nineteenth century the United States experienced an unprecedented transformation from the combined effects of urbanization, immigration, and industrialization. Population grew and wealth increased as the United States became the world's leading economy. At the same time, industry centralized and wealthy capitalists dominated the economic and political spheres. This concentration of power and wealth threatened cherished American ideals and protest movements emerged to condemn this situation and to demand a more egalitarian society. In the 1890s, workers and farmers, who supported the rights of the producers and labor republicanism, used the labor movement, Farmers' Alliances, and populism to democratize America, but industrialists frustrated these efforts. However, periodic protests continued over the next century with the working class playing a pivotal role in these confrontations. For example, a massive strike wave idled millions of workers in 1919 as strikers demanded industrial democracy. They wanted unionization, higher wages, and shorter hours, but they also sought respect, power, and a broader definition of Americanism which would include recent immigrants. Once again, big business, aided by the state, prevailed. The depression era brought a more concerted challenge as industrial workers unionized under the CIO banner. This effort, undergirded by worker agitation, secured collective bargaining as well as wage gains, job security, and improved working conditions, but ownership and investment decisions remained in the owner's hands. Fringe benefits followed in the post–World War II era but signs of danger also became visible. The service sector and the global economy played larger roles in the 1970s and 1980s. In the industrial sector major domestic producers sought state aid, expanded international operations, and closed industrial heartland facilities. They also demanded and received significant concessions as wages and fringe benefits dropped, working conditions deteriorated, and job security atrophied. These developments devastated industrial workers and their families and communities and they reacted by turning to local unions and community groups in the absence of government and national union help.

Homestead, Pennsylvania, provides an excellent case study of these developments because of the crucial roles of the community and its labor force in experiencing industrialization and deindustrialization and mobilizing collective responses to its effects. It played a pivotal role in the rise of Carnegie's iron and steel empire as a producer and the site of the famous Homestead Lockout of 1892. Carnegie and Henry Clay Frick confronted the skilled ironworkers and the Amalgamated Association of Iron and Steel Workers backed by the rest of the labor force, Homestead residents and leaders, and the national worker-farmer protest movement. They triumphed in this labor war as the intervention of the state militia and the judiciary turned the tide in their favor after their foes repulsed the Pinkertons in the first battle. This victory undermined the union and the skilled workers and allowed Carnegie to install a new steel technology, hire many recent immigrants, and create a company town. Carnegie reaped large profits and maintained control, but sporadic opposition, both strikes and political activism, punctuated the next several decades and culminated in the steel strike of 1919. The strikers demanded collective bargaining, shorter hours, and higher wages, but they also sought more respect and recognition. U.S. Steel, Carnegie's successor, won this struggle aided by its own wealth, state aid, and a fragmented labor force. This defeat again undermined effective collective action, but the onset of the Depression produced another resurgence of labor activism. Aided by the Wagner Act and public support, steelworkers mobilized under the banner of the CIO and SWOC. They forged an industrial union which overcame many skill and ethnic barriers and won higher wages, job security, and collective bargaining. After World War II fringe benefit packages became commonplace, but management rights, including control over investment decisions, remained sacrosanct. This issue became important in the 1970s and 1980s as Germany and Japan became leading steel exporters. Major integrated steel companies in the United States virtually ignored the new technologies used by their foreign competitors and instead demanded aid from the state and concessions from workers and turned to diversification rather than reinvestment. These decisions devastated steel towns and caused massive layoffs. In this crisis the steel companies denied their responsibility and the state and the national leadership of the United Steel Workers of America provided little assistance to the unemployed. Some of these workers turned to their local unions and community groups who responded with emergency aid and projects for long-term amelioration. These efforts provided a critique and alternative to the mainstream, as did its predecessors a century earlier. However, corporate power and its state allies controlled and benefited from deindustrialization as Carnegie and Frick and their associates of the later nineteenth century reaped the rewards of industrialization.

In 1883 Carnegie purchased a virtually new Homestead iron facility and undertook a massive expansion program which included installing modern open-hearth furnaces, hydraulic cranes, and electric lighting. While Carnegie made these major investment decisions, the skilled ironworkers continued to exercise considerable autonomy at the work site. They adhered to egalitarian work rules and used their solidarity and the power of the Amalgamated Association of Iron and Steel Workers to obtain high wages and gain employer acceptance of their work code. Though the Amalgamated excluded unskilled laborers, who were usually recent eastern European immigrants, from their ranks, special circumstances, such as industrial accidents, led to temporary solidarity which bridged skill and ethnic divisions. Skilled workers also played prominent roles in the community as they organized picnics, parades, and singing societies. They and their allies not only voted, but held political office. This dual position of strength enabled them to resist an 1889 Carnegie attempt to reduce wages and negotiate individual contracts.

However, Carnegie resented the three-year contract which resulted from the successful strike and sought an opportunity to assert unilateral control and lower labor costs. The purchase of the modern Duquesne facility in 1890 and the shift to steel production improved Carnegie's position. He took advantage of these circumstances by demanding wage concessions and a different contract expiration date. The workers rejected this ultimatum and the Homestead Lockout and Strike of 1892 ensued. Carnegie and Henry Clay Frick, his major partner, prepared for this confrontation by hiring Pinkertons, constructing a fence around their facility, and stockpiling steel. The skilled workers and the Amalgamated also prepared for battle as unskilled workers joined the ranks of the strikers and town residents and political officials offered their support.

Both sides understood the importance of this battle in the struggle over the division of wealth and power in an industrial society. Carnegie and his supporters upheld the inviolate nature of the individual right to own and use private property, which included the employment of nonunion workers. Homestead workers and their allies counterposed the rights of the community and the public good. They linked their struggle for unionism to the preservation of cherished national values such as liberty, independence, and the rule of law. Their rhetoric of labor republicanism and citizen rights had wide appeal, especially after the invasion of the Pinkertons linked the conflict to the preservation of jobs, families, and homes. They depicted corporate power as evil and a threat to the American way of life including the imposition of "wage slavery" and the dependence of the industrial labor force and other producers. Although the strikers generated much support, the wealth and power of Carnegie, combined with his political allies, overwhelmed the workers. Carnegie's triumph provided him with free rein to introduce a new steel technology, hire recent immigrants, and forge a company town.

In the 1890s the Amalgamated conducted several organizing drives and workers protested at the workplace and in the community. Support for the Populist Party and the industrial armies also provided outlets for discontent by residents who sought political and economic changes. Several strikes by the Amalgamated occurred in the early twentieth century, but protest politics provided the major channel for discontent. The presidential candidacy of Eugene Debs in 1912 aroused significant support because of his stand in the Homestead strike of 1892 while others appreciated his integrity, his critique of industrial capitalism, and his advocacy of an egalitarian society. The outbreak of World War I provided new opportunities for advocates of a transformed society. The curtailment of European immigration improved the bargaining position of the labor force which sought a fair share of the productivity gains of the steel industry. For a time the federal government added leverage to their demands as the need for mobilization made the contribution of the industrial labor force more essential. To rally public support, President Woodrow Wilson used a rhetoric focused on democracy and self-determination. The War Labor Board, led by Frank Walsh, gave specificity to his message by supporting labor demands for higher wages and collective bargaining and invoking the term "industrial democracy." This vague but dynamic concept provided a rallying cry for labor leaders and workers in the strike wave of 1919. Millions struck as leading employers and labor battled over the labor-management agenda of the postwar society. Both sides evoked Americanism in behalf of their cause as employers, including Judge Elbert Gary of U.S. Steel, hailed the American plan with its open-shop agenda while labor called for working-class Americanism and industrial democracy.

The American Federation of Labor, the house of labor which included the Amalgamated Association of Iron and Steel Workers, responded to pressure from less-skilled workers and established the National Committee to Organize Iron and Steel Workers under the leadership of John Fitzpatrick and William Z. Foster. This structure included the twenty-four trade unions which claimed jurisdiction in the steel industry and combined craft jurisdiction with elements of de facto industrial unionism. By mid-1919, pressure for a strike intensified as workers experienced renewed discrimination and galloping inflation. Less skilled eastern and southern European workers played the pivotal role in demanding that union leaders set a strike date and seek higher wages, shorter hours, and union recognition.

More than three hundred thousand steelworkers heeded the strike call on September 22 with immigrant workers providing the backbone of the strike and skilled workers, unlike the Homestead Lockout and Strike of 1892, playing a more marginal role. As a result of a systematic campaign by the steel companies, many strikers faced repression and terror as state power reinforced company wealth. The Coal and Iron Police, a poorly disciplined force under the control of corporations, conducted a campaign of violence and intimidation against strikers and their allies which led to mass jailings in a setting of the suppression of civil liberties. The sheriff of Allegheny County swore in thousands of strikebreakers as deputies and forbade outdoor meetings. In Homestead strikers had great difficulty securing a hall to hold meetings because of an ordinance which prohibited meetings conducted in languages other than English. This policy reflected the position of the town elite and local officials who supported U.S. Steel, in contrast to community support for the strikers in 1892. State troopers added to the repression of the strike by clubbing and kicking residents, using their horses to intimidate, and arresting and fining residents for legal activities. The clergy and the press added to the onslaught against the strike, unlike their position in 1892, as most clergy admonished strikers and called on them to return to work and the press carried editorials, articles, and advertisements in support of U.S. Steel and the other steel companies. Pittsburgh newspapers published numerous full-page advertisements featuring Uncle Sam calling on strikers to return to work.

In addition to the power struggle in which the steel companies commanded the advantage of wealth and support from local, state, and federal governments, a rhetorical battle focused around contrasting versions of Americanism ensued. Employers invoked patriotism and the dangers of Bolshevism to elicit public support and divide the strikers. They appealed to skilled, native-born workers and contrasted them with the less affluent, less educated, and less Americanized unskilled, immigrant strikers. In their appeals to the public, steel companies conducted a two-pronged offensive: they appealed to patriotism and offered the American Plan, open-shop approach, as a sound basis for labor-management relations and condemned less-skilled workers and William Z. Foster for radicalism. In hurling the Bolshevism charge, they pinpointed Foster and associated him with the Industrial Workers of the World and syndicalism. Steel strikers and Foster offered a working-class Americanism as a basis for postwar society as they demanded union recognition, an American standard of living, and the rudiments of political and economic democracy. However, the steel companies also won the propaganda battle and by December the steelworkers and the Amalgamated, reeling from the combined effects of internal division, a powerful foe, and state repression, suffered another crushing defeat.

The 1920s brought continued company domination of the workplace and the community although workers gained an eight-hour day in 1923 and the underground economy provided a limited countervailing force to company domination. Nevertheless, the open shop and the Republican Party prevailed and most steelworkers remained excluded from the prosperity of the 1920s. The onset of the Great Depression intensified the problems of Homestead steelworkers as income plummeted with skyrocketing unemployment. However, the election of Franklin D. Roosevelt and the inauguration of the New Deal provided a ray of hope, particularly the passage of the National Industrial Recovery Act of 1933. Section 7A of the law guaranteed workers the rights to organize and bargain collectively and established a board to enforce its provisions.

This legislation sparked major organizing drives among garment workers, coal miners, and steelworkers. In 1933 Homestead steelworkers established a lodge of the Amalgamated Association, the "Spirit of 1892," which recruited a large membership and elected officers. Later in the year an Employee Representation Plan (ERP) also emerged at the Homestead Works. Nevertheless, many Homestead rank-and-filers sought to energize the Amalgamated Association and provide an alternative to the lethargic and conservative national leadership of Michael Tighe. They held district meetings to plan strategy, demanded union recognition, and set a strike date. However, both progressive intellectuals and labor leaders persuaded rank-and-file leaders to seek the support of the Roosevelt administration rather than strike, but this strategy backfired as local membership declined and remained at a local ebb in 1935.

However, 1936 brought major changes on several fronts which improved the position of steelworkers. On July 5, Thomas Kennedy, lieutenant governor of Pennsylvania and a United Mine Workers leader, addressed a rally of local steelworkers, and the Steel Workers Organizing Committee (SWOC), a CIO unit headed by Philip Murray, dispatched organizers and Murray delivered many addresses. An important political development paralleled this labor activism. At the state level, the election of 1934 brought Governor George Earle, Senator Joseph Guffey, and Lieutenant Governor Thomas Kennedy to office and inaugurated a "Little New Deal." In 1936 Homestead voters provided strong support for Franklin Roosevelt, and the following year John McLean became burgess as he defeated John Cavanaugh and his long-entrenched Republican machine. Homestead steelworkers could also take solace from the Lewis-Taylor agreement negotiated in 1937 which provided for U.S. Steel recognition of SWOC and a one-year contract as well as company guarantees on wages, seniority, hours, and a grievance procedure. However, the drive for unionization still required a long, hard struggle by union leaders and organizers. A special "Flying Squadron," dispatched to Homestead by SWOC in March 1937, played a pivotal role in this process. Members talked to workers at the mill and their houses and distributed specially printed appeals to Homestead workers. This concerted drive helped to abate the distrust of unions by these workers, especially members of the ERP. SWOC unionized the Homestead steelworkers in spite of determined company efforts to promote the ERP and to undermine the CIO and SWOC. Antiunion literature distributed by U.S. Steel tried to exploit the fears of Homestead steelworkers about their abandonment by the Amalgamated and the danger of control by dictatorial elements led by John L. Lewis.

Appeals to African American steelworkers also played a role in company strategy, although this tactic proved less effective than in the 1919 strike when racial divisions crippled labor solidarity. A more inclusive policy by the Amalgamated lodges brought more African Americans into the union in the 1930s and helped to pave the way for SWOC. The Urban League, the NAACP, and especially the National Negro Congress lent their support along with black churches and prominent Pittsburgh area black leaders including Ernest Rice McKinney, Homer Brown, and Robert Vann who published the *Pittsburgh Courier*. However, rank-and-file steelworkers and coal miners who became union organizers often secured the most converts with Homestead one of their most fertile territories. Although organizers encountered strong company opposition and some African American steelworkers remained skeptical of SWOC's racial equality promises, the inclusion of contract provisions for higher wages, a seniority system, and a grievance procedure appealed to most African American workers in spite of ongoing discrimination.

SWOC leaders and organizers achieved even more success in unionizing the ethnic labor force, aided by the efforts of ethnic associations, particularly the German Turners Association, the Romanian Beneficial Society, and the International Workers Order. Catholic clergy, especially Father Charles Owen Rice, also played a helpful role in the unionizing drive. Ironically, the campaign allied clergy and Communists in a common struggle on behalf of steelworkers and industrial unionism. The Steel and Metal Workers Industrial Union and the Unemployed Councils spearheaded the Communist effort with the struggle of the unemployed providing a more fertile ground for activism. Unemployed Councils led demonstrations and stopped evictions, provided participants with experience in the power of collective action, and trained future organizers for SWOC.

The CIO and SWOC registered important gains for the labor movement and steelworkers in the late 1930s and early 1940s. Public officials and public opinion became more supportive of labor unions and the working class. Steelworkers made wage gains, secured the protection of unionization, and obtained a grievance procedure and seniority provisions. They also played a role in the rising Democratic Party in the steel towns of the Pittsburgh region. However, without minimizing the important gains steelworkers achieved on the job, in their standard of living, and in the political realm, several limitations of these advances must also be considered. The era of Republican Party hegemony and the leadership of Burgess John Cavanaugh in Homestead ended with the impressive victory of Franklin Roosevelt in the election of 1936; John McLean replaced Burgess Cavanaugh the following year and that started a long-term Democratic Party dominance of local politics. Although the Homestead Democratic Party closely identified with the New Deal, many members, including Burgess Cavanaugh, were recycled Republicans. Union activists didn't play a large role in the Democratic Party, whose leadership came from merchants and professionals. Nevertheless, the political process became more open as some millworkers became office seekers and officeholders, ethnics and the Catholic Church became more active, and some connections emerged between the McLean administration and some African American leaders. At the state level the election of Lieutenant Governor Thomas Kennedy produced a more favorable climate for workers and the labor movement in the state government and built on the gains secured by Governor Gifford Pinchot who placed some limits on the coal and iron police and on the issuance of injunctions. Earle made some gains for labor through his "Little Fireside Chats," although the Republican-controlled state senate stymied enactment of his "Little New Deal."

At the national level, the Roosevelt administration and the Congress gave more support to labor than the national government of the 1920s. The passage of the National Industrial Recovery Act, especially section 7A, gave labor solace and support and contributed to a burgeoning of the industrial labor movement. The legislation energized the organizing drives of autoworkers, coal miners, and steelworkers and contributed to labor ferment in Homestead. However, the obstacles to unionization and civil liberties proved formidable as Burgess Cavanaugh's administration prevented U.S. Secretary of Labor Frances Perkins from getting a permit for a labor meeting in September 1933, so she had to speak on post-office property. While contemporaries and historians view the hearings held by the La Follette Committee on workers and civil liberties as valuable to labor in exposing illegal employer tactics, the results of the National Labor Relations Act are more controversial. The legislation recognized organized labor as a collective entity which deserved state protection and this shield aided workers in achieving some important gains in wages and protection against discriminatory practices by employers. Nevertheless, large companies retained the upper hand with wide latitude for the exercise of management rights, while workers and unions remained in a subordinate, but upgraded position.

Steelworkers and SWOC soon faced a new set of issues, however, as war clouds hovered over Europe and Asia by the end of the 1930s and Franklin Roosevelt shifted his priorities from the New Deal to mobilization for war. Most major, national labor leaders strongly supported the war effort and signed "no strike" pledges for the duration of the conflict. In exchange, the federal government aided the labor movement by pressuring recalcitrant employers such as Ford and Bethlehem Steel to accept unionization in order to be eligible for lucrative defense contracts. The federal government also supported maintenance of membership clauses in collective bargaining agreements. This provision enlarged union membership and treasuries. However, World War II produced a mixed picture for the labor force with white men making the largest strides, and blacks and women securing some advances in employment opportunities and wages. Unemployment tumbled and money wages rose, buoyed by overtime, but the "Little Steel Formula" placed a cap on wage gains and the burgeoning labor movement, including the United Steel Workers of America (the new name for SWOC), became more centralized and bureaucratized and the distance between national leaders and the rank-and-file increased. In addition, the bonds between the Democratic Party and the state and the labor movement tightened, workers and the labor movement lost some independence, and the sphere for their own initiatives constricted.

Homestead workers and residents experienced another facet of the new order as the federal government selected the Homestead Works of U.S. Steel for the nation's largest wartime expansion of a steelmaking facility, which included an open-hearth plant as well as a slabbing mill, a sheared-plate mill, and a forge shop. These additions stimulated increasing profits, production, and employment, but carried a high cost. Businesses, churches, and homes in the ward were destroyed and over fifteen hundred families, nearly one-half of Homestead's population, were uprooted. Homestead residents viewed this displacement in diverse ways. Advocates of modernization saw it as slum clearance which benefited the borough financially and upgraded the quality of life. African Americans and ethnics, who bore the brunt of the displacement, stressed the costs of community destruction.

The new power of national labor leaders, including Philip Murray of the United Steel Workers of America (USWA), increased the gap between the rank-and-file and labor union heads, but a common interest in production and patriotism in the World War II era created strong bonds of unity. At Homestead, production for war took priority, but black workers protested, nevertheless, and won some concessions. By the end of the war many workers became more vocal in their opposition to lagging wages, the no-strike pledge, and the high profits and the high salaries of major companies and their executives. Workers responded to these grievances with wildcat strikes in which Homestead workers participated. In 1946 almost 800,00 steelworkers struck for a fair share of the wealth they produced, including members of Local 1397. Homestead workers benefited from an elaborate planning system coordinated by Elmer Kish, chairman of strike preparations, who organized an intricate picketing system, obtained support from sympathetic women and other allies, and coordinated rallies. The strike attracted support from local merchants and politicians. However, the red scare changed the character of the labor movement as Elmer Kish and other local activists lost their union offices and the major industrial unions, including the USWA, became more conservative. These developments not only deprived labor unions of some of their strongest supporters of workers, women, and black rights but robbed the labor movement of individuals capable of raising questions about rights and power, the responsibilities of corporations to host communities, and the rights of workers to participate in discussions that involved their lives in the wake of deindustrialization and the flight of manufacturing jobs. Some steelworkers suburbanized and purchased consumer durables, but many blacks and women lost some of their limited World War II gains as veterans reclaimed many industrial jobs while women returned to the home or the underpaid pink-collar sector.

The end of World War II left the United States as the dominant power in the world and the only major nation with a viable economy. For more than two decades the United States held this special position as it accumulated vast wealth, pursued suburbanization, and shifted its economy from an industrial to a service sector base. These developments affected Homestead steelworkers as they witnessed a rising national standard of living in which they participated to a limited extent and a change in the geographical focus of the steel industry. The Chicago-Gary area, which produced steel for the burgeoning automobile industry, improved its relative position compared to the Mon Valley. In the 1950s the USWA conducted frequent strikes to reinforce its position and to secure wage and fringe benefits gains for its membership.

Fringe benefits gains continued in the 1960s, but the basic wage of the steelworkers provided a limited income. Steelworkers faced a mixed picture in the 1970s as fringe benefits improved and the average hourly earnings grew, but employment became a major problem for many steelworkers. The standard-of-living situation had demographic implications for the population of steel towns and the process of suburbanization. Homestead lost much of its population base, beginning with the mill expansion of the 1940s. However, union officers at the Homestead Works usually lived in Homestead or a nearby industrial town, as did most Homestead mill employees. These workers did not join the suburbanization process of the 1950s and their participation in suburbanization was limited and late.

The unemployment crisis which struck the Mon Valley in the late 1970s and 1980s had its roots in national and international developments in the 1960s and 1970s. In the two decades following the end of World War II the United States dominated the world economy and the production and profits of big American companies benefited from this unique situation. Some unionized workers also derived some gains from the wealth generated by economic growth and steelworkers won wage and fringe benefit improvements. However, unchallenged dominance bred a sense of complacency in businessmen and political leaders. This attitude contributed to the growing economic problems which faced the United States after 1965. Japanese and German steel producers built well-located modern facilities equipped with state-of-the-art technology while our corporate executives responded much more cautiously to breakthroughs in steel-production technology. By the late 1960s these conditions enabled them to dominate their domestic markets and to become major exporters to the United States. To counter this growing crisis, steel company executives sought government aid and demanded lower labor costs. By the late 1970s Youngstown experienced a wave of plant closings and the Mon Valley followed in the 1980s.

These international developments had implications for national labor leaders and steelworkers as well as steel company executives. The labor-management environment in the steel industry changed in the aftermath of the lengthy 1959 strike as workers secured some wage and fringe benefit gains and labor leaders won some recognition from their corporate counterparts in exchange for a strike-free environment. In return for these advances, the workers and the union accepted management rights and acted jointly with management to increase productivity and limit imports. These informal arrangements received more formal recognition in the Experimental Negotiating Agreement of 1973 which forbade strikes, but provided workers with cost-of-living allowances and a bonus. This agreement and the centralized national leadership of the union produced some dissatisfaction from workers and activists, many of whom belonged to a new generation of steelworkers influenced by the protest movements of the 1960s and 1970s.

Young workers, often better educated and more independent than the older generation, resented the dictatorial methods on the shop floor and the unresponsive national union leadership, helped to build pockets of resistance, and rallied around the candidacy of Ed Sadlowski in the 1977 presidential election. Sadlowski founded Steel Workers Fight Back and conducted a strong, but unsuccessful campaign against Lloyd McBride focused on the union democracy issue. A core of activists emerged in Homestead who viewed the Experimental Negotiating Agreement as undermining the shop-floor power of steelworkers, who witnessed the closing of Open Hearth 4 in

1974 and who disagreed with the policies of the incumbent local leadership. The Sadlowski campaign provided the dissidents with an opportunity to try to democratize their local as they reached out to the membership with leaflets, fund-raisers, and a newspaper. Activists built solidarity at rallies which protested against the closing of the Youngstown mills and won election as delegates to the convention of the USWA in 1976 where they advocated union democracy. Ron Weisen, elected as a delegate and later a Sadlowski supporter, became president of Local 1397 in 1979 as he and his running mates unseated the incumbents and became effective champions of the increasingly embattled Homestead workers, devoting particular attention to white men, who dominated the membership of the local.

Pressure from the civil rights movement and the women's movement temporarily diversified the labor force of heavy industry in the 1970s as more women became steelworkers. The wages, fringe benefits, and unionization features of steel industry employment attracted some women. The passage of the Civil Rights Act of 1964 and the creation of the Equal Employment Opportunity Commission (EEOC), which had the major responsibility for enforcement of the equal opportunity provisions, began the long process which culminated in the hiring of more female steelworkers. Initially, the commission focused on racial discrimination, but under pressure from the National Organization for Women and other women's rights groups, gender discrimination received increasing attention, culminating in a Justice Department consent decree in 1974 which benefited women and African Americans. The agreement provided compensation for victims of discrimination and changed seniority arrangements and other discriminatory practices. Especially in communities with limited employment opportunities for women, such as Homestead, steel employment offered an attractive alternative to lower-paying, traditional female-sector employment. Ironically, however, these gains proved ephemeral as deindustrialization caused widespread unemployment and female steelworkers, lacking seniority, suffered layoffs less than a decade after winning their long struggle. In the face of this adversity, little aid was forthcoming as the Reagan and Bush administrations had other priorities, the national leadership of the United Steelworkers of America lacked an adequate response to the crisis, and even local unions and community groups in the Mon Valley which responded to other aspects of deindustrialization failed to address the problems of former female steelworkers. Under these circumstances these workers depended on their own initiative and resources, the aid of family and friends, and female networks. Their plight paralleled the situation of female workers in nontraditional jobs such as coal miners, autoworkers, and the building trades.

African American men became an important presence in the steel industry in the early twentieth century, but ongoing discrimination led them to turn to protest and federal government aid in the 1960s and 1970s along with aspiring female steelworkers. World War II opened jobs for black steelworkers in Western Pennsylvania and in 1944 they comprised 14 percent of the mill employees. However, by 1950 their proportion of the labor force fell to half that figure and they continued to suffer from a disproportionate concentration in unskilled and semiskilled occupations with little opportunity for promotion. Philip Murray and the other national leaders failed to respond to this pattern of discrimination in the 1950s. As a result of this indifference at the national and local levels of the union, some black workers took the initiative. For example, Albert Everett, a black steelworker, addressed a meeting of Local 1397 in Homestead and condemned leaders of the local for their hostility to the promotion of blacks and their reluctance to submit the grievances of black steelworkers. The Fair Share Group of Steelworkers emerged at the same time and wrote to David McDonald and to George Meany to protest the neglect of the problems of black workers by national labor leaders. However, the passage of the Civil Rights Act of 1964 and the creation of the EEOC provided black workers with a weapon to pressure recalcitrant company officials and union leaders. Some improvements occurred in the late 1960s, but discrimination persisted and black steelworkers and their allies turned to the federal government for assistance. This initiative resulted in a 1974 consent decree in which steel companies and the union acknowledged their discriminatory practices, agreed to change seniority arrangements and other restrictive practices, and the steel companies compensated victims of past discrimination. In the late 1970s blacks made significance gains in the steel industry, but the massive layoffs of the 1980s turned their triumph into a Pyrrhic victory. Their suffering elicited no more positive responses from the government, the industry, and the labor movement than did the similar plight of women workers.

Weisen and his slate won office when steel company executives sought lower labor costs by curtailing production, laying off workers, and combining jobs in an era of "concessions" bargaining. Homestead workers experienced job eliminations and job combinations as well as reduced wages and lower fringe benefits. These developments placed tremendous pressures on the standard of living and a way of life of Homestead residents. The community had been characterized by high levels of residential stability; a strong sense of neighborhood; and close family, ethnic, and church ties. The rising tide of unemployment caused problems for local high school graduates seeking a secure job and unemployed steelworkers confronting monthly mortgage payments. Increasing health problems and declining social services added to the woes of residents. Corporate officials disclaimed responsibility for the effects of their decisions and politicians and national labor leaders provided little tangible aid. This emergency left unemployed steelworkers searching for other avenues of assistance.

Local 1397 provided an important local response to the crisis with a variety of programs and initiatives designed to aid the unemployed and their families. Ron Weisen began publicizing the plight of the unemployed and its causes and condemned U.S. Steel for using overtime to eliminate jobs and taking advantage of widespread job insecurity to impose unsafe working conditions and overbearing supervisors on the steelworkers who remained at work. He called on the company to finance the modernization of the Homestead Works rather than spend billions to purchase Marathon Oil. Weisen also condemned the district and national leadership of the union and made two unsuccessful runs for the leadership of District 15. He indicted Lloyd McBride, president of the USWA, for his failure to aid laid-off steelworkers. On the other hand, Local 1397 gave a high priority to programs which aided the unemployed and their families including a variety of fund-raisers, a food bank which distributed food to the unemployed, and a job bank which matched the unemployed seeking part-time employment with community residents who needed workers.

New community organizations also emerged to aid residents in confronting the crisis by offering an explanation of these developments, emergency assistance, and a program for the future: The Denominational Ministerial Strategy, the Mon Valley Unemployed Committee, and Tri-State Conference on Steel. The Denominational Ministerial Strategy was composed of a core of Protestant ministers who specialized in research on the Pittsburgh economic elite and dramatic direct actions which captured media attention, especially the Mellon Bank campaign. The ministers, mostly Lutheran clergy, indicted the region's power elite for practicing corporate evil by using profits, rather than Christian principles, as a basis for investment decisions. This indictment brought a counterattack from the elite which undermined the ministers' funding sources and applied pressure which eventually led to their removal from the pulpit. The ministers reacted to this campaign by redirecting their assault away from business power centers and concentrating on the churches. This move cost them the support of sympathetic local labor leaders, including Ron Weisen, and public opinion and contributed to their increasing marginalization and the eventual demise of their organization. The Mon Valley Unemployed Committee followed a different path which focused on responding to the emergencies facing unemployed steelworkers and their families. It won extended unemployment compensation, expanded food banks, and renegotiated mortgage payments for the unemployed. Initially, its organizers mobilized the unemployed who held demonstrations which frightened politicians and produced some limited initiatives from the political system. However, they shifted their tactics to working within the system through lobbying and responding to individual complaints received on their hot line. The Tri-State Conference on Steel, which grew out of the crisis resulting from the steel plant closings in

Youngstown and the threat of layoffs in the Mon Valley, brought together activists, clergy, and workers in a campaign to revitalize the Mon Valley steel industry. Their plan proposed the use of eminent domain to acquire property to restart steel facilities. The steel produced in the plants would be used to construct infrastructure facilities and to build mass-transit vehicles including the experimental Maglev train. The campaign to save Dorothy Six, the Duquesne blast furnace, generated widespread grassroots support and extensive publicity. However, the results of a detailed feasibility study doomed this project in 1985 because of the need for massive expenditures. The South Side electric furnace project, a later undertaking to restart part of the Jones and Laughlin steel facility in Pittsburgh, suffered the same fate, but generated some public and political support during the campaign. Nevertheless, the leaders of the Tri-State Conference on Steel could take solace in the pivotal role which they played in the creation of the Steel Valley Authority (SVA), the hosting of numerous conferences on deindustrialization and reindustrialization, and the establishment of the City Pride Bakery.

The SVA was founded in 1986 to provide a mechanism for regional economic development modeled on the Tennessee Valley Authority. It sought to prevent the destruction of jobs and factories by using the power of eminent domain to give communities and workers a voice in how capital should be invested in the Pittsburgh area. The City Pride Bakery project mobilized a worker/community coalition to provide jobs and bread while providing a model for revitalizing industrial communities. The model featured a tripartite ownership structure composed of private ownership, worker ownership, and community ownership. By the early 1990s activists and workers could take pride in this project to reshape the local economy. The temporary success of this small project, which provided several hundred jobs, owed much to the efforts of Tom Croft, executive director of the SVA. Croft also sought to retain the regional manufacturing base by developing an early warning system which spurred communication with management and workers at troubled companies. Most recently, the SVA has embarked on a major new initiative, the sustainable Manufacturing Project, which seeks to attract new firms to brownfield sites—previously occupied industrial sites—in the Mon Valley.

In spite of these local and regional initiatives, Homestead steelworkers faced difficult times in the late 1980s. By the mid-1980s it was clear that the steel mills would never reopen and communities such as Homestead faced unemployment rates of 25 percent and the exhaustion of both unemployment benefits and supplemental unemployment benefits. On July 25, 1986, the Homestead Works closed and changed the nature of Homestead. Families broke up, houses deteriorated, and less affluent residents moved into town. Despair became more common as the potholes remained unrepaired and the tax base fell. As poorer people moved into the town, violence, drug abuse, and robbery became more commonplace. Stores along Eighth Avenue, such as Woolworth's and W. T. Grant, closed while Goodwill and other thrift shops opened. Despair affected the young as well as adults and some pupils turned to drinking and drugs. Students lacked big dreams and only a handful of Steel Valley High School pupils talked about going to a four-year college, while many students decided to enter military service. The school system suffered from declining funds which led to a smaller faculty, the elimination of drama and music programs, and extra teaching assignments for the faculty. Declining revenues also undermined town services as the park maintenance and street paving were neglected. Church attendance declined and few young people went to church. In late 1988 Local 1397's union hall closed, ending an era; now there was no union in Homestead. By 1990 signs of decline and decay proliferated. The 1990 census recorded a town population of less than 4,200 residents, a decline of almost one thousand since the last census. Other markers of deterioration included the closing of the borough building and the closing of the last Roman Catholic school in Homestead. The Park Corporation, which purchased the Homestead Works, destroyed the old mills.

The tragedy of Homestead attracted interest from organizations hoping to redevelop Homestead and preserve its historic sites. Plans from the federal government and the Pittsburgh elite focused on a museum and a park, a Mon Valley highway, and exhibition halls. These plans had little chance of implementation and local activists had a different vision for the valley. They wanted revitalized steel mills and jobs. The destruction of the mill and the town ended America's heavy industrial era with a community and a way of life in ruins. The corporation proved too powerful for the communities, activists, and workers to overcome. However, the destruction of Homestead played out against a background of complaint and new initiatives for worker and community empowerment.

In the past century two major changes, with vast economic and societal repercussions, transformed American society. Industrialization enhanced the wealth of the country, while raising questions about decision making and wealth distribution. The deindustrialization of many former industrial heartlands devastated many communities and created a bipolarized service sector and undermined the regional standing of the North, the East, and the Middle West. At the same time, corporate giants diversified and sought good business climates, low labor costs, and supportive government policies inside and outside the national borders.

The steel industry played a pivotal role in both developments with the Mon Valley, especially Homestead, an important element in this process. Homestead, along with Braddock and Duquesne, provided the keystone of the Carnegie empire. In the 1890s the shift from iron to steel production contributed to Carnegie's success in establishing production and unilateral control over decision making and garnering the lion's share of the wealth in the aftermath of his victory in the Homestead Lockout of 1892. This triumph owed much to his wealth and determination, but the aid of the state and the power of the dominant ideology also played pivotal roles. The struggle at Homestead paralleled other major battles of the 1880s and 1890s as workers and other producers offered alternative conceptions of the good society focused on mutual aid, economic justice, and democracy, and fought for their realization. They turned to labor unions, politics, and community groups, but the superior wealth and power of the business elite overwhelmed their efforts.

Although this elite maintained its control over the next century, periodic challenges to its hegemony emerged, particularly the candidacy of Eugene Debs in 1912 and the steel strike of 1919. Beginning in the 1930s, critics of industrial capitalism built buffers which provided a modicum of protection to industrial workers to secure limited portions of the wealth which they created. Using the federal government, the USWA, and the Democratic Party, they won higher wages, fringe benefits, and some political power. However, new international economic conditions emerged in the 1970s with the reindustrialization of Germany and Japan, the fuel crisis, and the focus on defense expenditures and high technology. Faced by rising imports and competition from minimills, the leading integrated steel companies diversified and sought aid from the government, the union, and workers rather than building new facilities and introducing the new steel technology. These tactics failed to deal with the crisis and by the late 1970s and early 1980s massive layoffs and plant closings became commonplace for many steel companies and workers. This policy resulted in industrial devastation and human tragedies steelworkers and their families suffered.

Facing despair, steelworkers in Homestead received little solace and support from U.S. Steel, the Reagan and Bush administrations, and even the national leadership of the USWA. This lack of national initiative left the responsibility to respond to the crisis to the limited community resources. Local unions and community organizations condemned this indifference and offered an alternative value system based on mutual aid and social justice as well as innovative survival and economic and community reconstruction programs. Homestead, following the lead of Youngstown, built a vigorous grassroots movement with support from Local 1397, sympathetic clergy, and activists, unlike most steel towns which failed to mount a strong response and left conservative forces in complete charge. The community groups built some public support, publicized the human trauma of deindustrialization, and formulated alternative plans and the SVA. They also provided emergency aid and pursued direct action. Nevertheless, the power and wealth of the steel companies, state support, and cultural hegemony determined the outcome. Unlike some industrial nations experiencing similar traumatic changes, the United States provided relatively little aid to displaced workers and afflicted communities and regions. These options and the alternatives proposed by dissident groups in the United States remained virtually unexplored by politicians and historians unwilling to challenge the dominant institutions and values of the society.

Brief Bibliographical Essay on Deindustrialization and Historians

Industrialization became a vital element in the creation of our national wealth and power in the late nineteenth century. However, even as the steel, auto, and petroleum industries undergirded our growing national economic base, other industrial sectors such as the New England textile industry, the New Jersey textile industry, and the anthracite coal industry suffered setbacks. This process continued in the early twentieth century as the Gary-Chicago region steel complex replaced the Pittsburgh area as the hub of the steel industry. Deindustrialization accelerated and expanded in the post–World War II era as part of the transformation of the American and world economies. A new global economy emerged and the service and high-technology sectors became dominant features of the domestic economy and labor force. Journalists, social scientists, and policy analysts have described and analyzed the nature and effects of recent deindustrialization. Nineteen ninety-five was a big year for recognition of the deindustrialization issue by journalists, although their articles focus on downsizing and pay particular attention to the effects of economic changes on white-collar workers and middle-level managers. The *New York Times* and the *Christian Science Monitor* published a series of articles on the topic and the *Atlantic Monthly, Foreign Affairs,* and *Harper's* featured articles on the state of the American economy. However, historians, until very recently, have seldom studied this topic although their scholarship on industrialization has been illuminating and the presence of a historical context is vital to understanding the process and consequences of deindustrialization and the alternatives available to the public and policy makers.

Historians of Europe have been somewhat more willing to describe deindustrialization as a long-term process, most notably Christopher H. Johnson, *The Life and Death of Industrial Languedoc, 1700–1920: The Politics of Deindustrialization* (New York: Oxford University Press, 1995). Bryan D. Palmer, a Canadian history scholar, has also made an important contribution in his book, *Goodyear Invades the Backcountry: The Corporate Takeover of a Rival Town* (New York: Monthly Review Press, 1994). Historians of the United States in the twentieth century usually neglect this topic with John Cumbler's valuable book the major exception (John Cumbler, *A Social History of Economic Decline: Business, Politics and Work in Trenton* [New Brunswick, N.J.: Rutgers University Press, 1989]) along with George Lipsitz, *Rainbow at Midnight: Labor and Culture in the 1940s* (Urbana: University of Illinois Press, 1994); Mike Davis, *City of Quartz: Excavating the Future in Los Angeles* (New York: Verso, 1990); and Robin D. G. Kelley, *Race Rebels: Culture, Politics and the Black Working Class* (New York: Free Press, 1994). Several other very recent developments indicate some awakening of interest in this topic. Walter Licht and Thomas Dublin delivered papers at the North American Labor History Conference (1995) and the American Historical Association Conference (1996) on the decline of the anthracite coal industry and Thomas J. Sugrue published a very suggestive article on deindustrialization and the auto industry of the early 1950s (Thomas J. Sugrue, "Forget About Your Inalienable Right to Work: Deindustrialization and Its Discontent at Ford, 1950–1953," *International Labor and Working-Class History* [fall 1995]: 112–30).

19

THE ROLE OF LABOR TODAY

Reflections on the Past Throw Light on the Road Ahead

JAMES J. MATLES

INTRODUCTION[1]

At the Thirty-Ninth UE International Convention, in 1974, James J. Matles had announced that he would not seek reelection as the union's general secretary-treasurer, an office he had held since 1962, following the death of Julius Emspak. Prior to that he served as the union's first director of organization.

When he addressed the Fortieth International Convention his remarks were selected and shaped by the fact that it would be the last time he addressed a convention as an officer of the union.

As was his custom, he spoke without prepared text. He looked back over the thirty-eight years he had served as a UE officer and the more than two-score years he has been involved in the struggles of the working people of America.

It was a brief summing up with touches of humor and nostalgia to season the sharp insights developed in those years—lessons from the past to give guidance for the future.

No one could know it was to be his last address to any UE members.

From *The Role of Labor Today* (pamphlet). ©1976 United Electrical, Radio, and Machine Workers of America. Reprinted by permission.

Five days later, Jim Matles was dead of a sudden heart attack. He had just finished talking with workers at a UE organizing meeting.

He had died as he lived—in the heart of the struggle to bring a better life to working people. His farewell speech does not probe the depths of that struggle, nor his role in it, but it does touch both most effectively.

Mr. Chairman, Brothers and Sisters, Friends: You have elected me thirty-eight times. Before I talk about some of my own personal reflections, I want to talk a little about what this convention is all about and the situation we are facing.

During the past several months I have attended a number of district council meetings and a number of local meetings. And those of you who were present at those meetings know that I have raised some questions of a nature that are, by far, more serious than the questions we officers of the union have raised with you for many years.

Our country is in the deepest trouble. I have spent my time, the time that I could spare during the past year, in trying to find out what has brought this about, and I have been reading what some of the chief corporate executives of this country have to say about our corporate profits system.

I felt it would be helpful in meeting our problem, to know what the other side is thinking and saying.

I say to you today, as I have in a number of the district meetings recently, I haven't heard the kind of discussions coming from the corporate executives of this country today since the Thirties when many of them were scared to death that this setup may go down the drain.

THE THIRTIES AND FDR

When we look back to the Thirties we often think about Franklin D. Roosevelt. We think of FDR sometimes as the savior of our people, the great humanitarian. It is true, Roosevelt was not Tom Girdler of Republic Steel who had the strikers shot down in Chicago. No, FDR was not that kind of a man. He was what you would call a liberal man.

But Franklin D. Roosevelt did represent the corporate interests in America and he knew that the setup was in trouble. He knew that the policies and actions of Herbert Hoover and Wall Street were running it into the ground. He knew and understood the trouble that was boiling in America and the rebellion that was arising in America and that you couldn't settle it with guns, as Hoover was doing—shooting down the veterans and the hunger marchers.

Roosevelt knew that this system had to make concessions in order to save itself, and he proceeded on a course to do just that, to save the corporate system in America. But most of the bosses were too dumb to realize what he was doing for them. They were too dumb to appreciate it.

THE NEW DEAL

But he saved the system. Yes, under the pressure of the millions, he gave ground. He put through some of the outstanding labor and social legislation of our time: the minimum wage and hour law, the Wagner Act, unemployment compensation, social security. Not since those early years of the New Deal have we seen a single gain of special importance to the working people and to the people of America. Not one significant piece of social legislation of the same magnitude.

When the system was saved, they clamped down again.

Yes, we have made progress, the working people have made progress in forty years. They made progress but for every bit of progress they made they had to drag the system along, kicking and scratching and screaming all the time. Not a single concession was made willingly; no matter what the working people have done for the system, not a single concession.

THE "SYSTEM" IN TROUBLE AGAIN

And so today, following the discussion by the top executives of corporate interests in America, reading every word that I could, I have found that they concluded as far as a year ago that the corporate system is running out of money. Don't laugh. They say that the corporate system must get $4.5 trillion. A trillion is one thousand billion. They say that unless that's done, this system cannot be saved.

While they say they are running out of money, nine million people are running out of bread and butter. And their answer to that is: "If we get the money, eventually some of it is going to trickle down to the people."

That's what Hoover said. That's what Herbert Hoover said. That's where we came in. That's where we came in.

SAME CRISIS—SAME SLOGANS

Twenty-six million people still live in poverty in America. Sure we have made progress, but we again face the same crisis and hear the same empty slogans.

The unemployment that we are having is not temporary and the growing pool of unemployed will continue to grow.

I confronted an executive of a corporation and I asked him, "Is it reasonable to assume that the corporations in America expect that, when this recession eases and production starts climbing up again, that you expect to put out as much work as you have put out before this recession started with 20 or 25 percent fewer workers than were in those plants before?"

He didn't say yes, but neither did he say no. And I firmly believe that's the plan. That's the plan.

They say we are suffering from a consumer society. That's a fancy way of saying that the people have too much. They say we have to transfer over to a capital accumulation society. That can be done in two ways: fewer workers in the shop and increased productivity, and the reduction of taxes for the corporations—reduction of taxes for the corporations, a greater burden on those who remain working.

PLAN BURDEN FOR THE PEOPLE

You didn't hear them raise any cry about [needing to go] from thirty-nine weeks to fifty-two weeks of unemployment benefits. When we went from twenty-six to thirty-nine, this union started the fight for thirty-nine weeks, believe it or not. This union went to Washington and at that time the Speaker of the House was Congressman McCormick. This union went there. And this union started to push for the thirty-nine weeks.

The Speaker of the House heard about it for the first time from us. And he said, "I'll try, I will see. I think you boys have something, you know."

You know, nobody else started that, but the NAM [National Association of Manufacturers] fought it, the Chamber of Commerce fought it, industry fought it. Why didn't they fight the fifty-two weeks? Why didn't they fight the sixty-five weeks?

They didn't because they figured that that's a small enough price to pay. In fact they've got it figured out so they're not going to pay at all. The working people who still have jobs will pay the bill, and when unemployment compensation runs out, those that remain working will pay the welfare. Instead of tax reform there will be more favorable tax laws for the corporations so that they can get this $4.5 trillion during the next ten years. That's what they are saying.

This being the case—and in our judgment it is—we are in for the most difficult days ahead.

That's where the corporations stand today.

THE LABOR MOVEMENT

Now we have to address ourselves to the shape of the labor movement. If the CIO was not split. If the CIO was not wrecked by the corporations and their flunkies in Congress, and if the labor leadership had not caved in and crawled on its belly, this country would be in different shape today.

For one thing, by this time we would have a labor party in America. That's what we would have had. (Applause)

When we started to organize GE and Westinghouse, there was an entrenched company union in Schenectady and an entrenched company union in East Pittsburgh. Today we have two great big company unions in America: A Republican union and a Democratic company union. That's a new standard. (Applause)

A COMPANY UNION IS A COMPANY UNION

And in answer to those who say one company union is better than the other, let me tell you what happened to me in my first shop meeting in the shop I worked when we started to organize. The president of my local union, Joe Wild, of the Machinists, was in the chair, and one of the fellows got up to make a report—we were making reports on what's going on in the shop as to how we were organizing. And he said, "We got a rough time. We got a lousy foreman in my department."

And I got up—I didn't talk too well then; didn't know how to talk English at all, I don't know it much better now—and I said, "Mr. Chairman, we have a good foreman in my department."

And he said, "Son, when you learn how to speak English better, you won't say that. You will say, 'My foreman is not as lousy as the other one.' That's what you will say." (Applause)

Don't let anyone get up and talk about one company union being better than the other. They are all lousy. Here and there you have a company union official in one state—he may be a Republican or a Democrat— who doesn't cut your throat quite as much as the other one. At least he hides it better.

POLITICAL ACTION VERSUS PLAYING POLITICS

Joe Borgia asked me at a district meeting—he's head of the legislative committee of District 6—he said: "What's the trouble with our political action?"

My answer to that was, there is a difference between political action and playing politics. When we fought the politicians and we won that legislation we did, we didn't play politics; we engaged in political action. We didn't rub bellies with politicians. There was plenty of air between us. You could see the light. You could see light all the time. Today try and find some air and light between the bellies of the labor leaders and the bellies of the politicians. No go. You won't find it. They are playing politics. (Laughter and applause)

In 1947 while the Taft-Hartley Bill was before Congress, the three officers—Emspak, Fitzgerald, and I—went into the CIO executive board, and we had the unmitigated gall to propose, while the bill was still going through Congress, that the CIO recommend to all affiliated unions that they take a referendum to shut it down. Take a vote first. Do it in a democratic way, but shut down every plant in the country.

NEED FOR GENERAL STRIKE

The CIO could have shut it down. The people would have voted to shut it down. But we were told that that would be a political strike against the government of the United States. That's what we were told.

And when the wage freeze came from Nixon in 1971 and the labor leaders crawled in to serve on their wage and price board, and we spoke out and we said, "Don't go on that board. Let's go to the rank and file. Let's make a recommendation. Let the AFL-CIO executive council for once in its life make a recommendation to the affiliated unions to take a vote and recommend they shut it down in protest."

And, again, we were told that that's a political strike against the government of the United States.

Now we are face to face with a question of nine million unemployed, and some news reporters asked George Meany: "Is the labor movement going to take some action on it?" George Meany said, "The AFL-CIO is pretty conservative in certain ways."

I don't know where he got the "certain ways" qualification. He said, "We believe in the American system. We don't take to the streets, and we don't call general strikes and we don't call political strikes."

"WE TOOK TO THE STREETS"

When we took to the streets in 1930 and succeeded in amending unemployment insurance, Meany's predecessor, William Green, the president of the AFL, and the executive council declared their opposition to unemployment insurance because it was a dole and because it was socialistic. That's a fact! They were opposed to unemployment insurance.

Two months ago a friend of mine, Charlie Rivers—many of you know him—he was an organizer of our union for many years, helped build, organize this union and the Metal Workers Industrial Union that preceded this union. He called me up and he said, "Jim, you come up for dinner to my house, I have a present for you."

Charlie has been an amateur photographer all his life. He went through his albums, and he says, "I have a snapshot," and there it was, a demonstration for unemployment insurance in Union Square, New York City, in 1930—125,000 strong.

And he said, "You see, you are there. I took your picture."

MEANING FOR TODAY

Yes, that brought back some memories—memories that have meaning for today. I am talking about that in order to point to where we will be compelled to go tomorrow and the day after tomorrow if anything is to be done about the nine million unemployed. If we don't act, it's going to be ten, and then its going to be eleven. It's going to grow unless we do something about it.

And that demonstration in Union Square was the first demonstration that I attended. I was one year and two months in this country.

And my fellow workers in the shop and I went to that demonstration. We were then organized in this little Metal Workers Industrial Union. And the mounted cops, several hundred of them, rode into that mighty big crowd, split it up, and started pressing us in different directions and forced us to disperse. The section of the people that I was with were pushed off Fifteenth Street and Union Square to an appropriate building, the Tammany Hall Building. That's where we were pressed, right on the steps. And the next thing I knew, I felt a mighty big club on my back and that was the end. And I want to tell you a club on your back that knocks you out makes you radical in quick time, fast. (Applause)

Mighty radical.

MEANY AND "POLITICAL STRIKES"

George Meany declared a few months ago that he is against political strikes. I'm grateful to him for one thing right now because he single-handedly declared a strike against grain shipments to Russia, he, finally engaged in a political strike. That's a political strike.

Now the argument is down the drain. He finally engaged in political strikes. But the only thing that is wrong with it, he did it himself, he did not put it to a vote to the longshoremen.

This evening he called it off. He had no business calling it off and he had no business calling it without getting the membership to vote on it.

For one thing I'm grateful; he finally showed that at eighty-one years of age he finds some good reason to engage in political strikes.

THE 1950S: THE "DIRTY DECADE"

This union bled, and this convention tells you that since 1936—how can any one of us that has gone through those days, months, and years ever forget it? I was talking to Fitz the other day, recalling the 1950s—for several years during the McCarthy period we knew that a few days before Christmas the Justice Department would serve papers on us, or the Un-American Committee would serve papers on us. Injunctions would be issued against us, always before Christmas! Make sure that everybody is sound asleep and then call us down; denaturalization proceedings, contempt of Congress proceedings, try to put us out of business by the Subversive Control Board; all of that, year after year, and the labor leaders and the corporations and their men in Congress and in the administration, all hooked up to do the job.

CORPORATIONS CALL THE TUNE

The "Dirty Decade" may be past but we are facing tough times today. Our big problem is not with Gerald Ford, our big problem is with Henry Ford. That's the problem.

Our big problem is not Congressman Murphy from somewhere; our big problem is with President Murphy of General Motors.

Our big problem is not with Senator Speer; our big problem is with President of U.S. Steel Speer.

And so you go down the line. That is where the big problem lies, with the heads of corporations. The politicians are the hired hands. I don't have to find out now what Gerald Ford is doing. I read what Reginald Jones, head of GE, said and I knew what Gerald Ford was going to do. He said it a year ago; the plan was set out by the corporations.

Nixon—he was a flunky, he was bought and paid for. Agnew was a flunky, bought and paid for. They are not the powers. Apply the pressure to the corporate setup. If they give the signal to do something and they get into trouble, Gerald Ford will move and their congressmen will move to try to save the game. Just remember that.

GROWING UP IN THE UNION MOVEMENT

Now, just a little bit of my own reflections. It is strange that after forty years that I should have to tell you a couple of things about myself. But I have a reason. I have a reason because it is with greatest pride, my greatest pride, is the fact that here you have an immigrant boy, nineteen years old, coming into this country, and as a result of what you have done, you pushed me up there to meet with the heads of General Electric and the heads of Westinghouse, with our committees, and with the heads of the large corporations in America. You considered it worthy that a fellow like myself or Emspak or Fitzgerald would be able to represent you.

The first job I got in the union—I joined it forty-five years ago—the Metal Workers Industrial Union—in a little shop.

I was elected secretary-treasurer. I was eminently qualified for that job but I had two minor problems. I didn't know how to read or write English. (Laughter)

I asked my president, Joe Wild, "Why do you do this?" He said, "You're young, you'll learn."

I will say the decision making there was not too monumental; if I missed something in the minutes, there wouldn't be a catastrophe. The treasury we had in the union was $1.46. That was the treasury.

I took my minutes—I was catching on already, taking a little bit English—I was writing it down in Rumanian. And as for translating, I had a girlfriend, she was born here, I would talk to her and she would make up my minutes in English.

There is where it all began. And I want to say to you I don't plan to quit UE or to quit the labor movement. That's not my plan at all. (Applause)

CONVICTIONS AND BELIEFS

You have given me a pension and I have that social security that we won back in the Thirties, and I think I helped do something about that. Whatever you find me doing in this union, you should know, if any question comes up, that not one penny in wages or salary will go to me for anything that I may do for this union, beginning November 1, when my term of office expires.

I do not equate working with the union or the labor movement with being an officer. Giving up office to me does not mean giving up my convictions and my beliefs.

Fitz said that I volunteered to do some work with organizers and local officers, to help them develop to the extent that I have learned anything, to see if I can pass any of it on. But anything I have learned you have paid for, not only in money. Not every strike we ever lost was because the other side was so powerful; we had our share of mistakes which in many cases also contributed to the loss. When we slipped up in contract negotiations and they put something over on us, you had to pay for it.

THE INTERESTS OF THE WORKING PEOPLE

Yes, I figured the organizers and local officers who can see beyond the nickel and dime unions, beyond the type of Meany unionism, beyond the type of business unionism, those who want to make a contribution and serve the interests of the working people in America—I figured maybe I may be able to be of help to them, just to pass on what I have learned.

My odometer has been rolling up and in 1971 I talked to my associate officers generally about my plans to get out as I saw this odometer kept running up and going up to the point of the first round. The first round on the odometer going up to ninety-nine thousand, nine hundred, and ninety-nine and that odometer will turn and the zeros will appear, six of them across, and then the first one will appear and I will start driving this buggy all over again. Not the same way but I will drive it.

I'm turning in my stripes, I'm not turning in my UE uniform, and I sure as hell am not turning in my M-1.

So thank you very much.

(The delegates arose and there was prolonged applause.)

In two minutes you're going to have a resolution and you're going back to work!

NOTE

1. Farewell address of the UE general-secretary-treasurer to the 40th Annual International Convention of the United Electrical, Radio, and Machine Workers of America (UE), San Francisco, California, September 10, 1975.

20

SEEDS OF A LABOR INSURGENCY

PETER RACHLEFF

I t was a decade in which technological change; a racial, ethnic, and gender recomposition of the workforce; structural economic shifts; and employer and government antiunionism decimated the labor movement. From 19.4 percent of the workforce ten years earlier, unionized labor plummeted to 10.2 percent. The strike had virtually disappeared as a weapon of labor. Where four million workers had hit the bricks a decade before, now only three hundred thousand dared to do so. As the labor movement withered, wages stagnated and the workweek lengthened despite a doubling of manufacturing output. Inequality grew, as the top one-tenth of 1 percent of the social pyramid took in as much income as the bottom 42 percent.

With unionized workers concentrated in declining industries and increasingly distant from the most rapidly growing sectors of the workforce—people of color, immigrants, women—the arbiters of public opinion proclaimed the imminent death of organized labor. Union leaders themselves advised a strategy of caution and cooperation. "Labor is understanding more and more," the head of the American Federation of Labor told a gathering of industrial engineers, "that high wages and tolerable conditions of employment can be brought about through excellency in service, the promotion of efficiency, and elimination of waste."

This was the 1920s. Now, at the other end of the century, when fifteen

Reprinted with permission from the February 21, 1994 issue of *The Nation*.

years of open, government-assisted assault on labor coupled with the unprecedented (and also government-assisted) mobility of capital have promoted pun-
dits again to write obituaries for organized labor, this dreary decade bears
recalling. For in the darkness of that antecedent period were glimmerings of
the movement that would be reborn a few years later. In 1933 and 1934 more
than two and a half million workers would strike. Over the next seven years,
eight million would join unions, many of them newly formed.

It would be facile to imagine that we stand today on the cusp of a replay
of the thirties—the political economy is vastly changed, as are the fortunes
and organizational discipline of the Left—but the past surely offers useful
signposts for considering the future.

In the aftermath of the NAFTA (North American Free Trade Agreement) vote especially, many have asked, what now for the labor movement? The response often centers on the global trends of capital or the
political leverage centers on the global trends of capital or the political
leverage unions might exert in Washington and in electoral contests around
the country—all relevant matters. But the beginnings of a more intriguing
answer can be found in developments, some as yet discernible only in faint
outline, that are changing the culture of the labor movements. Efforts to
organize the unorganized, to give greater voice to workers who have traditionally been silent, and to redefine the objectives of the already organized
point not merely to a labor "revival" but to a future movement that is
markedly different from the one that exists now as the CIO of the 1930s
was from the AFL of the 1920s.

Among organizing campaigns, the most exciting are those that
resemble social movements more than conventional trade unionism. For
more than ten years, Black Workers for Justice (BWFJ) has insisted that the
organization of the South, broadly speaking, is vital to the future of labor.

NEW CONSTITUENCIES, NEW IDEAS AND STRATEGIES ARE ENERGIZING THE LABOR MOVEMENT

Based in North Carolina—which has led the country in both attracting and
losing manufacturing jobs while remaining the least unionized state—the
group has promoted community and workplace organizing, fighting police
brutality and congressional redistricting as well as workplace inequities.
Signing up with an establishment union is rarely the first step. Rather,
BWFJ relies on techniques, like speak-outs and union elections held outside
the formal auspices of the National Labor Relations Board, that help build
power in communities and rally public support for workplace grievances.

In Southern California, Mexican drywall workers, many of them undocumented immigrants employed by exploitative subcontractors, have established roving pickets who disperse to job sites and recruit workers. They succeeded last summer in spreading their organizing from Los Angeles to San Diego, and in attracting not only thousands of new members but also the attention of the larger labor movement.

Also in Southern California, and a few cities elsewhere, the Service Employees International Union's (SEIU) "Justice for Janitors" campaign has similar elements. The workers—most of them immigrants, some undocumented—have been exploited through a network of subcontracting. The SEIU campaign targets building owners and contract cleaners alike, using mass protests to aim at a large part of the local industry rather than at particular employers. These protests involve workers' family members and neighbors, are solidly grounded in specific ethnic cultures, and make dramatic arguments for justice that have captured the imagination of non-immigrants. Since 1991 the union has signed unprecedented contracts with major cleaning companies in Los Angeles and Washington.

In other cities, self-organization among immigrant workers has also emerged. The AFL-CIO has encouraged the organization of Asian Pacific American Labor Alliances in San Francisco, Oakland, Seattle, Honolulu, Los Angeles, New York, and Washington. In Boston, a network of progressive local unions has helped set up an Immigrant Worker Resource Center, which offers legal aid and English classes, while also organizing picnics celebrating ethnic cultures and disseminating labor news in Spanish and in Haitian creole. In New York City, the long-standing Chinese Staff and Workers Association has promoted independent unionization in the garment, construction, and restaurant industries, while organizing protests in support of nonunion workers as well.

Much of the most innovative organizing prefigures new union structures: linking workplaces and communities; revolving around "work centers," as activists in La Mujer Obrera and Fuerza Unida have called their community-based labor organizations in El Paso and San Antonio, respectively; and breaking from some of the standard forms of union activity. At the same time progressives within the more traditional labor movement have seized on these efforts as sources of inspiration and education for their own union brothers and sisters.

Some of the most significant union victories in the past decade have come on college campuses, where mostly female clerical and technical workers have drawn heavily on feminist ideas. While different unions have formally organized in different places—the Hotel Employees and Restaurant workers at Yale; the American Federation of State, County and Municipal Employees at Harvard and the University of Minnesota—a common thread and common organizers have connected these campaigns, sometimes to the chagrin of their respective internationals, which see their centralized control challenged by an independent network of women organizers.

In 1960, women accounted for 18.3 percent of union membership. By 1990, it was 37 percent. In new organizations that are overwhelmingly female, it is not just a question of more women or more members but of altered approaches, from the time of day they meet and the expanded role of small group meetings to the kind of literature they produce and the issues they address.

Even in the building trades, new ideas have started to percolate. Fifteen unions, inspired by the International Brotherhood of Electrical Workers, have developed the Construction Organizing Membership Education Training (COMET) program, through which thousands of rank-and-filers have been trained as job-site organizers. Traditionally, these unions forbid members to work on nonunion jobs. Under COMET, they are encouraged to "salt" nonunion sites to draw members. Some even wear union jackets on the job, daring contractors to discharge them and threatening discrimination lawsuits.

Equally significant are the efforts afoot to reorganize the organized, to shift from a culture of business unionism to what activists are calling an "organizing model" and "social unionism."

Since the late 1970s and early 1980s, the postwar "social contract" between business and organized labor has been torn up. During its heyday, full-time officers, hired staff, lawyers, and lobbyists had carried the responsibility for the union, while rank-and-file members were expected to do little more than allow dues to be deducted from their paychecks. Bureaucracy and apathy became two sides of the same coin. Economic growth and employer tolerance provided union members with a rising standard of living. But when the historical context changed, business unionism became as discredited as the deal that spawned it.

Of course, the transformation of the Teamsters, still incomplete but guided by the grass-roots reform movement Teamsters for a Democratic Union, is the most dramatic example. But it is not a solitary one. Among rail workers over the past three years, a movement for cross-union solidarity has developed from the bottom up that would make Eugene Debs proud. It grew in the face of deregulation and employer-government collusion to unravel generations of union gains and projections. National union leaders are only beginning to discuss such basics as coordinated bargaining and pledges of mutual solidarity. But at a grass-roots level, from Glendive, Montana, and Alliance, Nebraska, to the Twin Cities, Chicago, and Philadelphia, rail workers have been coming together regardless of specific union affiliation to call for a united front against both their employers and the government. In small rail towns across the country, workers and their families have reached out to other workers, and to farmers and small business owners, to build a movement to withstand the greed of today's robber barons.

What rail workers and the "New Teamsters" have in common with each other, and with less visible struggles in dozens of unions—including those of the autoworkers, the postal workers, the paper workers—is a newly energized rank and file and a shift of greater information, responsibility, and power to it.

In some unions, leadership at different levels has consciously introduced elements of this new organizing model. In most, however, there has been significant opposition. Yet the thrust from below, from the ranks, has been unmistakable, and with it has come a new quality to the union, from the meeting hall to the workplace.

This new activist unionism has developed vehicles for communication, such as videos and computer bulletin boards, and organizational networks for mutual support. These include local centers such as the Youngstown Workers' Solidarity Club, the Twin Cities Meeting the Challenge Committee, and the Mid-State Central Labor Council in New York; ad hoc labor solidarity committees, which have sprung up around particular struggles like the Hormel strike of 1985–86 or the ongoing Staley lockout in Illinois; new regional bodies, like the Western Nebraska Central Labor Council and the Eastern Montana Central Labor Council; national umbrellas such as Labor Party Advocates and the Rainbow Coalition, both of which seek to promote independent labor action. Kim Moody of *Labor Notes*, an excellent monthly newsletter out of Detroit, calls such initiatives an expression of "solidarity consciousness."

THE BOSSES SEEK A UNION-FREE ENVIRONMENT; AS EVER, THEY HAVE A FRIEND IN GOVERNMENT

NAFTA boosted these developments, particularly in terms of coalition building outside the labor movement and beyond national borders. And the popular education, outreach, and organization that marked the anti-NAFTA campaign is continuing. The Teamsters, along with the United Electrical Workers (UE), the United Automobile Workers, and the Communication Workers, have developed relationships with Canadian and Mexican unions, usually to tackle employers who operate in all three countries.

These relationships have strengthened with the organization of the North American Worker-to-Worker Network (NAWWN), based in Rocky Mount, North Carolina. NAWWN's very name grows out of its commitment to rank-and-file involvement as a basis for international solidarity. Last December, members of twelve organizations met under its auspices in San Francisco and set an agenda for this year. Their priorities will be to support and expand the "Adopt an Organizer" program initiated by the UE and the Mexican Authentic Workers Front. The aim: to bring democratic union organization to the Mexican factories opened by U.S. multinationals; to bring Mexican activists to the United States to speak to local union meetings and community gatherings; and to develop an emergency network able to mobilize support in all three countries for workers facing a particular crisis.

No sooner was that relationship forged than it was put to the test, when Honeywell and General Electric fired union organizers at their plants in Juárez and Chihuahua. The UE, the Teamsters, and the Canadian Auto Workers, who represent workers employed by these multinationals, sprang into action with shop-floor leaflets, petitions, and protest campaigns aimed at the companies and President Clinton. More activities are being organized with the assistance of NAWWN and *Labor Notes*.

Here, then, are the seeds of the labor movement of the future: the introduction of new forces into the movement, the development of structures that link workplace and community, the evolution of new union cultures on the job and in the union hall, an energized rank and file in more and more unions, the building of coalitions with social movements outside the "house of labor," a rebirth of solidarity, and the emergence of cross-border organizing.

Of course, significant forces seek to halt the growth of these seeds. And they bear a striking resemblance to their 1920s–1930s forebears.

Employers now have more of a global arena in which to operate, to be sure, but their basic tactics are as old and crude as they ever were: divide and conquer, intimidate and co-opt. They alternate between browbeating and cajoling their workers to "compete"—that is, to produce more while earning less. And they rely on a veritable battalion of management consultants, lawyers, psychologists, and paramilitary types, all eager to bring about a "union-free environment."

As ever, the bosses have a friend in government. For a dozen years, overt antiunionism reigned in Washington and trickled down to the states and cities. The busting of the air traffic controllers union in 1981 was the clarion call of the era. In its wake, antiunion ideologies were put on the federal bench, on the National Labor Relations Board (NLRB), in the Labor Department, and in regulatory agencies. In their worship of the "free market"—translated as freedom for the corporate class and servitude for everyone else—one doesn't have to strain very hard to hear the echoes of the Republican administrations of the 1920s and early 1930s.

FDR's election and his pro-union posturing in 1933 and 1934 helped break open the floodgates for the tide of new mass labor activism. But when this resurgence—particularly the general strikes of 1934—threatened the deep structures of American capitalism, New Deal reforms such as the Wagner Act served to channel, and to blunt, this rebellion.

Bill Clinton represents a more blatant obstacle in the path of labor revival. At heart his agenda follows the same course that was chartered by the Republican stars of deregulation, privatization, and free trade. In the interests of "competition" it has a new theme: "labor-management cooperation." Secretary of Labor Robert Reich and Secretary of Commerce Ron Brown appointed a Commission for the Future of Worker-Management Relations whose mandate was summed up by Reich when he said, "The jury is still out on whether the traditional union is necessary for the new workplace." There was no mistaking that what he had in mind by way of alternative was not the kind of nontraditional unionism I've been talking about here. Their "reforms" would undermine union organization where it exists and prevent it from taking shape where it does not yet exist.

One final parallel to the 1920s and 1930s cannot be overlooked. The emerging labor movement must also face the resistance of its old bureaucratic leadership. As before, these leaders advise conciliation and cooperation with employers and the government, and they are willing to muster their remaining forces to try to strangle internal movements in their infancy.

Indeed, solidarity at the top level of the labor bureaucracy now stands for little more than sticking together against oppositional rank-and-file movements. In 1985–86, Bill Wynn, the president of the United Food and Commercial Workers Union, was able to count on the support of the entire AFL, CIO executive board when he set about destroying Local P-9 in Austin, Minnesota, which had dared to buck the corporate agenda of concessions and had garnered the support of three thousand local unions across the United States in doing so.

So the seeds of a new labor movement have a long way to go to bear fruit. They must connect with one another in ways that strengthen each— and all—of them. They must inspire the complacent, defy the cynical, make their own history.

This is a tall order, but as a historian I can tell my friends in the labor movement in all honesty that it's possible. Hell, it's been done before.

1996: CHANGE AND CONTINUITY

The past two years have challenged the new forces within the labor movement. Both business and government have continued on their antiworker, antiunion agenda. Long, hard-fought struggles at Caterpillar, A. E. Staley, Bridgestone/Firestone, and the *Detroit News/Free Press* galvanized considerable solidarity from union activists, but failed to deter the corporate juggernaut of job cuts, contracting out, lower pay, and increased work intensity.

At the heart of the antiworker agenda remain deregulation, privatization, and free trade. Together, these forces pit one group of workers against another in a competitive downspiral in which none can win. The insecurity which flows in their wake has swept over not only blue-collar wage earners but has now engulfed most layers of frontline supervision and middle management. Every day the mass media makes some note of these "new" fears and tensions, while GOP presidential candidate Pat Buchanan found them fertile soil for his campaign. Even the *New York Times* ("all the news that's fit to print") has discovered Main Street's deep fears about Wall Street's penchant to reward downsizing.

These developments have continued to send tremors through the labor movement. In 1995, they shook the upper echelons of the AFL-CIO bureaucracy, leading to the first open election contest in the history of the modern labor movement. Losses in membership, workplace power, bargaining power, and public prestige finally caught up with the "leaders" of the labor movement.

But there was more involved. New forces were brewing within the labor movement. At its heart, some long-standing unions undertook campaigns to change their internal cultures, seeking to break out of the death waltz danced by bureaucratic leadership and apathetic membership. And at its margins, workers who had once pressed their noses against the glass behind which unionized workers enjoyed better wages, benefits, and job security, began to organize themselves, even creating new forms dissimilar from the craft unions and industrial unions of the AFL-CIO.

These *possibilities* played as important a role in the Donahue-Sweeney struggle for the leadership of the AFL-CIO as did the Kirkland administration's woeful track record of membership loss and declining power. Both candidates pledged to promote organization of the unorganized and an increased voice for those previously underrepresented, such as women and workers of color. The victor—John Sweeney of the SEIU, one of the few unions to have *grown* in the 1980s—went even further. He promised to adopt more militant tactics, such as nonviolent civil disobedience, in an effort to increase the labor movement's power. And he pledged to spend millions of dollars on bringing new members into the fold. In the summer of 1996, the AFL-CIO launched "Union Summer," a program meant to recall the civil rights movement's "Freedom Summer" of 1964. More than one thousand college students were hired for three-week internships and placed in organizing campaigns in eighteen cities. While "Union Summer's" practical gains may be slight, its symbolic expression of energy, hope, and a vibrant future is undeniable.

How successful such campaigns will be—indeed, whether Sweeney will live up to his promises—is an open question, but these developments reflect an increasing militancy within the ranks of the labor movement. In turn, they might also give rise to new ideas and aspirations, and once the rank-and-file genie is out of the bottle, even "progressive" business unionists may not be able to stuff it back in.

Another product of the changed times—both the frustration rooted in years of retrogression within the system and the hopes let loose by the new forces percolating within and around the labor movement—is the newly created Labor Party. In June 1996, 1,367 delegates, representing unions with more than one million members and a complex array of forces, met in Cleveland to establish a Labor Party based first and foremost on the labor movement. The most prominent leadership hailed from the Oil, Chemical and Atomic Workers (OCAW), which deals with some of the world's most powerful transnational corporations employing the most modern technology. Also playing an important role were unions with older progressive traditions, such as the UE, the International Longshoremen and Warehousemen's Union (ILWU), and the United Mine Workers of America (UMWA). Much of these unions' progressive traditions had spent the past two or three decades in mothballs. But they were still there, to be dusted off, updated, and reenergized. Others reflected a recent radicalization of a more traditional base, such as the Brotherhood of Maintenance of Way Employees (railroad workers who had been badly hurt by the rapidly changing rules in the transportation industry which had deregulated management while maintaining government intervention in labor conflicts) and a number of building trades councils and locals (whose world based on collaboration with contractors and government agencies had come crashing down). A sense of betrayal and outrage directed at the Democratic Party ran through these unions.

And then there were the refreshingly new forces—such as the California Nurses Association, the Farm Labor Organizing Committee, and the Black Workers for Justice. They brought the experiences and voices of women, immigrants, and African Americans directly into the dialogue and debate. With these voices, they insisted that the new Labor Party fight for the interests of *all* working people—the foreign-born as well as the native-born; women as well as men; workers of color as well as white; service-sector, white-collar, and professional as well as blue-collar industrial. Their new perspectives did not always mesh smoothly with those of the more traditional unionists present, but even when their voices represented dissonance the result was usually a creative tension and, ultimately, mutual respect and accommodation of some sort.

Like many other developments in and around the labor movement, it is hard to say where the Labor Party will go. The delegates adopted a constitution and platform which postpones the endorsing and running of candidates for at least two years while seeking to organize "sufficient numbers of workers" to be a political force. In the meanwhile, local chapters and endorsing unions will attempt to model an "organizing approach to politics" through petition, initiative, and referendum campaigns; holding public forums and educational projects; and using informational picketing and other vehicles to pressure the political process around issues of corporate behavior, standards for wages, benefits and working conditions, health care, and the environment.

Even if the Labor Party itself fails to become a political force in its own right, its very existence helps activists to discuss alternatives to the existing political terrain while articulating a sense of class which has been absent from the labor movement for more than a generation. The Labor Party might also provide fertile soil for the diverse new forces in and around the labor movement to intersect, commingle, and generate even newer forces and dynamics. As with so many other new developments, its ultimate course remains in the hands of the activists who have worked so hard to bring it into existence—and their ability to capture the imaginations and energies of their less-involved fellow workers.

Another important expression of increased militancy—and source of future developments—is linked to changes in internal union dynamics. Rank-and-file members and their families have played key roles in such life-or-death recent struggles as Hormel, Staley, and the Detroit newspapers. In less pressurized situations, some local activists are employing versions of what its devotees call an "organizing model." They encourage stewards to reorient their activities from "solving" members' problems to organizing the members to be more powerful at solving their own problems. Rank-and-filers take new responsibility through in-plant communications and mobilization networks, "solidarity committees," and union subcommittees for internal organizing, outreach, and community action. Examples of this transformation can be found all over the labor movement (often reported on in the pages of *Labor Notes* magazine), but they are still largely isolated and ad hoc. Their success depends as much on the initiative and effectiveness of the local activists present as it does on the situation and shared experiences of particular workplaces or industries.

Some unions are transforming themselves internally while seeking to organize others. They are training and using rank-and-file members as "volunteer" organizers with exciting successes which not only bring in new members but also energize the cultures of the existing unions. Building trade unions have turned to "salting" nonunion worksites, as their members hire on and explain the benefits of organization to their coworkers. During and after their 1994 freight strike, rank-and-file Teamsters leafleted nonunion barns, talked at length with truckers, and went on home visits. The Laborers have enlisted dozens of rank-and-file members, particularly Spanish-speakers, to help with their organizing campaign in the southern poultry industry. At a more general level, the AFL-CIO Organizing Institute has not only recruited young, college-educated union organizers, but it has also trained hundreds of rank-and-file union members in the skills and techniques of organizing. These men and women don't just organize others; they also become more active in their own unions.

Some of the most exciting developments are taking place at the very margins of the labor movement. There, a new workforce—women, immigrants, people of color, contingent workers, some highly educated workers—in such typically nonunion sectors as service, retail, and high tech have been making efforts to organize themselves. The organizations they form look different from conventional unions, and some of the activities they engage in expand the parameters of the "labor movement." They are the future of the labor movement, however it is defined, but, as yet, their efforts at self-organization have had little relationship to the existing institutional labor movement.

One of the most dramatic examples is provided by New York City's Chinese Staff and Workers Association (CSWA). They grew out of a number of struggles in Chinatown, particularly by restaurant workers. The CSWA provides a variety of direct services, links labor and civil rights organizations within Chinatown, and fights for workers' rights in a variety of ways. Recently, it identified itself as part of the "workers center" movement, which groups twelve organizations—CSWA, Appalachian Women Empowered, Asian Immigrant Women Advocates (Oakland), Center for Women's Economic Alternatives (North Carolina), Immigrant Workers Resource Center (Boston), Korean Immigrant Workers Advocates (Los Angeles), La Cooperativa (New York), Latino Workers Center (NY), La Mujer Obrera (El Paso), Southwest Florida Farmworker Project, the Workplace Project (Long Island), and South Asian Women vs. Domestic Violence—in a loose but evolving coalition.

Each of these organizations has some unique characteristics, but all are grounded in their particular communities, with members among the economically marginalized—women, immigrants, and people of color. Their organization is community-based, and it is able to marshal broad community resources in support of workplace conflicts. Sometimes, the organization throws its resources into what might be defined as "community" as opposed to workplace struggles, but their activists tend to reject this distinction as irrelevent for their constituency. And their impressive results in the past two to three years bear testimony to the effectiveness of their approach.

The CSWA has been among the most impressive and their activities among the most diverse. They have organized community support for workers' rights. CSWA maintained a community boycott of a prominent restaurant which was trying to break its workers' union. They organized demonstrations against racism in the construction industry, and they filed a lawsuit alleging antiunion discrimination by Chinatown contractors. These efforts led to a back-pay settlement for undocumented workers as well as legal immigrants and opened up construction jobs for Chinese immigrant women. They have also organized a Garment Industry Working Group, seeking to reach the more than twenty-five thousand Chinese garment workers in Manhattan alone.

CSWA provides individual legal assistance for workers and English as a Second Language classes. They have organized internal support groups for senior citizens, women, and young people. Their activities include community forums, small group discussions, and recreational and social activities. CSWA also publishes a quarterly newsletter, produces videos for cable television, and holds an annual "Labor Fair" which promotes not only employment opportunities but also workers' rights. They have made a top concern out of the media's depiction of Chinese immigrant workers as "willing to work like slaves." They have also organized around community issues, such as opposition to the opening of an Off-Track Betting Parlor in Chinatown.

While the CSWA is deeply rooted in the particularities of Chinatown and the exploitation of immigrant workers there, they have also reached out to other, similar, organizations. As already mentioned, they have participated in the formation of a national coalition of twelve workers' centers. They have also helped to organize the Lower East Side Workers Center, which includes blacks, Latinos, and non-Chinese Asians, and the Coalition to End Racism in Construction, which includes fifteen Latino, black, and Asian organizations. These coalitions are beginning to build bridges among different immigrant communities and communities of color, even as each organization remains grounded in the culture of its constituency.

The CSWA is but one example of the newly emerging "workers' centers." Similar organizations have emerged among other immigrant workers in such cities as Boston, New York City, Los Angeles, and El Paso. Interestingly, the new Labor Party offers representation and a place at the table for such formations, and some unions, such as UNITE (the merged Amalgamated Clothing and Textile Workers and the Ladies Garment Workers), have sponsored immigrant workers' centers of their own. Yet, the AFL-CIO, its state and central body organizations, have remained oblivious to their development, which is at the heart of the larger processes of self-organization going on among workers who have never been part of the institutional labor movement.

This is demonstrated most clearly in the experience of the North Carolina–based Black Workers for Justice (BWFJ), whose approach *begins* with criticism of the standard "hot shop" and NLRB election orientation of AFL-CIO affiliated unions. Given the low level of unionization in the South, the deep problems posed by racism, the hostility of Southern state governments, and the power of employers, a shop-by-shop approach which revolves around getting cards signed and then winning an election and gaining a first contract seems to be a recipe for failure. Moreover, BWFJ points out, unions typically leave town the day after a failed election, only demoralizing workers all the more.

In the place of the "hot shop," BWFJ has developed a multilayered organizing strategy which includes in-plant committees, industry-wide networks, labor-community alliances, and support from solidarity networks reaching beyond the South to union activists around the country. All of their activities are designed to educate their participants, often from their own experiences, and empower them. Particular tactics—"speak-outs"; "nonmajority status" unions; unofficial "central labor bodies"; and the use of petitions, lawsuits, letter-writing campaigns, and public marches—carry out this strategy in such a way as to link dynamically the layers of organization and activism.

Even after fifteen years, it is hard to assess the "success" of BWFJ. They have certainly provided a glimmer of hope where once there was none. And they have brought new ideas about organizing into the wider labor movement. Whether they are succeeding in changing the environment in the South—and the ways that Southern workers (white as well as black, and new immigrants as well as the deeply rooted) think of themselves—may not be known for years. And, then again, there could be an explosion and a veritable prairie fire of organizing the day this article is published.

Black Workers for Justice, the CSWA, and other immigrant workers' centers take on forms as diverse as are the workers who are creating them. That's the key point about labor activism at the margins of the institutional movement. It's not just far from the center; it's genuinely different. And here we see a dynamism and a hopefulness not seen since the heady days of the sitdown strikes in the 1930s.

Taking all of these elements together, not only is it not hard to see the contours of a labor movement of the future, but it is hard not to be excited about its prospects. The seeds of the resurgence I wrote of in 1994 are still there. I might even say that some have sprouted and some have spread. But what each will grow into—and how all these parts will relate to each other—will have to wait for some more experiences—some more "history"—before we can provide more grounded answers.

21

THE STRUGGLE FOR SURVIVAL

GENERAL BAKER

General Baker is a longtime African American activist in Detroit, a member of the United Auto Workers (UAW), and a former member of the Dodge Revolutionary Union Movement. The following is a presentation made at the University of Pittsburgh on November 15, 1993, at a meeting sponsored by campus groups and the Alliance for Progressive Action.

I've been working in auto shops for thirty years. I'm a steelworker in an auto union. Ford was the only one of the Big Three [Ford, Chrysler, General Motors] that had its own steel mill. In the huge Rouge complex in Dearborn, Michigan, one of the fourteen plants is a steel mill. I'm in Local 600.

I'm the chairperson of the National Organizing Committee (NOC). We're a group of people who've come together to try to fight for what we consider to be a survival movement and give a focus and political direction to that movement. The movement for survival is a general category of people who find themselves in a situation where they're no longer needed in the workplace, and they have to fight for their daily needs in order to survive. We fight alongside the homeless section, welfare recipients, and others who've been displaced and have to fight for housing, health care, food, and other survival needs.

From *Bulletin in Defense of Marxism*, no. 113 (February 1994). Reprinted by permission.

Our experience and understanding of this comes from an estimate of the situation that we view this country is going through. We refer to it as a revolution in the economy that's taking place. We've reached a new stage of development in technology and robotization inside the shops where human labor in many instances is no longer needed to be productive.

Back in the 1960s, some body shops in the auto factories had between two and three thousand people spot welding. We based our organizing inside those large shops. Today, there's not a single human being in the modern body shop. The entire work is done by robots and computer-chip controls, with no human labor at all. The same thing has occurred in the paint shops. Slowly, the whole plant is being engrossed by robots and electronic technology. The final assembly plants still have human labor. Those are the departments where workers have to get inside of the car and put the ceiling cloth on, etc. These positions are more difficult for a robot to do. The costs are currently prohibitive in terms of getting a robot that's that flexible. As soon as costs are down, we assume that those positions will be taken too.

We call this a revolution in the economy in this country. We already went through an economic revolution in the steel mills. There are now coke ovens operating around the world that have no human labor left at all. Based on that, and our understanding of human history, a revolution usually takes place first in production, and then some social upheaval follows. We're trying to prepare for the social upheaval that's going to be a result of this economic revolution that goes on as we sit here and talk. We base ourselves in that section of society that's been thrown out of production.

In the greater metropolitan Detroit area, Chrysler Corporation used to be the largest employer in the 1970s, with twenty-nine plants. They employed fifty-seven thousand hourly employees in the city of Detroit alone. Today, Chrysler Corporation has fifty-five thousand employees nationally, and only two plants left in Detroit. Ford and General Motors plants also closed. People who used to work in those plants find themselves living in shelters and on welfare rolls, and trying to struggle for survival.

As a result of cutbacks in the number of hourly workers and a declining tax base, the state of Michigan's budget was thrown out of kilter. In response to that, Governor Engler and the state legislature cut off all ninety-five thousand general assistance recipients in 1991. So no aid comes for any single, able-bodied adult in the state of Michigan. What was left was the AFDC rolls [those on the federal Aid for Dependent Children program]. In the past two years, any time a family's oldest child reaches eighteen that family and that child are cut off of aid because there's no aid available for single adults. These cutbacks have forced a real crisis in Michigan.

The homeless population in the greater Detroit area is about fifty-five thousand people. We have numerous shelters concentrated in the Cass Corridor area where people try to fend for their daily lives. In Michigan a single adult can only get food stamps. People will trade these stamps each month for fuel in the winter to try and stay warm.

During the auto boom in the 1960s, Detroit led the nation in the number of single-family dwelling units. Plant closedowns left us with something like fifteen thousand vacant houses in Detroit. The homeless will develop a squatters movement to take over some of these homes and then use their food stamp money to heat the homes.

Let me say to the students in this room that one of the main lessons we've learned is if one does not support the struggle of that section of society, then obviously you cheapen your own trade or profession. We've seen all the money fall away from social science studies. We've seen the cheapening of labor and an attack on welfare workers across Michigan as a result of an attack on the section that they used to serve. There have been massive layoffs in the Department of Social Services offices across the state.

There is another aspect to this. There has been propaganda hype about the welfare recipient always being black, which results in the race question being used to divide the working class. Out of the ninety-five thousand cut off of aid in Michigan, the majority were white. One tactical question we face is a demand that the welfare cuts are not painted as black so that we can establish the broadest base of unity for the fightback.

The fundamental question that we deal with is: how do we now try to fight alongside a section of people who no longer are needed to be productive in society? How do we view society in the upcoming stages when human labor is not needed in production? Obviously, we need jobs in order to get money to participate in the economy and get the necessities of life. We can eat with food stamps, but we don't know if we're going to get rent stamps, clothing stamps, etc. Because of this, we've developed a tactic and an outlook, particularly around housing, that says we're prepared to take what we need; that we'll only get what we're organized to take.

In Detroit there are four thousand empty public housing units with heat and light. We set up a base of operations, kicked in the doors of empty public housing units, took the locks off, bought new locks, set up an extralegal housing authority, took people out of the homeless shelters, had them sign applications, and put them in the empty units. This brought us directly into confrontation with the state. Many of us were arrested and the people thrown out of the units. But we just regrouped and went back and took over other units. We had basic support from those already occupying public housing. For example, D Building in the Jeffries Project had 125 units and only nine occupied. The nine occupants felt safer with people living in the building. If we could keep the new tenants in a unit for thirty days, then we could use the Landlord-Tenant Court to prevent eviction. Now, after about a year and a half, we have one hundred homeless families in public housing projects. They don't pay rent because they have no income. We learned from that struggle that we have to seize what we need in order to live.

According to *USA Today,* two thousand people get pink slips every day in this country. That's five hundred more per day than last year. If this is going to be a growing section of society, then we need to learn the tactics and strategies of struggle and political outlook for this section. We are placing ourselves in what we call the survival end of the struggle. This is a critical struggle which actually tests the question of revolutionary development of society. We think this is a revolutionary section of society, not because it consciously thinks that, but because objectively it's forced to confront the government in a fundamental way in order to get the necessities of life. We're prepared to test the system to its limits. The question of organized or conscious discipline is not necessary. This is the outlook the National Organizing Committee has been pursuing.

Most of our experience has been gained out of the organization Up and Out of Poverty. The leadership there is from the National Homeless Union, the National Welfare Rights Union, and the Anti-Hunger Coalition. These bodies are headed up by women. The organizations are fighting for survival of these people.

We're not sure where the struggle's going. We didn't anticipate some of the confrontations that developed in the course of trying to seize the necessities of life. Once, when we were getting thrown out of the projects, a homeless person suggested that we get tents and set up sort of a revival meeting, like the churches do, that we could use as a base of operations. We set up tents, which became known as Tent City. Every night, the Detroit police would tear down the tents and arrest everybody. Past fellow travelers of mine, like the Detroit director of the Health Department, would claim the tents were health hazards. The police would arrest us for trespassing on property. But we had a right to be on that property because we had agreements with churches to set the tents up on their property. People got a great education about the role of the state and police.

We also ran into a lot of other difficulties. Homeless people, for instance, didn't have a right to vote because they didn't have an address and therefore couldn't register. We battled with the city and the state legislature and were able to use the shelter address to register to vote. We registered tens of thousands of people in Michigan to vote in order for them to sign a petition to recall Governor Engler. People would stand in line all day to register to vote so they could sign the petition. We battled with the board of education to use the shelter address to get homeless children in school. The way the system is set up, if you don't have an address you can't go to school.

These struggles taught us a lot. The Wayne County Homeless Union developed a daytime drop-in center to take the overflow from the shelters.

Most of the shelters throw people out on the street during the daytime. They don't want homeless people coming together during the day so that they could try to collectively solve their problems. So they have to roam the street during the day and come back by 6:30 P.M. to reclaim their beds. The Homeless Union also developed a rotating ministry that takes in one church every week of the year—fifty-two weeks. For one week, a church feeds dinner and breakfast to the homeless and lets them sleep in the basement. We take about 150 foam mattresses to these churches. Then the people come to the drop-in center during the daytime. This sensitizes a lot of church people to the plight of the homeless.

The NOC asks, How do we approach the question of a new society in which we're not needed any longer to be productive? We want to ask this of students of sociology and history. If we were archeologists digging up tools, we could decide what the form of society was, based on the tools of production. Tools mark different epochs and different kinds of social structures that follow in order to implement the tools. If we dug up the robotic tools of today, what kind of society would need to exist in correspondence to them? We think it's a real revolutionary potential. We need more help to study which way we're going. How will we approach a situation where there are masses of people who need to live but are no longer needed in the process of production? That's the contradiction that we're confronted with in society as a whole. The NOC was designed to be based in that particular section of the population.

This is an international phenomenon. We view the districts where our homeless people gather in this country—like Detroit's Cass Corridor—as our developing shantytowns. These shantytowns are all over the world. The largest is probably in Brazil, where close to a million people are in one shantytown. In the United States, shantytowns are developing in the midst of all this plenty. All the stores, warehouses, and car lots are full. There are supposed to be eleven million empty luxury housing units. There are six million homeless. Housing isn't built for people to live in, but for real estate companies to make money. That's basically the nature of the system. We realize that homeless people will not be given these housing units because other renters will stop paying rent. That will threaten the existence of capitalism as related to housing.

Well, those are the kinds of things we've been fighting around. I wanted to bring this message to Pittsburgh in terms of our experience. I hope we now can get an exchange of ideas from others in the room.

QUESTION-AND-ANSWER PERIOD

Q: Let me express my gratitude that you came to speak to us. It's a pleasure to listen to someone who's not afraid of the word "revolution." I'd like to ask you about the specific consciousness of the people you work with. How do they come to think about the state and the police in these actions you helped organize? How are they thinking about their own situation?

A: It's not been difficult working with the impoverished section. People have a lot of pride. Even homeless people and welfare recipients don't want you to know that they're homeless or on welfare. I guess this is a holdover from the American psyche. You first have to break that up. People have a tendency to blame themselves for their problems and don't see the social consequences that helped in their collapse. There's a little story: the National Homeless Union was first organized by two guys out of Philadelphia. They were going every day to New Jersey to pick fruit on the surplus labor market. Neither knew the other was homeless. Finally, one of them got thrown out of the abandoned building he was living in, and the other guy saw him on TV. People have such a pride, it's hard to break through that. The same is true of welfare recipients.

These pockets of people are already finding ways to survive. They do it kind of illegally. You can't make a legal movement out of it as long as there's illegal individual behavior. There were a lot of people stealing gas from Michigan Consolidated Gas Co. The gas company wanted to bring a case against them, but they were afraid of a Wayne County jury. And I don't blame them, because wasn't no jury gonna convict nobody for stealing no gas from the gas company. Nearly every time you see three or four people on the street corner, they're trying to figure some kind of way to get something that they need to live. Oftentimes, it's not nothing for pleasure, it's just things they need to live. How do you take this movement and make it legal and public and break the illegal cycle that exists within it?

To try to get at your question, the slogan of the homeless union is, We're homeless, not helpless. We hear that one-third of the homeless population in Los Angeles has college degrees. You're not talking about what people normally conceive of as homeless people. People gravitate to California and the South because they don't have to worry about the cold.

When we first started out, the big thrust was at the point when general assistance [GA] was cut off. That increased the number of people filling up the shelters. Most people believed they would not be cut off for long, that something benevolent was going to happen and they would get the GA back. General assistance is not much. We call them conduits [that is, the recipients are just a means for distributing money to the landlords]. The people themselves weren't getting any money. Most of the stuff they got was vended [paid directly to the landlord]. The social service office would vend the rent and utilities before the recipient would get it, so most of them would have only about $10 left each month. Matter of fact, the landlords were our allies to keep GA on. This was an odd coupling.

Mayor Coleman Young had such an attitude about our tents that he sent the police every night to tear down the tents. We hadn't anticipated that. We'd sit there at night. The later we waited and mobilized, the later they would come. The last time the tents were torn down was at 3:00 A.M. We'd try to mobilize the press and as many people as possible. After they would leave, here would come two hundred police officers. They'd line up in formation on the corner, march down, tear up the tents, and arrest everybody. And people on the street were getting outraged: Why don't you tear down the dope house over there, man? You know they're selling dope there? Why do you want to bother the tents?

People learned an awful lot about how the whole system works, particularly against them. They understood clearly that Michigan was trying to balance the budget on the backs of the poor, the most helpless section in the state. The real danger is that Governor Engler's plan will become a national plan. He's a national hero. Everybody wants to follow the Engler plan. He's a leading proponent of welfare reform. His welfare reform is to cut everybody off and let them fend for themselves, regardless of how they find themselves living.

My experience working with autoworkers is quite different. They go to work at 6 o'clock in the morning and are quite disciplined. When you work with homeless people, the discipline is over a period of time. A homeless person might run up on $30 and they're gonna disappear. You won't see them for another three or four days until that runs out, and they come back. You have to tune yourself to understand the life they're living.

In Michigan all our social service workers are organized in the United Auto Workers. They're the largest local in the UAW, Local 600. Their treatment of welfare recipients is atrocious. We have all kinds of difficult fights at the welfare office with the way welfare mothers are treated. That's a whole other level of associated struggles.

Q: I appreciated all your comments, especially about women's leadership. Could you talk about the particular organizing issues that women face?

A: There's a lot of them. When the Homeless Union first got organized in Detroit, we had to learn an awful lot about how to deal with some of these issues. When the Union was very infantile, the organizers would come in and stay in the shelters a few nights, talk to various people, and come up with some kind of public activity. This was used to call a founding convention among homeless people to develop a union.

We could not let women with children get arrested. Once they were arrested, the children were taken and sent to foster homes. We had to find single women. The housing authority would give homes to women with children, but not to single females and males. When we took over houses, we would put AFDC recipients in them. When we took over public housing units, we would put single males and females in them. Every step of the way we had to have a broad discussion on the questions of gender and children. There also were all kinds of health-care discussions around women's issues. I'm sorry [my wife] Marian isn't here to discuss this further. I can say, however, that women play a real critical role. If it don't be for the women that's fighting in this movement, we wouldn't have a survival movement.

Leona Smith out of Philadelphia is the president of the National Homeless Union. My wife, Marian Kramer, is the president of the National Welfare Rights Union, and Gloria Richardson is head of the National Hunger Coalition. The three basic organizations leading the fight are headed by women. And their ranks are full of women. A lot of men are in supportive roles, but actually the women are carrying the fight.

Q: I'm from Youngstown. It's a smaller version of Detroit, with vacant lots and an official unemployment rate of 15 percent. We're trying to make a connection between the failure of the labor movement to address job cuts and the situation we're in. What has your relationship been with the labor movement, particularly in labor-management cooperation, which we argue simply is a way to cut jobs?

A: I've been in auto for thirty years. I've been the past president of the coke oven blast furnace unit of UAW Local 600. We have a pitiful relationship with the survival movement. We struggle wherever we can. There's real hatred and misunderstanding of what welfare rolls are. There's a real difficulty in trying to break down the prejudices.

Welfare and general assistance were developed for the working class in this country. In Michigan, general assistance was created right before the Flint sitdowns. Model changeover in the auto industry used to last for six months. For six months of the year you would not work. General assistance was created so those people could survive during the changeover period. It's been a battle to get working people to understand that welfare belongs to you. It was created in your name. How can you turn around and hate it? Now, we got a changeover that takes fifteen minutes. You got a 1991 model here, and in two skips you got a 1992 model there. It's electronically done. The old logic of assistance is obviously gone, and it's probably the material basis of why they could cut it like they did. Now they don't ever need these workers, so they don't ever need to feed them.

But I have a pretty progressive UAW regional director, Bob King, and we have a homeless and hunger task force out of my region. We have weekly meetings with all forty-one locals in my region. We do supportive work, but don't try to provide leadership. At the same time, that's not the going trend inside the shop. Clearly, everybody is trying to work as much overtime as they can at the expense of other people being hired. The new auto contracts set up two tiers, so that now new hires work at 60 percent of the wage for three years. It's a new slap at the so-called unknown. In the trade union movement they ask, Why are you gonna fight for the unknown? I say, Well, they ain't unknown; that's my next-door neighbor that needs a job. It's a real struggle for us.

Q: What, if any, role are students and universities like Wayne State playing in relation to the struggle, either contributing or undermining?

A: We haven't had a lot of help from Wayne State. Wayne State sits right on the edge of the Cass Corridor. Homeless people have to be very careful not to run into the Wayne State security patrol. There's a hostility between homeless people and university security. They're always running those people off campus who might be trying to pick up pop cans that have a 10-cent deposit in Michigan. Occasionally, we use the university facilities for meetings and conferences, but that's about all. We haven't had much student input, either.

Early in the 1970s, we seized the Wayne State student newspaper, the *South End*. We won the editorship. We passed out that newspaper at the plant gates every day for a year. We left a couple hundred on the campus. We just stole that resource for what we considered to be the proper place for it. We didn't need no newspaper floating around the campus talking nonsense. If we could lead another section with this paper, let's take it and use it. But no, we've had little support from the universities.

Q: Are there any Community Development Corporations (CDCs) in Detroit, and what kind of roles do they play?

A: We've got CDCs. We've got a big CDC in the Cass Corridor. Homeless people *hate* the CDC. They'd like to overthrow it. The CDC says, There are too many shelters down here; we need to make our neighborhood a neighborhood; we don't want all these homeless people. We have a constant battle with the CDC. The CDC is based out of Cass United Methodist Church. A lot of us joined the church so we could get on the board and vote out the old leadership, so we could keep them from being in our way. The relationship between the CDC and the homeless struggle is antagonistic.

This CDC hustles all the state money. The state knows all these homeless people are down here. The CDC gets money on the basis of all these homeless being down there. They want to take the money and do some nonsensical stuff about rebuilding apartments and houses that will rent for $400 to $500 per month. Homeless people don't have that money. They do things in *your* name and use it for something else.

CONTRIBUTORS

GENERAL BAKER is a longtime union activist and socialist. He was an elected official of United Auto Workers' Local 600 before his unit in Ford's River Rouge plant, the coke ovens, was closed down. He was also active in the Dodge Revolutionary Union Movement, the League of Revolutionary Black Workers, and the League of Revolutionaries for a New America.

ELAINE BERNARD is executive director of the Trade Union Program at Harvard University. Prior to 1989, Bernard was the director of Labour Programs at Simon Fraser University and president of the British Columbia New Democratic Party. She is interested in the role of unions in promoting civil society and democracy and international comparative labor movements.

HARRY BRAVERMAN was active in the labor and revolutionary socialist movements from the 1930s through the 1950s. In the 1960s, he became closely associated with the independent socialist magazine *Monthly Review* and served for a number of years as director of Monthly Review Press. He is best known as the author of the Marxist classic *Labor and Monopoly Capital*.

LIZABETH COHEN is the Howard Mumford Jones Professor of American Studies. Professor Cohen is the author of *Making a New Deal: Industrial Workers in Chicago, 1919–1939*, which won the Bancroft Prize in 1991 and was a finalist for the Pulitzer Prize. She is now at work on a book entitled

A Consumer's Republic: The Politics of Consumption in Postwar America.
Her teaching and research interests include consumer culture, material
culture, and the political and social life of twentieth-century America.

DAVID DEMAREST, who taught cultural studies in the English Department at
Carnegie Mellon in Pittsburgh, is especially interested in literature and
media about labor history. In 1992, he was coeditor of *The River Ran Red*,
an anthology of period depictions of the Homestead Strike of 1892.

GENORA JOHNSON DOLLINGER, during the Flint sitdown strikes of 1936–37,
formed the Women's Emergency Brigade which played a crucial role in
building the United Auto Workers. A longtime Socialist, Dollinger was a
founder of the Labor Party Advocates and was inducted into the Michigan
Women's Hall of Fame. She died in 1995.

DAN GEORGAKAS has written extensively on labor and ethnic issues. He is
coeditor of *The Encyclopedia of the American Left* and *The Immigrant Left
in the United States*. He is also author of *Solidarity Forever: An Oral History of the IWW* and *Greek America at Work*. Currently, he is editor of a
series of labor books for Garland Publishers.

JOHN HINSHAW is assistant professor of history at Lebanon Valley College.
He is also the author of *Steel and Steelworkers in Pittsburgh: Race and
Class Struggles in the Twentieth Century* (State University of New York
Press, 2001).

ROBERT KORSTAD is assistant professor of public policy studies and history
at Duke University and codirector of Duke University's Center for Docu-
mentary Studies project, "Behind the Veil: Documenting African American
Life in the Jim Crow South." His study of unionism in North Carolina,
*Democracy Denied: Black Insurgency and the Metamorphosis of White
Supremacy*, will soon be published.

PAUL LE BLANC was a hospital worker, shipyard worker, autoworker, and
social service employee before teaching history at several colleges and
universities. He presently is assistant professor of history at LaRoche
College. He has produced a number of works on the labor and socialist
movements, including *From Marx to Gramsci* and *A Short History of the
U.S. Working Class*.

NELSON LICHTENSTEIN teaches history at the University of Virginia. In 1996
he was cochairman of "The Fight for America's Future: A Teach-in With
the Labor Movement," held at Columbia University. He is the author of

The Most Dangerous Man in Detroit: Walter Reuther and the Fate of American Labor (1995).

SHERRY LEE LINKON is codirector of the Center for Working-Class Studies and coordinator of American Studies at Youngstown State University. She is the editor of *Teaching Working Class* (University of Massachusetts, 1999) and coauthor, with John Russo, of *My Sweet Jenny: Work, Memory, and Erasure in a Working-Class Community* (University Press of Kansas, forthcoming).

ALICE AND STAUGHTON LYND edited *We Are the Union* from taped interviews with Ed Mann by historians Bruce Nelson, Pat Rosenthal, and themselves. An interview with Ed Mann and other members of the Rank-and-File Team (RAFT) at Local 1462 appears in *Rank and File: Personal Histories by Working-Class Organizers*, 3d ed., ed. Alice and Staughton Lynd (New York: Monthly Review Press, 1988), 259–78. Staughton Lynd tells the story of Ed Mann's role in the struggle against shutdowns in Youngstown in *The Fight Against Shutdowns: Youngstown's Steel Mill Closings* (San Pedro: Singlejack Books, 1982), 93–127 (Brier Hill), 149–59 (U.S. Steel).

ED MANN (1928–1992) was a longtime activist at the Brier Hill mill of the Youngstown Sheet and Tube Company, in Youngstown, Ohio. He was president of Local 1462, United Steel Workers of America from 1973 until the mill closed in 1979. He also participated in the local branch of the American Civil Liberties Union, directing its attention to labor-related struggles for civil rights. After Mann's retirement he was an active member of the Workers' Solidarity Club, Solidarity USA (a militant retiree organization), and the IWW. Because of Ed Mann's central role in a variety of labor and social movement, the Workers' Solidarity Club named the Ed Mann Labor School in his honor.

MANNING MARABLE has written on U.S. historical and social realities in such works as *How Capitalism Underdeveloped Black America* and *Beyond Black and White*. A prominent columnist for the African American press and a longtime political activist, he is professor of history and director of the Institute for Research in African American Studies at Columbia University.

IRWIN MARCUS is a professor of history at Indiana University of Pennsylvania where he has been on the faculty since 1965. In that period he has taught a wide variety of courses including the History of Pittsburgh, the History of California, and the History of the Automobile. His teaching specialties are the History of the American Working Class and the History of Twentieth-Century American Protest Movements. His research has focused on the history of the working class in Western Pennsylvania with particular emphasis on deindustrialization, the history of steelworkers, and the history of coal miners. Currently, he is exploring the history of workers' education in the United States in the 1920s and 1930s.

JAMES J. MATLES was born in Romania in 1909. In America, he worked in the metal trades and quickly became active in the left wing of the labor movement, rising to leadership of the Steel and Metal Workers Industrial Union. In 1936–37, this union merged with the International Association of Machinists, then became part of the United Electrical, Radio, and Machine Workers of America. Matles served as the UE's first organizing director and later its secretary-treasurer until shortly before his death in 1975. He was also the coauthor, with James Higgins, of *Them & Us: Struggles of a Rank-and-File Union* (Prentice-Hall, 1974), a history of the UE.

MARK McCOLLOCH is Vice President for Academic Affairs and a professor of history at the University of Pittsburgh-Greensburg. He has been a member and activist in the USWA, SEIU, and the AFT. He is the author of *White-Collar Workers in Transition: The Boom Years, 1940–1970* and *Cold War in the Working Class: The Rise and Decline of the United Electrical Workers* with Ronald Filippelli.

BILL MULLEN is associate professor of English at the University of Texas, San Antonio. He is the author of *Popular Fronts: Chicago and African American Cultural Politics, 1935–1946* (University of Illinois Press, 1999). He is a cofounder of the Youngstown State University Center for Working-Class Studies. He is presently at work on Afro-Orientalism.

KAREN OLSON worked for the Student Non-violent Coordinating Committee during 1965–1966, and served on the editorial board of *Women: A Journal of Liberation* from 1968–1974. Her dissertation, "When Women Get a Working Life: The Transformation of Gender Relations in a Steelmaking Community," was completed in 1994 in the American Studies Department at the University of Maryland. She teaches history and anthropology at Community College of Baltimore County.

KATHLEEN O'NAN is a longtime union, antiwar, abortion-rights, and civil rights activist. A former member of the Oil, Chemical and Atomic Workers and the United Auto Workers, O'Nan is the Los Angeles organizer for the Labor Party.

PETER RACHLEFF has taught labor history at Macalester College in St. Paul, Minnesota, since 1982. During the Hormel strike of 1985–86, he served as chairperson of the Twin Cities P-9 support committee. He has continued to be active in the labor movement in the Upper Midwest, helping in recent years to organize the "Meeting the Challenges" labor conferences which have brought together 500-plus labor activists. He is the author of numerous articles and books such as *Moving the Mail* (1980), *Black Labor in Richmond, 1865–1890* (1984), and *Hard-Pressed in the Heartland: The Hormel Strike and the Future of the Labor Movement* (1993).

DAVID RIEHLE is a railroad worker and local union officer. He has been active in the labor and socialist movements in the St. Paul-Minneapolis area since the 1960s. His family has been engaged in similar activities in the Midwest for more than a century.

JOHN RUSSO is a founding member of the Center for Working-Class Studies at Youngstown State University. He is the codirector of the CWCS and also serves as coordinator of the Labor Studies program. He has published widely on labor and social issues and is currently completing a book with Sherry Linkon entitled *My Sweet Jenny: Work, Memory, and Erasure in a Working-Class Community*.

SUSAN RUSSO is an affiliate member of the Center for Working-Class Studies at Youngstown State University. She is a professor of graphic design and has written and/or illustrated six books for children.

LINDA STROM is a member of the Center for Working-Class Studies at Youngstown State University. She is the coordinator of the Women's Studies Center and her interests include working-class literature and the teaching of writing.

JOE W. TROTTER is the Mellon Bank Professor of History and director of the Center for Afroamerican Urban Studies and the Economy at Carnegie Mellon University. He is the author of numerous articles and books on the black working-class experience, including: *Black Milwaukee: The Making of an Industrial Proletariat*; *Coal, Class and Color: Blacks in Southern West Virginia, 1915–1932*; and *The Great Migration in Historical Perspective: New Dimensions of Race, Class and Gender*.